'Battleship Bertie'

Politics in Ahern's Ireland

Enjoy!

© John Cooney

Beyond the Pale Columns in the *Western People*, 2004-2008

'Battleship Bertie'

Politics in Ahern's Ireland

First published 2008
All rights reserved. No part of this publication may be reproduced,
transmitted or stored in a retrieval system without the written
permission of the author and publisher.

Published by
Blantyremoy Publications, 34 Eaton Square, Terenure, Dublin 6W. Ireland
Printed by Westprint Ltd., Enniscrone, Co. Sligo. Ireland

ISBN 0 95 27334 9 8

Acknowledgements

I am grateful to James Laffey, editor, and Brian Feeney, managing editor, of the *Western People* for their permission to publish this compilation of articles from my weekly 'Beyond the Pale' column for a wider readership. News editor Fiona McGarry, Anthony Hickey, production editor, and picture editor Henry Wills were also helpful and encouraging.

A special thanks to Martyn Turner for his instantly recognisable and inimitable drawing of *Battleship Bertie* which has renewed a collaboration we first shared in 1979 when he illustrated the cover of my *The Race for Europe*.

I would like to thank Tom Bourke of Westprint for refusing to be sunk in tidal times off Enniscrone harbour. Not forgetting *the Mayo Brigade* especially Tony McGarry, Seán Hannick, Martin Gordon and Liam Tuffy.

I have benefitted greatly from the work of fellow journalists covering politics and the Tribunals, and especially acknowledge the insights of Seán Boyne and Noel Coghlan at our regular summits in *Bellagio's*.

Thanks are also due to the *Terenure Cabinet*, especially the sagacious headliner and raconteur Tony Gilroy, and Kevin Rutledge, John Vincent, Peter Savage and David Woolhead.

As always my biggest debt is to Liguori, Francis, Sarah and John.

John Cooney,
Dublin,
September 22, 2008

Bertie File

1951   Bartholmew Patrick Ahern born on September 26 in Drumcondra, Dublin.

1977   Elected to the Dáil for Fianna Fáil in Dublin Finglas constituency in Taoiseach Jack Lynch's landslide victory.

1979   Supports Charles Haughey for Taoiseach against George Colley.

1982   Appointed Minister of State at the Departments of Taoiseach and Defence with rank of Chief Whip. Comes To public prominence by acting as Haughey's friendly face during internal heaves against the Boss.

1982   Appointed Fianna Fáil Opposition Chief Whip in December.

1986   Lord Mayor of Dublin.

1987   Appointed Minister for Labour by Taoiseach Charles Haughey.

1989   Key negotiator in Fianna Fáil's first ever Coalition pact with the Progressive Democrats, and reappointed Minister for Labour.

1991   Appointed Minister for Finance, replacing Albert Reynolds who re signed after his unsuccessful attempt to remove Haughey.

1992   Retains Finance Ministry after Albert Reynolds succeeds Haughey

1994   Becomes Leader of Fianna Fáil after resignation of Albert Reynolds.

1997   Elected Taoiseach in June by Dáil Éireann, aged 45, the youngest ever, heading a Fianna Fáil - Progressive Government with Tanaiste Mary Harney.

1998   Co-signatory of the Good Friday (Belfast) Agreement.

2002   Wins second term as Taoiseach and renews PD pact with the support of Independents, Jackie Healy-Rea, Mildred Fox and Tom Gildea.

2007   Wins third term as Taoiseach of a motley but *'rocket-solid'* Fianna Fáil - Greens-PD Government.

2008   Resigns as Taoiseach on April 2, and demits office on May 7.

DEDICATION

The antecedents of the 'Beyond the Pale' column go back to the days of the late John *Backbencher* Healy, who began his illustrious career in journalism with the *Western People* under the editorship of the legendary Fred De Vere. I was privileged to work with John during his regular visits to Strasbourg for *The Irish Times*. After his sudden death on January 6, 1991, I represented Agriculture Commissioner, Ray MacSharry, as the Commission Spokesman on Agriculture and Rural Development, at his funeral in the Church of the Three Patrons in Rathgar. John must have chuckled from the great above at my outranking in protocol my former *Irish Times* bosses, the late Douglas Gageby, Conor Brady and Major Tom McDowell. I was seated an eminent third in the pew pecking order to President Mary Robinson and Taoiseach Charles Haughey! This was a symbol of John's passion for "A Europe of the Regions". This book is dedicated to John's memory – and hopefully will rekindle fond memories for Evelyn of our many merry evenings spent dining in Strasbourg's *La Petite France - Mayo!*

It is also co-dedicated to the Nobel Peace Laureate, John Hume, who would often join us as at our more up-market rendezvous in the *Maison des Tanneurs*, where he would not only sing Phil Coulter's *The Town I Love So Well* but also picked up the handsome bills! It was John Hume's tireless work for the SDLP in 'spilling his sweat, not his blood' that provided the blueprint for a peaceful and inclusive Ireland, modelled on post World War II Franco-German reconciliation in a united Europe. John's emphasis on respect for the principle of cultural and individual diversity has influenced me since the beginnings of our friendship in my Brussels period as *Irish Times* European Correspondent This began in 1977 after his surprise appointment as a special adviser to Commissioner Dick Burke through the far-sighted influence of Noel Coghlan, then deputy chef de Cabinet of the exceptionally talented Burke inner team which also included Alan Dukes, Donal Kerr, Michael Lillis, Joe Carroll and the late Liam Hourican.

The uniqueness of Hume's contribution is summed up by former diplomat, Seán Donlon, in his remark that the Derryman changed the definition of one word in the English language – unity. For Hume, unity was not about feuding over control of two pieces of land, but about uniting people of different outlooks to work in harmony on the one piece of land. He would often recall his father telling him: "Son, you cannot eat the flag".

In Brussels and Strasbourg I received many *Humespeak* tutorials from John in which he would define the formula of the three strands that were to be embodied in the Irish Peace Process: Strand One concerned the internal political system for the governance of Northern Ireland. Strand Two defines North-South relations, and the East-West Strand redefines the relationship of North and South with Britain – all hinging on his conviction that economic development of people and regions, not least his native Derry, is integral to the peace philosophy. Hume earned his unique place as the statesman who changed mindsets about the nature of national identity and the real meaning of Irish Republicanism. Arguably, the greatest converts to Hume's definition have been the Sinn Féin leaders, Gerry Adams and Martin McGuinness.

The third co-dedication is to Bill Heaney, my first editor, who took the gamble of employing the young schoolteacher from the village of Blantyre on the *Scottish Catholic Observer*, and taught me how to write news stories, not just history essays.

I also dedicate this book to the memory of my late father, Frank Cooney.

Introduction: 'The Bert'

"Mr Consensus, a man whose words can mean whatever you want them to".
- OLIVIA O'LEARY

"The social loner". - ENDA KENNY

The Bertie Ahern Era was heralded on the steps of Government Buildings on Saturday November 1, 1994, immediately after the northside Dubliner was elected unanimously as the sixth and youngest leader, at 43, of Fianna Fáil. The closing of a divisive and turbulent chapter lasting a quarter of a century in the history of the country's largest political party, founded in 1926 by Eamon de Valera, was symbolised in the appearance of Albert Reynolds alongside Bertie. Not since 1959 when the reins of power passed from the elderly and blind Dev to the dynamic but no longer young Seán Lemass had the leadership succession and a generational change within Fianna Fáil been effected without trauma and turmoil, or both.

Despite the crisis circumstances which had been exploited by Tanaiste Dick Spring to force Albert's resignation as Taoiseach, the party's rallying to Bertie meant that there was none of the in-house fragmentation which took place in 1966 after the surprise resignation of Lemass when Jack Lynch emerged victorious as a compromise over more dominant personalities such as Haughey, Neil Blaney and George Colley.

In Haughey's moment of triumph in late December 1979, there was no public salute for him from Lynch who had timed his departure to favour Colley's candidature. Nor did Charlie conceal his disdain for Albert when the Longford man succeeded him in 1992 after his position became untenable following the RTE *Nighthawks* claims made to presenter Shay Healy by former Minister for Justice, an aggrieved Seán Doherty, that Haughey had authorised the illegal tapping of the telephones of journalists Bruce Arnold and Geraldine Kennedy.

As if the mild autumnal weather that Saturday was a blessing to a Fianna Fáil suddenly at peace with itself after the cataclysmic storms of the Harry Whelehan and Father Brendan Smyth controversies, a crestfallen but dignified Reynolds conferred the succession on the youthful Ahern as they stood together for the cameras. The strength of Bertie's position within Fianna Fáil was confirmed by unanimity following the late withdrawal from the leadership of Marie Geoghegan Quinn, whose caucus had mustered a mere dozen pledges in the 66-strong parliamentary party.

In a well prepared manifesto at his first news conference as party leader, Bertie struck the right note to signal a generational change in Irish politics. His frankness, not least in his admission of the breakdown of his marriage to his wife Miriam and his new relationship with Celia Larkin, impressed journalists that he was genuinely committed to an open information policy. The question by the flamboyant editor of the *Irish Sun*, Paddy Clancy, had provoked an outcry of hissing from party faithful, but Bertie overrode them and took the question head-on.

Afterwards in conversation with him for the *Irish Press*, I had the opportunity of wishing him well in a role which I knew he coveted since we had first met in 1986 when he was organising a business conference to garner financial support for Fianna Fáil as Charlie Haughey's acolyte. His pledge to be a consensus leader matched Irish society's quest for greater openness and transparency in its political system and public discourse.

Some time earlier Bertie introduced me to a party worker – Celia – on one of his rare incursions into the Dáil bar: both of them were wearing anoraks! A teenager in the 1960s when Irish society began to dislodge at least the tip of the iceberg of monolithic insularity of the de Valera decades, he accepted that the post-1922 Independence system of closed government needed to be modernised in order to cope with more complex times. Ireland seemed to be on the threshold of a new beginning, with one commentator describing Bertie as a working class version of Tony Blair, now leader of the Labour Party in Britain after the untimely death of John Smith, but not yet Prime Minister.

That November Saturday in 1994 it was universally taken for granted that within days Bertie would do a deal with Spring and become Taoiseach of a new Fianna Fáil-Labour Government. This proved not to be so. We were in for blustery changing times. For reasons still inadequately explained, but apparently owing to a strong resistance to a re-union with Fianna Fáil on the part of Spring's adviser, Fergus Finlay, he pulled-out of the deal at the last moment and condemned Bertie to troop a traumatised Fianna Fáil into the Opposition benches.

Opposition, as Seán Lemass ruefully observed, is particularly difficult for Fianna Fáil, which believed itself to be – and acted accordingly - like the natural party of government. Lemass, Lynch, Haughey and Reynolds all had the good fortune of becoming Taoiseach when the party was in power. Not Bertie. He would have to win power.

In the event, Opposition was to be his lot for 30 testy months. It was not easy for Bertie, an experienced member of Government in the pivotal Labour and Finance portfolios under Haughey and Reynolds, but as yet an unproven leader. It took him some time to learn the art of tabling questions to the usurper Taoiseach chosen by Spring, Fine Gael's John Bruton. Nor did it help Bertie that Bruton was a more polished Dáil speaker. Often, at Question Times, Bertie was out-called and left behind by the eloquent and quick-witted leader of the Progressive Democrats, Mary Harney. Conciliatory by nature, he was frequently less aggressive than an Opposition leader must be on occasions such as the revelations leading to the resignation of the Minister for Public Enterprise, Michael Lowry, that super-market owner Ben Dunne had paid for extensive renovation of his home in Tipperary.

During the passages of the Abortion Information Bill in the Dáil and the divorce referendum in 1995, I observed how ill at ease Bertie was with such contentious ethical issues, coded by the media as the liberal agenda, in a party which retained a fundamentalist Catholic wing that looked to Des Hanafin for moral guidance. In the ups-and-downs of political life, the more sartorially groomed Bertie had an appetite for hard work. With the assistance of Dr Martin Mansergh, previously Charlie Haughey's backroom intellectual amanuensis, he paid special attention to Northern Ireland with forays north of Dundalk. Through such visits, reported as events but without details, Bertie branded himself as the guardian of the Downing Street peace process brokered by Albert Reynolds with John Major. He also positioned himself as the voice of the Catholic nationalist minority, at a time when the well-meaning but Redmonite Bruton was making heavy Meath-rancher hay as John Unionist to the dismay of Sinn Féin.

Bertie's appointment of Mary O'Rourke as the party's first deputy leader gave his frontbench gender balance and media firepower, with the *Lady from Athlone* incising a cutting-edge which Bertie lacked. Bertie was leader but he was not a solo ego in a party hungry to regain power. His disappointment at losing a by-election in Wicklow caused by the death of Johnny Fox notched up the party's fifth unsuccessful outing. This, however, turned to relief and elation with the victories in Dublin West and Donegal North-East following the deaths of the veterans Brian Lenihan and Neil Blaney.

While opinion polls were regularly positive towards Ahern's Fianna Fáil, they cast doubts, surprisingly, on his vote-gathering appeal in Dublin. Some critics claimed that he had not yet clinched the support of the middle class in the capital; nor attracted the loyalty of the recently dispossessed country and western wing of Fianna Fáil. Pol Corrs wondered over the odd glass in the Dáil bar, though not in print, if Bertie would become the first Fianna Fáil leader never to become Taoiseach!

Of this political heresy, colleague Tim Ryan and I would be disabused by Bertie's close supporter as Director of Elections, P.J. Mara - immortalised but caricatured by the late Dermot Morgan in his *Scrap Saturday* satirical programme as Haughey's fawning bagman MARA, P.J. scoffed at such intemperate speculation as typical of a Dublin bias against Fianna Fáil. He would scold us that we needed to pay more attention to what was actually happening outside of the Leinster Hot-House – a steady flow of new policy documents, grassroots cumman reorganisation and a review of constituency candidates that were putting the party on election footing under the chairmanship of former Minister and EU Commissioner, Ray MacSharry.

In nods and winks at off-the-record 'guidance' sessions, it was sheepishly admitted that it would be difficult, probably impossible, for Bertie to secure an overall single-party FF majority last harvested by *Honest Jack* Lynch in 1977. Improving vote-transfers to Fianna Fáil in Ireland's multi-seat system of proportional representation at the next general election would be critical. The cunning Bertie, meanwhile, could be observed cosying up to Mary Harney's PDs in Opposition stratagems, presciently building up the basis of an uncosy reunion in the next government. Cunningly, too, Bertie spoke softly to the prickly Kerry spring rose, even though the rank-and-file of *the Soldiers of Destiny* were egging him on to gut the pugilistic-prone Springer.

At lunches and briefings, Bertie's Chef de Cabinet, Paddy Duffy, a former headmaster and superb communicator, would stress to me Bertie's innate reformist leanings in his determination to distance his Fianna Fáil from old FF. Paddy reinforced P.J's exhortations to get out into the constituencies to see at first hand Bertie's popular appeal. On an occasional Monday, a non-Dáil day, I would find out which routine constituency engagement/(s) Bertie was attending and go there to observe his inimitable inter-action with his people. This was never newsworthy but invariably instructive.

As a general election ticked closer, Bertie's media handlers were zealous in presenting their man as Taoiseach-material by arranging a number of agenda-setting speeches in which he attacked 'the Rainbow Coalition' of Bruton, Spring and Proinsias De Rossa. Emphasis was put on Bertie's credentials as Taoiseach-in-Waiting: the deliverer of the Haughey minority Government's national pact with employers and trades unions; his negotiating skills in beef deals that entranced even Libya's Colonel Gadhaffi; the endearing go-between who negotiated the formation of Haughey's unprecedented coalition with Des O'Malley's Progressive Democrats in 1988 and Reynolds' second Government in 1992 with Labour's Dick Spring. He was spoken of as the Finance Minister who balanced the books; and as Ireland's signatory of the EU's Social Chapter in 1988 and of the Maastricht Treaty in 1992.

Meanwhile, a strong political bond was being forged by Bertie and Mary Harney for their mutual advantage. In the general election called prematurely and misguidedly by Bruton at the behest of Spring for 2002, the Dublin duo issued joint policies to reduce personal income tax, a PD mantra but one not alien to FF. This appealed more than the Rainbow's more nuanced proposal for tax reform targeting the lower income.

Bingo Bertie! The Lotto Prize read: FF 77 (+8 from 1992), FG 54 (+13), Labour 17 (-16), Democratic Left 4 (4), Sinn Féin 1 (0), the Socialist Party aka Joe Higgins 1, (0), Independents 6 – but with the PDs down to 4 (-6). *Bertie the Wizard* and the *Fairy Queen Mary* waved their magic wand to form a Government with the support of 3 Independents, Jackie Healy-Rea, Mildred Fox and Tom Gildea.

In November Bertie beamed to the cameras with the new President, Mary McAleese. Dick Spring resigned and Ruairi Quinn defeated Brendan Howlin. Labour began rebuilding its base with an amalgamation with Democratic Left.

First Term, 1997-2002

The writer Frank O'Connor likened the reading of a Seanad debate on censorship of books in the Ireland of 1943 to "a long slow swim through a sewage bed". His damning image appeared an apt description for the record of the 28th Dáil, during whose duration the scale of political corruption was highlighted with constant revelations from the ever expanding Tribunals of Inquiry.

The Lowry resignation had opened up a series of disclosures about payments to politicians including that Dunne, Big Fella, had made substantial payments to Charles Haughey that were being investigated at the McCracken Tribunal. In late August 2002 the McCracken Report found that "if such gifts (to Haughey) were permissible, the potential for bribery and corruption would be enormous".

Bertie found himself embarrassed at the Moriarty Tribunal when he admitted that he had co-signed blank cheques for Haughey which were used to buy Charvet shirts and pay for sumptuous meals at *Le Coq Hardi* restaurant in Ballsbridge with his mistress Terry Keane. While accepting that Bertie had operated the blank cheque pre-signing practice for a proper purpose, Moriarty reported that "Mr Ahern facilitated the misuse of the account by Mr Haughey". It was a practice "which has to be viewed as both inappropriate and imprudent".

Although there were rumours centring on Ray Burke as having received 'donations' from businessmen in connection with land planning permissions in north Dublin, Bertie appointed him Minister for Foreign Affairs with direct responsibility for negotiations in Northern Ireland. A few months later Burke resigned both as a Minister and a Dáil deputy.

Bertie's mind was fixed on Belfast. He was rewarded for his intensive peace efforts with the landmark signing of the Good Friday Agreement in 1998. However, the public south of the Border was more engrossed in getting richer. Bertie's FF-PD Coalition took office just as the Celtic Tiger economy was taking-off, shooting to double figure growth. Unemployment dropped to 4pc from 10pc. The national debt was cut to below 35pc of GDP. Finance Minister Charlie McCreevy reduced the basic rate of tax from 26pc to 20pc and the higher rate from 48pc to 42pc.

Although in March 2002 Bertie's Government lost a Constitutional referendum proposing a return to the pro-life situation prior to the "X" case ruling by the Supreme Court by 50.42pc to 49.58pc, he remained the *Teflon Taoiseach*.

Contrary to the prophets of doom who had predicted his Government would not last, Bertie had presided over his Coalition in good economic times. So much so, he could boast his Coalition as "the longest and most successful government in peace time".

"It's showtime", quipped P.J. Mara on April 5, 2002 after Bertie dissolved the Dáil and launched a Fianna Fáil manifesto that claimed there would be no cut-backs even though the economy had dipped that year. In an otherwise appalling campaign by the PDs in which Mary Harney went to war with unmarried mothers, the highlight was the spectacle of Attorney-General Michael McDowell climbing up a lamp-post near his home in Ranelagh with the billboard slogan, "One party Government? NO thanks!" This showmanship deprived Bertie of an overall Fianna Fáil majority.

With an increased share of the vote from 39pc to 41pc, Fianna Fáil increased its Dáil seats from 77 to 81. The McDowell bounce doubled the PD representation to 8 on a mere 4pc of the vote. Under Michael Noonan's leadership Fine Gael slumped from 54 to 31, a loss of 23 seats including prominent casualties such as deputy leader Jim Mitchell, Alan Dukes, Charlie Flanagan, Norah Owen, Austin Currie, Frances FitzGerald and Alan Shatter. Noonan promptly resigned after leading Fine Gael to its worst general election defeat in over 50 years and was replaced by Enda Kenny. Pat Rabbitte, who had ruled out taking a seat in any FF-Labour Government, took over from Quinn. Residual public resentment at Spring's choice of Fianna Fáil in 1992, combined with a go-alone policy pro-gramme, saw Labour stay static at 21, losing ground to Sinn Féin which won 6.5pc of the vote and 5 Dáil seats. The other beneficiary of the election were the Greens with 4pc of the vote and 6 seats. Independents rose from 6 to 14 including Joe Higgins.

Second Term, 2002-2007

With a new Programme for Government Bertie reassembled his Coalition with the PDs and appointed McDowell Minister for Justice, while Harney retained her Enterprise portfolio. However, the introduction of public spending cuts and 'stealth' taxes such as bin charges saw FF's popularity fall in the polls. This trend was not helped with the publication of the damning Report by Mr Justice Flood against Ray Burke which caused public outrage.

Faced with local and European elections in mid-2004 Bertie used the March Árd Fheis at Dublin's Citywest to recall FF's republican roots and challenged Sinn Féin that there could be no half-way house between democracy and violence. In April he removed Beverley Flynn from Fianna Fáil. To boost his flagging ratings, he promised a Cabinet re-shuffle.

Bertie Ahern was, therefore, an unavoidable subject for incessant comment in my Beyond the Pale column, which began its weekly appearance in *The Western People* in June 2004. Its brief is primarily focused on current affairs, with a strong emphasis on politics interspersed with regular forays into religion, Europe and international affairs. This chronicle begins mid-way through Bertie's second term in Coalition with Harney's PDs. His skilful negotiation of the second Nice EU Treaty during the Irish Presidency in the first half of 2004 was acclaimed as one of his main achievements and contributed enormously to his rehabilitation in European capitals, an amazing turn around coming so soon after his loss of the first Nice referendum in 2001.

However, things were not running to course at home for Bertie. These columns open just as *Bertie the European* has suffered humiliating rebuffs in the June European and local elections that augured a revival in the fortunes of Fine Gael and Sinn Féin. For the first time Fine Gael won more seats than Fianna Fáil in the European Parliament and came a close second in the local elections.

Labour's performance was disappointing, largely because of rising support for Sinn Féin. In Dublin the legal high-flyer Ivana Bacik lost out to Sinn Féin's Mary Lou McDonald for a seat in the Strasbourg Parliament, where Proinsias de Rossa found himself operating in semi-detachment from Rabbitte.

Bertie's hegemony over the Irish political landscape was now under serious strain, if not threat, not least within his own jittery Fianna Fáil party.

Bertie Wilts as Sinn Féin Blossoms

(June 16, 2004)

Fianna Fáil was described memorably by Seán Lemass as "a slightly constitutional party" when the newly founded Republican Party was moving a Dáil motion to remove the oath of allegiance to the British Crown.

It was a double-edged remark made by Lemass in 1928 during a heated debate. His remark was seen as subversive by the ruling law and order Cumann na nGaedheal Government. But Lemass aimed to placate his former IRA comrades who still clung to the belief that political objectives could only be achieved by physical force. Seventy-five years later, Lemass's cryptic, even infamous utterance, is pointedly being levelled by the established political parties in Leinster House against Sinn Féin after its massive gains throughout the country at the expense of Fianna Fáil in both the local and European elections.

Lemass and the Chief, Eamon de Valera, who became revered as the founding fathers of Ireland's biggest political party, were at that time deeply concerned that the IRA had refused to surrender its arms dumps. Clearly, in those volatile days of 1927-28 both Dev and Lemass were keeping their option open for a resort to revolutionary militancy, if peace politics failed.

Today, a similar charge is being made against Gerry Adams and the Sinn Féin leadership: while taking the democratic route to Leinster House and the local council chambers, as well as to Stormont and Strasbourg, this process remains shrouded in ambiguity, because the IRA has failed to decommission its weapons in the North, while its members are engaged in criminal activities, notably in the lucrative drinks, fuel and drugs trade.

Despite the dead-lock in the implementation of the Good Friday Agreement and the warnings from Justice Minister, Michael McDowell, about continuing para-militarism, Sinn Féin has made what Martin McGuiness calls a break-through that will make the party become a major political force in the Republic. Already in the North, it has overtaken the SDLP as the prime nationalist party. Europe now beckons with Sinn Féin's Mary Lou McDonald taking a seat in the European Parliament for Dublin along with Barbara de Brún in the North.

Sinn Féin now represents a serious challenge to Fianna Fáil for the mantle of republicanism. Two self-proclaimed republican parties are confronting each other on a narrow pitch. The former is renowned for its pragmatic survival but is plagued by corruption from the Haughey era. The latter is "slightly constitutional", but is attracting the idealistic vote of those disaffected from FF.

This is a dangerous moment for Fianna Fáil – and one that may not be automatically solved by a change of Taoiseach, a cabinet reshuffle under a chastened Bertie, new found ministerial humility or even using exchequer money to bribe the electorate in the general election in 2006 or 2007. Nor are the Progressive Democrats in good shape. What is also worrying for the FF-PD Government is that both Fine Gael and Labour have made advances rather than losing ground to Sinn Féin. A resurgent Fine Gael and a reinvigorated Labour now offer a credible alternative administration.

Two powerful images emerge from these elections which have changed the political landscape. First is the absence of Bertie Ahern from the Dublin count centre as Gerry Adams beamed like the French soccer hero, Zinedine Zidane. The second is of Enda Kenny and Pat Rabbitte fraternising and lurking with intent to get Bertie out of Merrion Street – and to keep Gerry out.

But will Gerry take the Lemass route?

Bertie, Toast of Europe

(June 23, 2004)

Shortly after Celtic won the European Championships league cup in 1967, Jock Stein's Lisbon Lions lost the Glasgow Cup Final to their arch-rivals Rangers, resulting in the unforgettable headline: "Local team beats European Champions".

After his kicking in the local and European elections Bertie Ahern is savouring a similar sensation about the ups and downs of public life.

The old phrase of 'devil at home, angel abroad' is summed up in how one minute Bertie reads his obituary as Taoiseach, the next minute he is being acclaimed the uncrowned king of Europe for delivering an historic constitution.

More than a week after the local and European elections the question mark over his future as Taoiseach of this small island state of some four million squabbling souls remains unresolved, while the pressure mounts on the man who negotiated the EU Constitution for the world's biggest political union to become chief executive of the 25 nations serving a population of 450 million.

Be in doubt, Bertie may not be the flavour of the season among Fianna Fáil backbenchers, but he is the man of the moment in Europe.

An editorial in the *Sunday Tribune* was not exaggerating the scale of Bertie's success at the Brussels EU Summit with its headline: "A stunning historic achievement for Ahern".

Providing Europe with a new constitution that was beyond the reach of Italy's Silvio Berlusconi only six months ago ensures the Drumcondra man of an iconic place in the European history books, when his home-based critics want to dump him in the domestic political bin.

Whatever storms lie ahead in securing the Constitution's ratification, its negotiation last Friday in Brussels consummates a process that began in the early 1990s with the collapse of the Berlin Wall. June 18, 2004 is the date when the Cold War officially ended and the leaders of the European continent adopted a new democratic union. For Europe, the 20th century died last Friday.

In endowing Europe with a constitution for the 21st century, Bertie Ahern has acquired a stature in international politics greater than any previous Irish politician. No other politician in Europe knows the minds of his other 24 colleagues better than does Bertie. No one has a better knowledge of how the deal was done that reconciles the conflicting demands of those who want a Federal Europe and those who want a Europe of Nations.

So it is hardly surprising that the big names of Europe such as Jacques Chirac and Gerhard Schröder are still hoping that Bertie will change his mind and accept the nomination to succeed Italy's Romano Prodi as President of the European Commission for the next five years.

No Irishman has ever held the post of Commission President. It is one of the most important jobs in the world, even comparable to the Presidency of the United States in its power and prestige, the former Fianna Fáil MEP Mark Killilea noted in a timely statement issued before the Brussels Summit.

In a clear hint for the Taoiseach to go for it, Killilea urged that if it is on offer to an Irish person, "this is without doubt the greatest single opportunity which has been presented to this country and it should be taken up".

It is first class advice from the wise old owl of Galway politics to the most cunning Taoiseach of them all. It is in the Irish national interest that Bertie heads the new Europe rather than risk defeat at the hands of his local opponents, both inside and outside Fianna Fáil.

Dubya in Bertie's Ireland

(June 30, 2004)

An assignment from the BBC World Service as a political commentator during President George W. Bush's weekend visit to Dromoland Castle in County Clare provided me with an insight into how Bertie Ahern's Ireland is viewed on the international stage.

The biggest puzzle for listeners in far-away Jakarta or Nairobi was the quetion of why Ireland, which is so well-known for being pro-American in its social and diplomatic ties, had become so hostile to President Bush's Iraq policy.

The contrast between the adulation accorded to President John F. Kennedy in 1963 and the massive publicity four decades later that was centered on the anti-Bush war protesters appeared to be inexplicable.

Had Ireland become the Cuba of Europe in its strident opposition to President Bush?

Had the Irish, millions of whom had found new lives and prosperity in the Land of the Free, turned on its kith and kin?

To deal with such distorted perceptions, it was essential to stress that the public anger was not anti-Americanism. The Irish had not seceded from their special relationship with America. There had been no rift between the Irish and American Governments.

But clearly a fundamental shift in public attitudes had taken place in Ireland based on a moral conviction that President Bush - and British Prime Minister Tony Blair - had flaunted the rule of law embodied in the United Nations by waging war against Saddam Hussein's Iraq.

In particular, too, there was widespread antagonism towards Bush personally, because he is viewed as a doctrinaire fundamentalist who has a Texan cowboy's simplistic view of the world. In her controversial and courageous interview in the White House RTE's Washington Correspondent, Carole Coleman, had hit the Irish mood exactly when she charged the clearly agitated President with having made the world a more dangerous place.

This mood manifested itself on a smaller scale in 1984 when protesters including the Irish Catholic Bishops, led by Eamon Casey, boycotted a State reception for President Ronald Reagan in protest against his oppressive policies in

Central America, though the former B-movie film-star had deflected the criticisms by dint of his folksy personal charisma, a gift manifestly lacking in the drawl Bush.

George Dubya is no John F. Kennedy; nor a Ronald Reagan - and certainly not a Bill Clinton, who was feted for his charm and wayward eye - as well as for his role in the peace process in the North - when he visited Ireland in 1995.

Incidentally, a funny take on Bush's swaggering walk was penned by the *Irish Independent* columnist, Miriam Lord, who likened him to "an old cowboy with itching powder in his long johns".

Just to add to the merriment of the occasion Bertie again displayed his dexterity with the English language when he called the Guantanamo prison in Cuba as er, Guatapama. Bertie's slip of the tongue was a reassuring sign that the international statesman is still a fallible Dub.

Having negotiated the EU Constitution and nominated Portugal's Prime Minister, José Manuel Durao Barroso, for the Presidency of the EU Commission for the next five years, Bertie completed a triple triumph at Dromoland by healing the rift between Bush and the European Union. This achievement, one of the pivotal aims of the Irish EU Presidency, will help ease criticism of Bertie for having allowed the Americans to use Shannon Airport as a transport stop-over.

As one wag, unfamiliar with Drumcondra, suggested, Bush should grant Bertie American citizenship and enlist him as his Presidential running-mate. No chance – Bertie is unshiftable from his roots.

'Bertie Kissinger' hides
in Kerry

(July 14, 2004)

Bertie Ahern deserves a leisurely holiday in Kerry after his six months of globetrotting on behalf of the European Union Presidency as an Irish Henry Kissinger. Less satisfactory for the running of the country and the summer tranquillity of aspirant ministers is his foot-dragging over announcing his long-awaited Government reshuffle.

It was on the very first day of 2004 that Bertie confirmed his intention of a cabinet shake-up for the mid-year that would introduce fresh faces. For six months this tactical trick kept malcontents and wannabes silent in anticipation of preferment.

After Fianna Fáil's heavy hammering in the June local and European elections, the Taoiseach came under intense pressure from his angry backbenchers to make sweeping changes in his ministerial team, and to do so before the Dáil recess rather than drift into September or October. This he has ignored. He was too busy sorting out world affairs to sort-out the mess in his own political backyard. Worse still, like an absentee landlord from the era of Michael Davitt, Bertie did not even turn-up on the last day of the Dáil session before the long summer break.

Such occasions would be rippling with the atmosphere and excitement of a cup final day. The Opposition parties would mount an all-out attack on the competence of the Government, which, in turn, would defend its record and reaffirm its mandate to hold onto the trophy of power as the champions of the people.

Resigned to the reality that they did not have the numbers to defeat the Government, the Opposition deputies would shout foul by complaining bitterly at the excessively long holiday period stretching ahead from early July to late September. The Government parties would huff and puff about ongoing cabinet and committee meetings. Then, they would go off on holiday believing that they had given the public a thrilling battle.

In retrospect, such engagements may have been mere mock battles but they produced a drama which contrasts with the stand-in role for the Taoiseach by

Defence Minister, Michael Smith, as Bertie crossed the Irish Sea to accept an honorary degree from the University of Aberdeen. The Bonnie Prince Bertie celebrity circuit was more important than a rare appearance in Dáil Éireann!

As he has done for over six months, Bertie has left everyone guessing about his future intentions. After admitting that he was tempted to take the Presidency of the EU Commission – and that 21 of the 24 leaders backed him – Bertie hinted that he did not move to Brussels because he would retire at 60.

While a politician, like those in other professions, has a right to work to his own career schedule, the fact is that as a public representative Bertie has acquired negotiating skills which his EU peers admired so much that they wanted him to become the first Irishman to head the Commission.

In the national interest and out of a sense of patriotism, Bertie Ahern should have taken the Presidency. Bertie's departure to Brussels would have found him in a position where he could have served both Europe and Ireland, while Brian Cowen could have begun the task of revitalising Fianna Fáil as their first leader who had not served in a cabinet under Charles J Haughey.

Bertie, however, wants to go down in the history books as the man who won a third term in succession as Taoiseach.

Bertie Shafts Albert in Phoenix Park

(August 11, 2004)

As political biographies of Tony Blair come off the printing presses with the speed of yet another terrorist attack in Iraq, there remains only one biography of Bertie Ahern, even though the British Prime Minister and the Taoiseach are both in their eighth year in power.

Bertie Ahern – Taoiseach and Peacemaker by journalists Ken Whelan and Eugene Masterson, published in 1998, has not been updated to take account of the tumultuous events that have since cascaded on him. Yet, it remains an indispensable authority for understanding the personality of a Taoiseach whose driving ambition is to go down in history as one of the country's most successful statesmen, perhaps even greater than his boyhood hero, Seán Lemass. The book's reliability is based on the fact that Bertie cooperated extensively with the authors in its preparation, and was remarkably candid about his life story.

However, on the book's publication Bertie caused an almighty controversy by disputing some of its key revelations. Such was the frustration of the authors at his chameleon response to their collaborative effort that Eugene inscribed in my signed copy of their book, "Here's to the 'most cunning of them all' as we found out ourselves – eventually".

Re-reading the book is instructive in the light of how Charlie McCreevy has responded to his shafting by Ahern. Long after Charlie departs for Brussels a cryptic remark of the former Finance minister about the mystery of who Bertie Ahern really is will continue to haunt Irish politics. After the announcement of his nomination to the EU Commission, Charlie said that he knew Bertie 25pc – and that was 24pc more than anybody else he knew him. This admission prompted an unnamed Fianna Fáil politician to say that he detected a 75pc barb in McCreevy's comment, even though the Taoiseach had described the Kildareman as "my best and closest colleague".

Despite Bertie's angry disclaimers to the media that he did not push McCreevy out of the cabinet, the logic of the situation points to the Taoiseach at the very least using the anti-McCreevy sentiment among Fianna Fáil backbenchers to persuade his Finance minister that it was time to pack his bags for Brussels or risk humiliating ministerial demotion.

The McCreevy exile has also brought back memories of how Bertie is reputed to have shafted Albert Reynolds, his former Taoiseach, for the office of President of Ireland in 1997, even though he showed his voting card backing him at the Fianna Fáil party's candidate ballot which was won by outsider Mary McAleese.

This rekindles my own memory of how on the eve of the fatal ballot for Reynolds' future public career, I had been broadcasting radio bulletins on the hour for Independent Network News (INN) to all the country's regional stations. Late that evening after talking on the phone to Albert and to Michael O'Kennedy, the second Fianna Fáil candidate – I had been unable to contact Mary Mac – I sent out my final report of the evening. My report placed Albert as heading off a challenge next day from McAleese with O'Kennedy way behind as an also-ran candidate.

Shortly after the report's transmission, I received a call from a close aide of Taoiseach Bertie Ahern – I am still constrained today by journalistic ethics from naming the source - who told me that I was off-track and that support was swinging heavily towards McAleese who would win. The source's curt though friendly guidance was that I should correct the forecast in the morning's bulletins. While this tip-off sounded authoritative, I got back onto Albert to check it out. Without betraying the identity of my deep-throat, I found that Albert remained confident that he had the vote in the bag. Clearly, he was unaware of the shift towards *the Lady from the Ardoyne* in the Bertie camp. As Albert, no doubt, slept well in his bed that night in his Ailesbury Road mansion dreaming of his presidential destiny, I had a restless few hours slumber. Overnight, I wrested with the dilemma of what was really going on behind the scenes in the FF hinterland. It was inconceivable, I reckoned, that a Taoiseach would be organising a coup d'etat against his predecessor. It was equally unthinkable, however, that Fianna Fáil would be going for McAleese without either Bertie's connivance or even encouragement through intermediaries.

Yet, my source was adamant that McAleese, a failed Fianna Fáil Dáil candidate, had gained the upper-hand over a former Taoiseach who had built on the secret dialogue between John Hume and Gerry Adams to negotiate the Downing Street Declaration with British Prime Minister John Major before falling from executive power in a smokey squabble with Labour's Dick Spring over fugitive paedophile priests.

I wondered, too, if I was being used by the Bertie faction within Fianna Fáil to influence wavering members of the parliamentary party, many of whom would be listening to the morning bulletins on their car radios as they drove to Dublin for the crucial vote. Tipping McAleese to win could send a strong signal to them to get on the winning side. In my early morning bulletins, starting at 6am, I moved McAleese up the field, calling it a neck and neck race with the former Taoiseach. But I felt uneasy afterwards that I had been too cautious and should have called it in McAleese's favour.

As the drama unfolded that day, events from my inside knowledge assumed inevitability. Albert lost. Bertie consoled Albert by showing him his vote cast for him. McAleese emerged triumphant. Fianna Fáil ministers and deputies flocked to the *femme fatale* Mary as their new found champion. Albert acted with dignity that day, but he nursed deep suspicions about his successor's treachery which have become certitude in his own mind. The man they called *the Longford Leader* will go to his grave in the belief that Bertie destroyed his presidential prospect. I knew instinctively – and I still believe – that while Bertie had not plunged the dagger up-front Mark Anthony-style into Caesar – his hands, metaphorically speaking, were covered in Albert's blood, because of the background manoeuvres done with his knowledge and, most certainly, his bidding.

These recollections also bring back to my mind how at a public function in the summer of 1988 in Killala, County Mayo, Bertie, then Minister for Labour, named me as his favourite political journalist. I was most flattered then. Today, with the experiences of Albert Reynolds and Charlie McCreevy in mind, I shudder!

As Bertie enters his eighth year as Taoiseach, he does so with expectations of beginning a new phase of his leadership with a post-McCreevy cabinet reshuffle in the autumn. But McCreevy's cryptic remark about the unknowing side of Bertie's character will hang over the political and media landscape.

We badly need a new biography of Bertie Ahern, a political thriller.

Bertie looks after 'Cheekie Charlie'

(August 28, 2004)

Charlie McCreevy, Ireland's European Commissioner-designate, confided to a friend that he thought that Taoiseach Bertie Ahern had not secured a major economic portfolio for him, an apprehension which I shared.

Delighted, therefore, that Bertie cashed in on Ireland's highly successful six month stint as President of the EU Council, and has helped catapult his former Finance Minister into the inner group of Commissioners who will carry most weight in Brussels. McCreevy has been given a pivotal mid-field position in a strong team of 25 Commissioners whose challenge is to make the European Union a major economic and political force in international affairs.

The game plan for the next five years under the direction of manager José Manuel Durao Barroso, the former Portuguese Prime Minister, has two main drives. The first is to transform the enlarged EU of 25 nations – soon to become 27 – with its population of 450 million into the world's most dynamic economic bloc that will out-play America in terms of prosperity and trade. The second is to shape the enlarged EU into a more cohesive political power that will be taken as a serious ally by the globe's only real superpower, the US.

As Commissioner for the Internal Market and Services, McCreevy will be called on to consolidate the Single Market allowing free flow of people, goods and services within the EU by breaking-down protectionist barriers in the national systems. In this role, the man known as *Cheekie Charlie* will be the EU's financial policeman. Much of his work in Brussels will be regulatory. He will become a Eurocrat whose job will be to enforce free-trade principles on Government ministers who still think, as he did for seven years as Minister for Finance, in much narrower nationalist self-interested ways.

McCreevy's new boss, Barroso, a right-wing Thatcherite, is determined to put his own stamp on his team and to take overall direction of the economic and political grand plan.

I just wonder if Bertie has some private regrets that it is not the Ahern Commission.

Bertie Lies Low in Junket Season

(August 25, 2004)

Politicians develop thick skins that enable them to absorb oceans of abuse and insults from the media and their constituents, but the one criticism that they cannot cope with is to be accused of junketeering at the taxpayers' expense. This makes them go ballistic. They forget their sense of humour.

From over three decades observing the politico species, for whom I have enormous sympathy, even the most level-headed of them lose their common-sense – and usually their cool – at the slightest whiff of a suggestion that a foreign trip which they took on official business was really a junket with more time spent on play rather than work.

A defensive mechanism comes into play – oops, sorry about the Freudian slip! Let's try again. A defensive mechanism rears to life in their psychological make-up which transforms politicians into blustering moralists who bore you with the details of how they spent long hours gaining knowledge about how other societies organise the collection of rubbish, run their public transport services and operate a more effective tax regime.

As you begin to yawn and tell them to try pulling your other leg, their defensive mechanism summersaults and they go on the offensive in high dudgeon by counter-attacking the media for trivialising their civic endeavours. This latter reaction is called shooting the messenger.

A classic case-study of this response came last week from a senior politician, Mary Hanafin, the Government Chief Whip, who was one of the Magnificent Seven members of an Oireachtas delegation that visited Australia for two weeks on what was officially described as "a political mission". Along with Hanafin were Ceann Comhairle Rory O'Hanlon, Jim Glennon of Fianna Fáil, the PDs' Liz O'Donnell, Fine Gael's Bernard Durkan, the Dublin Independent T.D. Tony Gregory and Senator Rory Kiely.

On her return to her desk in the Taoiseach's office, Hanafin was contacted by reporters who asked her how she enjoyed her two-week junket. That Mary suffers from the defensive mechanism syndrome – and has a hand-bag to carry it in – can be vouched for by an *Evening Herald* reporter, who heard a blast coming from the Chief Whip thundering that "the group had worked very hard out there". So much of their time was spent in the Dáil's sister Parliament in Canberra explaining to their Aussie colleagues developments in Ireland, the stalled peace process in the North and the enlarged European Union, all prior to inspecting a cattle farm in Cairns, New South Wales!

On the pretext that these weighty subjects went unreported by the Irish media, an outraged Hanafin refused to give further details of this epic inter-parliamentary dialogue. What, however, really made Mary mad was the brazen tabloid coverage which their strenuous trip had received in her absence. This coverage included the Oz Seven posing for a group picture as they enjoyed the finest wines at the Jacob Creek visitor centre in the splendid Barossa Valley near Adelaide.

What affronted Mary even more was the wiliness of a photographer who snapped a picture of her, while she was soaking up the sun on a beach near the Great Barrier Reef, clad in a full length black swimming suit of the kind worn by a Mother Superior from an enclosed convent in the days before the Swinging Sixties. In contrast, the real pin-up girl in the photograph was the luscious Liz O'Donnell, who wore a skimpy bikini.

While Mary's abrupt reaction to the media might leave her open to the charge of engaging in a cover-up, she was merely indulging in the panic 'defensive mechanism-kill the messenger' response. Mary should have known better than to go on a rampage. She forgot the late John *Backbencher* Healy's advice that politicians should never fall-out with journalists: the scribblers will get even later on. Mary would also have been wiser to have followed the example of the affable Killaser-born Bernard Durkan, who took the trouble to explain by phone from Canberra that the Australian Government was paying for travel and accommodation in luxurious hotels Down Under, but that the group would be reimbursed from Dáil expenses for business class air fares to Australia, via Kuala Lumpur.

Durkan, a Fine Gael T.D. for Kildare North, was less credible when he spun the yarn that the seven flew business class for security reasons and that they were promoting trade with Australia! No doubt, when the Dáil eventually resumes after its long holidays, Sinn Féin and the Greens will want to know the real cost to the Irish tax-payer of the junket, which is estimated to be at between €7,000 and €10,000 a head.

As Hanafin is regarded as a certainty for promotion to a ministry in next month's cabinet reshuffle, commentators are now wondering if she has her sights set on replacing Brian Cowen as Minister for Foreign Affairs when the Offaly man replaces Commissioner-designate McCreevy in Finance. Hanafin has acquired a taste for global travel. Only last month she headed a nine-member Fianna Fáil Oireachtas group to China to promote trade links and discuss human rights issues. This ordeal entailed visits to the far-reaches of well-known Fianna Fáil strongholds in Beijing, Shanghai, Hangzhou and Xian!

Admitting that formal visits by a Government party, as opposed to an Oireachtas delegation, were unusual, Hanafin, no doubt, saw the visit to Red China as an excellent opportunity for Fianna Fáil to strengthen its links with Communists. This may not be as far-fetched as it sounds. After all, one of China's leaders, Deng Xiaoping, was a great admirer of Seán Lemass. So can we expect to see the Chinese either joining FF cumman in Killala and Chinese immigrants opening a Communist cell in Castlebar?

Getting back, however, to the traumas of Comrade Mary. A former secondary school teacher, Hanafin is widely tipped to be a safer pair of hands in Education than Noel Dempsey, who has upset parents and teachers alike with his half-baked reform schemes. She is also being mentioned for Health if Bertie decides to move Mícheál Martin. Other possibilities are that she could replace Mary Coughlan in Social Welfare, or perhaps even become the first woman Minister of Defence, if Bertie has enough bottle to dismiss her Tipperary county man, the defiant Michael Smith.

With Joe Walsh pre-empting a push from Bertie by announcing his retirement from Agriculture, the spotlight is now on a stand-off between Smith and Ahern. It will be more than interesting to see whether Bertie exerts his authority against Smith with the same determination as he drove Bev Flynn out of the FF party. Or has Smith something on Bertie?

Smith has a valid point when he maintains that Bertie's long run-up to the reshuffle is causing instability in Fianna Fáil. Seasoned professionals like Limerick's Willie O'Dea and Wicklow's Dick Roche live in hope of finally currying Bertie's favour, while younger talent like Mary Hanafin and Brian Lenihan are fretting about their prospects.

As Bertie plays the power game close to his chest in his Kerry hideaway, perhaps Hanafin was the most hard-necked of the new breed of political missionaries by going off on junkets. She is truly a high-flier!

Bertie v Mullingar Pact

(September 15, 2004)

The pained expression on Enda Kenny's face when I told him he would never be Taoiseach alerted me to the fact that my tongue had grown too loose and that straight talking by a journalist to a politician, while admirable in principle, can boomerang especially when delivered from a cosy bar stool.

Our conversation took place late one night in Powers' Hotel, where along with a group of politicians and journalists we had adjourned from Leinster House for a libation. One colleague was promising Enda, who only recently had succeeded Michael Noonan as leader of Fine Gael after the party's drubbing in the 2002 general election, that he would accept the job of Government Press Secretary when Enda became Taoiseach.

This was the cue which my big mouth could not resist. My gloomy prediction wiped the smile off Enda's normally cheery face. "Why won't I be Taoiseach?", the somewhat vexed Enda asked. Rather than backing off, I ploughed into deeper waters, explaining that while I would be personally delighted if he became Mayo's first Taoiseach, he was leading a moribund party which was beyond revival and which lacked appeal to young people who were turning away to Sinn Féin from both Fine Gael and Fianna Fáil.

As we explored the strengths and weaknesses of Fine Gael, Enda stunned me by saying, "John, you really don't want me to be Taoiseach." As I protested that he was misreading what I had been saying, the atmosphere returned to its lighter mood when Michael O'Regan of *The Irish Times* intervened to quip: "Well, John will certainly not be Enda's Press Secretary!"

The point is that relations between politicians and political journalists can oscillate between either being too cosy or too poisonous. I have long been critical of how some journalists receive favoured treatment because they are pliable and reliable. I abhor reportage, too prevalent today, which casts politicians as either knaves or fools. My approach has always been – well nearly always! – to speak my mind to politicians or bishops as I would write about them. Give credit when they make right decisions, hell when they cock-up or dither.

However, the maxim of publish without fear or favour that governs the Fourth Estate does not always work, as is illustrated by my mini-contretemps with Enda, with whom I struck up a friendly relationship since I first interviewed him 35 years ago on a snowy December day in Castlebar. That the politician-journalist relationship is often uneasy is confirmed in a stimulating book, *My Trade*, by Andrew Marr, the BBC's political editor. Writing about difficulties when friendships grow between politicians and journalists, he observes that "in the end, even honest journalists must behave like a shit – must build up close sources – and then betray them".

While Marr is talking about journalists publishing material that might break confidences or even break the reputation of politicians with whom they have established a degree of intimacy, there is also an in-between stage where frank exchanges of view can shatter the mirage that journalists are merely propaganists of politicians. Happy to relate, that when Enda and I next met at the Mayo Association dinner, there was no huffiness on his part, while I assured him that was no malice on mine. Happily, I go on the record that later events – Fine Gael's success in the European and local elections – have changed my mind. Enda could become Taoiseach. Obviously, I don't have a crystal ball to say with certainty that Enda will be Taoiseach; equally I can no longer say he will not be Taoiseach.

Indeed, the possibility of a Mayo Taoiseach and a Mayo Tanaiste has taken a step closer with the Mullingar Pact between Kenny and Labour leader, Pat Rabbitte. This tentative move by Fine Gael and Labour to form a Government possibly with the Greens after the next general election is timely, as it faces an early test in two by-elections next spring.

The by-elections in North Kildare and Meath caused by the appointments to the European Union of Charlie McCreevy and John Bruton as Ambassador in Washington are winnable by Fine Gael with the help of transfers from Labour and the Greens.

A double strike by Fine Gael would boost Kenny's image as a Taoiseach-in-Waiting and could provide a leadership crisis in Fianna Fáil for Bertie Ahern. It could destablise an already jittery partnership between Fianna Fáil and the PDs. At the very least, the by-elections will show if Fianna Fáil's new 'caring' policy, unveiled last week in Inchydoney by Socialist Bertie, will be lubricated with tax cuts and more public spending in the December Budget. The strategy is a tightrope. At the political level, Fianna Fáil must win back voters who deserted largely to Sinn Féin, in the June elections; at cabinet level, an abandonment of 'prudent' economic policy will alienate the PDs.

The North Kildare and Meath ballots will also provide the first indicator of the public's response to Bertie's cabinet reshuffle due on September 29 which he and

Tanaiste Mary Harney promise will inject a fresh dynamism into a jaded-looking coalition.

This fast-changing political landscape puts further pressure on Bertie to make a success of his reshuffle. The focus on battles ahead for Dáil seats is spoiling appetites for a Presidential election on October 22. Neither the coalition parties nor the Opposition want to be distracted from the looming contests. Fianna Fáil will throw the full might of a revamped party organisation into holding McCreevy's North Kildare stronghold, but a failure to do so – and Bertie has not won a single by-election since becoming Taoiseach in 1997 – could bring out into the open simmering questions about his leadership. Inevitably, those who will be disappointed may seize their chance to get rid of Bertie and install Brian Cowen as a Taoiseach who can best deal with what he dismissed as a posturing 'marriage of convenience' by the Mayo duet.

Fianna Fáil will try to discredit the credibility of a Kenny-Rabbitte cohabitation, pointing to the turbulent ideological differences experienced under previous FG-Labour administrations led by Garret FitzGerald and John Bruton with Dick Spring.

Perhaps a better model is to be found in the FG-Labour deal that brought Liam Cosgrave and Brendan Corish to power in 1973, when Enda and Pat were still in short trousers.

Although the Mullingar Pact was overshadowed in the media by Fianna Fáil's Inchydoney think-in, its architects need to move much closer a lot quicker than their original general election time-table, if they are to hit Fianna Fáil hard in the North Kildare and Meath by-elections.

Overall, Kenny's biggest task will be to persuade the undecided that he can offer a fresh team to take-over from a coalition showing signs of running out of steam. Pop broadcaster Ray D'Arcy may have shown himself to be politically illiterate in calling Enda "a pale boiled potato". The reality is that Kenny is becoming a hot political potato. The trick for Fine Gael strategists is to have Enda *Spud* Kenny on the boil when Bertie calls the general election.

Best of luck, Enda. You have tough battles ahead if you are to achieve a latter-day Races of Castlebar!

Bertie Bites Rabbitte

(September 22, 2004)

When Pat Rabbitte told Vincent Browne to shut up on a television programme in October 2002, the Dublin South West deputy's reprimand of the aggressive broadcaster guaranteed his election as the ninth leader of the Labour Party a few days later in the election to succeed Ruairi Quinn. As Browne gasped in disbelief, rank and file Labour members wondered what the Mayoman from Ballindine would do to Bertie.

Now, almost two years later, Labour supporters are asking themselves if Rabbitte will prove to be their Michael Noonan after his worse media mauling ever over his botched non-selection of a candidate for the Presidency of Ireland. The Sunday newspapers roasted the Dáil's star performer who learned his debating skills in St Colman's College, Claremorris, and University College Galway. For once, Rabbitte was on the receiving end for an uncharacteristic but spectacularly inept performance.

Leading the attack and getting his revenge was Browne, who argued in the *Sunday Business Post* that Rabbitte's decision "to funk the presidential election underlines the party's frivolity". In turn, Rabbitte was accused by others of doing a U-turn on his earlier call for a presidential election, and of shafting Labour's elder poet-statesman, Michael D. Higgins, who was bursting to run against the incumbent President, Mary McAleese.

Only by the narrowest of margins, by 13 to 12, did Labour's national executive endorse the 2-1 recommendation by its parliamentary party not to allow him to contest the election. A deflated Michael D. won new admirers by maintaining his dignity in such a humiliating debacle.

Labour's rebuff of Michael D. was a huge let-down for those in the Labour Party – and the public – who regard the Galway West deputy as an icon of the Left. Love him or loath him, his colourful speeches both edify and entertain. With his record of crusading causes, Higgins hoped his campaign would resonate with echoes of Mary Robinson's 1990 sea-change epic, and that he would have a platform to challenge President McAleese's "bland presentation and reflection on Ireland".

Back in the 1970s when he was a Senator, Higgins co-sponsored with Mary Robinson pioneering legislation of contraception and for the abolition of illegitimacy. In the 1980s he was an outspoken critic of the policies of President Ronald Reagan in El Salvador and Nicaragua. His crusading style resurfaced recently when he condemned the Iraq War by the Bush and Blair administrations as illegal.

Specifically, a Higgins presidential bid would have focussed on national identity, and the meaning of citizenship in an increasingly multi-cultural society. On economic policy, he would have pressed for more caring policies. But Michael D. was not given a platform. His colleagues agreed with Rabbitte that their priority was preparing for next spring's by-elections in Meath and North Kildare. Deep down, they believed Michael D. would be soundly trounced by Mary Mac.

While Rabbitte was saved further embarrassment by the withdrawal on Saturday of the candidature of Green Eamon Ryan, the political damage to his reputation had scaled Croagh Patrick heights. Rabbitte's floundering has strained Labour's relations with the Greens who enjoyed the high media profile given to the Ryan solo run for a few giddy days before its leadership grimaced at the his radio admission that he had smoked cannabis – and woke up to the fact that the Dublin South deputy was a political rookie whose ambition would put an enormous strain on the party's war-chest.

If money daunted the Greens, this was not the case for Labour. Michael D. insisted that the party would not face a financial problem, as he was confident of securing the 12.5pc share of the vote need to recoup up to €260,000 of his campaign costs.

Such a financial safety net cannot be assured Dana Rosemary Scallon, who is bombarding county councils for nominations. Prior to the loss of her European Parliament seat in the North-West to Marian Harkin in June, Dana lost here deposit when she stood in the 2002 general election for Galway West, where she won only 1,677 first preferences. Ominously for Dana, these two defeats indicate that the support which brought her into the European Parliament in 1999 as a defender of pro-life and family values has shrunk considerably. She has also clashed with leading Irish pro-life campaigners and the Catholic bishops over her uncompromising views on abortion.

This erosion of Dana's popular appeal suggests that her financial backing will be much smaller than seven years ago when she first stood for the Presidency after pro-life groups who felt voiceless in an increasingly secular Ireland contacted her in Alabama to stand as the champion of traditional values. To the liberal media's surprise, Dana was nominated by five Councils – Donegal, Longford, Wicklow,

Tipperary and Kerry – and she came third in a field of five to Mary McAleese, with 175,458 votes, roughly 14pc of the electorate.

This time Dana's door-knocking is going unheard, not least by Mayo County Council. It was hardly good political strategy for her to target Enda Kenny's back-door as her first call. With Fianna Fáil, Fine Gael, the PDs and Sinn Féin all backing *Mary Mac*, it will surely take a miracle for Dana to obtain the four nominations by the October 31 deadline. But assuming that Dana manages this near-impossible feat, she faces being massacred by McAleese. The former MEP would be hard put to win the 12.5pc of the vote to qualify for the €260,000 reimbursement.

With McAleese virtually assured of an uncontested second term in the Aras, the spotlight will fall on Rabbitte's performance since becoming leader. His decisive win two years ago in succession to Ruairi Quinn ensured that the blow-in from the merger with Democratic Left took charge of Labour with a mandate to fulfil his pledge to rejuvenate the party which he so lacerated when in Opposition.

Rabbitte's declaration that he would not serve in a Fianna Fáil-Labour Government under Bertie laid the foundation for his leadership victory over Brendan Howlin. His trump card was his pledge to make Labour the most effective voice in the Dáil.

Although Labour made some marginal gains in the last local elections and held its Dublin Euro seat with Proinsias de Rossa, the main winners were Sinn Féin and Fine Gael. Now Labour's first Mayo born leader faces four fall-outs from his presidential misadventure.

First, he has diminished the office of President by making it secondary to Oireachtas party politics. Kenny and Green leader Trevor Sargent are in a stronger position than Rabbitte to call for new rules allowing greater access to run for Head of State.

Second, Labour is again divided – and Michael D. may be sulking in the snipe-grass.

Third, Rabbitte's bungling contrasts unfavourably with Enda Kenny's sound judgement in not fielding a Fine Gael candidate. It strengthens Kenny's claim to be leader of the Opposition in the post-Mullingar period.

Fourth, Bertie Ahern must be chuckling as he prepares to announce his new cabinet and launch his offensive to win a third period as Taoiseach. The first Mayo-born leader of the Labour Party will need all his quick wit and brain-power to regain lost ground.

Bertie's 'Dream-team' Nightmare

(September 29, 2004)

During the long Dáil summer siesta Bertie Ahern has had plenty of time to hanker after the good old days before the era of Tribunals when the Real Fianna Fáil ruled the land. Overcome by nostalgia, he went to bed early one evening in his luxurious Kerry holiday hotel, and in a deep sleep he drew up his dream team.

For starters, he dropped those troublesome Progressive Democrats, Mary Harney and Michael McDowell, and blissfully selected his all-star FF team based on cronyism, nepotism and absolute power. In his dream it was D-Day, September 29, 2004, as he stood up before a hushed Dáil to announce his line-up.

Taoiseach, Bertie Ahern, with a mandate to seek Dáil approval on October 22 for the abolition of the Presidency, and to re-assign Head of State functions to the office of Taoiseach.

Tanaiste and Minister for Communications, Natural Resources & Marine, Noel Ahern. "This establishes the Ahern clan as the nation's number one family".

Finance, Dermot Ahern. "It keeps the Ahern name to the fore and it will keep Biffo wondering if his hour will ever come".

Foreign Affairs and Northern Ireland, Mary Hanafin. "Her recent trips to China, Australia and Medugore showed she is a high-flyer. If the DUP stall on the peace process, Mary can join *Big Ian* in prayer. She might even convert the North back to the True Faith".

Transport, Jackie Healy-Rea. "Jackie has agreed to rejoin Fianna Fáil. His construction of the Killorglin highway provides a model for getting Dublin back on the move".

Enterprise and Employment, Brian Cowen. "This will give *Biffo* experience in a heavy-weight economic ministry. His hour will surely come".

Environment and Local Government, John O'Donoghue. "John will be in charge of slush funding to win votes and outspend the Provos".

Justice, Beverely Cooper Flynn. "Bev is rejoining the Fianna Fáil family. Her banking experience is invaluable and she will bump up the fees for my lawyer friends at the Tribunals. She will keep Mayo quiet, thank God, and keep Pádraig from yapping".

Health, Martin Cullen. "A chain-smoker, Martin will repeal Micheál's anti-puffing ban, and get the smokers and vintners back on side."

Agriculture, Micheál Martin. "This will keep Mickey in Brussels for long spells in the smoke-filled rooms of late night meetings of of EU Agriculture ministers."

Social & Family Affairs, Michael Woods. "Woodsie's return will inspire the elderly. His special adviser on poverty will be Fr Seán Healy. Woodsie will also take over official responsibility for relations with the Churches to block David Norris's Bill legalising single sex unions".

Education, Michael Smith. "This will teach the Monsignor a lesson for taunting me all summer. He can update his academic qualifications".

Community, Rural and Gaeltacht Affairs, Séamus Brennan. "Séamus needs to sharpen his linguistic skills. He also needs country air after all that wasted time on Luas upsetting the unions".

Attorney General, Liam Lawlor. "I was impressed by his legal skills at the Tribunals. He would probably persuade the courts to pay my old pal Ray Burke's legal fees and reverse the stingy ruling by Judge Mahon".

At this point, Bertie awoke in a deep sweat. It had been a dreadful nightmare. As he turned on the bedroom light and sipped a glass of water, he comforted himself with the thought that under his leadership a new and more caring Fianna Fáil had come of age.

Unable, however, to get back to sleep, he drew up a draft cabinet to consolidate his FF-PD coalition and return him as Taoiseach for a record third term after the next general election. After humiliating losses to Sinn Féin in the June Euro and local elections, Bertie was under pressure to undertake radical surgery by cutting off accident-prone ministers such as Martin Cullen. But he knew he hated a blood bath. His minimum changes would be based largely on geographical factors to maximise the Fianna Fáil vote by spreading State cars nationwide. Three places were freed-up during the summer – Finance minister Charlie McCreevy was despatched to Brussels, Joe Walsh is retiring and Michael Smith had ensured his own dismissal by taunting Bertie to take him out.

Bertie's Winning Team:

Taoiseach Bertie Ahern – "Who else?"

Tanaiste and Minister for Education and Children, Mary Harney. "The PD leader will add the science-technology brief to education where she can engineer a new generation of PDs in her mould".

Finance, Brian Cowen. "With over a billion euro to spare in the kitty, *Biffo* can gear the December budget to relaunch the Government's popularity".

Foreign Affairs and Northern Ireland, Dermot Ahern. "From the Border's El Paso, the Dundalkman can speak the lingo of the Provos and sell the new EU Treaty to the electorate".

Transport, Martin Cullen. "A reprieve for the Waterfordman who messed up E-voting. A talker, he will be at home with Luas, the Unions, Aer Rianta and Ryan Air's Michael O'Leary".

Enterprise and Employment, Seamus Brennan. "This sideways move will not reduce his stature".

Environment and Local Government, John O'Donoghue. "An Ahern acolyte, he will direct funding locally to take on Sinn Féin".

Justice, Michael McDowell. "No change on the law and order front. *Mad Mullah* rule, Ok!"

Social and Family Affairs, Micheál Martin. "Another hardship portfolio for Micky".

Health, Mary Hanfin. "A disciple of the Nanny State, she can save the ailing hospital system".

Agriculture, Noel Dempsey. "His Meath base is important for next spring's by-election. He will impress the farmers with his command of EU lingo".

Communications, Natural Resources & Marine, Pat the Cope Gallagher. "The Cope was promised promotion for returning to Donegal from the European Parliament in the 2002 general election, and has earned his reward by directing the Euro-campaign that prevented Sinn Féin from taking a seat in Ulster-Connacht".

Community, Rural and Gaeltacht Affairs, Eamon Ó Cuív. "No change, Dev's grandson is committed to western development and should get on with his Irish language crusade".

Arts & Tourism, Síle de Valera. "With the thirtieth anniversary of Eamon de Valera's death next year, the Dev name will divert from the Haughey legacy".

Defence, Dick Roche. "Knows even more about the EU than Alan Dukes – and he will modernise the Armed Forces in line with EU policy".

Chief Whip, Mary Coughlan. "Mary can charm the begruders who are left out".

Attorney General, Rory Brady. "No change. He knows FF as well as the law".

If, dear reader, when Bertie announces a different team, this is because he changed his mind when he went back to sleep again!

Bertie's Reshuffle
Anti-climax

(October 6, 2004)

In the West and North West, where Ray MacSharry and Padraig Flynn once ruled like mighty chieftains in Fianna Fáil Governments, neither John Carty in Mayo nor Dr Jimmy Devins in Sligo-Leitrim were enlisted to the junior ranks of the FF-PD Coalition in Taoiseach Bertie Ahern's long-awaited but anti-climactic reshuffle.

Coming just days after Mayo's humbling defeat by Kerry in the All Ireland Final, Bertie's calculated concentration on more prosperous urban centres in the south and east of the country hardly provided a tonic to lift sore heads from Croagh Patrick to Ben Bulben via the Ox Mountains.

It is no consolation that Bertie's State Merc is the only one in northside Dublin, while south of the river Liffey is dotted with ministerial cars. Nor that Mícheál Martin, now Employment supremo, has the only cabinet chariot in Cork, with the departure of Joe Walsh.

In contrast to the absence of ministerial representation in Mayo and Sligo, Clare now boasts two juniors with the appointment of the energetic Tony Killeen in Enterprise Trade and Employment, while the veteran Síle de Valera stays in Education.

Just to add to the gloom, Michael Finneran in Longford-Roscommon did not manage to clamber on board Bertie's junior squad – while the popular Dr Jim McDaid in Donegal was sacked from his post as Minister of State for Transport, a deed which Bertie tried to disguise when he misleadingly told the Dáil that he had received his resignation.

The one crumb of comfort for the somewhat artificial BMW entity – the Border, Midlands and West region – in this ungenerous Ahern disposition of places - came with the overdue promotion of the able and likeable Cavan-Monaghan deputy, Brendan Smith, as Minister of State in the Department of Agriculture and Food. And of course, the farming organisations have already begun to woo Donegal South West's Mary Coughlan, who becomes the State's first female Minister for Agriculture and Food. Although Eamon Ó Cuív retains his roving brief as Minister for Community, Rural and Gaeltacht Affairs, he will shoulder an even more burdensome task in persuading the citizenry of the West and North West that Bertie still loves them.

Of importance for the development of the Corrib Gas project is the appointment of Noel Dempsey as Minister for Communications, Marine and Natural Resources, where he will be assisted by Pat *The Cope* Gallagher. In view, too, of the notoriously awful road network west of the Shannon considerable interest will focus on the new Transport Minister, Martin Cullen, a Waterford man who will be under pressure to ensure that the Dublin conurbation does not continue to virtually monopolise public expenditure. Interestingly, Cullen is on record as being supportive of the Atlantic Arc, a group of some 300 technology companies which are based on the west and south coast.

In spite of the upbeat talk from the Government spin-doctors that the Taoiseach had picked a winning team (minus Michael Smith), an undercurrent of discontent was detectable in the Dáil corridors as deputies expressed dismay that Bertie had not responded to the public's expectations of a more radical shake-up. There was widespread agreement even within the FF ranks with Fine Gael leader Enda Kenny's taunt that the Taoiseach laboured for three months to produce a political mouse, and with Labour leader Pat Rabbitte's verdict that he delivered "rancid old wine in new bottles". There was anger that Bertie shirked dismissing accident-prone ministers.

In opting for a minimalist cabinet reshuffle, Bertie deeply disappointed a large section of the Fianna Fáil parliamentary party with mutterings and mumblings already starting about a heave against his leadership if the new team does not reverse the Government's current unpopularity. "The bottom-line was that the voters punished us in the June local and European elections and gave us a message that they wanted to see heads roll, not deck chairs changed in cabinet", one Fianna Fáil activist told me.

This source was adamant that Bertie has swollen the number of dissidents and that he may not survive politically to lead his party into the next general election Angry backbenchers are tic-tacking privately to hatch an internal revolt that will lead to Bertie's being replaced as Taoiseach by Finance minister Brian Cowen by either next spring or the summer. The scenario is that the dissidents will canvass quietly among themselves to build up support for Cowen.

Bertie has gambled on a team that he hopes will result in his third general election win. But with such a nucleus already existing for discontent, he needs to hold the North Kildare seat vacated by the departure of Charlie McCreevy. FG should hold Meath after John Bruton takes up his post as EU Ambassador in Washington.

Insisting that he has picked the best people, the Taoiseach is relying to a large extent on Cowen producing a December Budget that will reduce taxes for the less well off and maintain Ireland's as "a model economy". Significantly, with the departure of the PD-minded McCreevy to Brussels, Bertie for the first time in his seven years in office will have control over economic policy, and he will work closely with Cowen. Indeed, some commentators compare the Bertie-Brian relationship with that of Tony Blair and Gordon Brown in Britain!

Ironically, with Mary Harney taking "the poisoned chalice" of Health, the Tanaiste's hold over Ahern is seen to be strengthened. The PD leader has an exit opt-out from Government if Fianna Fáil does not support her health reforms. Fianna Fáil backbenchers are convinced that she intervened behind the scenes to keep Séamus Brennan – seen as a covert PD – in cabinet as Minister for Social and Family Affairs at the expense of the able Brian Lenihan.

Both Ahern and Harney are gambling on newcomers Mary Hanafin in Education, Willie O'Dea in Defence and Dick Roche in Environment injecting a fresh dynamic into the nation's governance, and that the more seasoned members of Government, too, will deliver quality public services. However, in the new administration's first 24 hours we were subjected to old ways of doing business and to the prospect of a new dawn: John O'Donoghue, who remains in Arts, Sport and Tourism, announced €40m for Croke Park, while the Minister for Foreign Affairs, Dermot Ahern, and Bertie sat across the table with the ailing Ian Paisley.

On Friday it was confirmed that the Government will not be diverted from its new challenges when President Mary McAleese was returned unopposed for a second seven-year term in the Áras. In a magical sound-bite, she said that had cried with sheer joy on hearing Paisley talk of partnership and good neighbourliness. Close to tears for a different reason was Dana Rosemary Scallon, who had secured only one of the four County Council nominations required to contest the Presidency. Hopefully, the Government will make the rules governing the presidency more accessible to prospective candidates outside the main political parties.

As the Government gets down to the nitty gritty, working overtime will be the lot of Chief Whip, Tom Kitt. He will have to keep a close eye on his colleagues who were passed over for promotion.

Bertie's gamble may pay off. Yet by failing to meet expectations of a radical cabinet rehaul, he may yet be confronted by unruly backbenchers.

Big Ian Tempted by Bertie

(November 17, 2004)

"Brother Cooney, put today's lunch date into your diary," the late John *Backbencher* Healy advised me, raising a large glass of Cognac brandy in a toast to the Rev Ian Paisley with whom we had met in the European Parliament restaurant in Strasbourg.

"We have just lunched with the next Prime Minister of Northern Ireland", Healy, in expansive mood, predicted.

These words uttered almost 25 years ago came back to mind when I read a newspaper headline: "Paisley key to deal, governments feel". The story predicted that the Irish and British Governments are set this week to start the clock ticking for the sealing of an historic deal between Sinn Féin and the Democratic Unionist Party that could resolve the Ulster crisis.

According to diplomatic sources Gerry Adams and Paisley will be presented with the terms on which Taoiseach Bertie Ahern and Prime Minister Tony Blair are prepared to restore the Northern Ireland Executive and Assembly at Stormont. After all these years is Healy's prediction about to come true? Is Paisley, the noisy permanent outsider, about to come in from the Stormont cold, where he once threw snow-balls at Prime Minister Terence O'Neill as he welcomed Taoiseach Seán Lemass, into the inner sanctuary of Ulster Unionism? Is *Big Ian*, now an ailing old man close to his 79th birthday, about to end his days as head of a power-sharing Executive with his avowed enemy, Sinn Féin?

History did not take the turn sign-posted by Healy. Haughey and Thatcher fell out - and Paisley demonised them both. He opposed the 1985 Anglo-Irish Agreement negotiated with Maggie Thatcher by Garret FitzGerald. For a brief moment in 1990, Paisley sat down at talks in Stormont with ministers of the FF-PD Government of Haughey and Des O'Malley, but these broke down. In turn, he opposed the Downing Street Declaration agreed by Albert Reynolds and John Major, the Framework Document of John Bruton and Major, and the Good Friday Agreement which led to David Trimble taking over for a short but unsuccessful period the prime ministerial post which Healy had assigned for *Big Ian*.

Just over a year ago when Paisley's DUP overtook Trimble's party as the dominant force in Unionist politics and Sinn Féin outstripped the SDLP, a television journalist asked Paisley if he would talk to Sinn Féin. *Big Ian*, despite his age and frailty, seized the reporter by his lapel and roared: "I am not talking to Sinn Féin and my party is not talking to Sinn Féin, and anyone who talks to Sinn Féin will be out of my party".

Yet, we are now tantalisingly close to a deal, even though the DUP still wants to renegotiate the Good Friday Agreement. Gerry Adams has signalled the ending of the IRA. Paisley has been in Dublin for talks with Bertie.

If Paisley is still as ideologically aggressive as ever in the cause of Unionism, his physical decline has meant that his two main lieutenants, Peter Robinson and Nigel Dodds, have played a more up-front role in the negotiations. As the two DUP ministers who held portfolios in the Executive and worked the Agreement well, Robinson and Dodds are more pragmatic than their reverend master.

So, is Paisley for turning? One man who does not think so is Austin Currie, the former SDLP and later Fine Gael minister. In his autobiography, *All Hell Will Break Loose*, Currie recalls describing Paisley in 1966 as "a bigoted hangover from the seventeenth century" - and the passage of time has not given Austin any reason to change his mind. In one of the best books on the North written by a participant Currie writes that as a Paisley observer for more than 40 years, he believes that the parson-politician has contributed more to the intensity and the duration of the Troubles - and therefore to the deaths of so many people - than any other individual.

It is a harsh judgement, but one which I share. My view is that until Paisley steps down as leader or passes on to his eternal reward, his party is unlikely to make a Damascus-style journey from Ballymena to Stormont via West Belfast. If this proves to be correct, Paisley will assume a place in history similar to that of Yasser Arafat. Just as Paisley is revered by his followers as the champion of a Protestant Ulster, so too was Arafat idolised by his people as the advocate of a Palestinian homeland: both unsuccessful in achieving their goals.

The one exception which may make Paisley change his mind is the prospect of becoming the Prime Minister who caused the ending of the IRA. But both Sinn Féin and the SDLP fear that Paisley will demand a new Unionist veto to paralyse a new power-sharing Executive. Another remark made by Currie may also prove to be pertinent. Had Paisley been willing to take a pint, he writes, the whole history of Northern Ireland might have been different.

When Healy and I drank our Cognac brandy, Paisley warned us that the Devil's Buttermilk would be our undoing. I will raise my glass to Paisley if he proposes a toast to Sinn Féin.

Bertie, 'the Socialist'!

(November 24, 2004)

Bertie Ahern is "an extremely intelligent and able person who has thrived upon being underestimated for a very long time," according to journalist John Downing in a new political biography. Bertie's intelligence and ability are augmented by a phenomenal and single-minded work rate with days that usually stretch from 7 am to past midnight.

A few pints of Bass with his old friends in his Drumcondra watering-holes are among his few diversions which also include walking and attending sports events. Even when he travels abroad on Government business, he prefers when possible to be in Drumcondra before the pubs close.

Readers searching for insights, however, into the Taoiseach's career as a Socialist in this timely biography titled *Most skilful, most devious, most cunning*, will scour the pages feeling somewhat like United Nations inspector Hans Blick looking for weapons of mass destruction in Saddam Hussein's Iraq!

No doubt, Bertie Ahern's self-proclaimed Socialism was as surprising to Downing as it is to the rest of the political chattering class. Unless you are addicted to political spin, no such evidence is to be found, though his commitment to community development and his sense of patriotism are beyond question.

This Socialism fantasy does not deflect Downing, the Political Correspondent of the *Irish Star*, from producing a solidly workman-like book marking the first decade of Bertie's leadership of Fianna Fáil. It is, as Downing acknowledges, an interim report rather than a definitive verdict on Ahern's place in history. The book fills a gap in Irish political literature which I pointed to recently when I noted that unlike the numerous books on Tony Blair, there was only one on Bertie by Ken Whelan and Eugene Masterson which was published in 1998 as *Taoiseach and Peacemaker*.

When I wrote this, I did I not know that John Downing had embarked on this update publication. Nor did most of his colleagues in Dublin. John kept his labours quiet. Indeed, when I asked him the other day why he had not mentioned his project when he was in Ballina last July as a speaker at the International Humbert School, he confided that he was not sure at that time whether he would complete it for Bertie's tenth anniversary as leader of Fianna Fáil.

Despite a tight schedule, John has delivered a book which deserves a wide readership whether you love or loath Bertie. A Brussels veteran and now one of the most respected Pol Corrs in Leinster House, John draws on his wide experience and acute observation to give a coherence to the life story of Bartholomew Patrick Ahern.

During over seven of his ten years in charge of Fianna Fáil, Bertie has been in power as head of two FF-PD coalitions, and he aspires to lead a third Government, possibly with Sinn Féin. His aim is to quit politics for *la dolce vita* when he hits 60 in 2011.

Next to Fianna Fáil's founding father, Eamon de Valera, he is the longest-serving Taoiseach. While sympathetic to Ahern – though he puts the boot in when required – Downing, sensibly, avoids canonising Bertie, as his supporters do, as being even more successful in modernising Ireland than Seán Lemass.

Downing sets himself three main aims: to investigate how Bertie secured power, how he has kept that power and how he has used power. Given the secrecy of cabinet decision-making even in our so-called era of openness and accountability, Downing succeeds in his first two goals but is less enlightening on Bertie's exercise of power. For instance, there is no mention of the role of Gerry Hickey, his chief adviser, who has more clout than most cabinet ministers.

Where Downing is particularly good is in his highlighting of Bertie's mooching skills as a ward politician, operating from his Drumcondra power-house in St Luke's with a team of loyal assistants who weekly send out some 700 representations on behalf of constituents and supplicants.

Inevitably, Bertie's mentor, Charles J. Haughey, looms large in Downing's book. Downing's title is borrowed from Haughey's Svengalian description of Ahern, which continues to shroud his public image, but one which the author valiantly attempts to put in a more favourable 'consensus' context.

Noting the bonanza economic times of Celtic Tiger Ireland which have coincided with the country's rapid transformation from a religious to a materialist ethos, Downing identifies the consolidation of national partnerships with trade unions and business, the signing of the Good Friday Agreement in the North, and his negotiation of a new EU Treaty during the recent Irish Presidency as Bertie's main achievements.

Downing provides a readable and skilful summary of the Ahern years – but the real Bertie remains elusive. Downing, whose story takes us up to the recent cabinet reshuffle, accurately predicted that the appointment of Martin Cullen as Minister for Transport was a signal that Bertie will call the shots between now and the next general election.

Events have shown that Cullen has been handed 'the shitty end' of a pilot's stick by the Taoiseach in his unenviable task of keeping Aer Lingus airborne and profitable after the loss of chief executive Willie Walsh and his two key managers. Ambitious and a robust media performer, Cullen's replacement of Séamus Brennan was widely interpreted as a sop to the unions whom the Dublin South TD had alienated by his pro-privatisation policy for the public transport sector, including the break up of the airport authority, Aer Rianta, and the liberalisation of bus services.

Though an ex-PD and himself a pro-marketeer, Cullen is now charged with avoiding a showdown with the PDs, while finding replacements for Walsh and his two chief acolytes whom the Taoiseach has publicly demonised as trying to sell out in order to make themselves rich. A polarisation in positions rather than a difference in emphasis is emerging with Ahern showing no appetite to sell off part of the airline, and Harney insisting on new investment.

This latest row has more to do with Fianna Fáil running scared to the Left after its worst performance in the June local and Euro elections since 1927 than with aviation economics. Cullen's pragmatism is on trial. Does he show common-sense or follow the route mapped by *the Drumcondra Socialist*? On the answer, may depend the future not only of Aer Lingus but of the Government – and Bertie's prospects for a third term.

Bertie, Dumb and Glum

(December 8, 2004)

As Brian Cowen commended his first Budget to the Dáil last Tuesday and Fianna Fáil backbenchers cheered like born-again lobby voting fodder because of its emphasis on the poorer-off in society, the Taoiseach sat beside his Minister for Finance on the Government benches with the grim demeanour of a man in a dental waiting-room awaiting a painful tooth extraction.

That is how the biggest Dáil event in the annual political calendar appeared to me as I pondered why Bertie Ahern looked so glum when Brian Cowen released the first pre-election instalment of a calculated shift to the Left after the seven pro free-market enterprise budgets of Charlie McCreevy.

My first thought was that Bertie was troubled by the acclaimed popularity of the man known as *Biffo* who was establishing his undisputable claims as pretender to his prime ministerial office. This did not seem a convincing explaination, however, as Bertie stands to be the principal beneficiary in the public mind of a budget which he insisted should be more socially caring. And anyway, *Biffo* needs a few more years to restructure a tax system which continues to penalise the PAYE sector and to favour the wealthy.

No, the reason for Bertie's anxiety, it next occurred to me, was his realisation that earlier at Question Time the Fine Gael leader Enda Kenny had weedled out of him a premature admission that the four killers of Detective Garda, Jerry McCabe, would be released as part of a Northern Ireland deal.

Sure enough, this intuition was quickly confirmed. Cowen found himself sharing the media spotlight with unexpected controversy over the terms of a possible Northern settlement, as the widowed Ann McCabe complained that she had not been consulted by the Government about a development which would be in breach of the Good Friday Agreement - and which she had first heard on the news, while Paisley turned on the Taoiseach with a fury that threatened the prospects of a deal.

Indeed, the McCabe row upstaged post-budget commentary in the Sunday news-papers when the founder of the Progressive Democrats, Dessie O'Malley, accused Bertie of "appeasing terrorists" and of intimidating Mrs McCabe as "an obstacle to peace", because of her continued opposition to the release of "common criminals".

Confronted by a *Sunday Independent* phone poll showing four out of five people in the Republic against the release, and with Mrs McCabe's dignified protest that she was being treated unjustly by republicans, the Sinn Féin President, Gerry Adams, insisted that their release was covered under the Good Friday Agreement.

Until now, Mrs McCabe's position, and not that of Adams, was the firm commitment of the FF-PD Coalition. So it made for absorbing television viewing on Sunday evening to watch how the Tanaiste and PD leader, Mary Harney, dealt with the issue on Seán O'Rourke's *The Week in Politics* programme. In one of her best interviews for some time, Mary gave an impressive performance that captures the moral dilemma at the heart of this agonising issue. She highlighted past inconsistencies in Adams' attitude towards the murder of Jerry McCabe, and she stood-by a solemn commitment which she had given in Limerick that the four would not go free.

Significantly, she revealed that the Taoiseach had not yet obtained a Government decision on their release, but qualified her remark by admitting that in the context of a total end to paramilitarism in which the IRA laid down all their arms and stopped engaging in criminality, "then, and only then, will we even consider the possibility that these people might be released".

This was a spine-chilling insight into the complexities of peace-making in the North and of difficult compromises to be made in the process. Surely, there must have been confidential reports to the cabinet from Bertie and Minister for Foreign Affairs, Dermot Ahern that a U-turn on the McCabe case was under negotiation. Or, was it the case that the two Aherns kept their ministerial colleagues in the dark?

In my view, it is unlikely that Harney and other members of the Government, especially the Minister for Defence, Willie O'Dea, were not already briefed. It is likely that Enda Kenny got a whiff of this in the corridors of power and decided to put the Taoiseach on the spot at Question Time. Was Enda opportunistically seeking a political advantage to distract from Cowen's budget? Why had the leader of the main Opposition not been given a briefing in confidence by the Taoiseach in order to avoid a premature Dáil statement on the McCabe issue at a delicate time when the negotiations were on the proverbial knife-edge? Or was Bertie, as some commentators have suggested, using Budget Day to get out bad news on the McCabe front?

Having being caught out misleading the Dáil before, Bertie, I suspect, took the opportunity to prepare parliamentary and public opinion for what was deemed to be bad news for Mrs McCabe and for the families of the 302 Northern Ireland police officers killed in the Troubles. Hence, his down-cast visage during Cowen's Budget address. He must have known his admission would cause dismay, not least among the members of the Garda Representative Body, who are meeting this week - in of all places - Adare.

Paisley is due to give his decision on whether to accept the proposals of the two Governments to Tony Blair on Monday afternoon. The signs of his acceptance are not good. The man described by the late Brian Faulkner as the demon doctor insists that he will not be Trimbled by the IRA, of whom he will require the publication of photographed proof of complete destruction of their weapons and ammunition prior to his becoming the DUP's First Minister in a power-sharing Executive with Sinn Féin's Martin McGuinness as his deputy.

For his part, Gerry Adams has indicated that the IRA will not be forthcoming about photographic proof of a total decommissioning, especially after Paisley's outburst last week that republicans must be humiliated and wear "sackcloth and ashes". This week-end Paisley, who is bitter at learning that the IRA have not yet engaged directly with General John de Chastelain's International Commission on Decommissioning, taunted the Sinn Féin leader of being "a bloody and deceitful" man. In turn, Adams accused Paisley of using the language of humiliation that led to pogroms in the late 1960s.

All this sounds to me like a rehearsal of "the blame game". Although the two Governments claim a deal is tantalisingly close, I fear - but hope I am wrong – that when Bertie and Blair assemble in Belfast this Wednesday, they will be unveiling their proposals for a resumption of devolved government on their own - minus Paisley and Adams.

An indication that the North could once again be perilously close to further political and paramilitary instability came with a report in Monday's *Irish Independent* that on Sunday evening Gardaí foiled a plan by three members of the Real IRA to launch a new bombing campaign.

Unless there is a last minute restoration of trust, the scene seems set for frustration for Tony and Bertie in Belfast, while, in Dublin, Brian Cowen will be wondering why he will rank in history as the State's first Minister of Finance to find his first budget playing second news fiddle to the North.

Brian now knows that Bertie and Enda upstaged his big day.

Blame Game Stalls Bertie

(December 15, 2004)

"Well, my friends, you read in this column last week what no other political commentator would predict for you – that *Big Ian* and the Provos would not lie down together in a Stormont power-sharing bed".

In boastful language such as this the late John *Backbencher* Healy, a previous occupant of this column and to whose inspiration editor, James Laffey and myself often advert, might have crowed this morning in reminding you about my prediction last week that Bertie Ahern and Tony Blair would assemble in Belfast on Wednesday minus Ian Paisley and Gerry Adams for the unveiling of what they believed was the blueprint for a comprehensive settlement in the North.

As Ed Mulhall wrote in a perceptive essay which appeared in *Letters from a New Island*, Healy was proud of his ability to predict. "A prophecy come true, Lemass is for the country" was how Healy underlined his success in forecasting correctly the 1965 General Election, and in the 1977 General Election he was the only political writer with no egg on his face, because he alone had anticipated Jack Lynch's sweeping victory against Liam Cosgrave and Brendan Corish.

If he were writing this column to-day, Healy would have moderated his personal vanity with a dollop of homespun philosophy. "We have known better weeks, better times", he might note, as he did in his obituary of one of his heroes, Donagh O'Malley.

Healy would also have delved into the nature of Irish society to explain why a complex and secretive negotiation was reduced for the public to simply catch-phrases by Paisley and Adams, Bertie and Blair. "As in our politics, we had to simplify our history and, for a verbal people, the Slogan was all", he might be observing about the decommissioning issue, as he did in a brilliant essay on Michael Davitt in a *Western People* special supplement in 1979 to mark the centenary of the founding of the Land League.

Like Healy, I have had my fair share of accurate "prophecy" in the prediction game, such as that Charlie Haughey would beat George Colley for the leadership of Fianna Fáil, that Robin Eames would become the Church of Ireland Primate, that Bishop Cahal Daly would succeed Tomás Ó Fiaich as Cardinal Archbishop of

Armagh, that Diarmuid Martin would succeed Cardinal Desmond Connell as Archbishop of Dublin, that the first Nice Treaty referendum would be lost and the second won, and most recently that Cliff Taylor would be the new editor of *The Sunday Business Post*. For years, before any other journalist, I have tipped Brian Cowen to be the next leader of Fianna Fáil. The list of my clairvoyance is endless! Or so I deceive myself. For, like Healy, for every time I got it right, I could quote the occasions when I got it wrong, sometimes badly and embarrassingly so. It is one of the risks of a journalist's trade.

In this case, I wrote before the crucial meeting between Paisley and Blair in Downing Street that afternoon. Having followed the North closely since even before the Sunningdale Agreement in the early 1970s, and knowing all the main players in the current drive for a final settlement, I concluded that that "blame game" had already begun following Paisley's "sack-cloth and ashes" demands of the IRA, and that on Budget Day Bertie looked glum because of his Dáil disclosure to Enda Kenny about the release of Garda Jerry McCabe's killers.

Although I hoped that my prediction would be wrong, I knew I was taking a huge risk as *The Western* appears on Tuesday, just as the negotiations would be reaching their decisive phase and readers would have the advantage of knowing the outcome. At the back of my mind was the warning placed before all journalists of how *The Irish Press* headlined that Charlie Haughey was gone in a party purge when later that same day he did another of his famous Houdini survival acts.

On Monday evening when Paisley did not storm out of Downing Street but issued a statesmanlike soundbite that he would be prepared to enter government with Sinn Féin if the IRA allowed a total decommissioning of their arms to be photographed, I began to feel that I had done an *Irish Press*. Listening to Tommie Gorman's predictions on RTE that the deal was on, I braced myself for an egg rash on my face. On Tuesday morning as I collected *The Western* at Keane's on the Quay, I momentarily was tempted to take the honourable course and drive into the Moy after reading in *The Irish Times* that "Adams says SF can accept Anglo-Irish blueprint".

On mature reflection, I still calculated that Paisley and Adams were merely positioning themselves as apostles of sweetness and light ahead of the inevitable collapse of the talks which came around lunch-time when a breathless Charlie Bird informed us that the IRA were not accepting Paisley's diktat.

By now, many readers will have been turned off – and perhaps be confused – by the cascade of apologias and recriminations which have come from the participants in the still ongoing blame game. I shall not rehearse the ins and outs of the torrential outpourings of special pleadings and ingenious alibis from the squabbling politicians, but I do want to focus on what strikes me as important lessons to be learned from the revelations which have emerged about how negotiations were conducted.

First, Paisley has done us all a great service by refusing to be Trimbled by the IRA who remain equivocal in its refusal to have decommissioning visually verified.

Second, Tanaiste Mary Harney championed the public's right to know when she highlighted the IRA's refusal to commit itself to ending the criminal involvement of its members in knee-capping, the illicit booze trade and other Mafia-like scams.

Third, although Bertie had mentioned the need for the IRA to end criminality, he and Tony Blair gave the wrong impression at their joint press conference in Belfast's Waterfront Hall that the only outstanding issue was that of a photograph. By implication, the McCabe murderers could have been released in a side deal that would not have guaranteed an end to Provo gangsterism.

Fourth, the fine text of the proposals released by the two Governments shows that its sections on the election of a First (Paisley) and Deputy First Minister (Martin McGuinness) amounted to a substantial alteration of the Good Friday Agreement, one which would have Balkanised the North into a regime carved up by the DUP and Sinn Féin to the virtual exclusion of Trimble's Ulster Unionist Party and Mark Durkan's SDLP.

Bertie is due to meet Gerry Adams at Government Buildings, against the background of a row over whether the Taoiseach, as Adams claimed on the *Late Late Show*, nodded assent to the release of the McCabe murderers five years ago, but which Bertie has strenuously denied in several eloquent interviews.

According to Bertie the deal could be put right in a further nine hours of negotiations, and that the IRA have re-engaged over the weekend with General John De Chastelain. Hopefully, but I have my doubts. The deal has unravelled. Positions have hardened. The DUP will hold on until after next May's general election in the expectation of hammering Trimble. Tony Blair's focus will turn to Britain's EU Presidency and the winning of a third term.

As for Bertie, he wins my admiration for his commitment to the North, but he now faces a backlash for fudging the evasion of the IRA on its criminality.

As Healy might have observed, Bertie was Blair's poodle.

McDowell Outflanked
by Rome

(December 22, 2004)

D o you recall a provocative radio interview that Michael McDowell gave with Pat Kenny in which the Minister for Justice bragged that the canon law of the Catholic Church holds as much sway in Irish law as do the rules of a golf club? To refresh your memory. The interview took place in October 2002 shortly after RTE's *Prime Time* revealed that the Archdiocese of Dublin faced 450 separate legal actions against priests and members of Religious Orders who ran industrial schools.

Overnight everyone was talking about canon law as if it were a new pop record. The code of canon law is a compilation of the laws of the Catholic Church stretching back to the twelfth century but updated after the Second Vatican Council, which was an assembly of world bishops that met from 1962-65 to mordernise the Catholic Church.

Cardinal Desmond Connell had declined to appear on the programme, *Cardinal Secrets*, to defend his handling of eight cases. Tellingly, Fr Tom Doyle, an American expert on how the Catholic Church worldwide used secrecy to cover up the scale of youth rape by clergy, rated the Dublin archdiocese "right at the top of the heap".

In short, it is now on the record that the Dublin archdiocese for generations systematically engaged in a worse cover-up than occurred in Boston, Chicago, New York, Westminister or Sydney. Yet, instead of making himself publicly accountable via the national broadcaster, Cardinal Connell delegated the task to his chief canon lawyer and a church spindoctor.

Earlier, on April 1, Brendan Comiskey had resigned as Bishop of Ferns after the BBC television documentary, *Suing the Pope*, highlighted his mishandling of child sexual abuse cases by a number of clergy. While admitting that his best had not been good enough, Comiskey refused to answer questions about his handling of the paedophile priest, Fr Seán Fortune, who killed himself by drinking from a chalice filled with a lethal cocktail of whiskey and pills, while on bail awaiting trial after eight young men informed the Gardaí about their sexual abuse.

A picture of Fortune in conversation with the Pope stunned viewers, who were equally aghast to hear how the Papal Nuncio had claimed diplomatic immunity from giving evidence in an Irish court even though a predecessor, the Sicilian Archbishop Gaetano Alibrandi, was told of the allegations against Fortune.

Sensing a sea-change in public attitudes towards the Barque of Patrick, Health Minister Mícheál Martin announced an inquiry into the Fortune scandal by senior counsel, George Birmingham, who was to advise the Government on what format an inquiry into the Ferns diocese would take. One of Connell's right hand men, Bishop Eamonn Walsh, was sent as caretaker to Ferns with a pledge of co-operating with the inquiry.

The *Prime Time* programme further ignited public fury at the Cardinal's handling of the clerical sex abuse cases. A call for immediate Government intervention into the Dublin diocese was made by victims' leader Colm O'Gorman, who questioned the Church's internal inquiry then being set up under Judge Gillian Hussey, but later abandoned. An outraged media, reflecting public opinion, called on the Gardaí to seize the secret personnel files of all prelates and clergy of the Dublin archdiocese. *The Irish Examiner* called for Connell's resignation.

It was against this highly charged atmosphere that McDowell threw the secular gauntlet down at Mother Church. And as further heinous cases were reported in Donegal, Clare and Cork, Bishop Willie Walsh of Killaloe opted for zero tolerance against priest offenders. But Walsh's insistence that State law should take precedence over canon law was not shared by Connell, who merely offered "appropriate" co-operation, while maintaining that he was governed by the rules of canon law as to what material remains confidential.

Meanwhile, after meeting senior Gardaí and victims' representatives, McDowell announced a beefing-up of the specialist unit dealing with child abuse. Two days later Taoiseach Bertie Ahern told the Dáil that "the law of the land applies to all – irrespective of what status they hold," and he promised that sex abuse clerics would face the full rigours of the law.

More than two years later you were probably as stunned as I was to read a page one headline in the *Irish Independent*: 'Pope sacks priests – No appeal: Vatican orders dismissal of two convicted Ferns diocese abusers'. Even more surprised, I bet, was Mary Harney, who as successor to Mícheál Martin was expecting to receive the confidential report of the Ferns Inquiry before the Christmas holidays.

Next day, we learned that this report will not be ready for the Tánaiste until March. It was also revealed that before stepping down last April as Archbishop of Dublin Cardinal Connell persuaded Pope John Paul II to remove two of his diocesan priests from "the clerical state". On Friday the diocese of Kerry disclosed that in August the Pope defrocked one of its priests whom the Director of Public Prosecutions had decided a year ago not to prosecute in the Irish courts.

What's been going on in the corridors of Maynooth and the Vatican? A clue to how the State is being outflanked by Rome was given earlier this year in the only public speech Cardinal Connell, who can vote in a papal conclave until he is 80 in 2006, has given since his retirement: he reminded the Government that Rome's canon law governing the relationship between a bishop and his priests enjoys the status of foreign law. In coded language, he was telling McDowell that the Irish Catholic Church is not a golf club, it is a privileged institution.

Not only has Cardinal Connell's approach prevailed inside the Irish Hierarchy, his Eminence's reading of constitutional law is supported in an article in the Law Society's Gazette. "The Cardinal is right in that, if a relationship at issue is clearly subject to canon law, the courts will give effect to it", writes barrister, Henry Murdoch. The case cited by Cardinal Connell relates to 1925 (O'Callaghan v O'Sullivan) when the Supreme Court accepted the right of the Bishop of Kerry, O'Sullivan, to remove a parish priest in West Cork, Father O'Callaghan, against the cleric's wishes. On this basis, the Cardinal argues that the Supreme Court has recognised the sovereign authority of the Holy See in this sphere of law. Clearly, the Cardinal has shown himself in this instance to be a better lawyer than McDowell. Irish Catholics who are citizens of an independent sovereign Republic need to waken up to the reality that their Church operates as a 'State within a State'. Ruairi Quinn who famously proclaimed that Ireland was now a post-Catholic country will have to revise his opinion in the light of assertions from Catholic churchmen that they intend defending their prerogatives derived from canon law.

Breaking his silence, Cardinal Connell admitted that his retirement had helped the Church, because he had become the 'lightning rod' for public anger over the clerical sex abuse. His interview signals a more confident mood in the church.

However, the question must be asked: where does all this leave the Ferns Inquiry and a forthcoming Inquiry into the Archdiocese of Dublin? The answer will come from the Rev Ian Paisley – Rome Rule. The Catholic bishops have proved themselves to be more adept politicians and media spinners than Bertie's Government.

Politics in 'Bertieland' 2005

'Bertie Dev'

(January 19, 2005)

Some sixty-five years ago when the writer, Seán Ó Faoláin, was travelling around the West for his book, *An Irish Journey*, he told the grand story of "the non-Catholic IRA man" whom he believed came from somewhere in Mayo. Although this IRA man did not attend church often, his involvement in the movement had had the sympathy and support of his local Church of Ireland rector for some years. Then, one fine day the rector came to him with a sad tale.

"The bishop was coming on one of his rare visitations", Ó Faoláin explained. "As things stood it seemed more than likely, so small was the congregation that the church might very well be closed down". Would his old friend do him the great kindness of coming to church on the day of the bishop's visit? His old friend said he would consider it. The day came. The bishop took his place. The meagre – most meagre – congregation filed in.

"Suddenly the doorway darkened, and in came the rector's friend, and behind him tramped solidly the entire local battalion of the IRA. For one awful moment the rector thought it was a raid, but as the men took their places he realised the truth. Up got the bishop. He complimented the rector. It gave him especial joy, he declared, to see so many young, upstanding men in the congregation".

Today, the upstanding men of the Provisional IRA rob banks and line their own pockets rather than fill the pews of churches. For the second week-end running the not so upstanding men of the IRA received a hammering in the Sunday newspapers for their alleged €38m robbery from the Northern Bank, ranking second only to the massive coverage of the funeral in Midleton of schoolboy, Robert Holohan.

The solidarity shown by the public for the murdered youth – and the recent outpouring of solidarity for the victims of the tsunami disaster – reflect the same spirit evoked by Ó Faoláin in his benign, perhaps apocryphal story of "the non-Catholic" IRA man's rescue of the Church of Ireland rector – and they contrast dramatically with the pariah status of the current Sinn Féin-IRA.

Gerry Adams, the Sinn Féin President, was in a surly mood when he complained that his telephone calls to Taoiseach Bertie Ahern were not being returned, while on the BBC on Sunday, Martin McGuinness, the Sinn Féin chief negotiator, menacingly told David Frost that the Irish and British Governments would be moving "onto dangerous ground" if they attempted to discriminate against republicans for a robbery which he still maintains was not committed by the IRA.

While still in denial about IRA criminality, the two Sinn Féin leaders have been singing from the same hymn sheet of martyred innocence, with Gerry claiming that it would have been a "crossroads" for Sinn Féin had they been told of an intended IRA bank robbery, and Martin saying that if the IRA had been involved it would have been "a defining moment" which he would have found "totally and absolutely unacceptable".

It must be dawning on even Adams and McGuinness that their rhythmic rhetoric is being dismissed as stonewalling bluster. At a news conference in Belfast Adams snapped that he did not care whether anybody listening to him believed him, while on the *Frost Show* McGuinness urged anyone with information about the robbers to contact him rather than the police. When at the end of the interview, Frost asked McGuinness to contact him if he received any news from informers, I just burst out laughing at the Derryman's pow-face reaction to being given a frosty brush-off.

Meanwhile, Bertie has gone off to China, putting the proverbial Chinese Wall between him and the Sinn Féin leaders, and leaving the Minister for Foreign Affairs, Dermot Ahern, and Northern Secretary, Paul Murphy, to pick up the pieces of a shattered peace process. Some form of sanction against Sinn Féin is expected even by Sinn Féin.

Meanwhile, too, the Sinn Féin leadership is wrapping itself up in the mantle of exclusive ownership of the original Sinn Féin movement started 100 years ago by the pacifist and economic protectionist, Arthur Griffith, who advocated that the British monarch should be crowned in Dublin as well as at Westminister Abbey as the king and queen of an autonomous Ireland as part of a "dual" kingdom within the British Empire.

In a rewrite of twentieth century history, Gerry Adams is claiming direct lineage for today's Provisional IRA-Sinn Féin with Griffith's pro-Imperial movement, overlooking the fact that it was not until 1917 that Sinn Féin adopted a republican platform when the surviving Irish Republican Brotherhood leader of the 1916 Rising, Eamon de Valera, won control of a movement which he was to leave in 1926 to found Fianna Fáil, the Republican Party.

Well worth reading is Justice Minister, Michael McDowell's, blistering attack on the bogus claim being made by Adams to the Griffith legacy, which is as discredited as the Provo claim that it was not responsible for the 1987 Poppy Day massacre of Protestants in Enniskillen, as well as Adams' own denial of ever having been in the IRA.

McDowell is spot on in accusing Adams of attempting to hijack the Griffith legacy to popularise the delusion that the Provos are the legitimate goverment of an all-Ireland Republic founded in the 1916 Easter Rising on behalf of the Irish people.

If readers don't believe McDowell or me, my advice is to get a hold of Brian Feeney's book, *Sinn Féin: A Hundred Turbulent Years*, in which he traces the repeatedly reshaped identity of the Ourselves Alone movement from the days of its dual monarchy fantasy to the Provisionals dual strategy of the armelite in one hand and the ballot box in the other hand.

Although the failure of the IRA to decommission its arms and end its criminal activities has brought itself to its present isolation as "themselves alone", the lust for propagandistic certitude of the republican leaders has convinced them that their celebrations of Griffith this year will bring them new recruits in the college campuses and the working class estates forming a cumann in every electoral ward in the Republic.

To counteract Sinn Féin's blatant distortion of history – and to prevent the seduction of impressionable young minds – I would hope that every headmaster and headmistress places a copy of Feeney's book in their school library, and that every library around the country stocks his book.

Hopefully, too, China-bound Bertie has taken a copy with him along with his Chinese phrase book. He should be under no delusion that Gerry and the boys are out to steal de Valera's clothes and denude Fianna Fáil of its position as the largest political party in the State. After all, de Valera was a past master at stealing the republican clothes of Mary McSwiney, Father O'Flanagan, Count Plunkett, Austin Stack and the fanatical JJ Scelig O'Kelly.

I reckon that Bertie will be paying most attention to Feeney's section on how as Taoiseach Dev locked up and even executed his old comrades in arms. The stark choice for Adams and McGuinness is either to make their followers upstanding pillars of democracy – or be faced down by *Bertie Dev*.

It is Sinn Féin which is moving onto dangerous ground.

Rambo's Fall Floors Bertie

(January 26, 2005)

Ray Burke's spectacular fall from grace and high ministerial office to a felon's prison was sealed on Monday when he became the first senior politician to be given a custodial sentence arising from Tribunal inquiries into corruption. His six-month sentence at the Dublin Circuit Criminal Court for lodging false tax returns is a triumph for the Criminal Assets Bureau (CAB) which pursued him for tax evasion after the Flood Tribunal had investigated him for receiving more than €200,000 in payments from builders and businessmen.

The jailing of a former Minister for Justice will be applauded by the general public, which enraged at the spectacle of lawyers enriching themselves on hefty fees paid by taxpayers at the long-drawn out Dublin Castle hearings, were despairing of any major politician being given time for corruption.

This judgement will immortalise Burke, but it will make it even more difficult for Taoiseach Bertie Ahern to draw a line in the sand for today's Fianna Fáil from the era of Charles J Haughey.

Burke's disgrace is a personal blow for Bertie, who appointed his fellow Dublin northsider Minister for Foreign Affairs, and also put him in charge of the Northern Ireland negotiations. He did so in June 1997 despite expectations that Burke would be hauled before the Flood Tribunal.

The imprisonment of the man known as Rambo will also embarrass Tanaiste Mary Harney, who approved Burke's appointment to the third most powerful job in cabinet after then chief whip Dermot Ahern had cleared his colleague of any wrongdoing on being assured at a meeting in London with builder Joseph Murphy that no payments were made in return for favours.

Although the Taoiseach defended his minister, further revelations forced Burke to admit that autumn that he had received a £30,000 donation from Murphy's building firm. Not only did Burke resign from Government, he quit politics, becoming a reluctant and evasive figure at the Flood Tribunal.

Ironically, Raphael P. Burke, now a broken man, could have become a millionaire and a respected politician, perhaps even becoming Taoiseach, according to an old friend of his late father, P.J. Burke, a Mayo-born Dáil deputy for Dublin North.

"I knew Ray when he was a boy at school in Swords and later when he went into insurance and the estate agency business where he learned all the tricks about land development", this Burke family friend told me. "P.J. was the old school of Fianna Fáil, a man you could trust", he recalled. "He would turn up, sometimes on the altar, at every funeral in his constituency and was nicknamed the Bishop. But young Ray was part of the new Mohair suit generation in Fianna Fáil who had education and enjoyed a good lifestyle".

Shortly after Ray took over his father's Dáil seat in 1973, a newspaper report claimed that he was mixing business with politics. He was interviewed by Gardaí about reports of planning irregularities in North Dublin. This budding notoriety, however, did not deter Taoiseach Jack Lynch from appointing the young Rambo to the junior ministry of Industry and Commerce in 1977. Indeed, during the Irish EU Presidency two years later when senior ministers were distracted by the leadership battle between George Colley and Charles Haughey, Burke was headlined as a ray of sunshine for his able performances at Council meetings in Brussels.

With his breezy, cocky walk, his sociability in the Dáil bar and his straight talking, Burke personified the new outward-looking Ireland at the heart of Europe. Always well-dressed, he looked more like a business executive than a politician. Although Burke voted for Colley against Haughey, his undoubted ability was recognised by The Boss who promoted him to the cabinet as Minister for Energy and Communications. Burke became one of Haughey's social in-crowd.

In public, he cultivated a political hard-man image, especially on his pet subject of RTE bashing. In private, he regularly enjoyed a few pints in the Dáil bar with the late Brian Lenihan and the Government Press Secretary, P.J. Mara. As Minister for Environment, Burke entered political folklore for planting trees and shrubs during a by-election in Dublin West – and for ordering their removal when Fianna Fáil lost. While Fianna Fáil languished in Opposition in the Fitzgerald-Spring years from 1982 to 1987, Burke would arrive flamboyantly at Leinster House in his chauffeur-driven Mercedes as chairman of Dublin County Council.

On February 20, 1987, after a general election in which Haughey failed to win an overall majority, the media was full of speculation that C.J. would do a deal with Independents in return for their Dáil support. But at a lively lunch in Lock's restaurant at which I suggested that the Haughey administration might last a few months, P.J. Mara was adamant that Haughey would do no deals with the Independents, a view emphatically endorsed by Burke who pointed to a successful minority government led by Seán Lemass as providing the model for a stable Haughey III Government. My card was marked for my next day's front page story in *The Irish Times*!

Burke's political judgement proved to be woefully faulty two years later when he and Pádraig Flynn counselled Haughey to go for a snap early election which resulted in an FF coalition with Dessie O'Malley's hated Progressive Democrats.

As Minister for Justice, Burke's national profile rose. Rambo was a tough negotiator at the Anglo-Irish Conference. He went through a liberal phase when praise was heaped on him by Senator David Norris for including homosexuals in the Prohibition of Incitement to Hatred Act. A Haughey tone was detected in Burke's speech style and he was even mentioned as a future Taoiseach. But his critics, and they were not a few, said privately that the benevolent Burke image would not last. Question marks hung over him amid continuing rumours that he had received money-filled envelopes during planning controversies.

As Albert Reynolds has revealed, he dropped Burke from cabinet when he became Taoiseach in 1992, because of such rumours. On the fall of Albert two years later Burke's career was rescued by Bertie. On the eve before Ahern was elected Taoiseach in June 1997, Burke was enjoying a drink in the visitors' bar with journalists, including myself. He looked confident but was worried by the illness of a daughter. With rumours flying that Burke had received £30,000 from a builder, journalists, myself included, were convinced that Bertie would not appoint him to cabinet. Next day, we gasped in disbelief from the press gallery when Burke became Minister for Foreign Affairs. This week, Burke entered prison – and the history books – as the Celtic Tiger's most notorious political rogue.

Burke's sentence could not come at a worse time for Bertie Ahern as the Taoiseach prepared for his showdown meeting at Government Buildings with Sinn Féin leaders, Gerry Adams and Martin McGuinness, over the alleged involvement of the IRA in the €38 million Northern Bank robbery.

The Sinn Féin propaganda machine will try to deflect attention from the Taoiseach's claim that Adams and McGuinness had prior knowledge of the robbery to wag the finger at the depth of political corruption that existed in Fianna Fáil and that is now forever personified by Ray Burke.

Bertie Goes Game-Shooting

(February 2, 2005)

In a fraught week in which Ray Burke went to jail, Sinn Féin protested its innocence in IRA criminality and Martin Cullen was dazed by the Quigley Report on hefty public relations' contracts, Bertie Ahern bounced back as *the Teflon Taoiseach*.

Bertie's political stock grew when he treated Sinn Féin leaders Gerry Adams and Martin McGuinness, so long used to red carpet treatment in Government Buildings like ambassadorial swans of the Northern peace process, as the ugly ducklings of republican terrorism and bank robbery.

Bertie went game-shooting when he targeted and unplucked the Dáil's five Sinn Féin T.D.s who had no chance of gliding away swan-like over a choppy lake which once was tranquil Ireland under the peace process. Citing intelligence reports about resumed punishment beatings in Belfast, Bertie exposed the under-water paddling of their webbed feet to show that they had Matt Talbot holes in them.

On Thursday Bertie's impish remark about Martin Cullen needing to give a 100pc in future to his huge agenda as Transport Minister was a surprisingly public signal from the Taoiseach that he regards the accident prone Waterford man as the weakest link in the cabinet.

Even though clearly damaged politically, Cullen today is mightily relieved that he retains the Merc and perks of high office after being cleared by former Revenue Commissioner Dermot Quigley of any wrongdoing in his controversial hiring of the highly paid public relations consultant, Monica Leech. But Bertie's throw-away remark must surely send a chill down Cullen's spine that the fine print of the Quigley report effectively has called into question his political judgement in awarding contracts worth €390,000 of tax-payers' money to Ms Leech, a Fianna Fáil supporter, for part-time Government work from her homebase in Waterford.

This technical exoneration was underlined by Bertie when he noted that Quigley's findings showed that his minister had not broken any rules, and had not directed civil servants in his former Departments of the Office of Public Works and Environment to hire Ms Leech.

While the public may suspect that Quigley's technocratic report is an Irish

Hutton-style white-wash to shield the political establishment from censure, it has made a number of important recommendations for a tighter and more effective monitoring of how lucrative Government contracts are given to public relations "experts".

Indeed, the thrust of these proposals has enabled Bertie to take the initiative to establish a special unit under his control which will require ministers to seek his approval before hiring PR experts from either the public or private sectors.

If Bertie has come out of the Leech affair with his own power-base strengthened, the personal toll which the controversy has taken on Cullen was evident on his haggard and drawn face as he claimed vindication from Quigley's report. But his usual arrogance was absent from his voice.

Even Cullen knows that his survival in cabinet depends on his getting over the next big hurdle when the State's public ethics watchdog, the Standards in Public Office Commission, meets this week to decide whether to hold a full inquiry into Ms Leech's contracts. If this Committee's initial probe recommends dropping the investigation, Cullen will be in the clear to get on with the job of sorting out Aer Lingus, Aer Rianta and the national roads that Bertie wants him to get on with. If the Committee orders a full investigation, as advocated by Fine Gael leader Enda Kenny, Cullen will be forced to fall on his sword.

Further down the line, Cullen may also face further questions from the Auditor and General. This would be embarrassing for a minister whose reputation was already damaged by the over-inflated price which for he purchased Farmleigh as a State residence. And who forgets his €50 million mishandling of E-voting?

Cullen's vulnerability was overshadowed, however, by ill-judged and inappropriate comments by President Mary McAleese on Ulster's unholy war which deflected focus from a solemn remembrance of the extermination of Jews in Poland's Auschwitz concentration camp. Graciously, the President has apologised to aggrieved Ulster Unionist politicians, the Orange Order and the Church of Ireland for comparing Protestant treatment of Catholics in the North to the Nazi murder of six million Jews in death camps. In her interview the President should have spoken about Christian-Judaic reconciliation rather than adding to Ireland's shame by clumsily re-igniting outdated Catholic-Protestant animosities in the North. Rather than defending President McAleese's gaffe, Gerry Adams would be better advised to persuade the IRA to abandon completely its Nazi-like armed struggle and crude criminality.

Bertie Unfazed by IRA

(February 9, 2005)

First and mainly, the peace process - or what is left of it in the wake of last December's Northern Bank robbery which Taoiseach Bertie Ahern and British Prime Minister Tony Blair believe was carried off by the IRA with the advance knowledge of Sinn Féin leaders Gerry Adams and Martin McGuinness.

After petulant denials by Sinn Féin and an ominous silence by its armed wing, the IRA issued two statements, both of them menacing. It was only the second one which was taken seriously.

The IRA's manipulative mentality was demonstrated in this second statement implying a return to war. This was dictated to RTE's chief correspondent Charlie Bird minutes before Thursday evening's six o'clock television news. Charlie rushed onto the national air-waves breathlessly informing us of his latest scoop from some shadowy cousin of the legendary P. O'Neill.

For the record, the sinister two-line statement read: "The two Governments are trying to play down the importance of our statement, because they are making a mess of the peace process. Do not underestimate the seriousness of the situation".

In his rush to get the story on the bulletin, Charlie apparently had no time to probe his republican deep-throat about what the message actually meant. He could not offer any authoritative interpretation as to the unsettled state of the Provo mind. It was a chilly instance of spinning Provo-style.

This broadcast triggered angry reaction from politicians of all the main parties, North and South, as well as in Britain. It generated acres of print in the news-papers. It has given the IRA massive coverage with zero accountability. The context in which the IRA two-liner needs to be read is that republican leaders took umbrage at Taoiseach Bertie Ahern's refusal to take offence at their previous day's first message in which they tarred him as a fellow traveller of the Rev Ian Paisley.

In its first ominous communique, the IRA had announced withdrawal of its offer of arms decommissioning and accused Bertie and Tony Blair of pandering to Paisley's "rejectionist" Democratic Unionist Party. It muttered menacingly that it would not remain "quiescent".

Rather than quaking in his boots as the IRA hard-men expected, the Taoiseach responded in low-key, almost casual fashion, when speaking in Dundalk, he said that he had not read it in a negative fashion. What irked the Provos most was that Bertie made it clear that he was not for turning in the face of their veiled threat of a return to their armed struggle. Nor was he backing off from his belief that the IRA pulled off the €38 million Northern Bank robbery.

Just in case it had not sunk into the murky minds of the Provos and their ugly ducklings in Sinn Féin, Bertie reiterated that political progress could only be made when there is a complete end to criminality, paramilitary activity and the decommissioning issue. This is the substance of the Dáil motion tabled for debate this week by Fine Gael leader Enda Kenny, in time for the publication of the report of the Independent Monitoring Commission which is expected to recommend sanctions against Sinn Féin. While Tony Blair will be under pressure to withdraw Westminster facilities to abstentionist Sinn Féin M.P.s, the Irish Government takes the pragmatic view that retaliation will merely reinforce Sinn Féin's victim complex.

The members of the IRA Army Council, who delude themselves of constituting the supreme lawful authority on this island, continue to pose a challenge to the elected Government in the Republic. While ministers, deputies and councillors should maintain dialogue with Sinn Féin, relations should be formal, not cosy. The ugly ducklings of Irish democracy occupy fifth column status in the Dáil.

The biggest danger, meantime, is that the current stand-off in political negotiations will create a vacuum that will tempt the hawks and the crooks to ply their evil trade.

Defeat, however, for Sinn Féin candidates in the forthcoming North Kildare and Meath elections will give republicans notice to go back to the negotiating table.

This reality has not sunk into Adams, whose erratic utterances are worth as much scrutiny as the IRA's second statement. He has rounded on both Governments, threatening that the peace process could be as "transient" as Blair's time in Downing Street. He has drawled that it was "patent nonsense" for Bertie and Blair to say that the IRA was the only obstacle to a permanent peace. This came close to saying that the IRA will not go away.

On Saturday Adams hit a new low in vulgar discourse when he opined that the two Governments "need to dig their heads out of their asses", a remark which was deplored by Archbishop Seán Brady. On Sunday, the prelate called for calm. In contrast to Adams's verbal summersaults, Martin McGuinness gave a germ of hope when he described the Northern Bank robbery as "a criminal act" carried out by people who did not care a tuppence for the peace process. The Derryman could be preparing the ground for Sinn Féin's split from those militants who want to go back to violence.

Huffily, both Adams and McGuinness insist that Sinn Féin will no longer "interpret" for the IRA. The key question, therefore, is: does the second IRA statement reflect Sinn Féin's position? Or are Adams and McGuinness, as the Taoiseach believes, still speaking as members of the IRA Army Council?

Only the IRA knows.

Bertie Taunted by Sinn Féin

(February 16, 2005)

T he bravado of Gerry Adams taunting Taoiseach Bertie Ahern to arrest him in connection with the Northern Bank robbery reveals that the penny has not yet dropped in the Sinn Féin-IRA mind-set that they have lost credibility with the public.

If the "household" names in the Sinn Féin-IRA leadership continue refusing to renounce paramilitary crime, the Irish and British Governments will have no option but to direct their State security branches to make arrests and divest the republican movement of its ill-gotten booty. This is the stark choice confronting Bertie and British Prime Minister Tony Blair as they consider what sanctions to impose on Sinn Féin after the damning report from the Independent Monitoring Commission.

The clearest sign yet that the politics of the peace process are stuck in a cul de sac was made manifest in the public contempt shown by Sinn Féin President, Gerry Adams, towards the Taoiseach. Adams insulted the Irish people when he taunted this State's democratically-elected leader to arrest him and Martin McGuinness for the €38 million bank robbery. This wish may become a reality for the Sinn Féin leadership once the criminal investigations being pursued by the North's chief constable, Hugh Orde, and the Garda Commissioner, Noel Conroy, assemble the books of evidence for the courts!

Simultaneously, as suggested by Fine Gael leader, Enda Kenny, an outraged public on this side of the border will feel cheated if the Criminal Assets Bureau has not already started moving against the IRA god-fathers of crime with the same determination that they showed against drugs barons after the murder of Veronica Guerin. It would come as no surprise if the courts were to discover that the proceeds from IRA crime and fund-raising could substantially ease the national debt as well as augmenting the public service pension fund.

Nor is the Irish public taken in by Adams' claim that Bertie and Justice Minister, Michael McDowell, are playing "dirty politics" to save Fianna Fáil and the PDs from the rise of radical politics represented by the self-styled altar-boys and hand-maidens of Sinn Féin. Still cocooned in their roles as victims of a securocrat-led conspiracy, the republican leaders continue to ignore the demands from London and Dublin - including a Dáil resolution – to end criminality and to decommission their arms. For Lent, Gerry, Martin and other senior republican ventriloquists should shut up and study their Bibles about Paul of Tarsus's conversion on the way to Damascus. If not, in due course, and under due process, they may find Bertie calling their bluff.

On Sunday evening, however, Enda Kenny set the scene for a Dáil showdown when he announced his intention to move the writ for holding a by-election in Meath shortly before St Patrick's Day, a move which I suspect will be blocked by Bertie.

Normally, this move should just be a routine part of the parliamentary process but it signals a return to ding-dong Government versus Opposition politics after weeks of a united Dáil stance against Sinn Féin.

Kenny's timing of the writ is a calculated gamble to put Bertie and Fianna Fáil into a Catch 22 situation by casting them in an unfavourable light if they refuse to agree to his proposed date for the Meath by-election. Already Bertie has been taunted as running scared of an early poll when he suggested that the Meath contest to replace the former Taoiseach John Bruton, now EU Ambassador to the United States, should be held after Easter.

Bertie has suggested that it would be in the best interest of the country if the Meath contest is held on the same day as a by-election in North Kildare to replace former Finance Minister Charlie McCreevy, now EU Commissioner in Brussels. Under Dáil rules Kenny has the right to propose a date for filling the Meath seat which has been vacant since November 1, and his ideal dates would be Thursday, March 10 or Friday, March 11.

Kenny made his announcement on RTE's *Week in Politics* programme with an impish smile on his face, because he knows that Fianna Fáil's new and untried Meath candidate, Cllr Shane Cassells, needs time to prepare for his first Dáil battle. Apart from putting Fianna Fáil into electoral battles which it would prefer to postpone, Kenny's move has the potential to disrupt Government and Dáil business. It would come just as Government ministers would be preparing to set off on their annual global exodus at St Patrick's Day celebrations.

The Taoiseach complains that the timing of Kenny's move would distract from the Finance Bill and the Social Welfare Bill, a claim which Kenny dismisses as "nonsense". The reality is that both Government and the Dáil observe the St Patrick's Day holidays as an extended period of national promotion abroad and a lengthy rest from domestic politics.

Kenny contends that by-elections are governed under the Constitution, and that this obligation should direct the time-table, not Government travel itineraries or the Dáil schedule of the Government Chief Whip. But Bertie has the Dáil majority to refuse Kenny's move, even at the risk of being called chicken by Fine Gael and Labour. Bertie could out-manoeuvre Enda if he can get the message across to a concerned public that the fundamental spotlight should rest on Sinn Féin's need to embrace democratic politics fully, perhaps at a reconvened Forum for Peace and Reconciliation.

Sinn Féin will taunt Fianna Fáil that Bertie runs away from challenges.

Bertie Confronts 'Red Diesel' Republicans

(February 23, 2005)

T he peace process is dead and gone – it went missing with the €38 million stolen from the vaults of the Northern Bank in Belfast. The missing loot was gone and buried until part of it was recovered in Garda swoops in Cork, Meath, Westmeath, Louth, Dublin and numerous other places in the Republic.

The arrest of eight persons including a prominent member of Sinn Féin and a businessman was truly a defining moment for all the participants in what was the peace process.

'Cometh the hour, cometh the man.' Noel Conroy, the Mayo-born Garda Commissioner, is proving himself one of the most resolute chief police officers ever since Ireland achieved its independence in his major crack-down on IRA criminality which was threatening to undermine the State.

This most comprehensive Garda intelligence investigation ever undertaken into republican money-laundering under the direction of Commissioner Conroy has struck a huge blow to the credibility of Sinn Féin-IRA. It also brings to a head pressing but fundamental questions for the Irish and British Governments as well as for the established democratic political parties on both sides of the Border. To again paraphrase the poet W.B. Yeats, the political landscape has changed - changed utterly.

The squeeze from the Irish and British Governments will intensify on Sinn Féin this week to disband its IRA murder gangs and end its Mafia-style robberies and money-laundering. As Gardaí continue their investigation into republican money-laundering in Cork and other parts of the country, the police forces in the Republic and the North announced unprecedented cooperation to combat what Foreign Minister Dermot Ahern has called "red-diesel republicanism".

On Monday Justice Minister Michael McDowell signed a historic deal at Hillsborough Castle in County Down enabling Gardaí not only to join the Police Service of Northern Ireland (PSNI) but also take up senior posts in its ranks. Similarly members of the PSNI are being seconded to the Garda. Commissioner Conroy and PSNI Chief Constable, Hugh Orde, are in daily contact by phone. The Provos are seeing signs of a united Ireland police force!

In advance of the signing the heat was been turned up on the republican leadership by McDowell's public naming of Gerry Adams and Martin McGuinness - along with Kerry North T.D. Martin Ferris - as members of the IRA Army Council, a charge which has been bitterly contested as false on behalf of all three by McGuinness.

On Tuesday at Westminster Northern Secretary Paul Murphy was due to announce sanctions against Sinn Féin in line with recommendations by the Independent Monitoring Body. British Government sources in London indicate that Sinn Féin will lose its Westminster perks worth about €700,000.

This Wednesday Taoiseach Bertie Ahern was chairing a security summit to review the dramatic events which have revealed the Sinn Féin-IRA as operating as a state within a state with its own treasury, a standing army and social welfare system for its members.

In industrial trouble-shooter, Phil Flynn, the Garda clamp-down claimed as its first incidental victim a key figure in the creation of Ireland's Celtic Tiger economy.

While insisting that he is innocent of any wrong-doing, Flynn's links with the Chesterton Finance Company at the centre of the money-laundering racket were too embarrassing for him to continue in his plum roles as chairman of the Bank of Scotland (Ireland), his directorship with the VHI, and his chairing of the Government's decentralisation steering committee. His stepping aside represents another chapter in a remarkable life-story that saw him rise from working class boy in Dundalk, the El Paso of Provo bandit-land, to that of banking merchant prince and close counsellor of both Bertie and the Sinn Féin leadership.

As Flynn vowed to return to public life when vindicated, the public itself came to grips with the sheer scale of the attempted subversion by Sinn Féin-IRA of the Irish State. The screw was tightened by Gardaí and members of the Criminal Assets Bureau (CAB). What really alarms the subversives is that in addition to raids inside the Republic, where CAB officers can pursue orders to divest criminals of their "corrupt enrichment", they also have new powers to investigate suspected crime abroad in countries such as Libya, Turkey and Bulgaria, where republicans are suspected of extensive money-laundering operations.

In contrast to McGuinness's claim that he had seen no evidence to show IRA involvement in the €38 million Northern bank robbery, Defence Minister, Willie O'Dea, predicted that a definitive link would be established to the IRA with the money seized in Cork with the Northern bank robbery. The Government's hardening position was best summed up by O'Dea when he warned that it was no longer prepared to accept the "farce" that Sinn Féin and the IRA were separate: they were "indivisible". Adams and McGuinness, however, are continuing to be farcical. Neither McGuinness, who cat-calls McDowell the "Minister for by-passing Justice", and Adams, who appeared at a republican rally in Strabane on Sunday, has taken in the Government's message. Both continue to show no remorse. Pictures of Adams standing beside beret-clad republicans in army uniforms will further alienate public opinion in the Republic.

In the battle of words the republicans' pleas of being smeared in advance of by-elections in Meath and Kildare North – as well as Westminster elections in the North – cut little ice even with those who were favourable to their admission into democratic politics. RTE may pull the plug on its coverage of the Sinn Féin Árd Fheis on March 5, because of its closeness to the by-elections.

Even those sympathetic to the republican movement are being switched off by the Adams-McGuinness farce. Former Taoiseach, Albert Reynolds, has advised the republican movement to make a big push to show the IRA is going out of business once and for all, and author Tim Pat Coogan has expressed his disillusionment and sense of let down. If Gerry and Martin won't listen to Bertie and Blair, they should take heed of the advice from Albert and Tim Pat.

There is an urgent need for a radical rehaul of the basis on which such political dialogue can be conducted. In the Republic the Taoiseach may reconvene the Forum for Peace and Reconciliation. If so, the pre-condition for the admission of Sinn Féin into such talks should be that they take an oath of loyalty to the democratic institutions of the Irish State and abjure terrorism and criminality. Consideration should also be given by cabinet ministers to the devising of a similar solemn oath that would be sworn by all members of the Oireachtas including Sinn Féin.

In the North the women members of the McCartney family have shown out-standing courage in exposing Sinn Féin-IRA involvement in the murder of their brother Robert and in intimidation of witnesses. This has sown the seeds of a new civil rights movement coming from within Sinn Féin's own heartland against Sinn Féin-IRA's gangsterism. President George Bush has been briefed by his Belfast-based envoy. Sinn Féin-IRA is totally isolated.

Republicans are no longer perceived to be bona fide members of peace and democracy. They will pay a heavy price for their duplicity in both the Westminster elections and in the by-elections in Meath and Kildare North.

In fixing March 11 for the by-elections, Bertie and Mary Harney surprised us all by doing a U-turn when confronted by Enda Kenny and Pat Rabbitte's threat of obstructing Dáil business.

Alas, there is no sign of a U-turn by Adams and McGuinness. The farce drags on.

Hard-boiled Ian Blesses Bertie

(March 1, 2005)

Ian Paisley, 79 next month, and recovering from a cancer scare, is no longer the vigorous towering man of the cloth that he was. But a chuckling Paisley told RTE's indefatigable Tommie Gorman that he would still do business on the formation of a power-sharing Executie with Sinn Féin, provided the IRA totally ended insurrection and criminality.

Paisley's humour was as refreshing as the life-line which he threw to the beleagured republican movement, and I found myself chuckling at Paisley's recollection of his 'ecumenical' meeting with Taoiseach Bertie Ahern at the Irish Embassy in London, where he had been invited for a working breakfast. Before getting tucked into his two hard-boiled eggs – not a traditional Ulster fry! – Paisley said grace, while the Taoiseach crossed himself. "I take them off at the top myself so I know what is in them", Paisley guffawed with characteristic Scotch-Irish blarney.

The reciting of grace – and Paisley's statesman-like persona – reminded me of the lunch which the late John *Backbencher* Healy and I had with him in Strasbourg in 1980 when we had to bow our heads in silent prayer as he intoned the Lord's blessing over the meal. This was the occasion when at the end of the meal Healy predicted that we had just lunched with the next Prime Minister of Northern Ireland.

In an interview with RTE's Tommie Gorman, Ian Paisley has made it clear that he aspires to end his long and turbulent career as Northern Premier with a reformed Sinn Féin. He has announced his intention of defending his North Antrim seat in the Westminster general elections in May, when he expects his Democratic Unionist Party to confirm its supremacy over David Trimble's Ulster Unionists. Despite Sinn Féin's current troubles arising from the Northern Bank robbery and the Garda probe into the Rafia's money-laundering operations, it is still highly probable that the republicans will emerge victorious over the SDLP on the nationalist side of the electorate.

The major obstacle in the way of Sinn Féin sweeping the floor with the SDLP, of course, is the groundswell of support for the family of Robert McCartney after his murder at the end of January in a Belfast pub by up to 12 alleged members of the

IRA, who also covered up the forensic evidence for their bestial deed and intimidated witnesses from giving evidence to the Police Service of Northern Ireland.

At an unprecedented protest rally on Sunday in Belfast's East Strand Paula McCartney dismissed as inadequate – others would say cynical – the IRA's dismissal from its illegal organisation of three of its members who were allegedly involved in her brother's murder; and she renewed her call for all those involved to hand themselves into the police for trial by the courts.

What must also add acutely to Sinn Féin-IRA's embarrassment was the accusation made at the rally by Eamon McCann of engaging in "a second Bloody Sunday" cover-up of the McCartney atrocity. An indication of the pressure on republicans, meanwhile, was indicated in south Armagh by Sinn Féin President Gerry Adams, again ominously surrounded by black-beret clad, so-called republicans, that an even more dramatic concession must come from the IRA.

The scene is now set for a momentous Árd Fheis in Dublin. This will be the most significant test of the leadership of Adams and Martin McGuinness since the 1986 Árd Fheis when the Northerners took control of the movement for their twin armalite and ballot box strategy from the southerner Ruairi Ó Brádaigh.

It will be a particularly trying event for Adams, whose popularity has slumped by 31pc according to an *Irish Independent* poll. Lately, too, Gerry has given a number of tetchy and unimpressive media interviews. Now that his halo has slipped, his past record will be under further scrutiny as a result of the revelations contained in a new book, *Stakeknife – Britain's Secret Agents in Ireland* by Richard O'Rawe, who was the IRA spokesman in the Maze prison in 1981 during the Hunger Strikes that resulted in ten deaths including that of Bobby Sands.

Sensationally, O'Rawe discloses that just before the fifth hunger striker died an intermediary from Margaret Thatcher's Government, code-named the Mountain Climber, offered secret concessions to Adams that would have been acceptable to the prisoners, but were overruled by the IRA army council which wanted to use continuing sympathy for the hunger strike in order to win a by-election in Fermanagh-South Tyrone caused by Sands' death. While describing Adams as a Pontius Pilate, O'Rawe credits the Sinn Féin President for being pivotal in bringing about the peace process that began after the end of the hunger strike.

At this week-end's Árd Fheis Adams will be fighting for his own political life. He may have cause to bless Ian Paisley. But he knows the price will be the end to insurrection and criminality that the people will be able to see.

Bertie's Waiting Game

(March 8, 2005)

The television and newspaper pictures of Gerry Adams seated beside the sisters of the murdered Robert McCartney on the front-row of the Sinn Féin Árd Fheis was a public relations master-stroke by the *Big Boy* that helped limit some of the damage which the republican movement has inflicted on itself in the past three months.

The sisters' acceptance of his invitation to attend the RDS in Dublin for his presidential address on Saturday evening was an attempt by Adams to exorcise their slain-brother's ghost which enveloped the week-end debates.

It was a high risk strategy for the sisters to be welcomed into 'the republican family', but their strict neutrality during the address ensured that they were not being seduced by mere verbal assurances from the Sinn Féin President about bringing the suspected IRA and Sinn Féin killers before the courts. Most importantly, the level-headedness of the sisters was maintained in their post conference comment that they would judge Adams' words on whether convictions of the killers of their brother are secured.

With his own personal popularity down in the polls to support from less than one in three voters, Adams admitted that the McCartney murder was "a huge crisis" for the republican movement. Ahead of the Árd Fheis, moves to defuse the issue came with the IRA's suspension of three of its members and later Sinn Féin's suspension, without prejudice, of seven of its members alleged by the McCartney family to have been involved in their brother's murder.

Such was the badge of shame hanging over IRA-Sinn Féin that Adams had given their names to the Northern Ireland Ombudsman, Nuala O'Loan, in the knowledge that these suspects might face interrogation by the police and possible prosecution in the courts of the Northern 'statelet.' Yet, by Saturday, none of the 70 people who were in the Belfast pub had given evidence, some of them insisting on their right to silence either from earlier intimidation or fear of later being branded as informers.

Unless the suspended Sinn Féin members make "full and truthful" statements on the murder, Adams has warned that he will initiate an expulsion process against them, a threat which will be a test of his determination to move against the criminals inside IRA-Sinn Féin.

Overall, the Árd Fheis's claim to act as the dynamo of the peace process sat uneasily with motions upholding their armed struggle, such as those commending the discipline of the IRA, calling for the release of the murderers of Detective Garda Jerry McCabe and for the destruction of the criminal records of their Volunteers.

A vision of the Gaelic dreary Eden that republicans would have us return to was encapsulated in a motion calling for streets in new housing estates to be sign-posted in Irish. And there was no end to the revered references to the venality of the "Dublin Government" and its betrayal of the spirit of the nation represented by the Fenians, the Sinn Féin movement embodied by Arthur Griffith 100 years ago and, of course, the Men of 1916.

All stock rhetorical republican stuff, but this stale diet was deemed necessary by the leadership to maintain party morale – and Sinn Féin's poll rate of 9pc support – after three months of media censure in the wake of the Northern Bank robbery, the McCartney murder and the Garda money-laundering raids in the Republic. So, judged by the short-term goal of sustaining the fervour of their followers, it can be claimed by the leadership that this Árd Fheis was a success. It was business as usual.

Mock battles centred on the most despised hate figure in the republican repertoire of *bete noirs*. The Minister for Justice, Michael McDowell, was dubbed the new Margaret Thatcher. Former Taoiseach John Bruton's interview on American television in which he named Adams as a leading IRA member was broadcast after the Árd Fheis was over, thus depriving him of co-billing with McDowell!

Judged by McDowell's pre-Árd Fheis challenge to republicans to grasp the nettles of disbanding the IRA and ending paramilitary crime, the Árd Fheis was a non-event. But it was never going to be the scene for resolving these two crucial issues. The more accurate marker was Bertie's forecast that finding ways forward would come after the Árd Fheis. As an astute politician, Bertie realised the limits for manoeuvre placed on Adams and Martin McGuinness at what after all was their party's annual talking-shop. With the polls showing Bertie well placed for a third term as Taoiseach, he has time to play a waiting-game.

On the positive side at a time-marking Árd Fheis, Adams' pledge to the McCartney sisters means that he has given a solemn public commitment to deliver those whom he says have sullied republicanism, even at the risk of forcing a split in the ranks. With Westminster and local elections due in May, Adams needs to deliver quickly on this front. Otherwise, the bravery of other families who are following the McCartney example of speaking out against IRA-Sinn Féin criminality threatens to erode their electoral bases in the North.

In the fine print of Adams' speech, and that of Gerry Kelly, there were coded messages for Irish and British Government diplomats of their intent to meet Ian Paisley on a democratic playing-field and to enter a reformed policing system in the North. But these issues were left for another Árd Fheis after the May elections.

With a third national opinion poll confirming slippage in Sinn Féin support to 9pc, the leadership glossed over this. It could – and should – have been worse. But this means that its candidate in Friday's Meath by-election is an also-ran.

Banned from the White House on St Patrick's Day, censured in the Dáil and Westminster, and under investigation in the European Parliament, Sinn Féin is now marked out as a shunned sect.

Yet, neither Adams nor McGuinness were prepared to put patriotism before pragmatism by tabling the two resolutions which are demanded of them by the Irish and British Governments. Their defensive tactics this week-end contrasted dramatically with my recollection of how they operated with pre-planned skill at the 1986 Árd Fheis in Dublin's Mansion House when they took control away from Ruairi Ó Brádaigh.

The one ray of light for the future is that Bertie's hope that the "logic" of a full-commitment to democracy will prevail eventually in Sinn Féin.

Bertie's Washington Date

(March 15, 2005)

Easter 2005 finds the so-called republican movement at its most critical junction almost eleven years after its cease-fire in which its leaders Gerry Adams and Martin McGuinness must either finally take decisive action to disband the IRA or confront its psychopathic, rift-raft wing at the risk of a split.

The Easter Monday addresses of the republican leaders will be monitored closely by the Irish, British and American Governments. Bertie Ahern, Tony Blair and George W. Bush will be looking for a clear message from them that their period of masterly ambiguity is at an end and that a definite course of action is being charted inside their movement for its speedy liquidation on both its armed and criminal fronts.

As a result of the slamming of the doors of the White House and Congress on Adams on St Patrick's Day and their opening to the McCartney sisters and partner of the butchered Robert McCartney, the pressure has never been so intense on Sinn Féin -IRA to abandon its evil ways.

The omens of an Easter conversion, however, are far from good for four principal reasons.

First, neither Adams nor McGuinness have yet shown that they have come to terms with the gravity of the crisis confronting their movement, and that they possess the moral fibre needed to root out the evil in their ranks.

Even before the McCartneys left for Washington, McGuinness peevishly warned the wee lassies against being manipulated, and of consequently losing the support of tens of thousands of republicans sympathetic to their cause of obtaining justice in the courts for their murdered brother. Not only did this implicit threat reveal a male chauvinist streak in McGuinness, it showed him up to be a bully boy from the Bogside whose mask had slipped under pressure.

Similarly, Adams showed his two-faced lack of genuine sympathy for the McCartneys when he refused at an American Ireland Fund dinner to join in the applause which the American political and media establishments were showering on the McCartneys for their personal courage and moral integrity.

Indicative of Adams' incapacity to listen to the plain truth, the *Big Boy* stormed out of the dinner when Senator John McCain, the former Republican presidential candidate, said that "no one can honestly claim that the IRA is anything better than an organised crime syndicate that steals and murders to serve its members' private interests".

Nor did McCain let the Shinners' leader off the hook when he told Adams that there was no place in a democracy for a political party with a private army, and that the Sinn Féin leadership "should call for the IRA to disarm, demobilise and disband once and for all".

And what was Gerry's response when he went before a television camera? He blustered about how the storm would pass and that he faced more difficult moments in the past. Wrong, Gerry. This is not a storm. Your days of prevarication are over. Get real. Did you not listen to Senator Ted Kennedy, whom you insist was "ill-advised" in refusing to meet you?

Second, even as the McCartney sisters were receiving the support of the Americans, back in Belfast two of the republican suspects of their brother's murder were leading the St Patrick's Day parade in the Short Strand where the family lives. As Claire McCartney told the *Sunday Tribune*, this was a further insult to Robert's memory. It was an act of defiance against all those seeking justice.

Understandably, given that these two suspected killers were joined in a St Patrick's Day parade in the Short Strand by some hundred hangers-on, Gemma McCartney wrote a diary published in the *Sunday Telegraph* where with McCain-like forthrightness she saw parallels between the current generation of IRA thugs and the Nazis. All of this under the public banner of Sinn Féin!

Furthermore, on their return from Washington, the McCartneys and Ms Hagans learned that not only had there had still been no progress in the police investigation into Robert's murder, there were reports of continued intimidation against a driver who had taken many of the 70 republicans away from the pub scene of the murder.

So much for the promise given to Adams at the recent Sinn Féin Árd Fheis in Dublin that unless suspended Sinn Féin members made "full and truthful" statements on the murder, he would initiate an expulsion process against them. This pledge remains a threat which will test his determination to move against the criminals inside IRA-Sinn Féin. Do not expect an Easter Monday round-up by the republican movement of its own suspects, and their hand-over to the Police Service of Northern Ireland!

My third reason for not expecting an Easter break-through is that Bertie's promise of holding a substantial meeting with the Sinn Féin leaders after Easter will enable Adams and McGuinness to prolong their old game of cat-and-mouse with what the recent Árd Fheis still contemptuously called the "Dublin" Government.

So I nearly choked on my St Patrick's Day lunch when I heard from Washington that Bertie had had a meeting with Adams in Washington and had agreed to a follow-up meeting. This was a complete U-turn by the Taoiseach from the ultimatum which he issued to Adams and McGuinness at their meeting in Government Buildings on January 25 – to go away and only come back with their schedule for complete IRA decommissioning and the ending of criminality.

At the Sinn Féin Árd Fheis earlier this month neither Adams nor McGuinness tabled the two resolutions demanded of them by the Irish and British Governments. They ignored Justice Minister Michael McDowell's pre-Árd Fheis challenge to them to grasp the nettles of disbanding the IRA and ending paramilitary crime. They were given breathing space for making their annual talk-in a non-event from Bertie's forecast that finding ways forward would come after the Árd Fheis.

Then, incredibly, in Washington, just as the whole American political and media elites were giving Adams an icy reception – and the McCartney sisters had changed the whole dynamic of the peace process - Bertie has allowed Adams and McGuinness off the hook. Does Bertie not realise that he is not dealing with a trade union group?

My fourth reason for not expecting an Easter peace miracle is that Adams and McGuinness are still focused on maximising the Sinn Féin vote in the May Westminster and local elections. Adams knows he needs to deliver quickly on the promise which he made to the McCartney sisters at the Árd Fheis or face damage to Sinn Féin's electoral base in the North. He is engaged in damage limitation for Sinn Féin at the forthcoming elections; not in moving to end-game for the IRA.

If Bertie does not see this, Catherine McCartney does. In her strongest criticism of Sinn Féin yet, she pleaded for a breaking-down of the "wall of silence" which Sinn Féin has created to protect her bother's killers. In an indirect appeal to Bertie and Tony Blair to waken-up to what is happening, she called for "constructive help, not just words" from the Irish and British Governments to break down this wall of silence.

Bertie's Eight By-election Blows

(March 22, 2005)

The apology by the four Castlerea Prison IRA inmates regretting the killing in cold blood of detective Garda Jerry McCabe was a cheap public relations stunt to deflect attention from Senator Ted Kennedy's calling-off of his planned meeting in Washington this week with Sinn Féin President Gerry Adams.

Far from being a sign of moral remorse by the four killers, the Sunday evening statement was inspired by the Sinn Féin-IRA leadership via Kerry North deputy Martin Ferris with the damage limitation aim of upstaging the Kennedy cancellation for the top spot on Monday morning's main newspapers headlines and television-radio bulletins.

Arguably, the decision by the last of the Kennedy brothers to snub Adams because of the IRA's "ongoing criminal activity and contempt for the rule of law" is as psychologically as big a blow as the earlier decisions by President George W. Bush to ban Adams from the White House on St Patrick's Day and by the Speaker of the House of Representatives, Dennis Hastert, from the luncheon on Capitol Hill.

This is a huge mark of condemnation from Senator Kennedy, who was an enormous influence on former President Bill Clinton in enabling Adams to travel to America a decade ago and be feted as a peace envoy in the White House. Both Bill and Ted were urged to do so by America's then Ambassador to Ireland, Jean Kennedy Smith. The enormous influence exercised by Ted's sister in securing Adams' access to the White House was brought home to me by accident when I called at the US Embassy by appointment to interview the Ambassador for a television programme, only to find her in a private huddle in her office with Sinn Féin's Rita O'Hare.

So embarrassed was the Ambassador at my early arrival that she admonished me not to say a word about the person she had just been in dialogue with. Such was her tone of voice that I knew that this silence was a pre-condition of my conducting the interview. Presumably, Taoiseach Albert Reynolds was privy to this secret channel between Ambassador Kennedy Smith and Sinn Féin, but if word had spilled out then about the intimate relations between the US Envoy in Dublin and the republican leadership, there would have been a furious reaction from John Major's Government in London and from the Ulster Unionists.

In deciding not to meet Adams, Senator Kennedy is effectively rowing back from the act of faith made by his sister about the sincerity of Sinn Féin to become fully democratic, a disillusion which is shared by New York Republican Congressman Peter King, who said that the republican leadership was making the Rev Ian Paisley look good! That sincerity will be put to the test when Adams meets President Bush's envoy to the Irish peace process, Mitchell Reiss, who only wants to hear from the Sinn Féin President of its time-table for meeting the demands from the Irish and British Governments that the IRA is disbanded and that its members end their involvement in criminality.

Judged from this perspective, the statement from the Castlerea Four that their early release will be off the table in any future negotiations for the restoration of a devolved Government in Belfast – that was already removed by Taoiseach Bertie Ahern and Justice Minister Michael McDowell – falls woefully short of what is required of Sinn Féin-IRA.

Adams will also face a grilling from the American media who are giving massive coverage to the visit to the White House of the sisters and partner of murdered Belfastman Robert McCartney. It will not help Adams' cause that none of the 12 republicans identified by the McCartney sisters have yet given evidence to either the PSNI or the Police Ombudsman, and that a Sinn Féin Assembly candidate for Mid Ulster in 2003, Cora Groogan, who was among the 70 persons in the bar, claims she saw nothing and heard nothing. Perhaps the snub by Ted Kennedy will bring home Sinn Féin's international isolation to Adams.

This continued spotlight on Sinn Féin-IRA has also served to deflect attention on Fine Gael leader Enda Kenny's latest electoral triumph. The success of Shane McEntee in Meath not only means that Fine Gael has held the seat vacated by John Bruton on his appointment as EU Ambassador in Washington, it confirms Enda as a credible Taoiseach-in-Waiting.

The FG-Labour voting pact in the two week-end counts in the Meath and Kildare North by-elections is judged to have been a modest success which should encourage Enda's fellow Mayoman Pat Rabbitte to convince the Labour Party's annual conference in May to give him a mandate to negotiate a Government pact with Kenny for the general election.

The election in Kildare North of the impressive Catherine Murphy, a former Labour stalwart who left after being frustrated in her ambitions by party whip Emmet Stagg, will give a boost to the other 12 sitting Independents including Dr

Jerry Cowley of Mayo and Marian Harkin of Sligo for their brand of community advocacy. It signals that Independents could hold the balance of power in 2007.

In the short-term, the Opposition will be encouraged to intensify its clamour for the dismissal of Enterprise, Trade and Employment Minister, Micheál Martin, along with his former junior ministers in Health, Ivor Callely and Tim O'Malley, for the €2bn debacle over the illegal charges on the elderly in nursing homes.

What is most worrying for the Fianna Fáil-PD coalition is that the by-election set-backs in Meath and Kildare North confirm the endurance of an underlying public resentment against their rule that was delivered even more sharply in last June's local and European elections.

Nor can the FF-PD Government take any consolation in the extremely low-turn outs - 40.6pc in Meath and 38.2pc in Kildare North – by saying that their supporters did not bother to vote because the by-elections were not seen as important plebiscites affecting the balance of power in the Dáil where the Government continues to hold a commanding majority.

But this double blow for Fianna Fáil will bring about a dramatic change of mood in the Dáil, which will reinvigorate the challenge to Kenny and Rabbitte of providing an alternative administration to Bertie, whose curriculum vitae now carries a record-breaking stigma of having lost 8 by-elections in a row since becoming Taoiseach.

Although recent national opinion polls have shown that the Fianna Fáil-PD partnership has regained a level of popularity which gave it a second term in the June 1997 general election, Bertie can no longer take it for granted that he will win a third term, with or without Mary Harney. Despite the complacent, almost clownish, response of Marine and Communications Minister, Noel Dempsey, to the double-defeat, Bertie faces a major internal post-mortem if he is to address glaring weaknesses within the country's biggest political party.

There can be no disguising the blow to morale in FF from losing Kildare North, the seat held by former Finance Minister Charlie McCreevy before he was shunted by Bertie to Brussels as EU Commissioner. For the first time ever Fianna Fáil does not have a sitting deputy in Kildare North. Faction-fighting between McCreevyite loyalists and supporters of Áine Brady, who topped the poll in the first count, will have to be sorted out by FF headquarters.

Bertie must also confront the lesson from the 12pc showing of Sinn Féin's Joe Reilly in Meath that the Shinners have not vanished from the electoral map – and still threaten Fianna Fáil's republican credentials, despite their criminal and terrorist connections.

Blair's Power Weakens

(May 10, 2005)

Eight years after his youthful coming to power, Tony Blair, now looking prematurely aged and frazzled, stood at the election centre last Friday morning in his Edgefield constituency, victorious and heading for a historic third term as a Labour Prime Minister.

Yet, he looked as if he was attending his own wake. Nor could his mood have been cheered up when a few hours later the raucous Scottish voice of George Galloway, recently expelled from his safe Glasgow Labour constituency but elected as an Independent in London, summed up the reason for his reduced majority in the House of Commons: "Mr Blair, this for Iraq".

Nor could Blair have been happy next day to discover that deeper shades of orange and green represented by the Democratic Unionist Party and Sinn Féin define the electoral map of the North more starkly than ever along sectarian lines. In the North's tribal carve-up in which Ian Paisley and Gerry Adams now rule the roost, David Trimble is politically 'dead and gone'. But the SDLP has not gone away, you know.

With its expected surge, Paisley's DUP took 9 of the North's 18 Westminster seats, including Trimble's coveted scalp in his Upper Bann constituency, leaving Lady Sylvia Hermon, an avowed liberal unionist in North Down, as the token member at Westminster of the 100 year old parliamentary party which once embodied orange supremacy.

In a typical put-down by Paisley, Trimble was taunted as the author of his own downfall, a leader who had tried to do business with Sinn Féin-IRA, but had "took the wrong road". In other words, he was shafted by Sinn Féin. Trimble hit the dust as did two of his predecessors, Terence O'Neill and Brian Faulkner.

On the nationalist side the Sinn Féin juggernaut clocked up 5 of the North's 18 seats, as it added Seamus Mallon's Newry-Armagh bailiwick to the 4 seats which it took in the 2001 general election.

Thankfully and contrary to predictions, the Shinners failed to decimate the SDLP, whose party leader Mark Durkan, easily in the end, retained John Hume's seat in Foyle. This success was partly a result of Unionist tactical voting to keep out Sinn Féin's Mitchel McLaughlin. Mark has the capacity to grow in strength and rebuild the SDLP as a more enlightened and viable alternative to the 'slightly constitutional' Sinn Féin. Tactical voting by Unionists in South Belfast enabled the SDLP deputy leader, Dr Alasdair McDonnell, to become the first nationalist to hold this traditionally middle class Protestant stronghold, while the veteran Eddie McGrady beat off the Sinn Féin challenge in South Down.

The surprise survival of the SDLP's three musketeers indicated, contrary to what Sinn Féin claims, that the Northern Bank robbery and the murder of Robert McCartney had enough effect on voters to deprive republicans of a complete sweep of the nationalist deck. The unsettled question of Robert McCartney's murder will remain Adams' Iraq.

The story of the election, however, was how Trimble, the former First Minister and co-holder with John Hume of the Nobel Peace Prize, was defeated by a comfortable 5,400 votes by the DUP's David Simpson. This was a humiliating exit for the former academic lawyer whose arrogance annoyed middle-road nationalists who refused to come to his rescue.

As the new Northern Secretary, Peter Hain, installs himself in Stormont while doubling-up as Secretary of State for Wales, he plans to explore ways forward. But there will be no progress towards restored devolved government until Sinn Féin provides absolute proof of IRA arms decommissioning and disbandment, as well as an end to republican criminality.

I suspect, however, that Tony Blair will be gone from Downing Street before Sinn Féin proves its democratic credentials to *Big Ian*. We await Gordon Brown.

Bertie's EU Constitution Fatigue

(May 31, 2005)

Sad to say, the euphoric mood which accompanied Taoiseach Bertie Ahern's negotiation last June of the new European Constitution has evaporated, as fears grow that it will be rejected in France and the Netherlands. After a series of opinion polls showing a likely 'No' vote in France, the latest one has indicated a swing towards its acceptance. President Jacques Chirac has mounted a fight back to persuade a sullen electorate that a rejection of the Constitution would do France's prestige enormous harm. However, the former Socialist leader Lionel Jospin, who believes that the Constitution will be approved, acknowledges that it will be difficult for the pro-Europeans to win, because voters will be tempted to use the referendum to register a protest vote for domestic reasons against the unpopular Chirac.

Even if the Constitution is narrowly approved in France on May 29, the EU could still find itself in a pickle three days later when the Dutch go to the polls – and the signs are that the mood in traditionally pro-European Holland has swung decisively against accepting the Constitution.

Meanwhile, Bertie has confirmed that Ireland will hold a referendum irrespective of the outcome of the votes in France and the Netherlands, but no date has yet been fixed, though it is expected to be held in the autumn.

Negotiation of the Constitution was the major achievement of Ireland's EU Presidency, with Bertie being widely feted by his European colleagues for his diplomatic skills in securing agreement for the dense legal document that specifies the EU's powers and decision-making procedures. The new Constitution creates a new EU President and foreign minister, as well as an EU diplomatic service, with the aim of enhancing Europe's presence in international affairs, especially as a counter-weight to the dominance of the United States as the world's sole superpower.

On internal matters, it allows for more democratic control by the national parliaments and the European Parliament. It also provides the legal basis for the EU taking a greater coordinated role in tackling international crime, and in stream-lining policies governing asylum and immigration.

The underlying difficulty for the member state Governments is that the complex details of the constitution baffle their national electorates who have not been given an inspiring document about European identity similar to the easily read American constitution.

According to the European Commission in Brussels, all 25 member states must seek to ratify the Constitution updating the Nice Treaty either by referendum or by parliamentary approval regardless of the French outcome. The deadline for completing the ratification process is next summer. But if by then, 20 member States have ratified the Constitution and the other 5 have been unable to do so, the issue will be referred to a meeting of the European Council composed of the heads of Government.

So far only Spain has held a referendum which was carried, but the negative mood in France and Holland raises the prospect of the Constitution being still-born in these two founding member States of the original EEC in 1957. Luxembourg's Prime Minister, Jean-Claude Juncker, who is the current President of the European Council, has ruled out a renegotiation of the Constitution in the event of its defeat in France or Holland.

Britain's Prime Minister Tony Blair has promised to hold a referendum after achieving his record third general election victory, but he will be hard pressed to win it, given the deep-rooted hostility in Little England to Brussels rule. Similarly, in Denmark, there are strong anti-EU feelings.

In previous referendums, the Danes were forced by the EU to hold a second plebescite when they rejected the Maastricht Treaty, and after Ireland said 'No' to the Nice Treaty, the 'Yes' camp won on the second go. It is difficult to envisage this bullying tactic being imposed on the French if they say Non on May 29. The EU could face a period of paralysis from constitution fatigue.

At long last, my good friend David Haworth in Brussels informs me, the EU Commission has admitted its long-term botching up of its message to its citizens, and is devising a new strategy to communicate with the people of Europe. It needs to preach more about democracy and less about regulations.

The commemoration of the sixtieth anniversary of the ending of World War Two should remind us of how precious democracy is. We need to keep the bigger picture in mind if we are not to throw away what the writer, Timothy Garton Ash, describes as the rebirth of Europe.

Seán Doherty,
FF 'Pope of Cootehall'

(June 14, 2005)

The genuine emotion from political colleagues led by Taoiseach Bertie Ahern and the public towards Seán Doherty on his death from a brain haemorrhage while on holiday in Donegal has been mixed with critical assessments of the former Minister for Justice's controversial place in history.

Even his erstwhile political opponents joined in the consensus that the Roscommon man was an able and humorous character whose social company was delightful. The high regard in which he was held in his native Cootehall was expressed by Fr. Brian Conlon when he said that the Doc was the local people's Pope.

On the more negative side of the reaction to his death at only 60 were the recalling of his notoriety over the bugging of the phones of two prominent journalists, Geraldine Kennedy and Bruce Arnold, in 1982, and new material from former Taoiseach Albert Reynolds and public relations expert Terry Prone about the circumstances in which he publicly outed Charlie Haughey a decade later with his sensational revelations that The Boss had known about the phone-taps.

What was most striking in the massive publicity which accompanied his passing was a flood of anecdotes from friends and foes alike about the remarkable influence which his personality evoked on them.

The first time I met Seán was in 1982 when he came to Luxembourg for a stormy meeting of European Justice Ministers at which he stonewalled on the controversial issue of extraditing terrorists with the cavalier coolness of a Robert Redford look-alike. Young, clean-cut with striking reddish-blonde hair and dressed like a business executive, he personified the new generation of ambitious politicians who had brought Charles J. Haughey to power with the promise of redeeming a country that was sinking in hyper-inflation and grinding unemployment.

Before his return to Dublin the Doc met me in a corner of the Kirchberg conference centre for a briefing. With a cherubic smile, he disarmed questions as to why Ireland was stalling on a European Convention to provide for mutual extradition of suspected terrorists – mainly IRA – between the then ten EEC member states, especially between Ireland and Britain.

Some months later – at the start of 1983 when Haughey's administration had been swept out of office by the Fine Gael-Labour coalition of Garret FitzGerald and Dick Spring – I had returned to Dublin and was enjoying the novelty of watching RTE television after six and a half years in Brussels. Almost on my first night back a new and tough-talking Minister for Justice, Michael Noonan, came on the box, grim-faced, to reveal that his Fianna Fáil predecessor had abused his office by authorising warrants for tapping the phones of journalists Bruce Arnold and Geraldine Kennedy.

In the words of Maurice Manning, Doherty was now condemned in the public mind, especially with the Dublin 4 set, as the anti-Christ. The State's ex-sheriff had turned out to be a bad-guy, as stories abounded of his alleged involvement in other shady goings-on such as the fixing of a court case for his brother-in-law in the Dowra affair.

Details of how Doherty had built a huge wall around his Roscommon home at the taxpayers' expense swelled his image as an unscrupulous man-on-the-make from West of the Shannon who had come to represent what was sneeringly called the country and western wing of Fianna Fáil.

As time moved on and Doherty served his time in the relative obscurity of the Opposition back-benches, the legend of a new Seán Doherty was spun by his fellow Roscommon man, journalist John Waters in his classic book *Jiving at the Cross-roads*. That of the constituency fixer and ubiquitous attender of funerals with the glad-hand-shakes. The master of parish pump politics but motivated with a passion to advance the interests of his constituents.

By now a political journalist in Leinster House, I got to know Seán socially through conversations in the Dáil bar or across the road in Buswells Hotel. His humour and his astute reading of the political scene came to the fore. There was a sense of a lost talent in the black-sheep from Cootehall.

In 1992, just as I was returning to Dublin from a second stint in Brussels, the Doc was back in the news with a bang, as he took out his smouldering-gun to claim that Haughey had known about the phone tapping. But the coming to office of his fellow county man, Albert Reynolds, on the fall of Haughey, did not result in Seán's recall to cabinet.

As it dawned on him that his scandalous past had put him beyond the Pale as far as ministerial office was concerned, Seán proved his managerial skills as Cathaoirleach of the Senate and later as a member of the Dail's Public Accounts Committee investigating evasion of the Dirt Tax.

Seán had become a re-born Christian, who would often invite me to join him on a Marian pilgrimage to Medjugore in order to cleanse me of what he taunted was my wayward liberalism. While the banter was light, he would speak like an Old Testament preacher, with the potential to tap into the alienation of the Pro-Life lobby to found a fundamentalist political party as a West of Ireland Ian Paisley. This he never did, remaining loyal to Fianna Fáil.

Shortly before his retirement three years ago to spend more time with his devoted wife Maura and family, while becoming a successful businessman, he invited me to drop in anytime at his home.

Only a few weeks ago as I passed the signpost for Cootehall on my way from Mayo, I nearly did so, but was too hard-pressed to get back to Dublin. If only, I would have more up-to-date memories of a remarkable figure in Irish politics, who went in the wrong direction in his early professional days.

When all the good-will towards him evaporates with time, the name of Seán Doherty will find a permanent place in the history books as an Irish Richard Nixon, a man whose misguided sense of duty became a threat to democracy through his illegal attempts to undermine freedom of the press.

The role of doughty defender of the Doc's memory, however, was played by his Roscommon Boswell, John Waters, who castigated the Dublin liberals for constantly misreading and misunderstanding the pulse of rural Ireland which the Cootehall man knew so instinctively. Arguing in *The Irish Times* that the cloud that hung over Doherty was more in the eye of the beholder, John remained adamant that the justifications for his action offered by the Doc were "valid when you see things from where he, and his followers and supporters, saw them".

Supportive evidence for John's argument came from Terry Prone in her *Examiner* column, where she instanced how Seán had justified his phone-taps on the grounds that he was investigating treason by showing her the typescript of a conversation between the late George Colley and Geraldine Kennedy in which the anti-Haughey Colley made it clear that he wanted to bring down Haughey's Government.

Particularly poignant was the reported plea to a tearful Seán from his wife Maura: "You've taken enough. Covered up enough. You've been the fall-guy long enough. You've suffered plenty and so have all your family. You owe it to yourself. You owe it to us. To tell the truth now".

It has also been established by Albert Reynolds that he tried to stop Seán going public with his revelations. Clearly, Seán needed to purge his soul of his decades-long demon. May he rest in peace with his Lord.

Three Crises Swirl Bertie

(June 21, 2005)

C risis is the word to sum up events this mid-summer: crisis in the EU, crisis in the Gardaí, and ongoing crisis in the peace process in the North – and we cannot blame any of these woes on Charles J. Haughey!

Of these crises, the most far-reaching is that of the nasty stand-off in the EU between France's President Jacques Chirac and Britain's Tony Blair. Great importance should be attached to the admission of the current President, Luxembourg Prime Minister, Jean-Claude Juncker, at the end of the most messy summit meeting of European leaders in the Union's 48 year history that the EU is in "profound crisis".

This pessimistic diagnosis was given weight by the uncharacteristically despondent view of Taoiseach Bertie Ahern that relations were bad, and that the Brussels summit was the kind of meeting he did not like being at. As Bertie told the Minister for Foreign Affairs, Dermot Ahern, had he still been the European President, he would have blown the whistle earlier to stop the aggro mounting between Blair and Chirac. A guillotine on the proceedings might have saved the EU the shame of Blair's refusal of an offer from Poland on behalf of the new member states to fund Britain's budget rebate. Rightly, Blair's refusal was described by Chirac as "pathetic and tragic".

Blair, the Labour leader who eight years ago promised to bring Britain to the heart of Europe and end decades of friction between London and Brussels, is now an even bigger menace to European solidarity than his Conservative predecessor, Maggie Thatcher. I remember reporting the Dublin Castle Summit chaired by Jack Lynch in December 1979 when the meeting broke up in similar acrimony to Friday's Brussels bust-up. It was at this meeting that Maggie began her budget campaign for Britain to get its money back from the European kitty.

The sombre mood after the Dublin meeting was summed up in an *Irish Times* editorial, aptly headed "Trouble." I vividly remember that it was written by Dennis Kennedy, who showed me it in Dublin Castle before sending it to the office for publication. Dennis's sarcasm caught the mood exactly. "Mrs Thatcher is giving her EEC partners one chance. If they do not come up with her £1bn, or most of it by April, they will have to face the consequences. She is not threatening to leave the EEC; worse than that, she is threatening to stay in it".

Just change the term EEC – there were only nine members then – to EU, and substitute Mr Blair for Mrs Thatcher, and the same editorial could be reproduced to sum up the dilemma today.

On reflection, however, I would rate the current crisis is even more bitter than in 1979, because in today's Union of 25 members, Blair has the capacity to crusade for a weakening of the integration process, especially as he senses that Chirac and German Chancellor Schroder are lame-duck leaders with their own electorates. On the 190th anniversary of the Battle of Waterloo, Blair is playing the anti-French card to bolster his own shaky position as Prime Minister, and he aims to push his crusade during Britain's EU Presidency that begins on July 1.

His demands for a drastic rehaul of the common agricultural policy, even though the latest reform was agreed in 2003 to decouple prices from production, spell danger for the Union's cohesion. Blair, more than Thatcher, is a bigger danger to the survival of the EU. He should be opposed vigorously by Bertie. Indeed, General Charles De Gaulle, who vetoed British membership in the 1960s, was correct in his assessment of Perfidious Albion.

Yet, it was the insight of an Englishman, Lord Acton, who coined the famous dictum about the corrupting effect of absolute power, that can help us cast light on the institutional malaise that has taken a hold of An Garda Siochana. In two interim reports into police corruption in Donegal, one published in July 2004 and the second earlier this month, Mr Justice Frederick Morris, has found that the force operates in an authoritarian, corrupt, unaccountable and secretive manner.

Yet, despite the removal and early retirement on full pensions of a few officers after the media outcry that accompanied the initial report, little progress has been made on the reform agenda a year later, causing Justice Morris to repeat his original criticisms and to add even more censorious comments.

At the heart of the inquiry were complaints from publicans and night-club owners, Frank McBrearty and his son, Frank Junior, that they were framed and victimised by Donegal Gardaí for the murder of a cattle dealer, Richie Barron, in the early hours of Monday 14 October, 1996. Not only has Morris upheld the McBrearty complaints, he has discovered that Barron died as a result of a hit and run car accident. Consequently, he has found that the McBreartys, and others who were similarly harassed by the police, were innocent of any involvement in the death. He has concluded that the Garda investigation was "prejudiced, tendentious and utterly negligent in the highest degree".

Meanwhile, enraged at their maltreatment, the McBreartys are calling for the resignations of both the Minister for Justice, Michael McDowell, and the Garda

Commissioner, Noel Conroy, whom they accuse of having received and ignored earlier information about the circumstances surrounding their harrassment.

Irrespective of the outcome in the case of the McBreartys, I agree with Senator Maurice Hayes, the man appointed by the Government to oversee the implementation of Garda reform, that McDowell's legislation submitted to the Dáil prior to the Morris Reports, falls far short of what is needed to restore confidence. Specifically, Senator Hayes is critical of the establishment of a supervisory three-person body that would report to the Minister for Justice as lacking the independent clout exercised by a Police Ombudsman in Northern Ireland.

The first Morris Report was not even debated in the Dáil, and Irish politicians will soon be off on their summer holidays for four months. There is a widely held view that the politicians are scared of the police, and that it took exceptional courage on the part of Mayo's Jim Higgins and Wexford's Brendan Howlin to bring matters to light.

Thankfully, in the last few days we have been assured by Commissioner Conroy of a more pro-active approach to Garda reform. This is most urgent, especially as we are already into the ugly Orange marching season in the North, and Sinn Féin President Gerry Adams has not yet delivered an end to the IRA and its involvement in criminality. Rather than calling for Commissioner Conroy's resignation, as Vincent Browne is doing, I would prefer to see the Mayo-born head of the Garda, achieve his twin goals of reforming the force and making the IRA a bad historical memory.

Zero Tolerance Towards IRA

(July 12, 2005)

Given the close geographical connection between Ireland and Britain, - and the use of Shannon airport by American troops being transported to and from Iraq - there are serious security implications for this country in the wake of the merciless murder by al-Qaida-linked bombers mainly of British nationality of 70 innocent people in the London bomb blasts on Thursday July 7.

Intelligence reports on the movements of up to 40 al-Qaida sympathisers have been given by the Gardaí to the UK authorities. Some €2.5 million has been raised, according to security sources, from scams such as bogus welfare claims and charity fronts.

Taoiseach Bertie Ahern has admitted that intelligence services are watching certain individuals very closely. The Minister for Defence, Willie O'Dea, is to circulate a booklet to every home with information about how to deal with a terrorist attack in Ireland. Whether we like it or not, as individuals we are all caught up in the effects of the Iraq War. We now travel under the threat of the lurking terrorist bomb. Baghdad dominates our movements.

Eerily, it was Richard Ingrams, the editor of *Private Eye*, who has pointed out that one British tabloid on Friday carried the single-word headline, "Bastards", just as it had some 20 years ago in relation to an IRA bomb. Likewise, Ingrams quoted Tony Blair's remark that the terrorists "must not win", the exact phrase as used by Margaret Thatcher about the IRA.

As Ingrams also observed, the London bombers do not appear to have a clear-cut agenda such as the IRA's political aim of securing a British withdrawal from the North and the creation of a united Ireland. This vagueness means that it is virtually impossible for George W. Bush and Blair to fulfil their rhetorical promise "to finish the job".

The renewed focus on anti-terrorism in London and Washington has contributed to a zero tolerance atmosphere towards the IRA as we await the outcome of their long drawn-out consultation on arms decommissioning and an end to their roguish paramilitary criminality. In this context, an *Irish Times* report that the republican leadership is considering a "new mode" for the IRA – that of pursuing a united Ireland by purely peaceful means – distinctly smacks of yet another fudge.

More timely was Tom Brady's report in Monday's *Irish Independent* that senior Garda officers are satisfied that the Provos were involved in a money-laundering racket in Cork earlier this year to 'cleanse' at least €7.2 million taken from the Northern Bank robbery. It would seem that the file against senior IRA figures and associates is close to completion and that high profile prosecutions may be about to take place in the courts.

No announcement was expected from republicans until after the Orange marches. While the march in Drumcree passed without incident on Sunday, tensions were mounting in Belfast for Tuesday's traditional Twelfth parade. This recurrence of sectarianism in the North naturally draws parallels between the role of religion in IRA republicanism and Protestant or Loyalist beliefs within Unionism. Inevitably, the IRA and the Orangemen belong to the same generic category of fundamentalism that has spawned Zionism in Israel, the Christian Right in America and al-Qaida.

This is a crisis too deep to be dominated by the pious simplicities of George Bush and Tony Blair.

Shoot to Kill

(July 25, 2005)

O n Friday evening just after I had noticed on the headlines popping up on my computer news digest that a man had been shot dead in London by police after a number of renewed bomb attempts, I received a phone call from a friend, Maurice Regan, who expressed his shock at how a policeman had put five bullets into the man in a Tube train carriage in Stockwell underground station while other officers pinned him down on the ground.

That evening the Metropolitan police were gung-ho that the man was "directly linked" to last Thursday's abortive terrorism attempt in London, perhaps a suicide bomber, and that a shoot-to-kill policy was deemed to be the most effective response. However brutal this killing was – and it smacked of an execution – the message had gone out to terrorists that their murderous activities would be met with immediate counter-force.

Yet, I could not help sharing Maurice's disgust and unease at such a calculated killing in a circumstance where the police could have arrested the man and brought him in for interrogation. Unless a terrorist was clearly in the act of unleashing violence and mayhem, a shoot-to-kill policy by the police brings its own lethal form of injustice in a democratic society, as we have seen in the North during John Stalker's investigation into such a policy by the RUC in the 1980s and more recently by the Israelis against the Palestinians.

It later emerged that the victim was an innocent Brazilian electrician. Yet, despite this horrendous police blunder and the protests from Muslim leaders, Prime Minister Tony Blair and the Metropolitan Commissioner, Sir Ian Blair, insist that the shoot-to-kill policy will continue in the hunt for four escaped bombers. Over-looked, of course, by Blair is the damning report which came out earlier last week by Chatham House, Britain's most authoritative foreign policy think-tank, which concluded that "there is no doubt that the invasion of Iraq had left Britain more exposed to terrorist attacks. Blair was particularly narked by its stinging criticism that his Government had been playing to its masters in Washington.

With Blair still vulnerable to the charge that he went to war illegally in Iraq with President George W. Bush on false pretences, it is highly likely that he will try to hype the statement expected later this week from the IRA to claim a major diplomatic achievement rather than to scrutinise it critically for a definite end to both its armed struggle and paramilitary criminal activity. Likewise, there are signs that Taoiseach Bertie Ahern, himself under media siege in the more farcical row over cronyism with his appointment of his ex-girl friend Celia Larkin to the consumer body, will be carried away with the atmosphere of the Galway Races to accept the bona fides of the republican movement.

Hopefully, it will be a substantial statement, but like St Thomas the Apostle and the Ulster Unionists, I shall remain sceptical about the statement until we see its effect. I am not so impressed by the confirmation that Sinn Féin leaders Gerry Adams, Martin McGuinness and Martin Ferris have agreed to step down from the IRA's Army Council. After all, do they think that we have forgotten that for months – nay, years – they have time and again denied being on the Army Council? Do they think we are dupes? Do they think that we have forgotten the IRA's €38 million robbery of the Northern Bank and the involvement of leading Sinn Féin figures in the murder of Belfastman Robert McCartney?

It was, therefore, with some misgiving that I spotted Gerry Adams and Mitchel McLaughlin (mistakenly described as an M.P. by *The Irish Times*) at Saturday's rally in Dublin for the freeing of the Rossport 5. The protests in Mayo have been infiltrated – and perhaps master-minded by Sinn Féin – making a resolution of the health and safety issues with Shell & EP Ireland more fraught. Where, I ask myself, has the money for slogans, banners and publicity come from? Why were there so few Mayo faces to be seen in the Dublin march?

My friend Maurice also informed me that the Shinners including Pearse Doherty, the failed European Parliament candidate, were among those who heckled Marine Minister Noel Dempsey at the MacGill School in Glenties. The protesters were unamenable to rational debate and in the words of School director, Joe Mulholland, came close to hi-jacking the scheduled debate.

With Shell admitting a "technical breach" in its construction of the pipe-line, hopefully, at the time of writing this column on Monday morning, there will be scope for the release of the five protesters in the High Court later today that will provide an opening for a resolution of the conflict.

There must be no winners, nor losers, in this feud.

Bertie Too Soft on 'Pat's Army'

(August 2, 2005)

The IRA's formal order to its "volunteers" on Thursday July 28 "to dump arms" as an end to its armed campaign and to engage in exclusively peaceful activities is to be welcomed as being better late than never. It marks a potentially significant landmark in the chequered history of the North's peace process.

However, P. O'Neill has not gone away, you know. The IRA's decision not to disband or decommission its highly secretive military structure is a continuing cause of anxiety about its capacity to return to arms. Its reinvention of its murderous platoons into a democratic-political club is frankly mind-boggling. The formation of an Irish version of Dad's Army – oops, Pat's Army! - has united mainstream nationalism and Ulster Unionism into a wait-and-see hesitancy about the true degree of the republican movement's commitment to peace and democratic politics.

The relevant passage of the statement read out by Seanna Walsh, the IRA's longest-serving prisoner, instructs all its "volunteers" to assist in the development of purely political and democratic programmes through exclusively peaceful means.

Like me, many readers remain sceptical that these "volunteers", many of them thugs and psychopaths, will abandon their estimated €100-200 million money-laundering business, mainly from tobacco and diesel fuel scams, as well as their inflictions of punishment shootings and beatings on the streets of oppressed nationalist communities especially in Belfast.

The statement envisages that the IRA's "commissioned officers" will continue to command the "soldiers" of Óglaigh na hÉireann. In doing what? – presumably by becoming social workers, political debaters and apostles in a new secular order of monks! The statement allows for the indefinite retention of the IRA, an insurrectionary private army whose constitution is in defiant contradiction to the 1937 Constitution of the Irish Republic. From Gerry Adams and Martin McGuinness down, not one IRA member has renounced his oath of loyalty to the armed struggle. Nor has the IRA rule book been amended to prevent a return to violence if the circumstances to do so were deemed appropriate for the attainment of a united Ireland. It has not ordered all arms to be dumped.

In the statement there was no sign of remorse at the killings of the past 35 years. The armed struggle was defended as having been legitimate. It bore none of the spirit of Michael Davitt, the only prominent Fenian to have abjured his oath of loyalty to armed insurrection in favour of peaceful politics. So, like St Thomas the doubting Apostle and the Ulster Unionists, I remain sceptical about the statement until we see its effect.

There was a chilling opportunistic tone to Adams' rhetoric that there was a time for war then and a time for peace now. The statement's adoption was in line with the republican movement's calculated agenda to get into power on both sides of the border as an electoral avenue towards a united Ireland with a Sinn Féin sans-culotte hue.

With a general election in the Republic less than two years away, Fianna Fáil, Fine Gael and Labour will face a strong challenge from a reinvigorated Sinn Féin which could hold the balance of power in the next Dáil, perhaps even forming a Government with Fianna Fáil. In the North a genuine cessation of criminal activities such as oil and cigarette smuggling – and an end to punishment beatings – could see McGuinness sitting at the Stormont cabinet table as second in command to the DUP's Ian Paisley sometime in 2006.

Adams, McGuinness and Martin Ferris have agreed to step down from the IRA's Army Council, but their replacements will take their instructions from this triumvirate of slightly constitutional politicians. Thankfully, their bete noir, Justice Minister Michael McDowell, has not forgotten the IRA's €38 million robbery of the Northern Bank and the involvement of leading Sinn Féin figures in the murder of Belfastman Robert McCartney. He remains committed to seizing IRA illegal monies, and like Taoiseach Bertie Ahern, to the campaign of the McCartney sisters and Bridgeen Hagans to secure justice in Robert's case.

It would be begrudging, however, not to admit that it was a substantial statement in its intention to abandon the physical force tradition, one which if delivered eleven years ago in the immediate euphoria of the Good Friday Agreement would have been proclaimed as truly historic.

On the positive side, the internal consultation process launched by Adams in April appears to have shepherded the IRA's units into the peace lane which leaves both the Real IRA and the Continuity IRA as marginalised ruffians.

Early confirmation by the head of the International Decommissioning body, General John de Chastelain, of a comprehensive dumping of IRA arms and explosives would make a sizable impact on public opinion, especially as it will be verified by two churchmen, Catholic and Protestant, without the photographic pantomime of sack-cloth and ashes demanded by the Democratic Unionist Party last December.

The British Government's dismantling of watch-towers in south Armagh and elsewhere suggests a secret pact between republicans and London about pre-arranged set-moves that included last Wednesday's release of Shankill bomber Seán Kelly. The promise of Westminster legislation in the autumn will allow paramilitary fugitives to return to Ireland.

Taoiseach Bertie Ahern is satisfied that the IRA's pledge that its "volunteers" will pursue exclusively peaceful means corresponds with the Good Friday Agreement's repudiation of paramilitary criminality. Unlike last December, he has not succumbed to republican pressure to release the murderers of the late Garda Detective, Jerry McCabe.

It was intriguing that in his RTE radio interview with Gerald Barry on Sunday, Bertie mused aloud about the IRA's illegal status, suggesting that in "the longer haul" when it was no longer an organisation committed to war, a Government order could lift the proscribed ban under an arrangement devised by Eamon de Valera when he formulated the Offences Against the State Act in 1939. This was a clear admission from the head of Government that he had failed to secure the IRA's disbandment at private meetings which he had held with Adams since their stormy meeting at Government Buildings in January. Surely Bertie has not fallen for this nonsense of the IRA transforming itself into a club for peaceniks?

My hunch is that Bertie has been too soft on the republican leadership, partly because he may need their support to achieve his ambition of becoming a third term Taoiseach, but also because British Premier Tony Blair has been in over-drive to reach an accommodation with the Provos to allow himself to concentrate on "true" terrorism posed by al-Qaida in London.

On cue, George Bush's White House has reopened the congressional corridors of power in Washington to the foot-slogging Martin McGuinness and Rita O'Hare as part of their strategy of maintaining the good will – and financial donations – of the powerful Irish-American lobby.

On balance, I hope that at long last Pat's Army is as committed to jaw-jaw as the IRA was to semtex and bullets, and that Sinn Féin whom I have called the ugly ducklings of the political system are on their way to becoming beautiful democratic swans. A test of this will be justice for the McCartneys whose efforts did so much to bring about this statement. Bertie vows to press their case.

Bertie Goes Missing in 'Innishvicillaun'

(August 9, 2005)

Sinn Féin's purring at the undetected return to Ireland of the Colombia Three has made a laughing-stock of Bertie's Government, immigration officers and the Gardaí, as well as enraging Ulster Unionists and reducing the Northern peace process to the level of a music-hall farce.

No wonder, an exasperated Tanaiste Mary Harney, standing in as Justice Minister for Michael McDowell who is on holidays in Australia, vented her spleen on the Sinn Féin President, Gerry Adams, for expressing his delight at their furtive return on Sunday's lunchtime radio.

After demanding that Adams should ensure that the three men, James Monaghan, Niall Connolly and Martin McCauley, hand themselves in to the Gardaí, Harney described Adams' interview as "arrogant and offensive to ordinary Irish people".

In this outburst, she is undoubtedly correct but she failed to acknowledge that the national mood is also one of dismay at the spectacle of the Government and the institutions of the State being subjected to ridicule and contempt by the leader of Sinn Féin.

Nor did Taoiseach Bertie cover himself in glory by doing a Pontius Pilate-style interview from his holiday-hotel in Kerry rather than returning to Dublin to oversee the most embarrassing international crisis with which he has been confronted in his eight years as head of Government. The Colombian Government has an opportunity to castigate Ireland in the eyes of the world as turning a blind eye to the presence in its jurisdiction of escaped felons. Bogota is also appealing to President George W. Bush to endorse their efforts for the extradition of the three men as part of the international war on terrorism.

Yet, Bertie is peddling the facile line that this is not a matter to be dealt with by the Government. It is the responsibility of the Gardaí to find the men, interview them and decide whether to send a file – presumably for travelling on false passports – to the Director of Public Prosecution. Likewise, Bertie has shuttled the extradition question into the hands of the judiciary on the grounds that there is no treaty between Ireland and Colombia for the return of escaped prisoners. A mealy-mouthed article in Monday's *Irish Times*, signed by Bertie but written by a media minder, was no substitute for the Taoiseach's presence at his desk in Government Buildings. What will stick most in the public mind is Adams telling Bertie on the national air-waves that whatever the process, he must stand up and not send these gallant men back to Colombia.

With buck-passing Bertie bolted up in his Kerry retreat, Adams and the Sinn Féin spin-machine have been attempting to lull the public into thinking the republican way about how cosy it is for the families of the Columbia Three to have their men-folk back in their homesteads. Are we supposed to accord them a hero's-welcome and treat them like returned long-distance emigrants who were offering peacenik services to the Marxist Farc guerrillas? As Mary Harney noted, Adams spoke of the men as if they had been "ordinary tourists visiting Colombia".

In Harney's words, too, it will be "an affront to democracy", if Adams plays dumb about the whereabouts of his fellow-travellers in the republican movement, though he has acknowledged that Jim Monaghan told RTE's Charlie Bird that he is ready to talk to the Gardaí. The Gardaí, I am sure, will not be impressed that the fugitive Monaghan opted in the first instance to have his cosy chat with Charlie broadcast to the nation last Friday evening rather than making themselves available for interview. Another instance of Spin Féin.

What really was distasteful in the Adams interview – a soft one with the usually forensic Gerald Barry – was the Sinn Féin President's disclaimer that the return of Monaghan, Connolly and McCauley was not harmful to the peace process. Without any sign of a reddening on his beard, Adams claimed that the difficulties for the peace process lay with the ongoing Loyalist feud and the failure of Ian Paisley's Democratic Unionists to share power. This is both a misleading and self-serving statement from Adams that is straight out of "the big lie" propaganda of the old Soviet Union which the great English writer George Orwell so ably exposed in his novels such as *Nineteen Eighty Four* and *Animal Farm*. Another "big lie" from Big Brother is his latest mantra that "the political leadership of Unionism is out of tune with civic unionism".

The main question which the public needs to put to Adams and Co. is why they have planned the timing and location of their reappearance on Irish soil, south of the border, and not in the North from where they would be extradited by the Blair Government? The manipulation of RTE with the Bird interview of Monaghan came just eight days after the IRA statement pledging to "dump arms". Not only has there not yet been any decommissioning of a single bullet, the Blair

Government has pandered to the Provisionals with the release of Seán Kelly, the removal of watch-towers and its schedule to cut-back on regiment levels.

It is not just the Unionists who are questioning Sinn Féin's trustworthiness. There is growing disquiet inside the more reflective wing of Fianna Fáil that Bertie has not only appeased Adams in his "private" talks, but that he has exposed himself to the charge of doing side-deals with Adams. A blatant instance of this is Adams' claim that elected representatives in the North will have rights to speak in the Dáil. Though Bertie now counter-claims that he was only offering Adams limited access to a Dáil committee on Northern affairs, Fine Gael leader Enda Kenny is right in demanding explanations from the Taoiseach as to what exactly he promised Adams in his ill-considered dealings with him after the Northern Bank robbery and the brutal murder of Robert McCartney in Belfast.

Rightly or wrongly, the public perception is growing that Bertie is Gerry's poodle. Bertie's over-indulgent attitude to Sinn Féin smacks more of the collaborationist approach of the late Neil Blaney and Kevin Boland rather than the even-handed conduct of Jack Lynch and Paddy Hillery.

The underlying intent of the IRA statement was to engineer a speedy passage to power in both the North and the Republic. The events of the past days gives me an unpleasant shudder that both Blair and Bertie are being duped by this strategy, and that we are already well into the opening phase of a republican coup of the island by stealth that aims to marginalise the Unionists in the North and outflank Fianna Fáil in the South.

Fine Gael Senator, Brian Hayes, has warned that a vote for Fianna Fáil at the next general election will be a vote for Sinn Féin. There is a lot of truth in this remark. It remains to be seen if saner counsels in Fianna Fáil rescue Bertie from this Quisling approach to Sinn Féin. It will be a real test of the Progressive Democrats to either put a halt on *Bertie Adams*, or leave this Government.

Increasingly, it strikes me that only a Government led by Enda Kenny and Labour's Pat Rabbitte can save us from Sinn Féin bondage of Orwellian proportions.

Mo Mowlam: Politics Loses Great Idealist

(August 23, 2005)

Mo Mowlam, who was to New Labour what Princess Diana was to the British monarchy, was only 55 when she died on Friday after her long and heroic battle against a recurrent brain tumour. Her tragic death has reminded us all of how the Grim Reaper never takes time off even for a summer vacation.

"One hell of a woman" was the gauche and infelicitous description of Mo by former Labour leader Neill Kinnock – but we all knew that he was calling the former Northern Ireland Secretary a secular saint. And the recounted stories of her flamboyant style and uninhibited perkiness all testified to her remarkable hold over the affection of so many people.

No sooner had I heard word of Mo's death on radio on Friday morning than I received a call on my mobile from David, a producer with TV3's Ireland-AM chat show asking if I could get into studio pronto to pay tribute to her life. I snatched Mo's autobiography, *Momentum*, and Julia Langdon's biography, *Mo Mowlam*, from my bookshelves and sped from my home in Terenure to the studio in Ballymount at a pace that would have done Jackie Stewart proud even though I noticed that the red warning sign indicated that there was only a meagre drop of petrol left in the tank.

On arrival I found the staff were all genuinely shocked at the news of Mo's passing, and I found it an emotional experience to be speaking on television in the past tense about Mo, whose presence in film clips appeared to dominate the studio. It is difficult to sum up a public figure's life in a few words. Though I cannot claim to have been part of her circle, the occasions on which I met her remain fixed affectionately in my mind, and I treasure a photograph taken with her in her office at Westminster.

When I was first introduced to Mo at the bar in the Burlington Hotel in Dublin by John Hume, I asked her what she would like to drink. "A double brandy," she cheerfully ordered. "You have been around for some time on the political scene here, John. Tell me what you really think".

This switching of the spotlight on the person whom she was speaking to was an instance of how behind her extrovert personality, the real Mo was a private person. She had an extraordinary ability to put her own life into different compartments: working hard at school in Coventry and later at Durham University had been her way of coping with family rows caused by an alcoholic father; having fun with fellow students and boy friends at colleges in Newcastle, Barnsley and the United States were combined with diligent academic teaching of politics and later its practice as one of the architects of New Labour and the Good Friday Agreement.

Ironically, it was her popularity and down-to-earth approach which saw her fall foul of the more conventional Tony Blair and the socially puritanical David Trimble that caused her premature departure from politics when she was only 50. A north of England lass, she fought for social justice and equality for women with a passion that made her increasingly alienated from the Blair in-crowd and their addiction to government by spin and deceit. Her death only a week after that of Robin Cook leaves New Labour bereft of its idealistic wing.

Bertie Deplores North's Sectarianism

(September 13, 2005)

Something very worrying is happening when the Orange Order, an institution professing loyalty to the British Crown, is colluding with so-called Loyalist paramilitaries who in broad day light fire volleys of shots at police vehicles in Belfast with intent to shoot to kill.

The stark reality behind this sinister development was highlighted by the straight-talking of Sir Hugh Orde, the chief constable of the Police Service of Northern Ireland, when he laid the blame squarely on the Orange Order for Saturday's scenes of street violence in which over thirty policemen and soldiers were injured.

Describing the riots as the "worst violence ever faced by a police force in the UK", Sir Hugh said with grim candour: "Petrol bombs don't appear by accident, blast bombs do not appear by accident and certainly firearms have to be planned to be produced in the way they were produced".

The Chief Constable put on the public record how he himself had seen "members of the Orange Order in their sashes attacking my officers", and he witnessed bandsmen belonging to the Whiterock Orangemen, Shankill Protestant Boys and the Sons of Ulster stand next to masked men. "The Orange Order," he concluded, "must bear substantial responsibility for this. They publicly called people on to the street".

Sir Hugh's most telling point was his showing to journalists the 15 or more bullets that were lodged in a police vehicle. These had been intended to kill officers. Filmed footage showed that gunmen from both the Ulster Defence Association and the Ulster Volunteer Force had been involved – and were certainly not spending a leisurely Saturday afternoon on cease-fire! The accompanying pictures of devastation of cars caused by petrol bombs made Belfast look like a smokey New Orleans. Unlike New Orleans, however, the devastation in Belfast, was man-made. Remarkably, this worst instance of sectarian violence from Belfast in a decade was fomented deliberately by the Orange Order in collusion with Loyalist gunmen.

Yet, the reaction of Unionist politicians was to blame the Parades Commission for not allowing the Orangemen to march triumphantly through the Catholic Springfield Road. Their common hymn-sheet intoned the party line that the disturbances merely reflected the frustration of the majority Protestant community at the extent of the concessions made to nationalists and republicans in the stalled peace process.

What is also profoundly worrying is that the Orange Order's stoking up of the riots in Belfast spread like an uncontrollable bush-fire to other parts of the North such as Ballymena, Antrim, Carrickfergus, Larne, Ballyclare, Glengormley, Newtonabbey and Ahoghill.

Not surprisingly, a Catholic priest in the Harryville area of Ballymena changed the venue for his Mass to avoid the cars of his parishioners from being hijacked or blocked by Loyalist bully-boys. Catholic worship in Banbridge, County Down, was also impeded. Worse still, on Saturday morning a 29 year-old Catholic man sustained severe head injuries when he was beaten mercilessly by a gang of Protestant youths.

Not without reason the Minister for Foreign Affairs, Dermot Ahern, who last week visited Belfast to hear the concerns of SDLP and Sinn Féin representatives, referred to a "huge effort to intimidate nationalist communities". Dermot's anxiety, and his expressed fear of how a new generation was being spawned in sectarian hatred, was shared by the Catholic Primate of All Ireland and Archbishop of Armagh, Seán Brady, as well as by Taoiseach Bertie Ahern. Both Bertie and the Archbishop deplored the likely negative impact of this dangerous development on the already stalled peace process, and they appealed for community dialogue.

Yet, neither the Taoiseach nor the prelate offered a specific initiative to mobilise community support against the root-evil of sectarian hatred. Indeed, the Taoiseach lamented that "this cannot be sorted out by governments – this is for the communities themselves." In making this comment, Bertie, probably unwittingly, put his finger on a mismatch which lies at the heart of the efforts made to construct a power-sharing Executive since the first IRA ceasefire in 1994: the sharing of power by political representatives from the two sides of a divided community cannot hold while there is still such endemic mutual distrust and animosity prevailing from the grass-roots up to the Stormont cabinet room.

The constant obstacle to political success, right back to the Brian Faulkner-Gerry Fitt power-sharing Executive of 1973-74 to the foundered remakes of the 1990s onwards under David Trimble and Seamus Mallon is the evidence that sectarianism has flourished, not diminished in the North during the past three decades.

The spread of sectarianism is the ugly reality confronting political and church leaders in the North, despite the many heroic stances taken by John Hume, Gerry Adams and David Trimble, as well as by peace-padres such as the Redemptorist priest, the Rev Alec Reid and the Presbyterian former Moderator, John Dunlop.

Inevitably, this grimly unedifying situation raises the fundamental question as to why the Catholic and Protestant Churches in the North - which claim to represent the good news of peace and reconciliation taught by Jesus Christ – continue to harbour within their respective memberships followers who hate fellow Christians belonging to other religious denomination deriving from the sixteenth century Reformation?

Part of the answer to this dilemma is to be found in an article written in September 1973 in the Dominican theology journal, *Doctrine and Life*, "The Northern Ireland conflict and the Churches" by Brian de Burca. "For some time now our Church leaders have joined together in statements and have asked for peace and justice, for security and liberty alike for Protestant and Catholic," he noted. "It would be a tremendous sign if they could now come together in a public act of reconciliation, admitting their own personal guilt for the tragedy that is now a part of Northern Ireland's daily life. Time is running out".

That was written ahead of what was described as the first Inter-Church Summit meeting which took place in the Ballymascanlon Hotel near Dundalk. Despite protests by the leader of the Free Presbyterian Church, the Rev Ian Paisley, that historic meeting led to an era of inter-church meetings.

However, this process failed, because Protestant and Catholic Churchmen refused to make institutional concessions to one another on rules governing mixed marriages and separate religious schools. The churches have maintained institutional segregation that allows sectarianism to prevail.

With Paisley now suggesting a meeting with Archbishop Brady, the time is ripe for the reconvening of an Inter-Church Summit that would put collective remedial action against sectarianism to the top of their agenda. Such a meeting would be timely, as the IRA prepares to dump its arms against the background of reactivated Loyalist para-militarism.

It is long overdue for the proscribing of the Orange Order. This organisation is not a cultural club for Protestant identity. It is a conveyor of virulent sectarianism. This was understood as far back as 1798 by the Anglican Bishop of Killala, Joseph Stock, when he noted that the foundation of the Orange Order three years earlier had introduced an element into Protestantism that aimed at the "excision" of papists.

By turning against the Crown Forces last week-end who prevented a wholesale attack on Catholics, the Orange Order reached its lowest point in its sordid history. It should be banned by the British Government and disowned by Protestant churchmen.

Adams & McG Deliver
for Bertie

(September 27, 2005)

T he *Irish Independent's* front-page photograph of Gerry Adams and Martin McGuinness basking rapturously in the red and white colours of the Tyrone team on All Ireland cup final day instilled two immediate thoughts in me.

The first reaction was a quizzical "how dare a Belfastman and a Derryman posture gloatingly as Tyrone men?" Although I would be chuffed to be considered an adopted Mayoman, this instant response stemmed from an unconscious proprietorial claim which I have on County Tyrone, because my grandfather was from a small farm in Coalisland before he went to Scotland almost a hundred years ago to find work - and have a life free from Protestant Loyalist intimidation - in the coal-fields of the West of Scotland at Blantyre, Lanarkshire.

The second reaction was one of admiration at the spin-doctoring skills of *MacAdams* in timing the decommissioning in the week of the All Ireland, the return of the Dáil and the British Labour party conference in Brighton, as well as the opening of the Dundalk by-pass.

Unquestionably, Adams and McGuinness are sharp political operators with a strategy of securing power in both the North and the Republic on their way to their ultimate goal of a united socialist-republican Ireland. The slick way in which the details of the decommissioning were carefully choreographed yesterday confirms that Adams and McGuinness have succeeded in delivering their pledge, announced on July 28, to end the armed struggle. It was a historic day.

However, the secrecy imposed by legislation drafted by the British and Irish Governments meant that General John de Chastelain, the chairman of the International Independent Commission on Decommissioning, (IICD), was tormented by sceptical, even abrasive journalists at his news conference in the Culloden Hotel near Belfast.

Having met General de Chastelain, who loves fishing on the River Moy, just over a year ago at a function in Dublin with Matt Farrell of the Ballina Chamber of Commerce, I am convinced of his integrity, competence and commitment. It has taken him some six years to reach what he declared was the fourth and final act of decommissioning by the IRA.

The Canadian-born general of Scottish Presbyterian background confirmed that very large quantitises of arms were put beyond use – he and his two colleagues, Brigadier Tauno Nieminen of Finland and Ambassador Andrew Sens, stated their belief that all the arms in the IRA's possession were decommissioned. They came to this conclusion on the grounds that their inventory of arms was consistent with the estimates of arms which they had obtained from the British and Irish security forces.

Furthermore, ammunition which had been collected over a period of time from caches, individuals and service units had been brought to them in loose form.

He was honest enough to admit that the IRA may still retain some weapons. He declined to cite figures or publish his inventory which would only be handed over when the Commission completes its work with Loyalist paramilitaries. He had not asked the Provos for photographic evidence as he knew they would not do so. He had stuck to his mandate working last week from six o'clock in the morning till late at night. He had handled every weapon.

A difficult moment was when a hostile journalist of the Unionist persuasion questioned General de Chastelain's credibility by suggesting that he had overlooked weapons smuggled into the North from Florida in 1996. At times, the General may have been hard of hearing, but on this occasion his military expertise came across when he pointed out that hand-guns do not bear the date of their manufacture.

To my mind, the testimonies of the two independent witnesses were highly credible. Both the Rev Harold Good, a former President of the Methodist Conference, and Fr Alec Reid, the Redemptorist priest who since 1969 has worked with the Clonard peace ministry, were categorical in their assurances that the decommissioning by the IRA was now an accomplished fact. It was incontrovertible and beyond a shadow of a doubt.

Explaining that they had observed last week's destruction process of a huge amount of arms minute by minute from the beginning to end - and insisting that they had not been appointed to do so by the IRA - they declared that they were certain – utterly certain – about the exactitude of the de Chastelain report.

Also certain about the magnitude of the IRA's move was Martin McGuinness who described the event as a hugely historic advance that marks the final page in the final chapter of IRA arms.

"What more can we ask for?" he asked.

If the mood of the press conference reflected the doubts held by the Ulster Unionists who demanded an inventory of arms decommissioned, the prospect of a return to the negotiating table may yet take some time. This was indicated by the Minister for Foreign Affairs, Dermot Ahern, who noted that a clean bill of health may not be given to the IRA until January when he hopes real progress can be made to get the Unionists to share power with nationalists.

Having been critical of Sinn Féin-IRA since the foul murder of Robert McCartney and the Northern Bank robbery earlier this year, I hope that the decommissioning was as thorough and comprehensive as Tyrone's majestic victory over Kerry at Croke Park yesterday.

I also hope that this represents what Martin McGuiness describes as "the final page of the final chapter" with the disbandment of Pat's Army, as well as a definite end to republican involvement in criminality.

If so, it is now the Ulster Unionists, notably, Ian Paisley's hardline Democrtatic Unionists who are on trial. It was the late Brian Faulkner who called Ian Paisley the demon doctor. Many including myself have expressed doubts about his ability to compromise. Now that the IRA has effectively marched off the battle-field, will he be conciliatory and do the deal that ends the Ulster Question once and for all?

Former Taoiseach Garret FitzGerald hazards the guess that Paisley may go for a deal – but he is not sure. Nor am I. Much will depend on the abilities of the more pragmatic Peter Robinson and Nigel Dodds to coax *Big Ian* to end his days as First Minister. Or at least, that they can persuade him not to follow his son, Ian Junior's bigoted negativity. Unionism still badly needs leadership.

In this context, it is timely to recall the advice of the late Basil McIvor, the liberal Unionist who was Minister for Education in the short-lived Sunningdale power-sharing Executive in 1974. In his biography, *Hope deferred*, McIvor wrote: "Return to local democracy can only be achieved by courageous Unionist politicians who will dare to take risks, who will refuse to walk away from the unpleasant necessity of speaking to the enemy, who will be prepared to negotiate but always wary of the republicans edging towards a united Ireland".

To quote Shelley in *Prometheus Unbound*, we must continue

".... to hope till Hope creates
From its own wreck the thing it contemplates."

Both Tony Blair and Bertie Ahern have expressed their satisfaction that 11 years after the first IRA ceasefire and 7 years after the Good Friday Agreement the way is now clear for Loyalist paramilitaries to follow the route taken at last by the IRA.

Yesterday was a day of hope, one in which to give republicans the benefit of the doubt. Tyrone's two most public sons – Gerry and Martin – must not shatter the hopes of the whole island and the world.

Bertie Rules Out FF-SF Deal

(October 4, 2005)

The new Dáil session whose advance publicity from the Opposition had highlighted the combined strategy of Fine Gael, Labour and the Greens to pin the charge of Rip-off Ireland firmly on the record-sheet of the Fianna Fáil-PD Coalition has been overshadowed by the welcome release of the Rossport Five and the IRA's arms decommissioning.

Rightly so. Government ministers kicked off the political season worried that public vexation with rip-off prices and poor services – as well as further instances from the Auditor and Comptroller General of government wastage - will become the dominant nark of the electorate in the long run-up to a general election.

Realising that this mood of disenchantment could provide Enda Kenny and Pat Rabbitte with their passport to power, Taoiseach Bertie Ahern has come out fighting to scorn the credibility of an alternative FG-Labour-Greens formation – and to bury speculation that Fianna Fáil might join up with Sinn Féin in the next Government.

For a politician so renowned for double-speak and for keeping his options open, Bertie was remarkably cut-and dry when he told Tommie Gorman on RTE radio on Sunday that he could not see a FF-SF coalition lasting "five days, let alone five years". He also dismissed the prospect of a Rainbow Coalition with the put-down remark that Fine Gael, Labour and the Greens "cannot agree on the weather".

Not surprisingly, Bertie is talking up his success in securing IRA decommissioning by claiming that more progress had been made in the past decade in relation to political problems in Ireland than in the past 800 years. It is a claim that must stand the test of time. The way is now clear for making the Good Friday Agreement work in its totality by restoring not only the Executive and the Assembly in the North, but also of developing North-South economic links, an issue which was pushed strongly by the SDLP leader, Mark Durkan, when he met Bertie at Government Buildings.

One immediate effect of the IRA arms decommissioning has been the boost it has given to Tony Blair's determination to stay on as Prime Minister until as close as possible to the next British general election. No wonder Gordon Brown left Labour's annual conference in Brighton looking even gloomier than usual!

As so often in the past 35 years, the big unknown question remains how the leader of the Democratic Unionist Party will react. A modern Moses leading his Protestant fundamentalist tribe into an Ulster of peace or a latter-day King Canute raving in vain against the advancing tide to equality of Catholic nationalism? This is the stark choice confronting Ian Paisley after confirmation by General John de Chastelain, of the historic destruction by the IRA of its vast arsenal of bombs and bullets.

Last December *Big Ian* called it right when he pulled out of a power-sharing deal with Sinn Féin-IRA. His demand for photographic evidence of IRA arms decommissioning exposed the duplicity of republicans in sticking sneakily to their dual track armalite and the ballot box strategy. On that occasion, Paisley did public service to both a divided North and an indifferent Republic by drawing attention – along with Justice Minister Michael McDowell – to the criminal State within a State built by the republican God-fathers.

This time, *Big Ian* has misread the extent to which Sinn Féin has cut off its IRA persona after its worst press ever over its robbing of the Northern Bank and the involvement of its members in the foul murder of Belfastman Robert McCartney.

Either Paisley, who will be 80 next April, can continue to stonewall change and frustrate Bertie and Blair in their joint aim of restoring the Northern Executive and Assembly by next spring. Or he can show a pragmatic side to his demagogic character that would see him end his days as head of government in Stormont – standing side by side with his Deputy First Minister, Martin McGuinness.

Paisley has the opportunity to enter talks with republicans if they receive what the Minister for Foreign Affairs, Dermot Ahern, calls a clean bill of health in January when the International Monitoring Commission delivers a report on terrorism and paramilitary criminality. This report could pave the way for talks about talks which could lead to a power-sharing deal in the late spring. More likely, these 'talks about talks' could breakdown in June ahead of the marching season. But especially if the Loyalist paramilitaries follow the Provo path of decommissioning, the climate could be right for a new push next October.

This time next year, the Right Honourable, the Rev Dr Ian Richard Kyle Paisley, could be installed as First Minister presiding over a government with a Sinn Féin that embraces the new police service. It will be a nightmare for all of us in this island if the demon doctor opts for tribal obstructionism rather than inter-community partnership. It would be a start, at least, if Paisley would begin to decommission his bellicose rhetoric.

While Gerry Adams and Martin McGuinness await Paisley's response, like the two tramps in Samuel Beckett's play, *Waiting for Godot*, the Sinn Féin leadership have become more visible in their support of the Rossport Five cause as part of their drive to win more Dáil seats in the next election.

During the summer it became clear to me that the Shinners were exploiting the imprisonment of the Rossport Five and their families' genuine concerns about the safety of the Corrib gas pipeline so close to their homes for their own political purposes of securing a Dáil seat in Mayo. I heard at first hand from councillors and Gardaí in Mayo of cases of intimidation and harassment. I myself was also the target of outrageous smears for my efforts to convene a round table debate between Shell E&P Ireland, the Department of the Marine and the Shell to Sea Campaign.

So it was refreshing to hear the Fine Gael leader, Enda Kenny, telling Seán O'Rourke on Sunday's *The Week in Politics* programme that Sinn Féin protesters had targeted him in an "insidious campaign" for his speaking-out against any secret deal for the release of the IRA murderers of Garda Detective Jerry McCabe.

Unlike the opportunistic antics of Dr Jerry Cowley, and to a lesser extent Michael Ring, Enda kept a balanced view of the local safety anxieties and the national interest of developing the gas. His plea to the Government to appoint a mediator of stature has been acted on by the Minister for the Marine and Natural Resources, Noel Dempsey, with the Shell company's Andy Pyle also showing good-will by his accommodation in the High Court.

Hopefully, the pending appointment of a mediator, along with this month's public hearings under Senior Counsel John Gallagher, as well as the publication of the independent safety review by end of November, will create a climate of conciliation conducive to a settlement satisfactory to all sides of the dispute.

Alas, it is not in Sinn Féin's political self-interest for a settlement to be brokered.

However, it was good to hear the Minister for Education, Mary Hanafin, express her optimism that progress can be made, even though she too had observed how Sinn Féin leaders had been heading up to Mayo.

The less involvement of Sinn Féin in the Corrib talks, the better will be the chances of a successful resolution to a conflict that cast a shadow over the long nights of summer in Rossport.

Enda Circles Bumbling Bertie

(October 18, 2005)

"**M**ove over, Bertie, to the Opposition benches!" was the message from Enda Kenny that had the Fine Gael faithful gung-ho at his presidential dinner in Dublin's Burlington Hotel. Over 1,000 FG supporters who had paid €100 per head gave out a roar worthy of Croke Park to register their agreement with their Mayo leader that Bertie Ahern's long tenure as Taoiseach is coming to a close. Only last year the same event was half-empty.

With Government ministers reeling from the recent revelations of widespread wastage in flagship projects, Kenny zoomed into his main theme that on top of "the broken promises is now broken trust".

Above the rising applause, he roared: "The trust that the people had in the Government at the last election to manage effectively has been shattered. Nothing has illustrated this more than "their buck-passing of the past two weeks".

The temperature rose further when Enda observed that if everyone in our hospitals washed their hands as often as our Ministers, we'd eliminate MRSA. "With the current Government, cabinet members chase the publicity but run away from the responsibility".

In contrast, Fine Gael in Government would accept responsibility and be accountable for its performance "good or bad", and it would promote new people and fresh ideas to tackle the challenges facing Ireland today. Access to quality health care would be his priority. The gross wastage of recent years would be avoided.

It was exactly what the faithful wanted to hear. Not since the heyday of Garret FitzGerald had I detected a mood of confidence at a Fine Gael event that the political tide towards Government Building was running in their favour. The inflow of new blood into the party was also noticeable in the numbers of young people present, as well as the new smiles on older faces.

This expectation of a return to Government was also evident in the many chats I had with prominent figures in the party, as well as councillors hopeful of winning Dáil seats. However, this optimism was held in check by a detectable underlying anxiety that reports from around the country indicated that Pat Rabbitte's Labour Party was not doing well enough to put an alternative Rainbow Government in place.

More disquietingly, there was also an apprehension about the continued rise of Sinn Féin which threatens to expand its representation in the next Dáil, possibly holding the balance of power that could enable Bertie to fulfil his ambition of becoming a third term Taoiseach.

As a counter-move against Sinn Féin, Enda on Sunday took up the mantle of Michael Collins. Speaking at the launch of The Collins 22 Society, he rounded on Gerry Adams' Sinn Féin for undermining "the vision and aspirations of constitutional republicans" through claim to be spiritual descendants of Collins and Arthur Griffiths, who launched Sinn Féin 100 years ago. Through today's Sinn Féin association with the IRA and its criminal network stretching the length and breadth of Ireland and abroad, "the current users" of that title (Sinn Féin) had dishonoured the memory of Collins and Griffith.

As Enda was inaugurating the Collins 22 Society, Bertie was delivering his annual address to the *Soldiers of Destiny* in memory of Tone at Bodenstown. It will be tantalising at this week-end's Fianna Fáil Árd Fheis to watch how Bertie will try to regain the moral high-ground of republicanism in this three-way ideological battle between FF, FG and SF under the guise of Michael Collins versus Eamon de Valera versus Wolfe Tone for the soul of modern Ireland. His big card is his success in securing IRA arms decommissioning. His big test is securing a similar move by the Loyalist paramilitaries. His even bigger task is coaxing Ian Paisley's Democratic Unionists to return to the negotiating table on the formation of an Executive with Sinn Féin – the Gerry Adams one!

Bertie, Pal of Liam Lawlor

(October 25, 2005)

Not only did Liam Lawlor's sudden death in a Moscow Mercedes car crash on Saturday upstage Fianna Fáil's Árd Fheis in Killarney, the sensational covereage by the Sunday newspapers suggesting that he died in a red-light district, and that the female passenger was a lady of the night has provoked widespread disgust and outrage about declining ethical standards in the Irish media.

It now transpires that the sole survivor from the crash which also killed the Russian driver is Julia Kushnir, a 32 year Ukranian and mother of two who was acting as Lawlor's interpreter-secretary. The two had just arrived from Prague, where Lawlor had been conducting property business. Their luggage was in the wrecked car.

My sympathy goes out to Liam's wife and family who, naturally, have issued a statement deploring "the barrage of inaccurate, reckless and vindictive coverage" from "certain sections of the media".

Lawlor's role in the corruption of Irish politics is huge, yet he was a likeable rogue.

At the Flood and Mahon Tribunals into planning corruption Judges Feargus Flood and Alan Mahon have struggled to make sense of the web of dodgy practices which Lawlor was accused of, ranging from Quarryvale to Arlington Securities. As a result of his untimely death, the evidence against Lawlor may now never be fully known.

Lawlor's defiance of all-comers won him pariah status in the corridors of Leinster House. His gruff style ensured that he was never fazed by the legal eagles. Fearlessly, the former Dublin and Leinster hurler was always delighted to engage with journalists even when he knew they were trying to put him down. He was always trying to pull the wool over our eyes.

Many a reveller on the town were astonished to catch a glimpse of the former Dublin West deputy enjoying a gentle libation in a well-known Dublin hotel on either the eve of his latest of his three visits to prison for obstructing the work of the Planning Tribunal, or within hours of his release. I remember calling him on his mobile phone one Saturday afternoon when he was due to go to Mountjoy

Prison. When he answered, he was playing a game of golf. He, enthusiastically, attacked the Tribunal for being a waste of taxpayers' money – and a waste of his time!

At a popular level, he became an anti-hero. Yet, he was certainly no Robin Hood. Liam represented, unashamedly, the corrupt face of Irish politics. Unlike public relations consultant and former Government press secretary, Frank Dunlop Liam Lawlor truly had balls of iron.

Yet, his most difficult moment came last March. It must have looked even to Lawlor that the game was up for him. "A tissue of lies" was the damning comment hurled at Lawlor at the planning tribunal in Dublin Castle. The exasperation stemmed from discovery that for some six years Lawlor had concealed his involvement in the acquisition of 55 acres of land at Coolamber in West Dublin. Yet, even as a series of lawyers paraded weighty evidence against him, Lawlor, continued to interrupt them with his characteristic refrain –"This is a blatant lie."

Yet, the noose was getting tighter around Lawlor's bull-neck. The State lawyers showed that his company, Advance Proteins Ltd, was largely a front which he used as his own personal bank account. According to a senior counsel, Lawlor used this account to purchase his Mercedes car, pay stud fees and veterinary bills for fillies and foals. The former Synge Street Christian Brother who studied engineering at Dublin's College of Technology, owned Somerton House, a magnificent pile in Lucan. He was obliged to resign from Fianna Fáil in June 2000. In 2002 he quit politics.

Yet, despite Lawlor's financial misadventures, he was never expelled from Leinster House. He was protected by the club. The Oireachtas never passed an emergency law to have him thrown out in disgrace. Even in the spring of 2003, Lawlor shared a bar with his old pal, Taoiseach Bertie Ahern, in Prague after they apparently met by chance.

Yet, even though Bertie eventually had to disown Lawlor and throw him out of the Fianna Fáil parliamentary party, he appointed him chairman of the Ethics Committee. Bertie retained a bond of affection for Liam dating back to their arrival in Leinster House as part of the same intake of the 1977 general election that had brought Jack Lynch to power as the head of a single party Fianna Fáil Government. Lawlor had beaten Mary Harney, a protégé of Lynch, for a nomination to run in her home constituency of Dublin West.

Lawlor quickly proved that he was a politician with an eye on political promotion as well as business. He had been at Charlie Haughey's side as one of his drivers during his years of political exile on the chicken and chips circuit around the country. Yet, when Lynch retired, Lawlor supported George Colley against Haughey!

Under Haughey, Lawlor came to public notoriety when he refused to resign as chairman of the Dáil committee which dealt with State sponsored bodies when it became known that he had been appointed by beef-baron Larry Goodman to the board of his Food Industries which wanted to buy the Irish Sugar Company. Lawlor was accused of a conflict of interest. But he refused to stand down from the Dáil committee until he was forced to do so by Haughey.

In his book, *Yes, Taoiseach*, Frank Dunlop tells how Lawlor pestered Albert Reynolds for a junior ministry in his government. There was no way Albert would consider this.

"An exocet without a delivery system" was what Haughey had called Lawlor. Albert agreed. So, too, did the Fianna Fáil faithful in Killarney. The general sentiment was nostalgic. His old pal Bertie summed up the overall verdict that Liam Lawlor was "an engaging, witty and larger than life character".

This, he undoubtedly was. But as the *Ireland on Sunday* editorial read: "Tragic – but let's not be hypocrites".

Bertie's Unholy War with 'Luscious' Liz

(November 15, 2005)

"**A** national identity is built not only by looking to the future but also by looking back", said former European Commission President and prospective Prime Minister of Italy, Romano Prodi, as quoted by the Rome correspondent of *The Times*, Richard Owen.

The connection to be made between what is happening in Italy and what can be detected as taking place in the flow of Irish politics is the recent announcement by Taoiseach Bertie Ahern of his revival of the Easter Parade by the Army in Dublin's O'Connell Street, which has been matched by Fine Gael leader Enda Kenny's support for the Michael Collins Society.

Faced with the challenge of Sinn Féin, with its brash form of republicanism, both Bertie and Enda are reaffirming their claims to the title of founding fathers of the Irish State. Veneration of Ireland's republican tradition is back in vogue.

The same rebirth, however, does not extend to Catholicism which became so identified with the independent Irish State, but which is now in crisis as a result of the public revulsion over clerical child sex abuse. If anything, in the wake of the Ferns Report and ahead of the Commission of Investigation into the archdiocese of Dublin, the Catholic Church is undergoing unprecedented scrutiny by politicians and the media for its past misdeeds from the era of clerical arrogance.

The Government Report by Mr Justice Frank Murphy into sexual abuse of children by 21 priests of the diocese of Ferns over a 40 year period from the 1960s to 2003 will lead to the urgent introduction in the Dáil of greater child protection legislation.

However, Liz O'Donnell's searing attack against the Church has caused a serious rift between the outspoken former Foreign Affairs junior minister and Catholic card-carrying Bertie. O'Donnell's demand for an end to "cosy phone calls from All Hallows to Government Buildings" has been taken by Bertie as a personal insult on account of his close association with the Vincentians, the missionary religious order situated in his Drumcondra home-base.

In an angry rebuttal of O'Donnell's other specific call for the State to "radically address" Catholic Church ownership of 3,000 primary schools, the Taoiseach stoutly defended the church's role in education and its positive place in civil society. For her part, O'Donnell has said that she did not know of Bertie's Vicentian connections!

The feisty Liz's call for a "no more Mr Nice Guy" approach by the State against an "untruthful" church also contradicts her PD colleague, Michael McDowell. The Justice Minister dismissed any suggestion that the Government was launching "a Grand Inquisition" against the Catholic Church when he announced the terms of the Government's investigation into the Dublin archdiocese.

While McDowell says "the process of inquiry must lead to some tangible outcome", the Government's backing-off from Ferns-style inquiries into the arch-diocese of Tuam and the diocese of Elphin is most disappointing in view of the unrecorded level of child abuse by clergy in the west of Ireland.

If the usually cavalier McDowell is wary of a Grand Inquisition, it is exactly a secular crusade against the power of the Catholic Church which O'Donnell is pleading for. Her call for an audit of church wealth strikes a chord in view of former Education Minister Michael Wood's abuse indemnity of religious orders that will cost the tax-payer €1bn.

O'Donnell's contribution came in the Dáil Ferns Report debate in which she argued that late disclosure by Bishop Eamonn Walsh of files on five alleged priest child-abusers showed "the instinct for self-preservation and denial" was still alive at the top of the church. Her speech will rank as one of the most outspoken critiques of the Catholic Church in society ever made by an Irish politician since the foundation of the State in 1922. It will be seen as the strongest case yet made for a complete separation of church and state.

There is widespread support for her point that "if the church leadership, the hierarchy were a cabinet, it would resign en masse or be thrown out of office". No bishop has been prosecuted for covering-up sexual rapes of children in their care by priests, many of whom escaped trial. There has been no provision for accountability in the regulation of the Catholic Church's internal affairs which are dictated by the Vatican and its code of canon (church) law.

Feminists will applaud O'Donnell's demand for an end to consultation of churchmen on such matters as IVF, abortion services, stem-cell research, the Government's support for family planning in the Third World, contraception, adoption, homosexuality and civil marriage. But the emotional nature of her outburst – and her lack of accuracy and precision in some of her claims – weaken her case. Bishops did not edit page by page the drafts of the 1937 Constitution, though Eamon de Valera consulted Cardinal Joseph MacCrory on the special position of the Catholic Church. He also sought the approval of the Vatican for his Constitution before it was put for approval to the Dáil and the people through a referendum.

It is true that from the 1920s even into the 1970s there was "unrelenting deference" by the politicians to the bishops. Fear of "a belt of the crozier" was inbuilt into the psychology of politicians. Catholics feared going to hell for all eternity if they questioned the authority of bishops and priests.

Fifty years ago, Government ministers ended letters to the Archbishop of Dublin, John Charles McQuaid, with the obsequious phrase: "I remain your obedient and loyal servant." But the special position of the Catholic Church was removed by referendum in 1972, and a 30 year battle from the mid-1970s to the mid-1990s saw the liberal agenda succeed on issues such as contraception, divorce and homosexuality against opposition from the bishops.

O'Donnell's speech signals the urgent need for public debate to clarify the altered relationship between church and state in an increasingly multi-faith and secular society. A national forum on the role of religion in society rather than Italianate pilgrimages is what "the path to power and the spirit" requires today of Irish political leaders.

Euro-Gospel According to McCreevy

(November 22, 2005)

Now that the fall-out in Church-State relations from the Ferns Report has settled down, the political landscape is in limbo awaiting Finance Minister Brian Cowen's second budget next month.

Apart from the gun photo gaffe of Defence Minister, Willie *the Kid* O'Dea, non-budget political debate has focused on whether Bertie Ahern will need Sinn Féin's support to achieve his aim of a third term as Taoiseach after the next general election.

While the future role of Sinn Féin is undoubtedly an important topic for discussion, the Bertie versus Enda Kenny and Pat Rabbitte battle will not be resolved until the election takes place. Only then will we see the composition of the next government. As we do not yet know the actual timing and circumstances of the election, speculation at the moment is basically shadow-boxing. Everything has still to be played for.

A crucial factor in determining the outcome will be the Progressive Democrats, who are showing signs of strain and fatigue in their eight-year partnership with Fianna Fáil and are giving signals of a readiness to join a Fine Gael-led administration after the election. Indeed, it is Tanaiste Mary Harney who has the power to bring forward the election from 2007 to 2006 if she decides to pull-out of the present coalition which is showing signs of tiredness and maladministration.

Ironically, in all this speculation, the most interesting and zany topic of conversation around Leinster House these days is the future of the man banished a year ago from Irish politics – EU Commissioner Charlie McCreevy.

When a reluctant McCreevy was packing his bags for Brussels, I suggested in this column he would not fit into the collegial mould required of a member of the Commission. He was not a team-player, a quality essential in a Commission which puts a premium on managerial mediocrity.

Maverick McCreevy's Roy Keane style of independence and outspokenness fits him no better in José Manuel Barroso's Commission than has finally proved to be Keane's case in Sir Alex Ferguson's Manchester United.

You will recall that Bertie Ahern, acclaimed throughout the capitals of Europe for his diplomatic triumph in fashioning the now aborted EU Constitution, had for the taking the prize of succeeding Italy's Romano Prodi as Commission President. Instead the All Hallows boy delivered the nomination to Barroso, Portugal's Prime Minister. Berie followed this up by dumping McCreevy whom he wanted to dislodge from the Finance ministry into the slot reserved for Ireland on the Commission.

When a dazed McCreevy landed the job of Internal Market and Services, one of the four 'big money' portfolios in the right of centre Barroso Commission, Bertie predicted that Charlie would make "a significant contribution to the creation of a level playing field throughout the expanded EU allowing businesses to trade freely".

A significant weakness, however, in McCreevy's Brussels power base is that Barroso's Commission cannot of itself deliver a more competitive Europe that the EU leaders agreed in 2001. This agreement, known as the Lisbon Agenda, aims to make Europe the most competitive zone in the world by 2010. Already well behind schedule, despite last year's efforts by the Irish Presidency to re-kick start it, this objective can only by achieved by the member state governments. The Commission can persuade, but it cannot deliver. And the reality is that there is not a consensus among the member states to achieve their stated communal goal.

McCreevy has confided to friends that while Barroso was brave to single out the Lisbon agenda as one of his main goals, the Commission does not have power to implement this huge administrative agenda that involves deregulating the lumbering social protection systems in countries such as France, Germany, Belgium and Luxembourg. Their vision of a labour market where it is cheaper for employers to hire and fire workers is opposed by the unions.

McCreevy described the rejection of the EU Constitution in the French and Dutch referendums as set-backs that showed the plain people of Europe would revolt if the European elite continued to ride rough-shod over their concerns about high-tech jobs for their children in their pursuit of outdated social protectionism. The gospel according to McCreevy is that if we do not have a vibrant European economy, there will not be enough jobs, nor a decent standard of living or social inclusion, to defend. In McCreevy-speak, Europe is not within an ass's roar of growing at a rate to deal with the problems of tomorrow.

McCreevy's handling of a contentious draft Services Directive brought him into confrontation with France's President, Jacques Chirac. His forthright style has raised the hackles of Berlin's man inside the Commission, Gunter Verhaegen, who is in charge of Enterprise and Industry.

McCreevy next picked a public row with the governor of the bank of Italy for trying to block a Dutch takeover of an Italian bank. So unpopular did Charlie become in Italy that he now requires body-guard protection on his visits to the land of Caruso.

Last week Charlie's opponent was Barroso himself who took the Irishman to task for voicing his opinion that the Commission wants to do away with Ireland's privileged corporation tax system.

It is not his thoughts on the EU's future but his characteristically folksy remarks on the social mores of the nation that continues to keep the Irish media spotlight on McCreevy. His diagnosis of the working man as being interested only in a few pints, going to a game of football and having a bit of sex enraged the elder ladies who listen to the Joe Duffy radio programme.

Outwardly, however, McCreevy appears to be as happy as a sand-boy in Brussels. He is showing no stress. As a non-drinker, he does not smooch too often on the Brussels social scene. He enjoys playing golf and poker with wealthy cronies belonging to the Irish *Wild Geese* living in Brussels. Like most previous Commissioners from Ireland, McCreevy returns to Ireland - to his Sallins chateau in Co Kildare - virtually every week.

The question, therefore, is: does McCreevy harbour plans to settle scores with his old boss Bertie for sending him to Brussels? While both men have played-down publicly any personal differences, there is ample evidence that their relationship has been fractured. When McCreevy gave a farewell bash, Bertie was not invited but Albert Reynolds was.

More significantly, while McCreevy regards Tony Blair and Gordon Brown as his principal allies in forging his free-market economic philosophy on the New Europe, in contrast, Bertie blames Blair for failure to agree on an EU budget, and is outraged by Blair's attack on the common agricultural policy. Trade Commissioner, Peter Mandelson, has acted as Blair's cheer-leader, but McCreevy has not supported Bertie.

The Commission's proposed reform of the sugar industry which is being opposed by Agriculture Minister, Mary Coughlan, and the farm lobby as decimating Ireland's home-based crop, has elicited no word of protest from McCreevy who apparently endorsed them in the Commission.

My hunch is that McCreevy is biding his time to run for the Dáil in the next election. His supporters allowed Independent Catherine Murphy to take his old seat in Kildare North. He nurses a grudge that the Fianna Fáil backbench revolt that blamed him for last year's electoral debacle tarnished his record as Ireland's most successful ever Finance Minister.

Bertie Muzzles 'Ivor the Terrible'

(December 6, 2005)

With the Exchequer awash with money, the FF-PD Government is looking anxiously to Finance Minister Brian Cowen in his second Budget on Wednesday to restore its sliding political fortunes and thus lay the grounds for fulfilling Taoiseach Bertie Ahern's prediction that the next general election will not take place until 2007.

However, two opinion polls published on Sunday suggest that the political tide is running strongly in favour of an alternative government led by Fine Gael's Enda Kenny and Labour's Pat Rabbitte, both Mayomen.

Of particular worry for the Government is the *Sunday Tribune* poll recording a slump in support for Fianna Fáil, in contrast to a 5pc rise for Fine Gael, along with signs of an improvement in Labour's support particularly in Dublin where it has now reached the stage where it is on an equal footing with Fianna Fáil – a statistic that will cause a lot of worry for the *Soldiers of Destiny* as they prepare for the Battle of the Capital.

At 5pc vote-share the Greens could help make up the numbers required for an FG-Labour led administration, with the prospect too of being joined by the PDs who stand at a lowly 3pc.

Although Sinn Féin has moved up a point to 9pc, it has not made the spectacular advance which its leadership expected from the recent IRA decommissioning of its arms, but its potential for further growth remains, particularly in an election campaign when it is on the ground canvassing hard.

Another feature of the poll is a 2pc decline in support for Independents, which must cause Mayo's Dr Jerry Cowley and Sligo-Leitrim's Marian Harkin to shudder for the safety of their Dáil bases. The floating vote that brought Cowley, Harkin and many other independents to the Dáil in 2002 may be about to drift in the opposite direction.

Enter, therefore, Brian Cowen, with his €2 bn plus give-away budget. His childcare programme over five years at a cost of some €600m may help to ease a major social problem facing young couples, but continued public vexation with transport congestion, mismanagement of public money in abortive computer systems, the rise in interest rates, the ongoing chaos in the health services and the refusal of 1 in 9 civil servants to relocate from Dublin under the McCreevy decentralisation programme, as well as the unease for social partnership from the Irish Ferries row, all add up to continued public discontent with the Government's handling of the economy. Everything has still to be played for, and I would not be as confident as Bertie that there will not be an election in 2006.

Yet, Fianna Fáil's best asset remains Bertie's popularity on 51pc, compared with Kenny on 44pc, Rabbitte on 46pc, and Trevor Sargent on 36pc. But Bertie needs the egregious Ivor Callely like a hole in the head. The junior Transport minister has made himself the weakest link in the Government with his promotion of person-alised bill boards at the taxpayers' expense and his loss of four members of his personal staff.

Ivor, a smart dresser with a fondness for double-breasted suits and flashy platform shoes, revealed his naked ambition, literally, of becoming either Taoiseach or President, to journalist Katie Hannon, when he spoke of how he glued himself to television political shows from the age of three-and-a-half.

Ivor also waxed eloquently to the bemused Hannon as to how his boy-prodigy status was spotted by a soothsayer who told his mother Mary of his high political destiny. He recalled, starry-eyed, the famous occasion when still a pre-school toddler, he was travelling with his mum into Dublin city centre. A fortune-teller pointed at him and made the awesome prediction: "that man there is going to be President of Ireland".

A regular attender at funerals of constituents, Callely is "undoubtedly one of the hardest working deputies," notes one Dáil watcher. "He probably thinks he works even harder than Bertie". Not particularly popular with his colleagues, Callely's drive for power has embroiled him in open competition with constituency poll-topper Seán Haughey. More recently, Ivor saw off a challenge from Councillor Deirdre Heaney, despite her reputedly having the tacit support of the Taoiseach.

This is not the first time that Ivor has found himself off-message with party mandarins in Fianna Fáil. He has become the supreme subject for ridicule from the Opposition.

Fine Gael's transport spokeswoman, Olivia Mitchell, has dubbed him *Ivan the Terrible*, while Labour Senator, Derek McDowell, has called him *Calamity* Callely.

No wonder, Bertie has undertaken to monitor's Ivor's performance. Bertie also needs to take a tighter hold over FF's propaganda department. The report in the *Sunday Independent* that Fianna Fáil hoped to topple Rabbitte from the Labour leadership by offering a government deal with his successor bore the hallmarks of spin-mischief against the growing credibility of an FG-Labour formation. It was also clearly designed to distract attention from talk of a FF-SF pact.

It was Bertie's brother, Noel Ahern, who best spotted the PR gaffe when he growled on RTE's *The Week in Politics* programme that: "I sometimes wonder whether these reports are thought up in a pub".

Bertie might need to muzzle the brother, as well as Ivor!

Ivor's Train Careers
Off Track

(December 12, 2005)

Ivor Callely's eventual stepping down as junior Transport minister will rank as one of the most undignified and ignominious resignations in the history of Irish politics.

The tortuous Scarlet Pimpernel manner of his departure – they sought him here and they sought him there for days – embarrassed Taoiseach Bertie Ahern and deflected from the impact of Brian Cowen's record social welfare Budget.

The maverick Callely's bizarre behaviour also gifted the Opposition leaders, Enda Kenny and Pat Rabbitte, with the occasion for the most rowdy scenes in the Dáil for years. At the height of the confusion, the Dublin North Central T.D. had the brass-neck to go on the *Today with Pat Kenny* radio programme where he stonewalled questions about his resignation, and spewed out a long rambling defence of his untenable position as a Minister of State.

Showing signs of a conspiracy complex, Ivor *the Engine* ranted on about how he has been a victim of a former decorator whom he claimed was now an official in the Department of Transport. He pleaded for an investigation into what he claimed was "a mischievous and sinister campaign" to remove from high office his heroic self, one of the country's most upright and hard-working ministers.

Almost in tears, he distinguished between his own professional determination to hold onto office as Ivor Callely, the public figure, and Ivor Callely, the family man, who could no longer allow his wife and children to suffer the clamour of innuendo and media intrusion.

Ivor, the doughty champion of justice for himself, spoke as if his cabinet superiors, his ministerial colleagues and fellow parliamentarians were all offering unstinted support for his staying on in Government. The reality was that he was totally isolated. His colleagues were already speculating on his successor. This was adieu to the 47 year old Dubliner's ambition of becoming a future Taoiseach or President – or both!

It was a pathetic performance by a politician in total denial about the grave nature in the public mind of his acceptance of a freebie from one of the country's leading builders. Even though the decoration of his Victorian red brick pile in leafy Clontarf on Dublin's northside happened in 1992, this favour had remained unknown to the Taoiseach who has vowed to root out such practices as contrary to Fianna Fáil's new code of ethics.

As Callely gobbled up self-serving time on the national air-waves, Finance Minister Brian Cowen, who was due to do the annual fielding of listeners' questions with Kenny, found himself for the second day running being upstaged by his junior colleague. Nor did the snivelling manner of Callely's departure endear him at all with his boss Bertie, whose authority as Taoiseach he had so publicly flouted over a 36 hour period of utter political pantomime. When at their heart-to-heart chat in St Luke's, Bertie gave Ivor a last chance to get his act together with his civil servants – and to curb his mania for personal publicity – *The Engine* gave no indication of the skeleton about to jump out of his Clontarf cupboard.

On Tuesday night Bertie heard of rumours that a further *Calamity* scandal was about to be revealed by RTE's Charlie Bird. His attempt to contact Callely was rebuffed. Likewise, on Wednesday morning ahead of Dáil Question Time, Callely's continued unavailability to the head of Government meant that an abject Bertie was easy meat for Kenny and Rabbitte. Bertie was forced to admit to the House that he could not contact his northside subordinate turned insubordinate north-sider. Even though Bertie managed to tell Callely how unimpressed he was with his antics at a meeting before Cowen stood up to deliver his Budget, Ivor begged to have time to talk to his family.

His delaying tactics meant that Bertie had to hold a meeting with Tanaiste Mary Harney at which they decided that Callely would have to be sacked at a special cabinet meeting if he did not do the honourable thing and fall on his sword. A solemn-faced Bertie made it clear that Ivor knew what he would do if he did not resign.

Yet, Callely continued to tell reporters that Bertie was not looking for his head. Bertie's belated announcement that the ongoing controversies made it impossible for Callely to continue his ministerial activities was met with ribald disdain by the Opposition. To the bitter end, Callely humiliated his Taoiseach and embarrassed the Government on arguably the most important Budget day since the foundation of the State.

Ivor believes he is a martyr. Most of his colleagues will find it hard to forgive him for his attempt to put his own career above the interests of party and nation. Worse was to follow with revelations that Callely refused to leave his ministerial office, and that he has not declared his full property holdings in the Dáil register of members' interests. He could face a Dáil inquiry. But the aggrieved Callely, with his mania for self-publicity, is unlikely to be reconciled to his new role as a mere passive backbencher. He will mount a fierce counter-campaign against attempts to portray his forced resignation as the proverbial 'storm in a tea-cup'.

The Callely Affair has posed unseasonal headaches for Bertie. Callely's defiance has made Bertie look accident-prone. Bertie now has a ministerial vacancy to fill in Dublin North Central. He appears to be waiting for a few weeks before doing so.

Three names are being touted in political circles - Callely's constituency colleague Seán Haughey, Pat Carey of Dublin North West, and Jim Glennon in Dublin North.

Bertie is grappling with the pro and cons of his selection. To upgrade Haughey will be interpreted as an indirect rehabilitation of his father, former Taoiseach Charlie Haughey. To pick Carey would mean two junior ministers in Dublin North West, where Bertie's brother Noel is already installed. To give the nod to Glennon, a first term Dáil member, would breach Bertie's guideline of giving priority to experience. If Bertie turns to Seán Ardagh in Dublin South Central, he will face criticism of abandoning the northside, where Sinn Féin is poised to make inroads.

Bertie's postponement of a decision will be seized upon by a resurgent Opposition which will label him as dithering. Callely has done Bertie no favours. His refusal to make a resignation statement in the Dáil has made him a target for renewed attack from the Opposition. Kenny and Rabbitte will shower abuse on Ivor to prolong Bertie's discomfort.

However, a bullish *Biffo* Cowen believes that his Budget is making the impact the FF-PD Government expected it to make. It has been described by Fr Seán Healy of CORI, the Justice Commission of the Conference of Religious, as most welcome in "taking significant steps to promote the development of Ireland as a society characterised by fairness and wellbeing".

Although Ivor *the Engine* finds his career path stuck in a cul-de-sac, his fiery style of populist politics gives him the capacity to effect the direction of events in the run up to the general election. He could quit Fianna Fáil knowing he has a sufficiently strong base in his constituency to be returned to the next Dáil as an Independent.

If he takes this option, Ivor has as a precedent the model of the late Neil Blaney, the legendary Doneglman. Ivor is no Blaney.

Stormontgate Baffles Bertie

(December 20, 2005)

In crime writer Ian Rankin's thriller, *Witch Hunt*, an investigator called Michael Barclay does not think of himself as a spy. If pressed about his job, he would nod to people that he was in 'Intelligence'. Barclay liked the word 'Intelligence'. For Barclay, the word 'Intelligence' meant knowing at least as much and preferably more than anyone else. He did not like the word 'spy'. "It belonged to the old days, the Cold War days and before," writes Rankin.

"Breaking and entering, sleeping with the enemy, microfilm and microphones in ties and tunnels under embassies," Barclay muses. "These days there was no black and white: everyone spied on everyone else."

No sooner had I read this passage on Friday evening than glum-faced Gerry Adams and equally glum-faced Martin McGuinness were side by side on RTE television with Sinn Féin's former senior administrator at Stormont Castle, Denis Donaldson, who was pole-facedly admitting to have been an MI5 spy for Britain for over two decades.

Donaldson's public confession could have come straight out of a Rankin fiction. "My name is Denis Donaldson," the small-bespectacled 55 year old with the look of a rabbit caught immobile in the glare of car beam lights.

"I worked as a Sinn Féin Assembly group administrator in Parliament Buildings at the time of the PSNI raid on the Sin Féin offices in October 2002 – the so called Stormontgate affair.

"I was a British agent at the time. I was recruited in the 1980s after compromising myself during a vulnerable time in my life. Since then I have worked with British intelligence" – note the Michael Barclay terminology! – "and the RUC/SPNI Special Branch. Over that period I was paid money".

Donaldson went on to claim that his last two contacts with Special Branch took place two days before his arrest in October 2002 and the previous evening when he was brought to a meeting. Then followed his spin on his 'intelligence' role. "I was not involved in any republican spy ring in Stormont. The so called Stormontgate affairs was a scam and a fiction. It never existed. It was created by Special Branch".

This was the carefully constructed cue for the Sinn Féin President to insist that the alleged republican spy ring at Stormont was "a carefully constructed lie created by British Special Branch". Nodding in agreement with Gerry, Martin added that the only spy ring which operated at Stormont was run by the British intelligence services.

Just as well for the sheepish Donaldson that the IRA has abandoned its war for peaceful democratic methods, I muttered to myself. Otherwise he would be found in a County Down ditch with a bullet in his head. Yet here was Gerry Adams describing a republican traitor as a mere victim of British securocrats!

Yet old film footage of a younger Donaldson with a Beatles-style hair-cut showed him to be a close mate of the hunger striker-turned-martyr, the late Bobby Sands. One speculation was that Donaldson turned tout to save a family member from serving time in prison on Her Majesty's pleasure.

"What the hell is going on?" I asked myself, as I tried to get back to the more credible world of Rankin's *Witch Hunt*. I couldn't get back into the book. It was tame compared with the real enigma coming out of Belfast. I was puzzled. Send for Sherlock Holmes.

No wonder, when the cameras switched to Brussels, where the Taoiseach was attending the EU Summit, I was relieved to hear that Bertie Ahern was expressing his bafflement with the "bizarre" *Stormontgate affair*. He had always been "totally sceptical" about the police circus that led to the downfall of David Trimble's power-sharing Executive.

"Remember what happened," Bertie, with his best Humphrey Bogart accent, reminded us. "That film piece that they still show of all of the storm troopers charging up the stairs with heavy armoury to collect a few files, and to arrest a few people, it never added up…. it created enormous grief for us, because the whole institutions were brought down."

"This was a huge case", drawled Bertie who does not seem to be familiar with Rankin's world of spooks and spivs. "It doesn't get bigger than bringing down democratically-elected institutions that people voted for. What this is about I just don't know".

But reading between Bertie's lines, I sensed that the Drumcondra boy had a good idea that both Sinn Féin and British intelligence had been up to no good. Perhaps Bertie does know who Mr Big is.

The plot thickened when the SDLP claimed that Donaldson was taking the rap to save Sinn Féin the embarrassment of having to reveal the identity of a bigger mole from within its ranks.

Adams, the SDLP also claimed, was singing the praises of Donaldson, an arch-British agent, instead of accepting that the buck stopped with him. "The only option now open is for Gerry Adams to resign".

As Sunday newspapers hinted that another Sinn Féin household name in the Republic had been in the pay of the Gardaí, a new twist to the story came when the Northern Ireland Secretary Peter Hain told ITV's Jonathan Dimbleby that he defended the police operation in October 2002 and stuck to the line that there had been a Sinn Féin spy ring in Stormont. Something like a thousand documents had gone missing and turned up in west Belfast. Oh for the simple days of Agatha Christie when Inspector Poirot could reveal all!

Paradoxically, we now have a situation where Ulster Unionists are clamouring for a public inquiry into what they believe has been a British cover-up, while Tanaiste Mary Harney does not think that it would be a good thing for the North to take the road of tribunals which have become part of the political landscape south of the Border.

In contrast, the Fine Gael Justice spokesman Jim O'Keeffe, is proposing the formation of an Oireachtas Security Committee which would have the powers to investigate such mysterious matters.

Although Bertie is convinced that Tony Blair knew nothing about how and why the case against Donaldson and two other Sinn Féin members was dropped last month without an official explanation as to why its hearing in court was deemed not to be in the public interest, the British Prime Minister is under increasing pressure to speak out on the issue.

Whatever further disclosures are about to come into the public domain, this whole murky episode represents a further set-back to the prospect of a restoration of the Executive some time in 2006. DUP leader Ian Paisley has yet another reason for not going into Government with Sinn Féin. Perhaps Adams is not so paranoid, after all, when he claims that a militarist-minded section within the police is out to wreck the Good Friday Agreement.

If only Peter Sellars were still alive, I am sure that Inspector Clouseau would get to the bottom of this latest saga in what has been called the North's dirty war.

Stormontgate smells. And the stink may get even worse in London and Dublin as well as Belfast and Derry.

Bertie's 'Showtime' Ace

(January, 10, 2006)

The New Year has opened with own goals from Enda Kenny and Pat Rabbitte that may dent their shine as leaders of a Government-in-waiting, though their indiscretions may not be as humiliating or costly as Roy Keane's Celtic debut defeat to Clyde in the Scottish Cup. Kenny drew criticism on himself on account of remarks which he made about how the Government's decentralisation policy is in shambles. He argued that this policy has been badly planned and threatens chaos in the civil service.

This analysis of the mess which its architect Charlie McCreevy left before his departure to the European Commission in Brussels was sound. The logic in the argument is for a Fine Gael Government to retain those elements of the plan which are working but to revise the arrangements in order to maintain those departments in Dublin whose work would be more effectively performed in the capital city.

However, Enda enraged commentators by his acceptance of decentralisation as a *fait accompli*, even though it is still vehemently opposed by most civil servants. In power, he would not reverse the scheme whose locations include Knock in County Mayo. "Knock will happen". said Enda. "There are quite a number of people from the west who want to go down to that region".

While this may be true, critics rounded on Enda for defending the type of parish pump politics which they claim was at the heart of the McCreevy project. While these critics have a point, I felt that the way the boot went into Kenny's Mayo groin was done with the same kind of glee that befell Roy Keane and Celtic manager Gordon Strachan after their crumbling to Clyde on Sunday.

More serious than Kenny's indiscretion is the way in which Pat Rabbitte has engineered a controversial shift to the Right in the Labour Party with his implied personal support for introducing a work permit system for immigrants including those from EU countries.

His call for a rethink of immigration policy, floated in an *Irish Times* interview with Stephen Collins, places strong emphasis on how an Irish Ferries-style out-sourcing of jobs could lead to displacement of Irish workers across a range of industries. In a candid interview the Labour Party leader referred to stories which he had heard about displacement already happening in meat factories, the hospitality industry and in the building sector.

Although Rabbitte qualified his concern for the maintenance of Irish jobs by using cautious language, his message sounded closer to an alarmist anti-immigrant nativist than to the traditionally-caring approach of a Left-wing leader to disadvantaged newcomers to Irish society. "The time may be coming," he suggested, "when we will have to sit down and examine whether we would have to look at whether a work permit regime ought to be implemented in terms of some of this non-national labour, even for countries in the European Union."

The uncharacteristic humming-and-hawing in Rabbitte's choice of words makes it difficult to interpret just exactly what he is saying. But his direction towards a more defensive rather than open position on immigration is not in any doubt. Indeed, there is a detectable, dramatic change of tone by Rabbitte from neighbourly international socialist to wary protector of jobs for home-based nationals.

But the Tallaght-based deputy's change of gear has been too subtle for an immediate reaction from his political opponents. Politicians are still on their extended holidays, with Taoiseach Bertie Ahern about to make a tour of India cast as a colonial grandee from the European Union in search of new markets for trade and investment.

Uppermost in Rabbitte's mind is his concern about the possible effect on existing national labour markets in the 25 EU member States of a services directive that is being proposed in Brussels by Commissioner McCreevy, Ireland's former pro-free market Minister for Finance. "If the EU services directive goes ahead you can establish a company in Poland or Latvia and come over here on contract and do an Irish Ferries," Rabbitte has warned. "You can get an agency to employ the workers here at domestic rates in Poland or Latvia. It is a big issue."

According to Rabbitte, unless basic standards for workers are established across the EU, Irish jobs will be threatened. This protectionist line of thinking has earned Rabbitte a 'belt of the crozier' for Euro-heresy from the Archbishop of Dublin, Diarmuid Martin, who has dismissed any talk in favour of a permit system when the Celtic Tiger economy needs workers and managed migration. "Borders should be open. It's what the entire EU exercise is about," the former Vatican diplomat thundered at a Festival of Peoples' Mass in Dublin's Pro-Cathedral.

Fianna Fáil politicians today must be taking a degree of pleasure from the spectacle of a self-righteous Labour leader being taken to task in public by Ireland's senior Catholic churchman.

But it should worry Fianna Fáil that Rabbitte is targeting their vote by signalling that Labour in Government would defend Irish jobs and not allow total, free access from Eastern European countries. Rabbitte would appear to be tapping into the wider social implications of the pre-Christmas mass demonstration of workers and trade unions against 'out-sourcing' of jobs by Irish Ferries. Many workers joined this protest because of fears that the Irish Ferries case represented the thin-end-of-the wedge for their own jobs in other sectors. The FF-PD Government's hesitancy caused further concern for the future of the national wage agreement. No doubt, some of the protesters are none too comradely towards immigrants.

Whatever his motive, Rabbitte has moved a long way from his days as a member of *the Stickies*, The Workers Party. His appeal to the Right and mainstream Centre is a calculated bid for voters who would not normally vote Labour. He has identified an issue that will figure prominently in partnership talks between the Government, management and unions.

To my surprise, Fianna Fáil was slow to react to Rabbitte's comments. It took several days before the Minister for Enterprise, Micheál Martin, called on the Labour leader to clarify whether his "mid-air" remarks amounted to his "playing the racist card." With some justification, Martin noted that Rabbitte would have been the first person out condemning a Fianna Fáil TD with huge indignation if he or she had made that kind of remark. Pointing out that the economy needs about 50,000 migrant workers a year over the next four or five years to sustain growth levels, Martin concluded that the buttons which Rabbitte was pressing have far more to do with an electoral, political agenda than a genuine medium-term economic strategy for Ireland.

The extent to which the political system is on election footing was evident in the excitement surrounding Sunday's Fianna Fáil selection convention for the new Longford-Westmeath constituency at which the leader of the Seanad and former Minister, Mary O'Rourke, paved the way for a Dáil come-back when she beat Councillor Kevin *Boxer* Moran for the nomination. A sign of the changing times, however, was the furore which accompanied the ebullient Mary's congratulations to her campaign workers for working "like blacks". Immigrants may not yet feature prominently on ballot papers but their presence will be felt at all layers of society.

Amid all these side-shows, Taoiseach Bertie Ahern walzed his way through the Christmas and New Year season in a series of interviews where he reminisced about his favourite music and sports. His first serious interview came on Sunday when he emphasised the importance of getting democracy working again in the North.

Democracy in the Republic is now geared to the general election. The one ace which Bertie has is its timing. He says next year.

Bertie Buries Hatchet
with C. J.

(January 17, 2006)

"Haughey and old pal Ahern bury the hatchet" was the eye-catching front-page headline in the *Sunday Independent* that revealed how Bertie has been paying regular private visits over the past four years to his mentor at Charlie's Abbeville home in Kinsealy.

According to Jody Corcoran, two such visits have taken place since September after Bertie's Dublin Central constituency organisation sent Charlie a set of gold cuff-links for his eightieth birthday. The second encounter reportedly lasted for two hours at Christmas time.

Officially, the two men had fallen out badly in 1997 when details of Haughey's financial affairs and life-style were coming into the public domain, prompting Ahern, newly installed as Taoiseach, to voice strong public criticism that his former political patron had acted contrary to Fianna Fáil's "benchmark of honour". Not surprisingly, the Lord of Kinsealy did not take kindly to this censure which was made by his protégé at the Fianna Fáil Árd Fheis. Even more to Charlie's loathing were Bertie's comments to journalists disparaging people with large houses and pleasure yachts.

However, before this rupture I had heard from political contacts in Leinster House that relations between Charlie and Bertie had become fragile since Bertie took over the leadership of Fianna Fáil in 1994 while the party was in Opposition. A source of friction was reputed to be Bertie's down-playing of his previous association with Charlie who had famously described the Drumcondra ward-boss as "the most skilful, most devious, most cunning".

News of the Kinsealy-Drumcondra reconciliation is reported to have been eased by the passage of time which has made Bertie regret the sharpness of his tone, and for Charlie to acknowledge Bertie's political necessity in distancing himself from his former Boss, not least on account of the damage being done to him following the revelation at the Dublin Castle Inquiry that he had signed cheques to Haughey that, in part, sustained his *Champagne Charlie* lifestyle.

No doubt, when the Dáil reconvenes later this month, Bertie will come under attack from the Opposition for being soft on Haughey's corruption, and will be accused of being a Haugheyite in sheep's clothing.

This rapprochement sets the scene for a State funeral when Haughey, now severely ailing from prostate cancer, dies. In the immediate short-term, their renewed friendship could signal the promotion of his son, Seán, to the junior ministry so reluctantly vacated last month by the disgraced Ivor Callely. If so, the Haughey name will be inscribed in a new generation of government leaders.

Bertie Booster

(January 31, 2006)

With no date for a general election announced – and with Taoiseach Bertie Ahern still adamant that it will not take place until late spring–early summer in 2007 – the bombardment of opinion polls about the state of the political parties is confusing.

It is confusing in that newspapers and pollsters are "tracking" trends in public thinking on different method-bases from each other, and at different times.

Already this year, we have had two weighty polls on the popularity stakes which, as we are constantly reminded by both pollsters and politicians, are nothing more than snap-shots of the public mood at the time they were taken.

Both the *Sunday Business Post/Red C* poll and the *Irish Times/TNSMRBI* poll show a recovery for the Fianna-Fáil PD Coalition largely as a result of the largesse doled out by Finance Minister Brian Cowen in the December budget. Consequently, this means a slippage in the popularity of the alternative government being offered by Fine Gael's Enda Kenny and Labour's Pat Rabbitte as prospective Taoiseach and Tanaiste respectively.

So far, so good. Maybe this general trend is all that you need to know – at least until voting time when in the ballot box you can make up your mind. If we dig a bit deeper, the strength of the parties gets a bit more complicated.

For instance, the *Irish Times* poll, published on Saturday January 21, found that "voters favour Coalition over FG-Labour option". It showed that 39pc would prefer FF-PDS to form the next Government, compared with 33pc supporting a Fine Gael-Labour-Greens coalition. A clear six point lead for the Bertie Ahern-Mary Harney leadership.

In interpreting this poll, the key factor to bear in mind is that the pollster was testing the public pulse on the basis of its comparison with its previous findings which were taken last September. On this time-scale, there was an eight pc swing towards the incumbent FF-PD Government, but only a three pc dip in the ratings for the FG-Labour-Greens. Twelve pc of those interviewed are still undecided as to how they will vote, and a sizable 16pc don't want a government led by either of the two main parties, Fianna Fáil or Fine Gael.

In the more recent poll published in the *Sunday Business Post* on January 29, it highlighted that "FF support grows at FG's expense". Yet, in broad terms, it put the FF-PD partnership on 40pc support, and the FG, Labour and Green alternative at 43pc. A three per cent lead for the Government contenders.

While we should bear in mind that polling companies issue a health warning that there can be a 3pc margin of error in their findings, The *Irish Times* poll signalled a third term for the FF-PD Coalition, but the *Sunday Business Post* declared that neither the current Government nor a Fine Gael-Labour alternative would be in a position to form an administration without additional support if a general election were held now.

If you read the fine print of the *Post* poll, you will find that it is tracking public attitudes since its last poll conducted in December. In those seven weeks, Fianna Fáil's popularity has risen by three points to 37pc, while Fine Gael has slipped back four points to 23pc, and Labour had not budged from its 13pc rating.

The general message in both polls is a boost for Bertie and a set-back for Enda and Pat. But politicians are not political scientists, so on radio on Sunday Pat Rabbitte's clever line was that if an election took place this week, Bertie and Mary would not be returned for a third term.

With the Dáil only back in session last Wednesday after the lengthy Christmas recess, the Labour leader argues that there is plenty of time for the Opposition to get the people to opt for a change of Government, as it is in the interests of democracy to have a change. This line of argument, of course, is cutting no ice with Bertie, fresh from his trip to India. Perhaps it was the good news from the opinion polls that inspired him last Friday evening to check-in to the K Club.

What disappointed Fianna Fáil backbenchers, especially the hopefuls, was the chilling-out Bertie's decision to hold-off for a few days in announcing his junior minister to replace Ivor Callely.

There were grumblings that it was typical of Bertie to keep the aspirants hanging on in suspense.

Big Ian Doesn't Fancy Mary Mac

(February 7, 2006)

As the negotiations for the restoration of a devolved administration began in Stormont on Monday, the prospects for success were minimal. The DUP leader, the Rev Ian Paisley, has again refused to be in the same room as Sinn Féin. He remains distrustful of Sinn Féin on the grounds that the IRA still exists and that republicans are involved in criminality.

According to *Big Ian*, the big issue is that the IRA must prove that it is finished for all time. He regards Gerry Adams and Martin McGuinness as bluffers. He says he will not be cracking. He wants a deal that will stick and which he can sell to the Unionist people. *Big Ian* prides himself on being the leader of the people who want to maintain the Union with Britain, and at his party's annual conference last weekend, he made it clear that he does not like "the President of the Irish Republic" Mary McAleese.

In Big Ian's dictionary President McAleese, a Northerner, hates Northern Ireland and distrusts the Police Service of Northern Ireland, charges which have been dismissed by Taoiseach Berie Ahern who claims she has done more than anyone to reach out to all communities in the North.

President McAleese, however, has been heavily criticised for a recent speech which she gave in Cork during which she praised the 1916 Rising as an inclusive event. It was a controversial speech.

'Chicken Bertie' and 'Bearded One'

(February 21, 2006)

T he political correspondents of the national newspapers in Leinster House were busily polishing their prepared profiles of Seán Haughey last Tuesday morning, while sub-editors in the newspapers' HQ's were honing their headlines for an emblazoned return of the Haughey name in an Irish Government.

Even at mid-day the Taoiseach's media handlers were still reassuring the Pol Corrs that Seán Haughey was getting the nod from Bertie to join the junior ministerial ranks in succession to the disgraced Ivor *the Engine* Callely.

But in the immortal words of Sligo poet William Butler Yeats "all changed, changed utterly" after Dáil deputies shuffled expectantly that afternoon into the chamber. Suddenly, Bertie was no longer *the Almighty Ahern*.

In a terse statement, *Bungling Bertie* announced that Deputy Mary Wallace of the East Meath constituency had been appointed by the FF-PD Coalition to serve as Minister of State in the Department of Agriculture. Pat *the Cope* Gallagher moved from Fisheries into Transport, a hot seat in view of the latest deaths of Latvians on the Donegal roads. It has not gone unnoticed that Bertie had still nothing for Mayo's John Carty, his only party standard bearer in a constituency that once held three of the five seats!

Anger and frustration at Bertie's style of leadership erupted among FF back-benchers. In general, resentment was directed at his cat-and-mouse game of keeping everyone waiting for nine weeks in replacing Callely. In particular, it was fuelled by the Grand Old Duke of York manner in which Bertie had led Seán Haughey up the hill to Government office only to march him back down to the backbench seat which he has occupied for twenty years.

The Dublin North Central deputy was so humiliated that he took this passing-over as a snub to the Haughey family name and political dynasty. In venting his disappointment on national radio, the normally mild-mannered Seán showed he had inherited the steel of his grandfather, Seán Lemass, as well as that of his father, Charles J.

Seán's announcement that he would be considering his future in politics over the Easter period escalated the story, and knocked the smug smile off Bertie's face.

But in another move which was seen as a sign of his having lost his political touch, Bertie compounded his own discomfort when he went on *Clare FM* radio to destabilise Síle de Valera's position in the junior ranks, a move that the granddaughter of Eamon de Valera reacted to with stubborn contempt. This left Bertie grovelling to her at the Ógra Fianna Fáil assembly in Ennis, where he told her to get on with the job.

All of this political pantomime gave commentators a field day as they attempted to dissect Bertie's mind. *Chicken Bertie* was the unflattering description coined by former FF adviser Noel Whelan in his column in *The Examiner*.

The return of Mary Wallace, who had been in the huff since being dropped in 2004 was also a source of annoyance to backbenchers who felt that her Dáil absences and poor voting record were being appeased by a weak Taoiseach. She is known as *Wednesday Wallace* for missing other Dáil days, having turned up for 51 out of 233 votes.

Fianna Fáil's disarray was Sinn Féin's opportunity at its annual Árd Fheis over the week-end in Dublin's RDS. As a piece of rhetorical oratory, Gerry Adams' presidential speech was top of the range. Gerry had some good party one-liners: "Sinn Féin did not hijack 1916". "Sinn Féin is not for going away". "Ian is your war over?". "Any move to sideline (the) Irish (language) should be opposed". "Sinn Féin would effectively tax the fat cats".

With lobbyist Frank Dunlop and Labour Leader Pat Rabbitte locked in dispute at the Mahon Tribunal, this gave *the Bearded One* an opening to poke fun at the brown envelope culture endemic in the political system, a line which appeals to working class voters and city dwellers, on whose votes Sinn Féin hopes to win 10 to 15 seats at the next general election.

It was with some relief – a considerable degree of arm-twisting – that the leadership secured the adoption of a resolution giving discretion to go into power in the event of holding the balance of power after the general election. Power is the name of the game for the Árd Fheis at its first meeting since the decommissioning of IRA arms last year. But Sinn Féin's relationship with policing in the North still remains an unresolved issue. Tony Blair's Government appears to be offering concessions to Ian Paisley's DUP in regard to its two phased fall-back plan of reconvening the Stormont Assembly ahead of a restoration of an Executive.

With the twenty-fifth anniversary due soon of the H-Block hunger strike, Gerry wrapped himself in the fame of the Bobbie Sands and the late rebel balladeer, Luke Kelly, and he paid tribute to the Shell to Sea campaigners. He also pledged to continue to support the McCartney family in their campaign for justice for their murdered brother Robert. All this is good catch-all politics.

Adams even adopted a carrot and big stick approach to the Real IRA when he offered to open talks with "dissidents", while warning them that "no one should harbour the notion that the republican struggle can be advanced any further by an armed campaign".

On the lighter side, the best line of all, however, came from the country's best sketch writer, Miriam Lord. Referring to the recent leg – and thigh – baring performance on the *Late Late Show* of the dashing Toireasa Ferris, the Mayor of Kerry and blond bombshell daughter of Martin, Miriam quipped that Sinn Féin is now known as *Skin Féin*.

It was the Shinners' moment of carnival!

Bertie's Hot-line to God

(March 7, 2006)

The veteran chat show interviewer Michael Parkinson produced a moment of viewer incredulity on ITV television when he interviewed the increasingly pathetic Tony Blair. After a bit of banal banter characteristic of dummed-down television, Parkinson probed the British Prime Minister about his decision to send troops to Iraq during the 2003 invasion.

Blair waffled about his struggle with his conscience to do the right thing because people's lives were at stake. Invoking his faith, the prematurely ageing Blair hinted that he was only co-responsible for his decision. There was another force at work, he seemed vaguely to hint.

This was the opening for Parkinson to elicit from Blair the astounding admission that his decision-making partner was God. "If you believe in God, (the judgement) is made by God", Blair said. "The only thing you can take a decision like that is to try to do the right thing according to your conscience".

It was thunderbolt television. Like the President of the United States, the Prime Minister of Britain had gone to war on the instructions of God. Like George W. Bush, Blair believes he was guided by the deity in conducting one of the most misguided wars in human history. Yet, as blithely as Bush, Blair could shrug this off with further spiritual blather that God and history would eventually judge the decision. His one concession to common sense was that history's verdict will depend on how things turn-out. Actually, the war is not going too well for Tony's God! Has George not told him so?

As a result, too, of the publication of the now infamous Mohammad cartoons by newspapers in Denmark and elsewhere including *The Irish Star*, the Arab world is no longer a safe place for any Westerner to travel around. The world is infinitely more unsafe today. God's work, no doubt!

So far I have not heard one reputable theologian attack Blair's theological nonsense. Where in theology does it say that if a religious believer reaches a decision on a complex issue such as going to war that God has made that decision for him? Where in theology does it say that an unelected God makes decisions for democratically-elected political leaders relating to realpolitik? Politicians like Blair and Bush should stop passing the buck to God.

Yet, God-talk is cool. Last week at a major conference in Croke Park on the Catholic Church's social teaching I listened to Taoiseach Bertie Ahern, ICTU general secretary David Begg and Northern Ireland Ombudsman Nuala O'Loan, all waxing eloquently about bringing the God factor into their public lives. It would seem that these leaders now parade themselves as "celebrity Catholics".

The biggest conference on social issues ever organised by the Irish Catholic bishops was attended by only two politicians – Bertie and Green party deputy, Eamon Ryan. Representatives of all the political parties in the Dáil had been invited to attend the prestigious one day conference under the auspices of the Irish Commission on Justice and Social Affairs. Martin Long, the press secretary for the bishops, told me that invitations went to the spokespersons on social affairs and the environment of all the main parties in the Dáil.

With Croke Park in his constituency, Bertie arrived early and delivered a broad-ranging speech in which he spoke of his commitment to the dignity of the individual, social commitment and the rights of the trade union movement. The dignity of the human person has been at the heart of his political vision, Bertie revealed. "The emphasis in Catholic social teaching on the rights of labour is to me one of its most attractive features", he said modestly, adding that he subscribed "totally to the importance of the concept of the common good as the sum total of social conditions which allow people either as groups or individuals to reach their fulfilment more fully or more easily".

Lay preacher Bertie has come close to giving Ireland's social partnership negotiations between the Government, trade unions and management the imprimatur of the Catholic Church's *Compendium of Social Doctrine*.

The common good, he explained, has been at the heart of the partnership model of economic planning that has been employed successfully in recent decades. With reports this week-end of the current partnership talks close to breakdown, I hope Bertie still has his hot-line to God to do a quick fix.

'Mad Mullah' Excites Bertie

(March 28 2006)

Judging by how Michael McDowell dominates news bulletins, my hunch is that either he is going bonkers or he is on course to break-up the Fianna Fáil-Progressive Democrats Coalition. On balance, it is more likely that the man known as *The Mad Mullah* will bring the eight years-and nine months FF-PD partnership to a premature divorce rather than his self-imploding emotionally. The Minister for Justice thrives on public controversy. He is one of the best debaters in the Dáil and in the media. Not since Garrett FitzGerald has a senior Irish politician produced so many blueprints for the reform of society.

At the same time, McDowell's sharp tongue has given him the aura of a macho man who loves nothing better than a street corner brawl. If only the late Dermot Morgan were still around, McDowell would fill endless *Scrap Saturday* radio programmes.

However, there can be little doubt at all that McDowell's outburst against Fine Gael's Richard Bruton over Garda manning levels went too far and has damaged his professional reputation as a politician of stature. His crude invective against the politely-spoken, inoffensive and mannerly Bruton whom he likened to Joseph Goebbles, Hitler's propaganda minister, marked a low point in the increasing tendency of politicians to substitute proper adversarial debate on policy issues with grubby name-calling.

Yet, it must be admitted that his apoplectic performance on live radio bulletins was a most entertaining piece of slapstick politics unmatched since comedian John Cleese of *Fawlty Towers'* fame did his anti-Nazi goose-stepping.

With McDowell lashing into anyone in sight, not least his Dublin South East rival. John Gormley of the Green Party, I could hear in my ears Gerry Rafferty's song, *Already Gone* as the swan-song of a Coalition that is increasingly floundering, not least on the crime front with the M50 gang shoot-out being compared to Wild West L.A.

You will recall that only a few weeks ago McDowell suggested that it was of little consequence if Bertie Ahern or Enda Kenny led the Government. This was a sure sign that McDowell is thinking in terms of election strategy rather than completing his legislative agenda through this Dáil. Bertie and FF are showing signs of tolerance fatigue with McDowell's bravado solo-runs and reaching the stage of 'enough is enough' of his megalomaniac style of self-promotion.

It must also be occurring to Bertie that the sooner he cuts the umbilical chord with the PDs and goes to the country, the better his chance of securing a third term as Taoiseach will be. For the third time in succession FF's vote has slipped in the *Sunday Business Post* poll. The longer he delays, the more likely it becomes that he will dependent on power in the next Dáil on Sinn Féin.

The two per cent rise in support nationally for the Greens – and a 12pc growth since the last election in the transport-strangulated Dublin belt - makes them a factor in the balance of power – and they are playing hard to get with their no pacts policy in regard to a pre-election alliance with the alternative FG-Labour formation. The Greens' week-end party conference in Kilkenny saw a new spring in their sandals, and a fine-tuning of their policies to secure greater electoral appeal. The Greens could make a breakthrough

Sinn Féin may be static on paper polls but its organisation has been boosted with the decision of the Basque terrorist group ETA to take the ceasefire route with the assistance of Fr Alec Reid, Gerry Adams' confessor and mentor.

So, a real downside consequence of Michael McDowell's hari-kari politics is that the Minister for Justice has made himself an easy target for the Shinners to dismiss as further gobbledy-gook his attacks on them as Nazis and unreconstructed democrats.

Not only could McDowell precipitate the break-up of the Bertie Ahern-Mary Harney partnership this year, he could be helping Gerry and the boys into power by the backdoor with Fianna Fáil, a party which is increasingly looking vulnerable to a Sinn Féin ascendancy as happened to the SDLP in the North.

McDowell needs to stop his dangerous sleep-walking histrionics.

Bertie's Easter Rising

(April 18, 2006)

The Easter Sunday Parade in commemoration of the ninetieth anniversary of the 1916 Rising fulfilled Taoiseach Bertie Ahern's declared aim that it was about "discharging one generation's debt of honour to another".

Watched by over 100,000 spectators on a mild spring day, the march in Dublin by some 2,500 members of the Defence Forces was the centre-piece of the occasion. This was in line with the Taoiseach's stress that the event would be focused on Óglaigh na hÉireann as the successors of the 1916 men. It was symptomatic of the collective desire for a peaceful Ireland that Sinn Féin representatives were in the attendance alongside Her Britannic Majesty's Ambassador.

If, as the Taoiseach maintained, the GPO Rising unleashed an "unstoppable process that led to this country's political independence", it was obvious in Bertie's demeanour that he was unstoppable in his determination to commemorate the event in style. Because of Bertie's announcement of his commemoration plans at last October's Fianna Fáil Árd Fheis, the parade's preparations had been mired in the inevitable political squabbling engendered by inter-party rivalry. This suspicion was compounded by comments of historians that the political context to the 2006 commemoration was clearly related to the Taoiseach's perceived threat from Sinn Féin to his party's republican credentials.

In the run-up to the Parade, there was some political gamesmanship. Bertie identified 1916 with three subsequent Fianna Fáil-inspired landmarks in modern history: Eamon de Valera's Constitution in 1937; Ireland's entry in 1973 into the European Economic Community under Jack Lynch and his own signing of the Good Friday Agreement in 1997.

In turn, we had Fine Gael leader Enda Kenny protesting that the Taoiseach had ignored the contributions of his predecessors: W.T. Cosgrave's establishment of a stable democratic system in the first decade after the Civil War, John A. Costello's proclamation of the Republic in 1948/9, and Garret FitzGerald's negotiation of the Anglo-Irish Agreement in 1985. With Gerry Adams highlighting the need to implement the First Dáil's radical social programme, Labour's Pat Rabbitte hastened to don James Connolly's socialist dungarees.

On the big day, however, the Parade was carried off with decorum. President Mary McAleese and the leaders of the main political parties all dutifully performed their constitutional roles, while the music stirred genuine sentiments of national pride and a shared identity. As has been the case when hosting the European Union Presidency summits and European song contests, the Parade was organised by our civil servants and event managers with finesse and class.

It was not a day for political mischief. I could agree heartily with the Minister for Justice, Michael McDowell's verdict that the "open, inclusive" debate preceding the parade had brought a new generation of young people into contact with 1916.

Its resounding success amounted to a vindication of the Taoiseach's decision to hold the biggest commemoration ever on its ninetieth anniversary. The massive publicity surrounding the event, and its live coverage on RTE television, ensured its success, even though the absence of Ulster Unionists offered the spectacle of a Celtic Hamlet without the Orange Prince.

While I was numbered among those with reservations about a military parade, I was impressed by the emphasis on the Army's involvement in UN peace-keeping. Like many others, I was surprised at the modernity of the Army's weaponry and equipment, a comforting thought in our age of international terrorism.

As to where we go from here, Enda Kenny reckoned that Sunday's parade could be considered a long dress rehearsal for the centenary commemorations in 2016, while Bertie said that he had no difficulty with how the event should evolve, and he also indicated that the aim for the future decade should be to commemorate in 2016 what would be by then 100 years since the foundation of the State.

This is a great suggestion, one which I hope will inspire historians to get down to the hard work of chronicling and assessing in greater detail than has been done till now the full story of the development of Ireland as an independent State. There is much work to be done. Where are the biographers of W.T. Cosgrave and John A. Costello? When will we have well-researched accounts of Ireland, as it really was, in the lost decades of the 1920s, 1930s, 1940s and the 1950s?

As well as careful study of the decision-making processes of our political leaders and civil servants – now largely available to scholars in the national archive – we need to examine more closely the lives of ordinary Irish people in the times when religion and social hardship were the order of the day.

Now that Ireland has been a member of the European Union for over thirty years, scholars need to explore in more detail how the European experience transformed Ireland from an insular and poverty-stricken land, bolstered by ill-conceived protectionist policies, into today's modern and multi-cultural State at the heart of an enlarged Europe. Much good working has already been done. For instance, Tom Garvin's pioneering study of *Why was Ireland so poor for so long?*, and the recently published work by Brian Girvin on *The Emergency – Neutral Ireland, 1939-45* that argues that Eamon de Valera's pursuit of neutrality during World War II cost him his ultimate prize – a united Ireland.

Central to this future research programme will be a thorough examination of the rise and decline of the Catholic Church in twentieth century Ireland, detailing how the Church exercised power through its control of schooling, the hospitals and institutions such as reformatories and the Magdalene laundries. Side-by side with this focus on how the institutional church became corrupt in the run-up to its internal explosion with the child clerical abuse scandals will be an examination of how the Irish moved from unquestioning religious piety to one of growing secularisation.

The curmudgeonly side-line barbs of holding the Easter parade on the morning of Christianity's most important day by the two Archbishops of Dublin, Diarmuid Martin and John Neill, served also to reinforce their strictures about ambiguities in our more secularised culture.

Sunday was the day of commemorating two Easter Risings in which the Church militant sought to transcend the State's military celebration of national independence with the salvation message for humankind of Jesus Christ. On the day, Pearse won.

An abiding impression for me was of how most of the 1916 rebels died for God and the honour of Ireland, in contrast to the marginal role last week-end of churchmen. The ninetieth commemoration of 1916 may come to be seen as an official severing of the bond of faith and fatherland. It remains to be seen, too, how the political establishment and our more diverse society will define our identity in 2016.

Bertie, Go-between
DUP and SF

(April 25, 2006)

This week's decision of Ian Paisley's Democratic Unionist Party to address the British-Irish Inter Parliamentary Body in Killarney marks a highpoint in that body which was born as the ugly duckling of the 1985 Hillsborough Agreement.

To mix the image, more precisely it was the brain-child to a large extent of then Taoiseach Garret FitzGerald who signed that landmark accord with British Prime Minister Maggie Thatcher on November 15.

For some time the Ulster Unionists led by the dour James Molyneaux and the DUPs' roaring *Big Ian* mounted a massive agitation against Thatcher's sell-out to the Republic. Indeed, Garret's plans for the inter-parliamentary assembly looked like a dead duck!

However, the fledgling assembly was given what seemed artificial life – minus the Ulster Unionists, the DUP and Sinn Féin – and some years later when Charlie Haughey had come to power – I recall attending my first session of the body which was then co-chaired by Peter Temple Morris and Dermot Ahern, a rising backbencher and now Minister for Foreign Affairs. Peter and Dermot formed a thrilling partnership. They took their roles seriously, were full of ideas for the body's expansion and they networked well with the members. In short, they bonded. As did the MPs and TDs.

An inspired move was the appointment of Mike Burns, RTE's former London editor, as its PR officer. This most sociable of men secured a budget to invite journalists from both sides of the Irish Sea to the twice annual proceedings, a spring venue in Ireland, and Britain in autumn. A permanent fixture of these events – indeed, its life and soul – was – and still is – Aidan Hennigan, the Ballina-born doyen of the Irish press corps in London.

Admittedly, in those early days it was hard to produce stories, but bit by bit the stories got better. So too did the debates among the politicians. The news value of the meetings became assured by the attendance for key-note addresses of Irish Ministers for Foreign Affairs and Northern Ireland Secretaries of State, among them the late and unforgettable Mo Mowlam, as well as the easy-going Labour *Celtic Mafia* of John Reid and Paul Murphy.

The debates also carried a wealth of experience in the contributions of former Northern Secretaries such as the late Mervyn Rees, and Peter Brooke. Austin Currie's eloquent interventions were always a guarantee of a headline as well as engendering awe in his Coalisland oratory among his audience. Mayo's Tom Moffatt and Michael Ring added to the cultural mix.

Our meetings in London were an opportunity gleefully seized by Mike Burns to set up meetings for the Irish press corps at Downing Street with John Major. This access to the British Prime Minister was also granted by Tony Blair. However, the spin-obsessed Blair was less comfortable with answering our questions in the Cabinet Room than the more open Major. We only met Blair once in his Downing Street den, in 1998. He and his press secretary Alasdair Campbell dropped the annual encounter with us.

The social side of the British-Irish meetings were probably as important, if not more so, than the public speeches, reports and statements. Over long lunches, dinners in country houses and drink-talk into the wee' early hours of the morning, friendships grew among the politicians, the civil servants and the journalists. Particularly entertaining, as well as informative and insightful, were breakfast or dinner table conversations which I had with Peter Brooke, especially when he recalled how Gay Byrne encouraged him to sing *Clementine* on the *Late Late Show*, and Mervyn Rees, as he defended his record under Harold Wilson over the collapse of the power-sharing Executive in the North in 1974.

Although *Big Ian* is not in Kerry this week, and his colleagues led by Peter Robinson, are attending as special guest speakers, Paul Murphy is correct in predicting that sooner rather than later the DUP will sign up for membership of this unique talking-shop, as did the Ulster Unionists and Sinn Féin in the intervening years of the peace process. The Killarney encounter will bring Sinn Féin members and the DUP leaders into direct round-table talk.

If the give-and-take spirit of the British-Irish Parliamentary Body marks these exchanges, they will be less acrimonious than the continued barrage from Michael McDowell at last week-end's conference of the Progressive Democrats. True to form the Justice Minister warned that Sinn Féin could hold the balance of power after the next general election with up to 16 or so seats. His belief is that this is not inevitable, but that the electorate needs to waken up to the reality that the general election could endow the Shinners with the power to decide which Dáil alliance led by either Bertie Ahern or Enda Kenny takes power.

A two horse race, but people should waken up to the reality that after the votes are counted the Shinners could hold the power to decide which Dáil alliance led by either Bertie or Enda assumes conditional cabinet power.

One way or the other, McDowell's record in Justice and Mary Harney's *Angolan* battles in Health will stand centre stage in the election campaign even if the PD era of promised tax cuts is not yet ended.

Bertie Stands Out, Eames Stands Down

(May 16, 2006)

I t has been a good week for Bertie Ahern with high profile newspaper and television interviews with Sam Smyth and on the *Tubridy Tonight* show, as well as the gala celebrations of the eightieth anniversary of the founding of Fianna Fáil. You would be forgiven for thinking that Bertie has begun his election campaign for a third consecutive terms as Taoiseach – and you would be right, with May 11, 2007 now being signalled as voting day.

In the course of his interviews, Bertie again proved himself to have the common touch and a capacity to poke fun at his more extravagant moments on the world stage. The former anorak man was most entertaining in his account of how he made his most colourful fashion gaffe at the G8 summit in Georgia during the Irish Presidency of the EU two years ago. This was his wearing *the banana split*, or sour cream yellow jacket and trousers, which brought him international ridicule. He stuck out like a sore thumb walking for a relaxed photo-call on Sea Island along with the more casually dressed George W. Bush and other world leaders.

There was hilarious laughter from the studio audience when the master of the photo-call opportunity recalled: "I was there with Putin, Chirac and Bush, so I had no chance (to be noticed!). I had to stand out some way. Now everybody remembers the jacket and no one remembers the meeting". This self-mocking admission provided a revealing insight of the psychology of how politicians are obsessed with appearing prominently in news pictures. This is a central part of projecting their images, often at the expense of substance.

But in his interview *blitzkrieg* Bertie expedited some serious political business. He admitted that the FF-PD Government had been too ambitious in effecting its decentralisation of the civil service, and has put it up to the alternative Fine Gael-Labour alliance to spell out just what part of the decentralisation plan they would implement, modify or drop.

This is good political ball-hopping on Bertie's part that will force Enda Kenny and Pat Rabbitte to be more precise on an issue which along with crime, immigration and the health services will figure prominently in the election campaign. After all, Enda will not want to see Knock lose out in the original plan championed by Eamonn Ó Cuív.

Bertie was politically acute in his radio interview on Sunday when he dealt with the prospects of restoring the Northern Ireland Executive by its mid-November deadline. Speaking the day before the gathering of the Northern Irish political parties in the Stormont Assembly, he disclosed that he would prefer to resolve the issues in six days rather than six months. Insisting that it was time to stop running around the mulberry bush, Bertie showed his exasperation when he said that if the Northern politicians could not do a deal in six months, they would be unlikely to do so this side of 20 years. Tellingly, he added that this was also Tony Blair's belief.

It is also the belief of Robin Eames, the Church of Ireland Primate who has announced that he is retiring after twenty years as Archbishop of Armagh during which he played a pivotal role in both The Troubles and the Peace Process. Only minutes after announcing his shock resignation to the General Synod, the Archbishop urged the leaders of Ulster Unionism and republicanism to do a deal before it was too late. He, too, said that if the DUP and Sinn Féin do not reach an accommodation, the opportunity would not return for some time. Like the Taoiseach during his address at the Fianna Fáil eightieth anniversary Lord Eames appealed to Sinn Féin to make an act of faith towards accepting policing and the other necessary measures needed for peace for all the community.

In his parting peace message Eames said he was convinced that Sinn Féin's signing up for thr Northern Ireland Policing Board would help reduce lingering Unionist Suspicions of PIRA's armed struggle. While further doubts could be raised, both sides needed to trust each other, and "draw a line in the sand".

Looking back on his twenty years as Archbishop of Armagh, he acknowledged that the Orange Order riots in Drumcree against the local Catholic population had been the most difficult ordeal for him. But more optimistically, he had seen a declining tension in Drumcree, though it was "something which remains finally to be resolved", and he detected a new determination to get parading right.

Responding emotionally to the sectarian murder by a Loyalist gang in Ballymena of the 15 year old Catholic boy, Michael McIveen, Dr Eames warned: "More innocent lives will be lost if we do not get a hold of ourselves".

This brutal murder has highlighted the absolute need for politicians, civic leaders and churchmen to deal, at long last, with the sectarian cancer which is at the heart of the conflict in the North. Archbishop Eames has been an outspoken campaigner against sectarianism and he disowned his former connections with the Masonic Order. His 1992 book, *Breaking the Chains* enhanced his international reputation as a rare liberal voice from the North advocating moderation in a deeply sectarian society.

The Archbishop's latest project, *The Hard Gospel* initiative aims to remove sectarian features in the Church of Ireland's parliamentary and governing structure, as well as in society. This initiative is taking root at the grass-roots level and could produce good results.

However, I detected a fudge when the Synod went on to allow membership of the Masonic Lodge to be a matter for individuals even though it recognised that aspects of its rituals fall short of the full Christian message.

The end of the Eames era was a moment of nostalgia for both of us, as I was the only journalist present at his valedictory press conference who was around when he was first consecrated as a Bishop in 1975. We found ourselves talking about the same subject now, as then, - the importance of tackling sectarianism in the North. He paid tribute to Albert Reynolds as a Taoiseach whom he could trust. He also admired Bertie Ahern's tenacity.

Tenacity, indeed, is what Bertie needs to show in the difficult months ahead.

C. J. Haughey:
'I'll Expect You at 11'

(June 20, 2006)

S ix years ago an official in Fianna Fáil suggested to me over lunch that I
should approach Charles J. Haughey formally with a view to seeking his
approval to write his biography.

His main arguments were that it was known that Haughey was favourably
disposed to me; that I had reported politics and Europe while CJ was at the height
of his power, observing him close-up at key moments in Ireland, the North,
European capitals and Washington; that I had been close to the late John Healy
from whom I had absorbed the spirit of Charlie's earlier career; that I was
familiar with the Lemass era on which I had scripted a television documentary for
RTE, and that I had worked with Ray MacSharry when he was a Commissioner in
Brussels and knew all the main political players in all the parties.

It was also known within political circles that a few years previously I had been
involved with Tim Ryan and P.J. Mara in reading – and advising – on the draft
text of Tim's biography, *Mara*. The Fianna Fáil strategist also argued that as a
history graduate and the author of a major biography of Archbishop John Charles
McQuaid that was published at the end of 1999 I had acquired the academic
expertise required in undertaking such a huge project.

Such a project, I pointed out, would require - in addition to pouring over the
vast acres of Dáil reports, newspaper reports, radio and television interviews -
access to Haughey's private papers as well as his cooperation in doing lengthy
taped interviews. The FF man said he was sure that CJ would be positive to an
official approach from me on this basis. I said I would give his proposal careful
consideration. When I thought about it, I became hesitant about moving on the
proposal.

Two factors struck me as major obstacles in writing Haughey's biography. The
first was that the revelations at the Tribunals of Inquiry about CJ's wealth meant
that his financial affairs had become a source of public scrutiny. It was obvious
that some journalists covering the Tribunals would be writing books on this murky
side of Haughey's life and these would become important books in their own right.

This turned out to be the case with the publication of Sam Smyth's book, *Thanks a Million Big Fella* (about the "unholy trinity" of Charles Haughey, Ben Dunne and Michael Lowry), and Colm Keena's more exhaustive and more scathing book, *Haughey's Mi££ions – Charlie's Money Trail.*

With Haughey embroiled in the Moriarty proceedings and in negotiations with the Revenue Commissioners, I calculated that it would be a very testy task to elicit from the former Taoiseach his real thoughts about his messy and patently corrupt financial affairs.

The second reservation in my mind was how to handle his long affair with the journalist Terry Keane. It was an open secret that Charlie and Terry had conducted their affair for decades, though at that time no Irish journalist had publicised the affair. The closest to publication came from Terry herself in her *Sunday Independent* Keane Edge column, but that was craftily coded. Not to deal with the Haughey-Keane affair would have meant that the biography would be dishonest in not providing readers with the details of a relationship that dominated so much of Haughey's private life.

On the other hand, it was equally obvious that any biographer raising this affair with CJ would be unceremoniously thrown out the front-door of his Abbeville mansion in Kinsealy. It was to be a few years later that Terry published her kiss and tell story about Sweetie to *The Sunday Times.* In doing so, Keano broke the wall of silence and a shamed CJ broke off their affair.

However, a third factor also preoccupied me. I learned from various Haughey insiders that either Anthony Cronin, the writer and poet who had known Haughey since their student days and had worked as his cultural adviser in Government, or Martin Mansergh, his adviser and scriptwriter on the North, the economy, Europe and international affairs, were already embarked on writing the definitive biography.

In the light of these three factors, I did not pursue the Haughey book project. In any event, I was immersed in day to day journalism at that time as the Political Correspondent of *Ireland on Sunday.*

Around this time, spring 2000, I answered a telephone call in my Terenure office from a woman who startled me with the politely-spoken request, "Will you hold to take a call from Mr Haughey?"

At first, I thought it must be a journalist colleague playing a practical joke on me, After all, every journalist in the land was then chasing the disgraced Haughey for an interview or for at least an informal chat over a bottle of fine wine. The seconds dragged on, while I was left hanging onto an awesomely silent telephone line.

Yet, in spite of my initial scepticism about the *bona fide* nature of the call, I felt a nervous tremble which so many Government ministers and civil servant mandarins must have experienced in the years when *The Boss* was the revered but feared political ruler of Ireland.

"Good morning, John", the unmistakeable voice of CJ whistled down the line.

"Have you sent that book which you promised me?"

Somewhat embarrassed, I apologised that I had not yet sent him a copy of my biography *John Charles McQuaid, Ruler of Catholic Ireland*. During my research for the book CJ had given me several juicy stories about the formidable Archbishop of Dublin. I told him that I would send a signed copy by post that very morning.

Why don't you bring it out to Abbeville?" CJ interrupted in the decisive tone of voice that amounted to a command.

"I'll expect you at eleven o'clock tomorrow morning".

Next day, I arrived slightly ahead of the appointed time at his luxurious Georgian home in north county Dublin. I had been there once before when doing the Lemass documentary for an interview with CJ and afterwards had enjoyed his hospitality in his in-house bar that was designed as a boat.

After being cleared at the Garda checkpoint at the entry to his estate, I drove up the drive-way and parked my car. When I rang the bell, his secretary ushered me into a side-room and offered me coffee. She apologised that Mr Haughey was tied up at a meeting which had cropped up unexpectedly.

This was good news as it gave me the chance to explore his well-stocked book shelves laden with a diverse range of books covering history, heraldry and marine-related subjects.

About half an hour later I could hear CJ taking his leave of his senior financial adviser, accountant Des Peelo. I quickly surmised that this emergency meeting had been convened after the Moriarty Tribunal had announced the day before that the former Taoiseach had received £8.6 million in personal donations from 'a golden circle' of wealthy businessmen over seventeen years. The media that morning had been predicting that he would appear before the Tribunal before the end of the summer to contest that figure, which he later did.

When he came into the side-room, CJ invited me to accompany him to his nearby study. Although he had been diagnosed as having prostate cancer, he still looked remarkable fit for a 74 year old. But he was clearly psychologically worn by his court battles and, above all, he seemed to be extremely lonely.

He was delighted to receive the McQuaid book which he said would bring back memories of a happy era. He obviously had admired McQuaid's authoritarian style but did not share the Archbishop's antediluvian attitudes to public morality.

When I enquired if he had imitated McQuaid's imperial style and gliding walk that made him the centre of attention from the assembled gathering in any room which he entered, Charlie dismissed this with a McQuaid-like wave of his hand. So I did not believe his disavowal but did not press the point!

For an hour we sat and talked about the highs and lows of his political career. He made it clear that he did not want to become involved in any further public controversies. "I want to keep as low a profile as possible", he said. He declined to be interviewed for my newspaper.

But on the understanding that I would not use any of his observations until after his death, he spoke his mind on a number of hurts which he felt deeply.

On the big political scandal of that spring, he relished with unconcealed glee the political difficulties of Tanaiste Mary Harney. This was over the row that had broken out following her approval of the nomination to sit on the European Investment Bank of disgraced former Supreme Court judge, Hugh O'Flaherty.

"Mary always had a strong moralistic streak in her make-up when she was in Fianna Fáil", he remarked. "It must be chastening for her to be so heavily criticised for extending patronage to her so-called *golden circle*".

At the recall of Harney's co-founding of the Progressive Democrats in 1985 with Desmond O'Malley, CJ did not hide his contempt for their politics. "Their contribution to modern Irish politics has been negative", he hissed. "They introduced the pursuit of personalised vendettas into Irish politics".

On a lighter note, CJ chuckled at a newspaper report that morning that businessman Patrick Gallagher (who died earlier this year) had offered to pay up to £3 million to cut CJ's tax bill. "Patrick is well intentioned but he is living in a world of mirages", he remarked with a shrug that dismissed his would-be financial saviour.

Next, CJ attacked the hype being given in the news to remarks of a moral theologian about low standards of morality in Irish public life. Haughey's response indicated to me that he felt neither guilt nor remorse for having taken money from "public spirited people" who had wanted to alleviate his financial difficulties and let him get on with the vocation of modernising the country.

It struck me that Charlie really believed that he had done no wrong in taking money from wealthy figures who supported his political career by enabling him to live in a princely style. He knew that Winston Churchill had been looked after by friends, and that even Charles Stewart Parnell was assisted by friends when he ran into money difficulties over the running of his Avondale estate in Wicklow. In his younger days, too, Charlie had heard of how Archbishop McQuaid was subject to rumours of having been helped by wealthy Freemason friends when he bought and furnished a magnificent Gothic mansion in Killiney, County Dublin.

But the most striking revelation came at the end of our hour long conversation when he was accompanying me to the main door. I noticed a photograph on the table in the hallway of C.J. smiling engagingly with the Socialist Chancellor Schmidt at a press conference in Bonn in March 1981.

"You were there", he remarked.

"Yes", I said. "You won Schmidt's support for putting pressure on Maggie Thatcher to internationalise the Northern problem and end the tradition that the North was an internal UK problem that should not be discussed by European leaders.

"That's true", Charlie chirped. "But there was also other business that was done on that trip that was never reported by the media".

Charlie proceeded to tell me that the snuff-pinching Chancellor had entertained him royally at a castle on the Rhine known as Schloss Gymnich. There Charlie observed Helmut engaging in lively political exchanges with wealthy industrialists and powerful trades union leaders. Deals were being fixed that made West Germany Europe's economic dynamo and the envy of inflation-ridden Ireland.

"This made me curious," CJ said. "I asked Schmidt to explain how the negotiations were conducted. His analysis of their system sowed the seed in my mind for the Social Partnership agreements which I introduced in 1987".

With an impish smile, he spoke of how his then Minister for Labour – now Taoiseach Bertie Ahern - had been claiming the credit for himself of social partnership as one of his major achievements in government.

Mischievously, CJ added: "Bertie claims to be the author of social partnership, but it was thanks to Helmut Schmidt that I took the idea up. You can tell that story when I am gone. You can remind Bertie that social partnership was my initiative".

Now that CJ is gone, only days before the conclusion of the latest Social Partnership agreement, the Celtic Tiger generation which reviled him in his retirement can better understand how *The Boss* created the economic framework for the country's prosperity today.

Last Wednesday morning when I was waiting to go on air for TV3's *Ireland AM* breakfast programme with Senator Martin Mansergh to discuss the Haughey Legacy, I asked him if was preparing the biography of CJ. Martin told me that he would not be publishing in the near future, because he hopes to win a seat at the next general election in his home county of Tipperary.

During the programme Martin cited social partnership as CJ's greatest achievement, and I chipped in with my story about the Germanic origins of how CJ conceived social partnership during an economics tutorial from Chancellor Schmidt in a Rhineland castle.

As Martin and I left the studio, he told me that the Schmidt connection was totally new to him and that it was a genuine contribution to historical research on Haughey. This view was also taken a few days later by former Government minister and EU Commissioner Pádraig Flynn when we spoke on the phone.

The responses of both Martin and Pádraig who were both at the centre of events in the Haughey era made me think to myself, "Maybe, after all, I should have put a bid to CJ to have become his official Bosworth".

The role of latter day Boswell has been assumed by CJ's erstwhile severest critic, Vincent Browne, who became a regular visitor to Abbeville over the past five years.

But I have so say that I felt that Vincent was a bit too vulgar and insensitive in published descriptions in the current issue of his *Village* magazine of how frail and sick Charles Haughey had become in the final period of his illness.

Other journalists such as Frank McDonald and Liam Collins have also been writing up their Abbeville conversations with CJ, all of which make interesting additions to the Haughey literature. It is also reported that CJ kept a diary of his illness which may be published as a best-seller.

In all the debate as to whether history will be kinder to Charles Haughey than the media of his day, it would seem that no consensus about his role may ever be reached. What is certain is that the first historian who takes up the challenge to produce the first academic work on the life and times of Charles Haughey will have a formidable, perhaps even impossible task.

McDowell versus Harney

(June 27, 2006)

Reporting politics is frequently the mundane task of reporting a series of set-pieces directed by sparse accounts of cabinet meetings dictated by Government Press Secretaries and spin-doctors, predictable Dáil debates and the big occasions such as the Budget.

In an age of a celebrity-driven media, even political correspondents are being forced to concentrate on personalities. Hence, the big licks that are given to Bertie's relations with women post-Celia Larkin, the Taoiseach's extravagant make-up spend, Dr Jim McDaid's drink driving, the soaring rise of personal expenses for ministers and deputies, and the cost to the taxpayer of political junkets.

With the passing of Charles J. Haughey, there was a detectable note of nostalgia in political commentaries for the days when politics were dominated by crises involving political in-fighting and factionalism.

As if on cue, last week we suddenly found ourselves gifted with two big stories that sent shock-waves around the country as we witnessed an old-fashioned back-bench revolt in Fianna Fáil and a leadership struggle under the previously prim and proper Progressive Democrats. The cliché that Oppositions do not win elections but that Governments lose them made a roaring come-back in the latest Leinster house dramatic society's piece of theatre.

Suddenly, political correspondents found themselves reinvented as theatre critics!

Act One, scene one. By courtesy of Stephen Collins's programme note in *The Irish Times*, a pandora's box from behind the curtains of the PDs' party chambers is thrust into the centre of the political stage. It is revealed that a titanic power struggle has been taking place between Tanaiste and Health minister Mary Harney and Justice Minister Michael McDowell for the soul of the PDs. Or, rather more accurately, a naked power struggle for the leadership.

An aggrieved and emotional McDowell is claiming to PD colleagues that he has an arrangement with the embarrased Harney that she will step-down before the next general election. Making his bid to become the PDs' principal character, McDowell proclaims that the time has come for the promised change of leadership. *Michael the Great* himself is ready, nay eager even, to don the mantle of leadership.

Act one, scene two. Coyly, Queen Mary demurs and appeals for loyalty from her PD vassals. She is not willing to step aside. She will not abdicate. Her magnificent work in healing the sick is not yet fully accomplished. A majority of her subjects rally to her defence and *Michael the Pretender* is isolated.

Act one, scene three. A lonesome Mick grits his teeth and tells reporters that there never was a leadership fight. For good measure, he throws in his well-rehearsed party-line that he and Queen Mary are "absolutely and completely united about where the party is going".

An unconvincing performance, the scribes bellow from the wings.

Act one, scene four. Tight-lipped, Her Majesty, Mary the First, (not President Mary McAleese!), disdainfully refuses to confirm to the bemused scribes that her disloyal lieutenant had dared to grab her throne. "Lots of issues were raised at the meeting", she said regally in the grand manner of Marie Antoinette. But the scribes are not satisfied with eating mere bread. They smell a gobfest in the melt-down of the PD body politic.

Just as Opposition leaders Enda Kenny and Pat Rabbitte are ready to dance on the PDs' marked grave, the curtain on a side-show is unveiled by publicity-starved backbenchers of the *Soldiers of No Destiny*.

Act Two, scene one. Enter *the Gang of 16*. In a dingy backroom deep in the bowels of Leinster House sixteen Fianna Fáil backbenchers sign a letter in support of the establishment of a ginger group modelled on the British Conservative Party's 1922 group. Nobly, they proclaim that they are motivated by the patriotic desire to exercise more direct influence on ministerial decision-making in the national interest. In reality, they are fed up being controlled into submission at meetings of the parliamentary party and in the run-up to the general election they are in full panic about saving their seats and their own skins.

As Bertie pandered to them as long lost cousins, and commentators rehearsed their lines on the demise of the PDs, Act Three this week will focus on how the Mayo Opposition duo, Enda and Pat, try to put the nails in the FF-PD coffin. Only the summer holidays will save such a dysfunctional shower. *The Death of a Coalition* promises to be a protracted farce.

Perhaps Bertie should take Michael Ring's advice and run to the country now – before the walls of two houses of parliament – Leinster House and Stormont – crumble on top of himself and Queen Mary. It would be the end of the affair.

Battered Bertie Buys Time

(July 11, 2006)

T he FF-PD Government has scrambled to the safety net provided by the Dáil's three month summer break with its internal cohesion and sense of national direction badly dented.

The palpable loss of composure in the Government's ranks could almost match the bursting of the morale of the French soccer team after the sending off of its captain Zinedine Zidane for a gangland-style head-butt on the chest of Italy's Marco Materazzi during Sunday's World Cup Final in Berlin.

The quarantine period provided by the long vacation will be used by Bertie and Mary to nurse their wounds and damaged egos from their bunker in Government Buildings.

But both Ahern and Harney know that for their ten year old partnership, the game is up. Their increasingly dysfunctional administration is in extra time. The team spirit has gone.

In the no confidence motion against the Government Fine Gael leader Enda Kenny claimed that the Government was showing all the signs of heart failure – confused, memory loss, sick in the stomach, suffering from pressure and palpitations, tiredness and fatigue, as well as anxiety, restlessness and impaired thinking.

Just reading the list of ailments would bring on a heart attack!

Although the Fine Gael-Labour motion had no chance of success – and no one in the Dáil including those on the Opposition benches relished the prospect of a summer general election – the point of the exercise was to brand the Government team as losers on 13 issues of public concern.

The list of Government own goals has included the continuing chaos in the Health service, school classroom sizes that are the second highest in the EU, the slaughter on our roads, epidemic suicide, the crime on our streets, the abolition of the First Time Home Buyers grant and a VAT hike on houses. Not forgetting the appalling wastage of taxpayers' money over the electronic voting fiasco.

To add insult to injury, Enda reminded Bertie of former team captain Charlie Haughey's verdict on his squad: "The worst Government in the history of the State. They have no plan. Nothing works". The only real question to preoccupy ministers this summer is whether the penalty shoot-out of a general election will come in the autumn or early spring – or whether they can put off the final whistle until next summer.

Michael McDowell is the Government's Zinedine Zidane. He has lost his head on numerous occasions – trying to take Mary Harney's headship of the PDs, fighting with the Gardaí on police reform, the media on libel law reform, losing his head when criticised by Fine Gael's Richard Bruton, and again losing his head in the recent rape law crisis. Unlike Zidane, who had a marvellous playing career and will remain one of the world's soccer greats despite his moment of malevolent madness, *Mad Mullah's* record as a reformist Justice Minister is a chronicle of high-flowing promises and abysmal delivery.

Senior civil servant Eddie Sullivan has given the benefit of the doubt to a bedraggled McDowell and the Government by delivering a report that concluded that there was an "administrative error" made by an official, This had left the Government unaware of the pending Mr 'A' case which led to the Supreme Court striking down the 1935 law on statutory rape. His report thus cleared Attorney General Rory Brady from the criticism of not knowing about the case, because the unnamed official did not tell him about it on six possible occasions!

Quite rightly, the O'Sullivan report was dismissed by the Opposition and the media as a white-wash that raised more questions than it answered. After all, the system of referral that was put in place at the time of the fall of Taoiseach Albert Reynolds over the Fr Brendan Smyth extradition case was designed to be full-proof. Had the summer vacation not intervened, the Ahern-Harney Government would probably have been forced to call a general election. By holding on, it only buys time. It has minimal possibility of recovery.

The underlying trend against the Government was consolidated as a medium-term pattern in last week's *Sunday Business Post* opinion poll that shows the tide steadily in favour of a change towards the alternative administration of Kenny and Rabbitte and Trevor Sargent's Green Party. It can only get worse.

This summer will not grant the Government immunity from bad press. Already tensions are being highlighted inside Fianna Fáil between Education Minister Mary Hanafin and the FF chairman of the Joint Oireachtas committee on Finance, Seán Fleming, over the publication of the schools' examination results. Hanafin, a former school teacher, is against publication on the grounds that this will lead to misleading league tables. For publication are Fleming's committee and other members of the party.

Confidence is low in Fianna Fáil with twenty or more backbenchers fearing the loss of their seats. The Harney-McDowell leadership struggle has raised questions about the survival of the PDs as a political entity. The Labour Party has stood firmly behind Pat Rabbitte's anti-Fianna Fáil approach, despite Bertie's mischief in trying to spin the line that a Labour Party not led by Rabbitte would coalesce with him in his third administration.

Not even the support of Sinn Féin is likely to save Bertie's skin. The IRA's insistence that the murdered Belfast mother of ten children, Jean McConville was an informer has enraged all decent thinking and casts further doubts on Sinn Féin's conversion to democracy.

As for the Opposition parties, it is true that considerable differences exist on policy issues. But a dynamic relationship is visibly emerging between Kenny and Rabbitte. Policy discussions are taking place with a view to working out a definite programme for Government.

As we come to the end of play report, Bertie appears to have lost his touch and the confidence of his backbenchers who are furtively looking to Brian Cowen as their saviour. Mary Harney looks down and out by the burden of the Health system and will be lucky to hold her Dáil seat.

Michael McDowell retains the capacity to do another Zidane that could result in not just his own sending-off, but also that of a dispirited and time-wasting cabinet. The time could be approaching for *Mad Mullah* to take off his boots and go back with his gown and wig to the Fourt Courts.

The end of term prize must go to the Mayo twins, Enda and Pat, for their presentation of a credible alternative to this shambolic Government. Their hour is fast approaching.

While Rabbitte has had the advantage of being a darling of the media for his ability to talk the talk, Kenny has had to upgrade his game and overcome prejudice against him among the Fourth Estate.

This Enda has done – and if he keeps up this form, he will prove a winner. Bertie and Mary face a massacre. Roll on September 27, the restart of the Big Match.

'Mother Harney'
Hatches 'Mullah'

(September 12, 2006)

It was the *Italian factor* that inspired Mary Harney to make her momentous decision to resign as leader of the Progressive Democrats. A mixture of *la dolce vita* and *memento mori* – the good life and a reminder of the brevity of life – confirmed an intuition which she had felt for some months that it was time to step-down after almost 13 years as leader.

While on a three week holiday in Italy with her husband Brian, Mary, in relaxed mode and away from what she described as the Dáil "hot-house", reflected on last June's traumatic events that caused her so much emotional strain. Not only was that period arduous personally for her on account of her mother's illness, it overlapped with the eruption of a power struggle within the PDs that brought her into a bare-knuckled public spat with Michael McDowell, who claimed that he had a pact with her to resign the leadership so that he could take over.

This open warfare between the PDs' two cabinet ministers surfaced at a time when the party's ratings in the polls had slumped to an almost invisible two pc, a foreboding indicator of its minimalist prospect of winning a third term in government with Bertie Ahern. With the polls consistently showing that Fianna Fáil will lose seats in the election, and with neither of the two leaders of the putative alternative government, Enda Kenny nor Pat Rabbitte, entertaining a courtship with the PDs, the future looked down-hill for Harney.

As Harney revealed last week after her unexpected announcement that she was stepping down as leader ahead of the autumn Dáil session, she had already made up her mind in June to stand down, but was persuaded to stay on by colleagues anxious to keep McDowell, the *Mad Mullah* from taking over. On holiday in Italy Harney resolved to implement what she had planned to do in June, and this she has done with aplomb. The appreciations of her leadership have gone a long way to restoring her reputation that had been on the slide on account of her stint in *Angola*, Brian Cowen's pithy description of the Department of Health. She looked the old bubbly Harney rather than the dowdy and defensive Minister for Health.

From the moment I heard of her resignation on an RTE news flash, I was never in doubt that McDowell's hour has come. Neither Liz O'Donnell nor Tom Parlon has cabinet experience, an essential qualification for a party leader who will also be Tanaiste and head of a senior ministry.

Whatever reservations some of his PD colleagues have about Michael's impetuosity and unpredictability, they are putting a higher store in his intellectual and organisational capabilities, as well as his knowledge of both the workings of government and the make-up of the PDs of which he was a founding member and chief strategist.

The reservations about McDowell weigh more heavily with Taoiseach Bertie Ahern and Fianna Fáil ministers who fear that there may be some truth in Labour leader Pat Rabbitte's prediction that the Minister for Justice will create an opportunity to pull out of government. Bertie was particularly sorry to see the end of his partnership with Mary with whom he had a definite arrangement to see the coalition through to the end of a full five year term, as had their first government from 1997-2002.

However, I take the view that it is in McDowell's interests to stay the full course with Bertie. He needs time to bring the PDs back up in the polls, select candidates and finalise his party's election manifesto.

Richard Bruton, the shrewd deputy Fine Gael leader, observed on *Prime Time* that the PDs are lumbered with ten years' baggage of having been in government for the past decade, and it will be difficult for them to transform themselves into something different than what they have been.

It will be up to McDowell to prove whether the PDs are radical or redundant. If the PDs don't hold their eight seats at the election, then it will be Michael not Mary who will carry the responsibility.

While it was a clever move for Bertie to hint straight away that he will look to Independents to prolong a minority Fianna Fáil Government – an option many ambitious FF deputies would relish in the expectation of promotion to cabinet – it is a non-runner. With so much cash flowing into the Exchequer, Bertie and Brian Cowen would be at the mercy of the demands of the Independents for their support, FF deputies would resent any economic favours being doled out to their Independent rivals, and, most of all, the public would not tolerate a return to pork barrel politics.

The McDowell leadership of the PDs will add a new dynamic to the long run-in to the general election that will ensure him massive media attention. The Sinn Féin leader, Gerry Adams, will have to eat his words that the departure of Mary

Harney was an irrelevancy. McDowell's attacks on Sinn Féin will be highly relevant in convincing voters that Fianna Fáil must not be allowed back into government with either the active participation or tacit support of the Shinners.

It is this middle class section of the electorate that McDowell needs to woo in order to secure the party's niche of 7or 8pc of voters. It is this sector which appears to be moving towards Fine Gael.

Now that Bertie has lost the inherent stability in his Government guaranteed by Mother Harney, the loss of Blair as Prime Minister would be a more serious blow, especially when Bertie and Tony are promising Ulster's politicians a working holiday in Scotland to work out a deal for the North by November 24 deadline.

Harney's sole task from here on of reforming the Health services begins to seem relatively manageable compared with the mounting problems for Bertie and Blair. Stepping down may have been Mary's finest hour, one to match the fact that if it had not been for her pugnacity twenty years ago, there would have been no PDs – and the best known slogan of modern Irish politics, *Breaking the Mould*, would never have been coined.

Old Lady Puts Bertie
On The Ropes

(September 26, 2006)

The Dáil's return has been preceded by the biggest news leak of the year that has boxed a stunned Bertie Ahern on the ropes as he fights for his survival as Taoiseach.

A media clamour has put huge pressure on Bertie to make a full statement clarifying the exact circumstances in which he received payments from wealthy friends to finance his legal separation with his wife Miriam 13 years ago when he was Minister for Finance.

Although two ministers, Séamus Brennan and Willie O'Dea, have come to his public aid, there is an awesome feeling of dread swelling up within the cabinet and among Fianna Fáil backbenchers that their man is vulnerable to a knock-out punch that could end prematurely his career as Taoiseach. Mindful of the fact that *the Teflon Taoiseach* has weathered previous storms, notably suing for libel after being accused of receiving £50,000 from a businessman, no one is rushing to write Bertie's political obituary yet.

The Opposition parties led by Fine Gael and Labour have been slow to intrude into the sensitive personal details of Bertie's marital settlement, but they have not accepted his initial response in Clare that the information which he supplied to the Mahon Tribunal relates to his own private business. Enda Kenny and Pat Rabbitte have demanded to know how much Ahern received in 1993, who were the 11 or so donors, was the money a gift or a loan, was tax paid, and whether any political favours were done in return.

Apart from any embarrassment about disclosing such information, the Taoiseach faces the difficult question of why he did not declare this money in his annual statement of interests to the Standards in Public Office Commission. Even assuming that Bertie manages to stonewall, or obfuscate these questions this week on the grounds that they are confidential matters, the issue will continue to distract him and his Government from running the country and preparing for the December Budget. On October 10 Bertie and Miriam are scheduled to have a High Court hearing of their application to prevent the disclosure to the Mahon Tribunal of information it is seeking in regard to their separation agreement.

As Monday's *Irish Times*, the newspaper which first broke the story, has reported, the Taoiseach is confronted with the legal dilemma that Tanaiste and Justice Minister Michael McDowell introduced a law last spring enabling the Tribunal to secure access to family breakdown cases. Section 40 of the Civil Liability and Courts Act, 2004, stipulates that the in camera rule in family law cases may not be used to prevent the production of a document, or the giving of information, to a hearing or inquiry established by law. It would seem that this section will require Judge Joseph Finnegan to order the Aherns to provide the information about the terms of their separation settlement to the Tribunal.

Even if this information remains known only to the Tribunal, for how long will that remain confidential? This question will be uppermost in the minds of the Taoiseach's colleagues, the Opposition, the media and the public. As long as it remains unanswered Bertie will be in the ring with his two gloves tied behind his back.

As the politicians return to Leinster House after their long summer rest, the speculation will intensify about Bertie's future. Already there is talk that he will go for a snap general election in October or November, but he would do so as a wounded Taoiseach leading a party which faces meltdown, according to the latest opinion poll from the *Sunday Business Post*.

Will the men in the grey suits inside Fianna Fáil tell Bertie that he is now a liability and suggest that he should resign as leader? How many Fianna Fáil ministers and deputies calculate that they would have a better chance saving their seats in the next election under the banner of Brian Cowen? How will the new leader of the Progressive Democrats, Michael McDowell, react, especially under goading from Pat Rabbitte to break his silence? Will he throw Bertie a life-line or will he advise that it is time for him to go?

Bertie's footwork in response to the body-blow he received from the *Old Lady of D'Olier Street* has been shaky and erratic. There is a degree of sympathy for his grievance about the leak. No one has accused him of taking bribes. No one wants to know about his communion, confirmation and birthday monies.

The Irish Times is sticking to its original claim that the gift to Ahern was between €50,000 and €100,000. It would hardly do so if it was not sure of its information.

At the level of principle, the Taoiseach's refusal so far to give more information is contradicted by his own response to the McCracken report into the sources of the late Charlie Haughey's wealth. "We could not condone the practice of senior politicians seeking or receiving from a single, large donor sums of money or services in kind", he told the Fianna Fáil Árd Fheis in 1997.

Also coming back to haunt Bertie is his other 1997 remark that "public representatives must not be under a personal financial obligation to anyone". Was he suffering from amnesia about his own affairs in 1993 when he said that four years on? This remark could prove to be his Achilles heel. It is reminder that New Fianna Fáil has not managed to distance itself from the Old FF, of which Bertie was a prominent figure in the era of Charles Haughey and Ray Burke.

Never before has a Dáil resumed for business with such a major question-mark hanging over the viability of a Taoiseach, the most senior and powerful politician in the land. Suddenly, the prospect has become a real possibility that Bertie Ahern could be gone as Taoiseach sooner than Tony Blair will stepdown as the Prime Minister of Britain.

What may become known as *Bertiegate* could have a negative impact on next month's crucial talks which Ahern and Blair have arranged with the Northern political parties at St Andrews in Scotland. These talks need to succeed if an agreement is to be reached by the November 24 deadline set by the two Governments for the restoration of the devolved Executive.

'Bertiegate' Crisis

(October 3, 2006)

The indications are that DUP leader Ian Paisley will demand that Sinn Féin must first endorse the Police Service of Northern Ireland and show that commitment for some months before doing any deal. This would require Sinn Féin to hold an Árd Fheis on the issue that could postpone any agreement until next spring.

In a speech in Belfast at the week-end the Catholic Primate of All Ireland, Archbishop Seán Brady, said he hoped that "the coming weeks and months will see all those who have power to do so, commit themselves totally to a shared and positive future, by putting in place a local power-sharing Assembly which has full community support for the institutions of law and order".

Whatever about the continued reluctance of Paisley to deal with Gerry Adams' Sinn Féin, the tragedy is that both Bertie and Blair have their own personal problems to preoccupy them.

The *Bertiegate* crisis has consumed the interest of the nation opening up a deep cleavage in society over whether the Taoiseach has been guilty of wrong-doing that merits either his resignation or removal from office.

The atmosphere in Leinster House and the surrounding watering-holes has been as electric as the heady days in the 1980s when heaves were being launched against Charlie Haughey's leadership of Fianna Fáil and of the fall of Albert Reynolds as Taoiseach in late 1994.

In no other EU country would a head of Government survive revelations that he accepted loans worth €50,000 from 12 friends when he was Minister for Finance in 1993-4, and that a whip around by businessmen endowed him with £8,000 during his visit to see Manchester United. The general view in Dublin is that barring any new bombshell overnight Bertie Ahern should survive Tuesday's crucial Dáil session with the support of Michael McDowell's PDs, if he offers an apology and resolves to adhere to higher standards in future.

In today's money value plus interest, the Taoiseach spent the weekend signing and sending cheques said to be worth over €90,000 to his benefactors as part of his debt of honour. As electricity bills shoot up this week, many a household will envy how the Taoiseach can release €90,000 from his bank account with such ease, and will take a cynical view that such money would never have been released if it had not been first exposed in *The Irish Times*.

Yet, in the convoluted words of Finance Minister, Brian Cowen, Bertie was not incorrect in what he did during his difficult times of a legal separation from his wife Miriam. The ambivalent attitude of the public towards Bertie's unorthodox handling of his own finances was represented in the *Sunday Independent* - he was wrong but should stay on as Taoiseach.

Even though Enda Kenny and Pat Rabbitte have relentlessly emphasised the Taoiseach's need to give a full account to the Dáil of his breach of the normal ministerial code of conduct – and the bulk of the national media has done likewise – Bertie's direct appeal for public sympathy through the RTE *Six One* interview with Bryan Dobson last Tuesday has rallied a significant section of the public to his side.

The survival PR campaign devised by Bertie's handlers has been rooted in using stalling procedures in the Dáil to deprive the Opposition of adequate time to quiz the Taoiseach.

It has also been constructed on the premise that Michael McDowell desperately wants to remain Tanaiste, even at the cost of jettisoning the PDs' reputation for being the moral watchdogs of Fianna Fáil. McDowell has calculated that a walk-out by the PDs from Government would see Fianna Fáil standing by Bertie as a minority Government dependent on doing deals with Independents, especially those from the so-called FF gene pool.

So we are an important juncture in the destinies of both the Republic and the North, with the formation of a power-sharing government at stake in the Stormont talks and the saving of the FF-PD coalition in the South. Pivotal to the outcome of both issues is Bertie Ahern. With Tony Blair, he has been a tower of strength in driving the Good Friday Agreement of 1998, but his reputation is under a cloud south of the border.

It may be some consolation to Bertie that Pope Benedict XVI has been put in the media dock for allegedly covering-up on child abusing priests for twenty years. Colm O'Gorman's *Panorama* documentary on Sunday was a powerful and moving piece of investigation. Some callers to radio chat shows have been calling for the Pope's resignation, while church lawyers have counter-attacked by suggesting that O'Gorman has misunderstood Vatican policy and maligned the German Pontiff.

In all this mess, it was good to hear the good news from the North that power-sharing and policing will dominate next week's historic summit between the Rev Ian Paisley and the leader of the Irish Catholic Church at Stormont.

Big Ian, who has always preferred to insult the Pope rather than talk to a Catholic prelate, will ask Archbishop Brady to seek Sinn Féin's support for the Police Service of Northern Ireland (PSNI).

Welcoming the meeting, Dr Brady told me that his first meeting with the leader of the biggest Unionist party would provide him with "an opportunity to discuss the situation in the North". The Archbishop said that at this delicate stage in the talks process, it was important for politicians to talk to one another and "to go the extra mile" to restore devolved government at Stormont.

This first ever encounter between a Catholic Primate and Dr Paisley, who is also the head of the strongly anti-ecumenical Free Presbyterian Church, will come days ahead of talks at St Andrews in Scotland between the North's political parties.

The Scottish venue has been chosen by Taoiseach Bertie Ahern and the British Prime Minister Tony Blair to break the deadlock before the expiry date of November 24 for a restoration of the Executive.

Last Sunday week Archbishop Brady, in an important address in Belfast to international churchmen, called on the politicians to "commit themselves totally to a shared and positive future, by putting in place a local power-sharing Assembly which has full community support for the institutions of law and order".

Archbishop Brady is the only religious leader of the mainstream Christian churches in the North whom Dr Paisley has not met. Over the past two years the DUP have met with the leaders of the other major Christian churches at Stormont.

The prospect of such an unprecedented meeting between the Catholic Primate and Dr Paisley first emerged in the course of a major speech which Dr Brady made in Italy 17 months ago. Speaking in Milan at the invitation of the British Ambassador to Italy, Sir Ivor Roberts, Dr Brady took the initiative of saying that as the Catholic Primate he looked forward to "engagement with ministers from all parties", including the DUP as part of a more mature and confident" Northern Ireland. In response to this initiative, DUP Assembly member for Derry, Gregory Campbell, wrote to the Primate proposing they meet to discuss matters of mutual concern.

In June Archbishop Brady became the first Catholic Primate to meet leaders of the Loyal Orange Orders, at their request, when they held a meeting at his residence in Armagh to discuss the contentious parades issue. These talks contributed to the most peaceful Orange walks of recent years during the traditional marching season.

Referring to the November 24 deadline set by the Irish and British Govern-ments for an agreement on the restoration of the Executive and the Assembly at Stormont, Dr Brady told me when we met for lunch at his residence in Armagh that "the situation is so serious that any improvement in the political situation is important". He is worried about a political vacuum continuing for a considerable time which would not be healthy for democracy.

Stirring times. *Big Ian* talking to the leading Irish papist. A Taoiseach fighting for his political life and the Pope being called to accountability.

Politics Loses in 'Bertiegate'

(October 10, 2006)

Irish politics is the big loser in the on-off-perhaps back-on partnership of the Fianna Fáil-Progressive Democrat Government, according to former Taoiseach Garret FitzGerald.

Surveying the extraordinary revelations of the past few weeks about Bertie Ahern's Drumcondra loans and Manchester monies, Dr FitzGerald has concluded that these events "now effectively deprived Taoiseach Bertie Ahern of the capacity to undertake one of the most crucial duties of his office".

This concerns the Taoiseach's capacity of ensuring that members of his Government observe high standards of public probity. It is a view which I share.

In claiming that he has done no wrong in accepting the monies in 1993-4 when he was Minister for Finance, and that he broke no ethics code, Bertie Ahern has failed to acknowledge that what he did was morally wrong for a Government Minister.

In the words of FitzGerald, one of the most honourable leaders of this country, Ahern has fatally undermined what has always been seen as a fundamental principle of political probity in Ireland, as in the rest of northern Europe.

On narrow legalistic grounds, Bertie has claimed a right to accept a gift of money when a minister. He has also failed to apply to himself the yardstick which he enunciated in 1994 when he demanded of the disgraced Fine Gael minister Michael Lowry that an undocumented loan must be treated as a gift.

It would best if Bertie held a general election now, as called for by the Fine Gael leader, Enda Kenny. However, at the time of writing on Monday, the indications were that Tanaiste and PD leader, Michael McDowell, was seeking assurances from the Taoiseach that will enable the PDs to retake their seats on the Government benches when the Dáil resumes on Tuesday.

With Fianna Fáil standing behind the beleagured Bertie, and with the option of a minority administration propped up by some Independents, the Taoiseach will be renewing his efforts to clinch what Tony Blair has called the final settlement in the North. Ironically, if Ian Paisley does a deal in the North, this could boost Bertie.

The DUP played-down the religious dimension of Monday's historic get together of the Catholic Archbishop of Armagh and Primate of All Ireland with the world's most famous anti-Roman parson-politician. DUP sources stressed that Dr Ian Kyle Paisley met Archbishop Seán Brady at Stormont Castle as head of the North's biggest political party, and not as the Moderator of the Free Presbyterian Church.

Yet, this political spin that the meeting was not about ecumenism cannot disguise the reality that the North's most rabid anti-papist made a U-turn parallel in religious history to St Paul's conversion to Christianity while on his way to Damascus.

This is not to suggest that *Big Ian* is about to convert to Rome, or learn how to say the Rosary. He will still shout *No Surrender* to the Pope whom he regards as the anti-Christ. He will still denounce the Catholic Church's doctrines as unscriptural.

But judged by his past record of anti-Catholic bigotry, his sitting down for formal talks with the Pope's chief representative in Ireland amounts to a miracle – one which many Catholics thought would never happen.

For such an encounter to have taken place between a *Papist* prelate and the anti-ecumenical leader is the measure of a profound transformation in Paisley's outlook, one which is being interpreted as a hopeful sign that he is edging closer to a deal on power-sharing with Sinn Féin at this week's political talks in the university town of St Andrews in Scotland.

The reality is that even though Paisley, the M.P. for North Antrim, has proved to be as much concerned for the well-being of his Catholic as well as for his Protestant constituents, he has built his political career on attacking popery. His career is conspicuous for his anti-Catholic stunts and bellicose religious language from the age of the seventeenth century Covenanters.

It was anti-Catholicism that made Paisley, then an unknown hot-gospeller in the crowded world of Ulster Protestant evangelism, a household name exactly half a century ago. This came about when he claimed that a 15 year old Irish Catholic, Maura Lyons, had converted to his Free Presbyterian Church. It did not help Paisley's cause when her parents and local priests from whom she had ran away claimed that she had been abducted by the champion of Protestant liberty.

When the girl eventually returned from Scotland to her home and 'the True Faith', many Northern Protestants were embarrassed by *Big Ian's* antics. But this strange episode had established him as a public personality – and his congregation expanded.

In the early 1960s Paisley became the towering foe of ecumenism after Pope John XXIII and the Second Vatican Council opened out to the world and joined the church unity movement.

In 1967 he became notorious when during a televised students' debate at Oxford University, he whipped out a wafer from his jacket pocket and showed his contempt for the Catholic belief of transubstantiation – that the wafer changes into the body of Christ.

When the Archbishop of Canterbury, Michael Ramsey, went to Rome to meet Pope Paul VI, the roaring Paisley managed to get a seat on the same plane – but on arrival in Rome he was not allowed to get through passport control and was bungled back on the plane by discerning *caribinieri*.

When the civil rights began in the North in the late 1960s he castigated it as "a Romish Plot" to coerce Ulster into a priest-ridden South.

In 1973, when the then Cardinal Primate of All Ireland, William Conway, headed a Catholic delegation at the first inter-church summit with the leaders of the main Protestant Churches at Ballymascanlon, near Dundalk, Paisley came across the border with a bus load of followers to protest against a sell-out to Rome. He denounced the late Cardinal Ó Fiaich as "the IRA bishop from Crossmaglen," and Cardinal Cahal Daly as "the Black Pope of the Republican Movement". In 1979 he led the street protests against Pope John Paul II's visit to Britain, and in 1988 he was unceremoniously hauled out of the chamber of the European Parliament in Strasbourg after protesting against a speech by Pope John Paul.

Paisley has long perfected his art of protesting against any Protestant church-man who engaged in dialogue with Roman prelates and papist clergy. Only two years ago he stormed the General Assembly of the main Presbyterian Church when its Moderator, the Rev Ken Newell, invited Archbishop Brady to attend the debates as his special guest.

What a change on Monday when *Big Ian* sat down in Stormont Castle for "very constructive and helpful" official talks with the Archbishop he had heckled in 2004. The range of topics discussed including poverty, the right to faith-based schools, the family and marriage are covered by the Pontifical Council for Justice and Peace's *Compendium of the Social Doctrine of the Church*.

Paisley will face an angry backlash, perhaps even a schism, from his followers who still regard the Archbishop as the anti-Christ. One woman could not bring herself to say the word archbishop and described him as *Mr Brady*.

But as he travels to St Andrews, Paisley holds a strong deck of cards in the negotiations, unlike both Bertie Ahern and Michael McDowell in their poker game about the errant Taoiseach's financing of his home.

Good Friday for Bertie

(October 17, 2006)

S t Andrews, the Scottish University town, is famous worldwide for its golf links. Its university is the oldest in Scotland. In olden times it was the ecclesiastical capital of Pictland. Now it has given its name to a process that could lead to the final settlement of the Irish Question.

After gloomy reports that negotiations in the Fairmont hotel in St Andrews were heading for failure between the DUP and Sinn Féin, the political landscape in Ulster transformed on Friday when Tony Blair and Bertie Ahern gave a joint press conference in the lecture theatre to announce the St Andrews Agreement.

At one level, this was a smart public relations stunt by the Irish and British premiers. What they were presenting was not a done deal agreed to by the Northern parties. It was a new framework for resolving the deadlock which has made the 1998 Good Friday Agreement, otherwise known as the Belfast Agreement, inoperable.

But in a day of rising hopes that saw serious engagement between the DUP and Sinn Féin, the new framework proposals from London and Dublin were enticing enough to hook the Rev Ian Paisley and Gerry Adams.

It may have been an oversell to sum up the outcome as 'Paisley says Yes'. But for once, a Friday the Thirteenth, normally associated with bad luck by the superstitious, was a good news day.

Friday October 13, 2006, is now a pivotal date in modern Irish history. Its status as the foundation date for a new phase in the Northern talks was due to be confirmed this Tuesday with the announcement that *Big Ian* and *the Bearded One* would meet face to face in Stormont Castle.

Tuesday October 17 will now enter the history books as the day that Paisley and Adams came together for a meeting of the Assembly's Programme for Government Committee to chart the way forward from St Andrews.

November 10 has been set as the last day for the Northern parties to sign up to the two governments' St Andrews' proposals. On November 20/1 legislation will be enacted at Westminster to make changes to the Good Friday Agreement and the enforcement of the St Andrews Agreement.

On November 24, the previous make or break date set by the two Governments for restored devolved government, the Assembly will convene at Stormont to Nominate Ian Paisley as the North's First Minister and Martin McGuinness as Deputy First Minister.

This, in turn, will pave the way for further negotiations and consultations among the political parties with the aim of a full restoration of the Executive by next March.

An important impetus to these talks is expected to come in January 2007 when the Independent Monitoring Commission issues its next report on the IRA and loyalist moves away from para-militarism and criminality.

Assuming the negotiations go to plan, elections in the North and a referendum in the Republic will be held to endorse the St Andrews Agreement. This will be followed on March 14 when the Northern parties nominate their ministers to the power-sharing Executive.

Twelve days later, on March 26, power will be devolved officially to the power-sharing Executive led by Paisley and McGuinness.

But to go back to Friday October 13, 2006. Behind the scenes in the St Andrews hotel Blair and Bertie had wooed *Big Ian* and his wife Eileen on the fiftieth anniversary of their wedding. Blair presented them with a crystal bowl. Bertie gave them a handcrafted wooden bowl hewn from a walnut tree on the site of the Battle of the Boyne between the victorious King William of Orange and King James Stuart in 1690.

This time, however, it appeared that there were only potential winners. The DUP had accepted the principle of sharing power with Sinn Féin, which in turn had signalled its willingness to address a range of issues, not least in policing.

Suddenly, the fortunes of Blair and Bertie, both of whom had been going through days of political doldrum, were revived, as they cast themselves as the statesmen architects of the St Andrews Agreement.

However, as the Taoiseach acknowledged on Sunday, the parties have to work out the minutiae of the deal. The timetable will have to be managed carefully. He hopes that not too many wrinkles will appear to upset *Big Ian's* political bethroal to Martin.

On its side, Sinn Féin's engagement in policing depends on the approval of its Árd Comhairle and then an Árd Fheis, probably in December. This will take some time. It is not an easy issue for them – and their debates will be watched closely by the DUP.

The Scottish outcome includes some concessions which will make it easier for Paisley and his lieutenants such as Peter Robinson, Nigel Dodds and Jeffrey Donaldson, to sell to their grassroots. These include the retention of the North's grammar schools, a cap on rates, lower corporation taxes to attract new industries.

As well as giving the Assembly new powers over water rates and the number of district councils, the St Andrews Agreement is to be bolstered by "a billion pound plus" aid package that is to be overseen by Finance Minister Brian Cowen and the Chancellor of the Exchequer, Gordon Brown.

Even before the extent of the St Andrews Agreement was unveiled, Bertie was taking a bow in the autumnal sunshine with the news in two opinion polls conducted by *The Irish Times* and the *Sunday Tribune* showing that his own and Fianna Fáil's popularity had gone up in the wake of the Drumcondra 'loans' and Manchester monies crisis, while that of Fine Gael's Enda Kenny and Labour's Pat Rabbitte had dipped.

These findings were hard for *Irish Times* editor Geraldine Kennedy to swallow, and on Friday she published a morally sour editorial which claimed that the people had made a show of themselves in not endorsing Bertie's removal from office. This contrasted with Bertie's chirpy note of thanks for the thousands of political get-well cards which he received in recent weeks from people whom he described as good and fair.

With the St Andrews deal bulging in his pocket, and with Brian Cowen preparing his December budget with a healthy treasure chest at his disposal, the political horizons look bright indeed for Bertie in his quest for a third term as Taoiseach.

Conversely, these are bad days for Fine Gael and Labour, especially for Enda Kenny, who must be hoping that Bertie's bounce-back has not become irreversible. In retrospect, Enda and Pat Rabbitte did not show Charlie Haughey-like steel in tabling a Dáil motion for Ahern's resignation. While Bertie maximised his family difficulties, and ran rings round them, Pat and Enda came across as two nice guys who were not hungry enough to go for the political kill. The Mayo two will have to pick themselves up and get tougher. But they have a mountain to climb.

As of now, Bertie has two winning cards in his hand: a Budget bonanza, and the St Andrews Agreement that could prove to be the consummation of the Sunningdale, Hillsborough and Good Friday Agreements.

October 13, 2006, was Bertie's personal 'Good Friday'. It was the day Bertie and Tony brought Ian Paisley in from the cold.

Bertie's Bandwagon
Gathers Pace

(November 7, 2006)

Bertie Ahern's triumphant Árd Fheis at the week-end highlighted his domination over Fianna Fáil which is now confident that his name on the election posters will sweep the country's largest political party back for a third successive term in next year's general election.

With his position boosted in recent opinion polls and reaffirmed at the City West love-in, it was not surprising that Bertie felt strong enough to look back on the difficult few weeks when he was nearly toppled over the Drumcondra and Manchester dig-outs when he was Minister for Finance in the early 1990s.

The Taoiseach did so discreetly in a brief reference in his Saturday night presidential address when he said, "while we would all, I am sure, lead perfect lives if hindsight were foresight, I am proud of my record and grateful for the chance you have given me to serve Ireland".

This 'ordinary guy' identification with the people, the technique which enabled him to appeal for popular support over the Dáil and the media during his recent crisis, did the trick again. The 5,000 FF faithful cheered and cheered. But in the one-to-one situation of the television studio on Sunday, Ursula Halligan, on her *Political Party* programme, had more time to coax Bertie to ruminate on his claim that there was a plot to take him out. He duly obliged. He believed that there was some big, bad enemy out there waiting to get him.

"This just wasn't off the back of a truck," he said. "This was a sinister, calculated set-up, there's no doubt about that". This "somebody or some group" had definitely set out to bury him in a cold, clinical way probably before the summer, but he didn't know who it might have been.

Asked if he meant *The Irish Times*, the Taoiseach replied: "Well, yeah, there were elements. They tried day-in, day-out, but you just had to get on with it and just had to keep on doing your job, and I did it to the best of my ability".

So, it's official, the man who broke the conventional code of ethics by taking payments when he was Minister for Finance was merely the victim of a conspiracy that was highly personalised and conducted by a newspaper. No mention here of how Bertie was saved by PD leader Michael McDowell's lust to stay in power as Tanaiste.

Bertie has given his seal of approval to the modern day myth of a Taoiseach being saved by public popularity from the sinister machinations of *Irish Times* editor and former PD politician, Geraldine Kennedy. James Joyce would relish this revisionist version of how Bertie Ahern survived by the will of the people, in contrast to how Charles Stewart Parnell was brought down by the bishops and a treacherous Home Rule Party.

Parnell's fall, like Bertie's resurrection, are both history now. Bertie's mind is set on a third term that he reckons will be clinched by the December Budget. His party believes this too.

The main message in his presidential address was that the country had achieved its prosperity in the past decade as a result of the practical policies of the two successive FF-PD coalitions, and that it the alternative government of Fine Gael and Labour took power next year, Enda Kenny and Pat Rabbitte would squander this by "spend-all" policies.

Bertie's formula will be to increase spending on health, education, welfare and infrastructure, while keeping employment and tax revenues strong, and redistributing wealth to the less well off. Peace in the North, prosperity and Bertie running a fairer and stronger Ireland are the election themes. It will be intriguing to see how Kenny and Rabbitte can come up with to stop this Bertie bandwagon.

Yet, looking beyond the Bertie hypnosis of current politics, there are issues which are still causing public anger.

A story which got huge public reaction was the revelation by Fionnán Sheahan in the *Irish Independent* that the basic pay of TDs has risen to €1,000 a day, based on 97 sitting days this year. The average Dáil salary for 2007 will rise to €103,500.

This enriching of the political class by the political class is a source of considerable provocation to the millions of families on social welfare who are finding it hard to pay for rising fuel, education and health costs.

This growing gap between the haves and have-nots of Celtic Tiger Ireland has been highlighted by the St Vincent de Paul Society in its pre-budget submission to the Minister for Finance, Brian Cowen. The Society's President, Professor John Monaghan, has called for special measures to boost low incomes, create more affordable housing, support education and overhaul the health service.

Another warning to politicians of not exploiting racist fears for "cheap political advantage" in the lead up to next year's general election was given on Sunday by the Church of Ireland former Bishop of Killala, Dr John Neill, who is now the Archbishop of Dublin. While there is a lot of anecdotal evidence of racist attitudes towards immigrants, it would be foolish for any of the political parties to try to stoke up fears.

Socialist Bertie,
No Seculariser

(December 12, 2006)

It was the week of Brian Cowen's election 'return ticket' Budget and the Catholic bishops' controversial come-back into the Church-State arena over the age of consent for teenage sex.

Once again, public debate in Ireland revolves around the traditional issues of mammon and morality! With the exchequer awash with a record €4.4bn surplus, much of it from the higher than anticipated €10bn yield from November's tax payments from the self-employed and business property, most of Biffo's third budget was in the public domain even before he stood up to deliver it last Wednesday in Leinster House.

The first real cheers during his triumphant Dáil speech came when Cowen announced that the Government was fulfilling its pledge to bring old age pensions up to €208 a week. This became the lead story from the budget. The 2007 Budget may go down in the history books as 'the year of the pensioner'.

An equally upbeat Minister for Social Welfare, Seamus Brennan, boasted that over 400,000 pensioners will benefit from the increases in what he described as "the largest ever welfare budget", which also increased the base rate of social welfare by €20 to €185.80 a week for 565,000 recipients.

The same kind of high-flown language as used by the Fianna Fáil ministers was echoed by Fr Seán Healy, the head of the Justice office of the Conference of Religious of Ireland (CORI). Budget 2007 marks "a historic breakthrough" for those on basic social welfare, according to Fr Healy who advised Fianna Fáil to meet this target when he addressed its parliamentary party at a think-tank meeting in Inchydoney two years ago.

Fr Healy was chuffed that the Government honoured the commitment it made in its National Anti-Poverty Strategy to benchmark the lowest social welfare payment for a single person at 30pc of gross average industrial earnings. The increases in social welfare rates would have a positive impact on those who are at risk of poverty, because 60pc of recipients were living in households headed by a person who is not in the labour force. Fr Healy, you will recall, is now one of the most famous priests in Ireland. He is attributed with producing the miracle of Inchydoney by St Patrick-like conversion of Taoiseach Bertie Ahern to "socialism" - and for having steered Fianna Fáil in the path of social reform following the seven years of Charlie McCreevy's maverick brand of Celtic Thatcherism.

Fr Healy's imprimatur of the social side of Brian Cowen's budget in his annual budgetary critique on behalf of the Religious consolidated the public image of him as Fianna Fáil's personal padre. When I teased him about this alliance with FF, he admitted that it was causing him some embarrassment, because he prides himself on being non-party. But he was clearly pleased with his obvious input into the direction of the Budget.

Fr Seán was also quick to point out that he was critical of the budget's reduction of the top tax rate by one per cent to 41pc as being not the fairest use of the available money. "For the same cost to the exchequer every person could have been given a tax credit of €90", he suggested.

The only people to have a net gain from this Government initiative were people earning more than €43,000 a year and couples (both employed) earning more than €86,000. The failure to provide substantial additional funding to community and voluntary organisations providing services in local areas was also disappointing as was the failure to improve the access to medical cards.

Media analysis of the budget concentrated on how Cowen, while claiming to exercise prudence, had given thousands of euro back to most sections of the electorate. Even smokers could hardly complain about the meagre 20 cent put on a packet of 20 fags, though the tobacco companies have seized their chance to add 30 cent on a packet of five Pikeur cigars.

If the Opposition parties were down-cast at the euphoria on the FF-PD benches that the budget would be their election tickets, the mood changed some-what next day with the rise in interest rates by the European Central Bank and the prospect of big health insurance increases in the near future. The gridlock on the notorious M50 after a car crash seemed to sum up a feeling that most people were still standing where they had been on Tuesday!

More complaints were to be heard from young people about the failure to cut stamp duty on house purchases, and from groups such as carers, that Cowen had not gone far enough in recognising their special needs.

Cowen's Dáil standing ovation on Wednesday turned to a reality check on Thursday's *Today with Pat Kenny Show* when he was confronted with the tears of pregnant Sligo mother, Catherine Finneran, and her sad tale of how the system was letting her down in providing for the needs of her disabled son, Keith. Other callers to the programme gave graphic descriptions of their routine road infrastructure nightmares!

These cases of ordinary daily woes made me think that despite the obvious giveaways in the Budget, it may not be the Government's automatic re-election ticket as they believe. Just as Jack Lynch suffered from his election landslide in 1977, so too there may be a psychological back-lash to this budget, because people's expectations have become so high - and the gap between the conspicuous welfare of the well-off and the struggle of the many to cope with rising prices has widened.

By Friday, the Catholic bishops had come centre-stage with their statement from Maynooth that they had reacted 'with alarm' to the proposal from the Oireachtas Joint Committee on Child Protection to lower the age of sexual consent among teenagers to 16. "This sends out the wrong signal to a young generation who, under the influence of teenage glossy magazines, peer pressure, and binge drinking, feel engaging in sexual activity as something trivial", the bishops thundered.

The Conference of Bishops also noted that the proposal to lower the age of consent sent out the wrong signal to parents, who were often confused as to how they should react in the face of their children's activities. "Parents also deserve the support of the State as well as the Church to help them in their difficult task of rearing children in an age dominated by moral indifference", they advised politicians and priests.

In this unexpected display of "crozier power" the bishops lashed out at the growing levels of teenage sex, binge drinking and general violence, which they identified as contributing to Irish society's "downward descent into moral chaos". In this maze, politicians were not upholding morality.

On hearing this indignant outburst from Maynooth, it must have instantly occurred to Bertie that his previous silence on the issue had allowed Fine Gael to present itself as the Bishops' political voice, in contrast to the 1980s when *Garret the Good* was deemed the liberal crusader and Charlie Haughey the episcopal ally.

Bertie was quick to distance himself from the Fianna Fáil-led committee graced by "the boring" Michael McDowell and Brian Lenihan, even going as far as to embrace their Lordships. Enda Kenny reminded the public that Fine Gael was for moral values and had opposed the proposal.

The stage is set for a most exciting election next year with much of the campaign centring on both purses and souls.

Bertie's Ring of Steel

(January 9, 2007)

Everyone knows that 2007 is general election year – but who would have anticipated that by the end of its opening week Bertie Ahern and Tony Blair would be scrambling to avert the DUP and Sinn Féin from parking the peace process in a cul-de-sac?

Or, more zanily, that Waterford T.D. John Deasy would be throwing the political scene into a tizzy over his egregious stunt to destabilise Enda Kenny's leadership of Fine Gael?

Little wonder, therefore, that there was a ring of steel in Taoiseach Bertie Ahern's customary New Year interview with Gerald Barry on Radio One's *This Week* programme on Sunday.

Bertie was remarkably concise in his newsbite comments that Ian Paisley needs to confirm his St Andrews commitment to power-sharing in the next few days, and that Sinn Féin should go ahead with its special Ard Comhairle later this month to ratify its acceptance of policing in the North: otherwise, the timetable for elections to Stormont and the restoration of the Executive could fall apart, a diagnosis confirmed by the British Prime Minister.

It hardly augurs well for the process that the DUP is still not engaging in direct talks with Gerry Adams and Martin McGuinness, and it makes me seriously question whether it will actually be beneficial for democracy in the North to be ruled by these two extreme political parties with their roots in the sickly sectarian polarisations of the past three decades.

Anyone in doubt about the past negative contributions of the DUP and Sinn Féin would be well advised to read Chris Ryder's riveting biography of the late Gerry Fitt, the first leader of the SDLP. *Fighting Fitt* shows how calamitous were Provisional Sinn Féin's deliberate sabotage of the civil rights movement and its unscrupulously frenzied engagement in terrorism that held back political progress for so long. In turn, the Provo's violence was exploited by Paisley when he gave his support to the Ulster Workers' strike in 1974 that undermined the power-sharing Executive led by Brian Faulkner and Fitt.

The sins of Paisley and the Provos have come back to haunt them both as they grapple with re-establishing the twin pillars of power sharing and policing that they toppled more than three decades ago.

Unlike Bertie Ahern, who said on Sunday that he will find it inexplicable if the timetable for the establishment of the Executive by March 26 falls, I believe that the ground-swell of distrust from previous polarisation of Northern society has not been adequately furrowed by the antidote medicine of communitarian reconciliation.

I tend to agree with the valedictory assessment of Robin Eames when he stepped down as Archbishop of Armagh and Primate of All Ireland that there will not be a return to violence but that society in the Republic does not adequately understand that it will take time for Unionists to get over the post-conflict trauma and get to grips with the task of creating a truly non-sectarian society based on partnership.

It also seems to me that at St Andrews in November Blair and Ahern pulled off a fast public relations mirage in claiming a done-deal was struck by Paisley with Sinn Féin. The scepticism about Sinn Féin's conversion to policing within the DUP as most vigorously articulated by Nigel Dodds is more widespread than is recognised by Sinn Féin and the two Governments in Dublin and London.

By all means, it is crucial that Sinn Féin and the DUP should grasp the future, and that we welcome the more far-seeing direction being charted by Gerry Adams and Martin McGuinness. But this search for progress should be done over a timescale that allows for trust to be built up, and not on the basis of a political formula that will marginalise the middle-ground of Mark Durkan's SDLP and Roy Empey's Ulster Unionists.

There is too much political self-interest and opportunism inherent in the present negotiating framework such as the need for Blair to have success in Northern Ireland on his list of achievements when he leaves Downing Street; for the octogenarian Paisley to end his public career as First Minister at Stormont, and, of course, an administration in the North by May would have roll-over political consequences for the Taoiseach and Sinn Féin in the Republic's summer general election.

It was therefore the first substantive political argument of 2007 – and a welcome break from the sham Punch and Judy antics of John Deasy – when Enda Kenny detected a "dramatic new shift" in Fianna Fáils Dáil position as a result of the Taoiseach's remark that while he would countenance no formal pact with Sinn Féin, he could not stop them voting for him as Taoiseach.

Despite the immediate rejoinder from Fianna Fáil minders that there was no change in policy and that FF will not do a deal with Sinn Féin, Kenny was right in pointing out how in an interview with the *Sunday Business Post* fourteen months ago, Bertie said that he would rather go into Opposition than rely on Sinn Féin.

In my view, this is a perceptible widening of Bertie's position that could give Sinn Féin a notable say in post-election balance of power. This would be a dangerous moment for the country. Here in Mayo, it has not gone unnoticed how disruptive was Sinn Féin's infiltration in the agitation against Shell over the Corrib gas plans. Sinn Féin is still far short of being a fully-committed democratic party.

The other notable development in 2007 has been the focus placed on "negative" advertising in the run-up to the general election. I have a gut feeling that the hiring by the political parties of American guru-pollsters in itself will introduce a negative factor into homespun politics that in themselves are always robust but now may become manifestly dirty.

The Fianna Fáil-PD campaigns will present themselves as positive by high-lighting the future of the country and building on the undoubted economic success of the past ten years. The Fine Gael and Labour communications strategies will be to highlight public disquiet over the lack of law and order, the in-adequacies of the health service and the congested transport system.

The rise in Bertie Ahern's public ratings after his survival from the financial dig-outs from his Drumcondra and Manchester friends when he was Minister for Finance have contributed to a widespread perception of his invincibility – and have tarred Enda Kenny and Pat Rabbitte with a rag-tag image of hand-wringing non-runners.

If that stereotype remains embedded in the voters's mind, Bertie should be home and dry for his third term with or without Michael McDowell. But the collective psyche of a nation rarely stands still, especially in an election year when so much is at stake.

Anyone who predicts that the election is over before it begins runs the risk of sounding as wifully naïve and incorrigibly infantile as John Deasy has shown himself to be for the sake of a week's publicity.

Bertie Well Ahead of Enda

(January 16, 2007)

The general election is still some five months away but already political debate in the opening weeks of 2007 has sizzled around two possible outcomes, both of which return Bertie Ahern for a third term as Taoiseach. The first is a Fianna Fáil-Labour Government; the second is a minority Fianna Fáil single party government with the Dail support of an enlarged Sinn Féin. Both of these outcomes assume that the Enda Kenny-Pat Rabbitte alternative of forming a Fine Gael-Labour after the mid-year general election probably with Trevor Sargent's Green Party does not obtain majority support.

In this first scenario, Rabbitte reneges on his pact with Kenny and leads Labour into coalition as Tanaiste; or, if Rabbitte sticks to his previous declarations of not coalescing with Bertie Ahern, he faces a revolt within Labour and loses in a leadership challenge to Brendan Howlin who becomes Tanaiste.

The second scenario which is to the fore in current media speculation is that Bertie forms either a Fianna Fáil-Sinn Féin Government or leads a minority Fianna Fáil administration dependent for its formation and continued survival on Sinn Féin's support in Dáil votes.

The striking feature in this speculation is the dominance of Fianna Fáil in spite of the Moriarty Report's damning findings against the late Charles J Haughey and other Tribunal probes against Ray Burke and the late Liam Lawlor, as well as last autumn's payments controversy involving Ahern himself.

Even though there is ample evidence of public anger at the short-comings of the health service, surging crime rates and the abysmal state of the nation's transport infrastructure, on current trends Fianna Fáil is likely to contain its inevitable losses from its 2002 return of 81 seats and to be returned with sufficient seats to enable it to form a coalition or to sustain an interim minority government.

Among the factors pointing to this outcome is the prevalence of a considerable toleration of corruption in Irish society, alongside a limited capacity to distinguish between the acceptable and unacceptable in relation to 'donations'. The great 'Bertie crisis' demonstrated this clearly.

Attacks on what in other European societies, especially Britain, would be regarded as quite unacceptable behaviour, rebounded on the attackers – Fianna Fáil's poll ratings soared, those of Labour and Fine Gael plummeted.

It would seem that Fianna Fáil's successful projection of a popularist 'can do' image provides a powerful defence against media moralising about political corruption. The party has emerged largely unscathed from tribunal findings.

As one political analyist with long experience in Belgium said to me "crass mismanagement of infra-structure projects is overlooked as motorways come on stream whilst an increasing individualisation of society, with its accompanying erosion of a sense of community and commonality, weakens the capacity (and desire) for effective protest".

This same pundit also stresses that neither Kenny nor Rabbitte have succeeded in projecting themselves as leaders of an alternative government. "While good in one-to-one encounters and at party meetings, where he demonstrates a mastery of his brief, Kenny's media performance lacks bite. He is perceived as inarticulate, hesitant and lacking in charisma, focused on rural rather than urban issues. His handling of the 'Bertie crisis' was weak and indecisive. Deasy's attack on his leadership, whilst ill judged, reflected a growing unease amongst back-benchers. In short, he has failed to demonstrate leadership qualities to a public which is increasingly detached from politics".

This pundit is equally severe on Rabbitte's performance. "Whilst better in terms of media presentation than Kenny, Rabbitte equally lacks focus. Responses to crises are expressed in generalities; comments are frequently uninformed, suggesting a lack of briefing whilst challenges are petulantly dismissed, reflecting an insensitivity to the broader political culture within which he must operate. Like his putative partner, Kenny, his handling of *Bertiegate* was lack-lustre and ineffective. Over-centralisation of policy and an excessive reliance on a narrow circle of recently recruited advisers have resulted in his being out of touch with both his parliamentary colleagues and the wider party membership. Like Kenny, Rabbitte's grip on the leadership is tenuous."

The major opposition parties have failed to put across alternatives to the policies presently being pursued by government. The result leaves voters feeling that the devil they know is better than that they don't know. Fine Gael will almost certainly improve its Dáil representation in the next election, from its low base of 31 in the 2002 election, but will be hard put to get beyond the low 40s in the 166-member Dáil. Its gains will likely be at the expense of Labour and the PDs.

Labour, which won 21 seats in 2002, is challenged on the left by Sinn Féin and on the right by the Greens and their partners, Fine Gael. A jump to the high mid-20s will be hard to achieve.

The Progressive Democrats, with six members, face an outgoing tide on account of Tanaiste Michael McDowell's abandonment of principle in saving Bertie's leadership, and they deserve to pay a heavy price for the failure of their ideologically-driven Thatcherite policies in regard to transport, health, Eircom, Aer Lingus and crime. It is unlikely that they will be a significant force in the next Dáil.

While Sinn Féin, currently with five Dáil deputies, aim to double their strength to 10 or 12 seats, they are dependent on voters in deprived areas, and may find it difficult to secure transfers from the mainstream parties. They may end up with a small gain of two to three seats.

On this reading of trends, therefore, the likely outcome of the next election is the return of a weakened Fianna Fáil, dependent (overtly or covertly) on Labour or Sinn Féin.

It was therefore interesting to note that Rabbitte, though reaffirming his bond with Fine Gael, has moved to open the door on a possible post-election deal with Bertie. There is substantial grass-roots support for such an outcome in Labour which would be troubled by the spectacle of Bertie playing footsie with Sinn Féin.

It was also telling that Bertie has issued a further statement saying that he would not accept Sinn Féin's support, a disclaimer which two out of three voters in a week-end newspaper poll did not believe! I find it difficult to see the pragmatic godfathers of Fianna Fáil and Sinn Féin not coming to a power sharing agreement, if necessary.

However, the first opinion poll of 2007 – in the *Sunday Tribune* – gives Kenny and Rabbitte some hope of getting back into the electoral ring. The significant finding is a three point slippage by Fianna Fáil to 39pc share of the national vote, in spite of the boost that would normally have been expected from Brian Cowen's December Budget.

Contrary to my earlier dismissal of the PDs, they rose one point, giving the FF-PD Government a lead of 44pc as against 39pc for the putative alternative of Fine Gael (at 22pc, one up), Labour (12, up two) and the Greens (5pc, down one).

On the key question of who would make the better Taoiseach, Bertie at 57pc towers above Enda on 25pc. Enda needs to put on his mountain boots if he is to become the country's first Mayo-born Taoiseach. He has five turbulent months to catch-up on the elusive Bertie.

What Kind of 'New Ireland'?

(January 30, 2007)

A public debate has begun on the nature of Irish identity involving three leaders of political parties, Enda Kenny, Michael McDowell and Gerry Adams.

Describing as truly historic Sunday's decision by the extraordinary Sinn Féin Árd Fheis to endorse the Police Service of Northern Ireland, Adams said: "This is one of the most important debates in the history of republicanism and of this country."

While Ian Paisley and the DUP have still to endorse the significance of the Sinn Féin move into the mainstream of politics by giving their imprimatur to power-sharing in the North, Adams went on to make some acute observations about the kind of Ireland he aspires to. His remarks are worth quoting.

"Irish republicanism is about people. It's about the future; it's about a new egalitarian society; it's about the new Irish and the indigenous Irish; it's about the Proclamation of 1916 becoming a reality. So it's bigger than us; it's bigger than Sinn Féin; it's in the common good."

The language of inclusivity used here is clearly designed to appeal to idealistic young people and newcomers to this island who want to change society for the better.

The changing nature of Irish society was approached from a different angle by Enda Kenny at a Fine Gael think-in in Clontarf Castle last Tuesday when he addressed the impact of immigration mainly from a law and order perspective.

But the phrase in his speech which caught media attention was his reference to the Irish as being "Celtic and Christian". This definition of Irishness provoked strong criticism led principally by Tanaiste and Minister for Justice, Michael McDowell.

"Does inward migration constitute a threat to some form of "Christian-Celtic Ireland?" McDowell asked in the course of an address on immigration which he delivered on Saturday to the Law Society.

The reason advanced by McDowell for standing against the Fine Gael leader's assertion that Ireland is a "Celtic and Christian people" was based on the republican tradition in Irish politics, dating back to the United Irishmen of the late eighteenth century, which is embodied in the tricolour's accommodation of diversity and identity.

In the republican order, no single identity and tradition is regarded as authentic or core-Irish to the exclusion of other identities and traditions, the PD leader asserted. Descendants of the Danes, the Normans, the old English, the Planters and the Anglo-Irish are as much part of authentic Ireland today as those who descended from the Gaelic, Celtic or pre-Celtic inhabitants of this island.

In a sustained attack on Kenny's comments, McDowell argued that it was unrealistic to base the national aspiration to unity on the notion that the Irish nation is to be regarded as a Celtic people. "The truth is more complex than that and the challenge of reconciling Orange and Green in Northern Ireland and throughout the island would be well nigh insuperable if we were to lapse into a mistaken and inaccurate view of ourselves which excluded from the concept of Irishness those who fall outside a mythical descent from the Celts or pre-Celts."

In this exchange Kenny is at a disadvantage, because his use of the phrase of "Celtic and Christian" was too narrowly presented and ill-judged. It boxes him into a cultural corner that was described by the doyen of Irish historians, Professor John A Murphy, as fatuous. The Mayoman's remarks also allowed McDowell to have another pot-shot at the Fine Gael vote which he is trying to attract to the PDs, a tactic which appears to be having some effect, according to the latest *Sunday Business Post* tracking-poll which gives the Fianna Fáil-PD coalition its biggest lead since this regular survey began a year ago.

In the contrasting speeches McDowell is challenging Sinn Féin's claim to be the custodian of republicanism, while also casting Kenny as a Catholic tradition-alist from the West. What is common to the speeches of Adams, Kenny and McDowell is their pitching of ideas about the fast-changing face of Irish society ahead of elections on both sides of the border, with the Sinn Féin leader having his eyes on Stormont as well as Leinster House.

The securing by Adams and Martin McGuinness of Sinn Féin's overwhelming decision on policing was an impressive display of political consultation, and was doubly significant coming days after the damning report of the North's Ombuds-man, Nuala O'Loan, on collusion between the old Royal Ulster Constabulary in ruthless paramilitary Loyalist informers.

Both Kenny and McDowell were making contributions to the immigration issue – one in ten people resident in Ireland today are not Irish-born – that looks like becoming a big issue in the summer general election in the Republic. While accepting the positive contribution of immigrants, Kenny's main thrust was to accuse the Minister for Justice of mismanaging immigration, and he pointed to its disproportionate impact on crime, road accidents and overcrowding in schools.

His concern was to integrate immigrants into Irish society and to deport those convicted of serious crime.

In contrast, McDowell's speech centred on his proposal in a Bill which he is to bring before the Dáil in coming weeks about what constitutes Irish citizenship. He plans to require applications for citizenship to pass a test requiring them to have knowledge of Ireland and to have some proficiency in the English language.

More contentiously, the McDowell proposal envisages establishing a network of detention centres for asylum speakers suspected of making false claims about being persecuted in their native countries. This appears to be based on the system operating in Britain.

While "the new Irish" may be a feature of the Republic's election campaign, the issue in the North's assembly elections in March will be the too familiar one of the Orange and the Green. Already the DUP's reaction to the Sinn Féin endorsement of policing is to demand instant "delivery" in day to day relations between police and republican communities, while the Árd Fheis specifically empowered its Árd Comhairle to implement the policing resolution when it is satisfied about arrangements for power-sharing as well as a transfer of policing and justice powers to a new Executive.

If an "historic" event has the irritating habit of being a long-drawn out process, some things never change in the Republic's political system. Fianna Fáil was getting on with its 'can-do' image with Finance Minister Brian Cowen's €184 billion National Development Plan 2007-2013 which was dismissed as recycled announcements and a long election leaflet.

If, too, Fianna Fáil is concentrating on economics rather than cultural philosophy, the difficulties of junior Labour Affairs minister Tony Killeen over his Clare constituency office's letters seeking the early release of a brutal killer have drawn attention to the continued role of such representations in the political system – and of yet another caught-out politician refusing to resign. The eloquence of the victim's mother, Nora Lynch, in calling for an end to such representations by TDs, has had an enormous impact on the public, and her decision to meet the hapless and contrite Killeen – and forgive him – offers a model which Ian Paisley might follow in regard to Sinn Féin.

Meanwhile, in the Republic we need to open real dialogue with immigrants about the changing way of life here, without letting it become a source of contention for political advantage in the general election.

In this context, Gerry Adams' reference to the common good could offer the spirit in which this national debate should be conducted.

Green 'Bertie-makers'

(February 6, 2007)

One opinion poll appears to have changed dramatically the political landscape in the run-up to this summer's general election. The four point jump to eight pc in support for the Greens recorded in the *tns mrbi* survey for *The Irish Times* has put the spotlight overnight on the thin frame of Trevor Sargent as potential Taoiseach-maker and prospective member of a new rainbow coalition with Fine Gael and Labour.

If this poll were to be replicated in June, Sargent, who has said he would not lead the Greens into government with Fianna Fáil on account of its "culture of bad planning, corruption and bad standards", though he would be open to negotiate a deal with "all parties."

While Sargent will fight the election on an independent Greens' platform, he hopes to double his party's existing six seats. If he achieves this, he could find himself in the position of king-maker by brokering a government with Enda Kenny and Pat Rabbitte.

This poll came as a shock to Bertie as it showed a slump in the PDs to an almost invisible one per cent, a development that has prompted commentators to talk about their demise after ten successive years in power with Fianna Fáil.

The possibility of a PD meltdown has resulted in reports that Mary Harney may decide to retire before the general election rather than face the risk of losing her Dáil seat. Certainly, last week was another woeful week for the Health Minister who first knew about Fermanagh businessman Seán Quinn's take-over of BUPA Ireland from a press release.

Quinn Direct's purchase used a legal loophole that Harney ignored some months ago which will enable it to claim the status of a new entrant to the Irish health insurance market and avoid it making risk equalisation subsidy payments to the VHI. Harney's troubles will worsen as a result of the determination of Vivas to switch to a new underwriter to avoid payments this October to the VHI. Harney will now find it virtually impossible to defend the current working of the community support rating system.

The opinion poll also indicated that a majority of those polled still expect a FF-Labour coalition to emerge in a hung Dáil, a finding that confirms the relevance of the media debate during January that centred on whether Pat Rabbitte would reverse his decision not to enter government with Fianna Fáil.

Significantly, however, the bulk of these voters do not want Rabbitte to give Bertie a third term as Taoiseach, with 53pc of Labour supporters compared to 36pc wanting their leader to form a government with Enda Kenny.

The broad picture thrown up by the poll was that of three possible coalitions: 32pc for the return of FF-PDs under Ahern and Tanaiste Michael McDowell; 29pc for the FG-Labour-Greens line-up of Kenny, Rabbitte and Sargent, and 13pc for Ahern and Rabbitte forming a FF-Labour administration.

The fourth possibility – either a FF-Sinn Féin Government or a minority Fianna Fáil Government dependent on the support of Sinn Féin – continues to cause concern among voters, with 44pc opposed to this but 46pc convinced that Bertie would talk to Sinn Féin if this became necessary for him to stay in power.

With Sinn Féin support rising to 11pc in this poll – and with the prospect of entering power in Stormont next month after the Northern elections on March 7 – it could still hold the balance of power in the Republic.

While we will be subjected to poll fatigue in the coming months, what gave this poll added zip was its coincidence with the publication in Paris of the authoritative verdict of world scientists that unless greenhouse gas emissions into the atmosphere are cut drastically, devastating climate change will occur within decades. If emissions continue to rise, average temperatures are likely to rise by 4pc but could soar as disastrously high as 6.4pc.

Most alarming of all was the confirmation by the United Nations Intergovernmental Panel on Climate Change that there is already "unequivocal" evidence that global warming has already begun. This finding will draw attention to the self-congratulatory tone of Environment Minister Dick Roche's recently published *Ireland's Progress towards Environmental Sustainability* and to a more considered look at Green policies.

One of the great vexations of modern living in Dublin is traffic congestion, a phenomenon also experienced in West of Ireland towns such as Ballina. Even in the 'village' of Terenure on Dublin's southside where I live, it is increasingly difficult to move or find car parking space largely as a result of SUV-driving middle class women running their children to and from school. This kind of jeep is not needed in urban centres and merely adds to emissions as well as posing dangers to other drivers. I would ban them!

In regard to assessing Green policies, I would refer readers to two books which have landed on my desk. The first is *A Journey to Change – 25 Years of the Green*

Party in Irish Politics, edited by Dan Boyle, their Cork T.D. It fills in our gaps in the party's history and it set out its vision of the future.

The second book is *Climate Change: the challenge to all of us*, by the Columban priest, Seán McDonagh. He devotes much of the book to explaining exactly what global warming is, and is an invaluable introduction to the subject that now is the number one global issue.

Our vulnerability to nature has also been highlighted again this week-end with the discovery of an avian flu outbreak in Britain after 160,000 turkeys were gassed on a commercial factory in Suffolk. Agriculture Minister Mary Coughlan has been quick off the mark to assure the public that her department's safety measures are "more than adequate", a claim disputed by Labour's agriculture spokesperson Dr Mary Upton who has expressed her concern that these measures do not include keeping Irish poultry indoors, and that it is only a matter of time until the deadly disease reaches Ireland.

All of this is a vastly changed environment from exactly ten years ago when Ireland was at the height of its 'moral civil war' during the bitterly divisive divorce referendum that, like the battle of Waterloo between Wellington and Napoleon, was "a damned close" battle – divorce was introduced by the narrowest of margins, 50.3pc against 49.7pc.

A measure of social change over the past decade is the finding that three out of four poll respondents (mainly women) say they would vote today for divorce. Contrary to the Catholic Right which predicted that divorce would be a Frankenstein monster destroying marriage, the poll confirms that most people believe that the institution of marriage has not been undermined.

These findings confirm my view that the recently established Iona Institute, a think-tank whose leading lights include such conservative writers David Quinn, Breda O'Brien and Fr Vincent Twomey who aim to promote Catholic social teaching on marriage and the family, is harking back to a Catholic Ireland that has gone for ever. What we need is an institute on environmental issues that can help preserve our planet, rather than an organisation harking back to saving souls.

Pulling Tax Rabbit out of Hat

(February 13, 2007)

Fianna Fáil has rushed to damn Pat Rabbitte's commitment to cut the standard tax rate from 20 to 18 pc within two years of Fine Gael and Labour getting into government as auction politics.

It was amusing to watch the speed with which Finance and Enterprise ministers Brian Cowen and Mícheál Martin came off their blocks to criticise Labour's tax cutting proposal promises to have strong appeal to low and middle income earners.

In short, as many commentators have noted, this unexpected move, announced by Rabbitte towards the end of his televised address on Saturday evening at the Labour Party conference in Dublin's Helix centre, had put Fianna Fáil on the back foot.

The charge of Labour indulging in auction politics by Cowen and Martin is somewhat amusing, given Fianna Fáil's past mastery of political auctioneering which was brought to a fine art by Jack Lynch thirty years ago when he swept into power with a massive majority after promising to abolish local rates.

Nor should it be forgotten that in his give-away Budget in December when Cowen reduced the top rate of tax by one per cent to 41pc, he pledged that a re-elected FF-PD Government would bring that down to 40pc.

While sharing the general public concern that auction politics – the seduction of voters by plying them with *goodies* - can lead to lavish spending promises that cause retrenchments further down the line, I welcome Rabbitte's proposal as a morally legitimate and crafty political initiative grounded in social equity. In my view, Rabbitte has highlighted a weakness in the FF-PD coalition that questions Bertie's claim to be a socialist, and casts the Taoiseach and Tanaiste Michael McDowell as pursuing economic policies that have favoured the rich rather than those less well-off.

My chief witness to back up this claim is Fr Seán Healy, the head of the Justice Commission of the Conference of Religious, who famously preached anti-poverty to the Fianna Fáil parliamentary party at its Inchydoney think-in. It was the same Fr Healy who applauded Cowen's December Budget as "a historic breakthrough" for basic social welfare recipients, but he went on to criticise the cut in the higher rate as not being the fairest use of the available public money.

Fr Healy reminded his wayward FF disciples that the only people to secure a net gain from this FF-PD so called give-away were reasonably well-off individuals earning more than €43,000 a year and couples who were both employed with joint earnings of over €86,000. The social apostle also pointed out that for the same cost to the exchequer every person could have been given a tax credit of €90. This would have been a much fairer use of the allocated exchequer money.

Labour's proposal, which is estimated to cost the exchequer just over one billion euro a year has been described by economist Moore McDowell as a political time-bomb. It has been welcomed by Fine Gael's Fergus O'Dowd as likely to help low and middle income families to cope with cost rises, while Green leader Trevor Sargent has given it his endorsement as being socially equitable.

Rabbitte's tax cut proposal has to be assessed in conjunction with his five personal commitments of one year free pre-school education for all children, more Gardai on the beat in communities, abolition of the means test for carers, more beds in clean hospitals, and Eamon Gilmore's seductive €2.5bn fund to enable young people to begin to buy a home.

But the biggest applause for Rabbitte's speech was not for these proposals but for his scathing attack on Health Minister Mary Harney whom he accused of failing to understand that "health is a community service, not a market commodity." The Mayo-born party leader also served notice that he would scrap Harney's plan to build "super private" clinics which threaten "to drive up insurance bills, damage public hospitals and create a two tier health system."

The auction is on!

For Labour's rank and file, long accustomed to undisciplined party conferences, the Helix was an orderly affair. There were no rows that marked the leadership days of the late Michael O'Leary and Dick Spring. But it paid the dividend of an innovative tax and social programme that carves out a distinctive niche for Labour.

Talking to Labour activists attending the conference I was struck by the remark of several of them that the biggest issue they were finding on the door-steps was the immigration issue, and there was praise for the recent call for a rational debate on this by Fine Gael leader Enda Kenny.

In this context, it was interesting to hear Dick Spring – who was in buoyant form on the Marian Finucane programme ahead of the Irish rugby team's tragic defeat by France at Croke Park on Sunday – lending his support to a national debate on immigration. Politicians, he said, were afraid to grapple with the issue for fear of being associated with "a taboo subject", and that Kenny's contribution had been poo-poohed by the intellectuals and others.

The most striking fact presented by Spring was that on current levels of immigration within four years one in five of the population in Ireland will be non-native Irish. The impact on schools is already severe on account of the paucity of teachers to teach children who have no English. The integration of immigrants, especially in rural Ireland, is fast emerging as a major social question.

On the immigration issue, Rabbitte noted that the right balance will have to be struck between diversity and integration, but he appeared to be somewhat nervous that the issue could be distorted in the run-up to the general election.

In the meantime, the Progressive Democrats have continued to discredit themselves as the party of the rich with the leak of Michael McDowell's begging letter to so called *rich fat cats* urging them to make €5,000 donations which would be just below the State disclosure levels. Ironically, McDowell's defends this blatant fiscal casuistry!

Weeks before Taoiseach Bertie Ahern dissolves the Dáil and goes to the country, the other political parties are holding their rallies over the next five weeks. The Labour conference has put shape on the election campaign.

Political Parties' Auction Race

(February 20, 2007)

When *God Save the Queen* is played at Croke Park, the shrine of the GAA, for the first time ever on Saturday when Ireland play England in the rugby championship, I will be turning the television sound down to silence for its duration.

This is my usual wont. I am a republican democrat. As a dual identity person – Scottish and Irish – I love to bellow out *Flower of Scotland* and *The Soldier's Song*, though I have the voice of a frog when it comes to singing. While these two national anthems stir up my patriotic pride, *God Save the Queen* arouses deep primordial antagonism in me.

I believe that the continued existence of monarchy is an anachronism in today's world. It is repugnant to the dignity of men and women living in Britain and Northern Ireland that they are classified as subjects of the Queen rather than as democratic citizens.

While I have many English friends, I find the English nation as a whole a most chauvinistic race whose sense of superiority over others is enshrined in its adherence to the ideology of royalty and the class structure which in themselves replicate the era of imperialism when *Britannia* ruled the world.

This misplaced sense of superiority among the English finds its most irritating expression on the sports fields, be it soccer, cricket or rugby. Its fans export their crude manifestations of English patriotism when travelling abroad, and the match reports of its sports commentators reflect this Great England mentality in their biased slants.

I must confess, too, that in my younger days when I attended Scotland versus England soccer matches at Glasgow's Hampden Park, I numbered myself among the section of the Scottish crowd who booed during the playing of *God Save the Queen*, and at Celtic-Rangers matches at Parkhead or Ibrox was even more vociferous in drowning out the Rangers' loyalist chants.

Thankfully, the Welsh and the Scots, have their own anthems. They constitute two independent nations distinct from the English, though they are currently part of the United Kingdom with England and Northern Ireland. I hope to see the day in the not too distant future that Scotland under the Scottish National Party's leadership of Alex Salmond breaks-away from England some three hundred years after the establishment of the Union. I would also like to see the Unionists in Northern Ireland joining a federal Ireland voluntarily as in being in their best interests rather than clinging on to their deluded attachment to the English Crown.

It seems to me that the English should come up with a new anthem more in keeping with the times rather than remaining servile to a Queen whose royal House of Windsor are hardly role models for today.

Yet, come Saturday, I hope that the *Star's* warning of "Riot threat to Croker" does not transpire when the band strikes up *God Save the Queen*. Dublin in not Glasgow, and any disturbance on Saturday would rebound badly in the media around the globe on Ireland's image as a confident democracy at the heart of Europe.

As the former MEP, Mary Banotti recommended, the Irish should have strong stomachs and a limp smile on their faces while the English anthem is played. Or, if you are watching the match at home, follow my advice by turning the sound off!

Bertie Ahern's attendance at Croke Park should come as a welcome relief for the Taoiseach from the escalating auction politics that has marked the pre-election conferences over the past two weeks held by the Labour Party and the Progressive Democrats.

What must enrage Bertie is that Michael McDowell made no mention of his 10 year Government partnership with Fianna Fáil in his address at the PDs' Wexford conference, which was devoted to reclaiming the Progressive Democrats' credentials as the tax-cutting party par excellence. Last week Tanaiste McDowell did the Taoiseach no favours when he appeared to favour shutting-down the Mahon Tribunal into political corruption which he claimed will cost the taxpayer €1bn, a figure openly contradicted by Judge Mahon who quoted a sum of €300m.

McDowell pulled back from threatening a closure of the Tribunal after Bertie had said he had not intention of ending its proceedings. The impression had been sown by McDowell that the Taoiseach was afraid of the Tribunal's next phase of investigation into claims that he received money from Cork builder, Owen O'Callaghan. The word from Fianna Fáil is that the Taoiseach is determined to clear his good name from this and other claims.

There are also signs within the Fianna Fáil parliamentary party that the Taoiseach should have gone to the country earlier and that he is now boxed in by the rush to auction politics started unexpectedly by Labour's Pat Rabbitte.

McDowell's week-end promises to cut stamp duty for first time home buyers and slash income tax was a move that catapulted him into the fast-lane in the pre-election auction politics race. In addition to raising the contributory old age pension to €300 by the year 2012, McDowell promised to introduce an SSIA-style scheme for pensions that will give lower and middle income earners €1 for every €2 saved.

On income tax, the PD leader will not only reduce the higher rate of tax from 41 to 38 pc, and the lower rate from 20pc to 18pc over the five year life-time of the next government, he will adjust tax bands so that a couple earning at least €100,000 will pay the revenue commissioners only at the standard rate of tax.

While McDowell claims that his proposals have been fully costed, its scale has been cited in the media as ranging as high as €7bn. This dwarfs the Labour Party's plan to give low and middle income earners a €650 saving by reducing the lower rate of tax to 18pc within two years of a Rainbow Government taking office.

With economists saying that the exchequer can afford such cuts and incentives, McDowell and Rabbitte have challenged Fianna Fáil and Fine Gael to present their stalls. Until now, Bertie and his equally irate Minister for Finance, Brian Cowen, have been decrying political auctioneering and are loudly protesting that the general election has got off to a false start.

All of this makes Cowen's historically high give-away Budget of last December look like a cautious concession to the people from a begrudging miser of the public purse.

So gung ho was McDowell on leaving Wexford that he virtually invited Enda Kenny to be his travelling companion when he reminded the Mayoman that Fine Gael was ideologically compatible with the Progressive Democrats.

Even more brazenly, McDowell, while still claiming that the PDs are ideologically compatible with Fianna Fáil, has departed from their plans to move towards a more socially just society. Since Charlie McCreevy's departure to Brussels, the only tax cut which the PDs achieved was the December Budget's reduction of the higher rate from 42 to 41pc.

The next ninety days inside Government Buildings promise to be tense between Bertie, the self proclaimed socialist, and tax-cutting McDowell, the self-style crusader of conviction politics.

If Bertie and FF want to get into the auction race, they will need to start playing catch up.

Sargent Needs Rub
of the Green

(February 27, 2007)

After the ecstasy, came the agony. That was how I felt on Saturday evening after Ireland's 43-13 rugby victory over England at Croke Park when Trevor Sargent took over a half hour of prime television time to deliver his presidential speech at the Green Party's pre-election conference in Galway.

Never before had so many sports commentators and spectators become carried away with emotional flights of nationalist rhetoric as they redefined the nature of Irish identity with a vigour that would surely have coaxed James Joyce from exile had he still been still alive to witness this new dawn in Croker.

It was little wonder that Tom McGurk and his team of commentators looked completely exhausted after watching not just the Ireland-England game but also Italy's surprise humiliation of Scotland at Murrayfield in Edinburgh and France's outflanking of a spirited Welsh squad in Paris.

As the rest of the nation continued with the celebrations, duty required me to switch over to politics to watch Trevor Sargent's bid to book a place for his Green Party on the next government line-up.

Admittedly, Trevor would need to have had the charisma and speaking charm of Bill Clinton to capitalise on this half hour slot of free public broadcasting. He was unlucky that after twenty-five years in the political wilderness, the Greens had clashed with the Ireland v England match in the timing of their dash to the big time.

Perhaps it was just as well that most of the nation's potential converts to the Green cause did not see Trevor's rank-amateur performance. Lacking in experience of delivering a live television script, he came across poorly and spoke too quickly. He was no Bill Clinton.

Paradoxically, therefore, Sargent enjoyed his most successful conference since he became leader almost six years ago of the Green Party. Outbidding both Labour and the Progressive Democrats in the auction stakes, Trevor's long list promised indexation of tax bands, pension rises. Luas lines for Cork and Galway, medical cards for children under six, smart electricity meters for every house and an end to corporate donations to politicians.

But amazingly, in spite of the real surge of anticipation among delegates that the Greens are "ready for Government", Sargent let himself down and allowed himself to be upstaged by his own party chairman and fellow Dáil deputy, John Gormley.

While Sargent delivered a mediocre presidential address, Gormley had the delegates excitedly on their feet ready for electoral battle when he gave his pep-talk just before lunch-time.

It was Gormley, not Sargent, who sounded like a leader who is itching to get into power. Letting it be known that he was from a Fianna Fáil background, and did not have a visceral hatred of FF – Gormley indicated that he would even do a deal with Bertie Ahern if the numbers do not stack up with the Greens' first preference of a Rainbow Coalition with Fine Gael and Labour.

It was Gormley, not Sargent, who produced the best one-liners which convinced the rank and file he was a heavy-weight who could ridicule not only *Planet Bertie* but mix it on equal terms with hard-hitters like Michael McDowell and Pat Rabbitte.

According to Gormley, McDowell has gone native with Fianna Fáil and has become the Tammy Wynette of Irish politics. It was courtesy of McDowell's support that the real government of Ireland was made up of corporate 'gods' in the Fianna Fáil tent at Ballybrit during the Galway races.

Yet it was Sargent, not Gormley, who provided the rope with which his party may yet hang him, politically speaking, if he does not achieve his objective of putting both Fianna Fáil and the PDs out of office in the general election.

Although he has been in national politics for 15 years and topped the poll in his North Dublin constituency, Sargent's rise in popularity has owed much to the public perception of him as a modern day Peter Pan. With his straight-back-hair and youthful looks he comes across, at 46, as a mix of an honourable boy scout and a perpetual choir boy in a Dáil jungle of place-seekers and self-promoters.

But in the recent past Sargent gave hostages to fortune when he said that he would not lead the Greens into Government with Fianna Fáil, though he would serve as a minister in a Fianna Fáil-Greens administration. On one occasion, he ruled out ever sitting around the same cabinet table with Dick Roche, Martin Cullen and Frank Fahey.

In other words, he adopted a lofty position similar to that taken by Pat Rabbitte's Labour Party. Like Rabbitte last month when Bertie was eyeing him up as a prospective partner, this position came back to haunt Sargent when commentators questioned him as to what he would do in the event of a hung Dáil in which the Greens were wooed by Bertie.

Ill at ease with such advances, Trevor's responses were unsatisfactory and inconsistent. One minute, he was rejecting Bertie as a suitor and offering his resignation as leader of the Greens. The next minute, he was sitting uncomfortably inside the cabinet with Bertie as a Green Minister.

In between, he was almost hysterical with nervous laughter when broadcaster John Bowman asked if he would take "the honourable position" and resign as party leader if he failed in his mandate to put Ahern and McDowell out of government.

Hoisted on this petard of his own making, Sargent did not show the kind of swift disentanglement from a danger-zone with which John Gormley got off such hypothetical questions.

Unfortunately for Sargent, this distracted from his presentation of Green policies at a time when public awareness of global warming has given them unprecedented attention, a special niche backed up by a week-end poll in the *Sunday Business Post* showing the Greens as the most likely holders of the balance of power after the May election.

The overall impression conveyed by Sargent's verbal contortions – and his dullish eagerness to talk traditional *green-speak* - was that he would not be a good negotiator in cabinet making with either the FF fixers or the FG-Labour aspirants. More skilful in this power game than Sargent will be Gormley, supported by the equally worldly-wise Eamon Ryan and Dan Boyle.

Sargent's best line at the week-end conference was his call for "action politics, not auctions", a rule he instantly broke in the small print of his extended list of promises.

With six T.D.s in the current Dáil, the Greens hope to return to Leinster House with at least nine or ten. This would put them in the ideal position to do a deal with either Bertie or the Enda Kenny-Pat Rabbitte duo.

If, however, in the long election campaign ahead Sargent does not prove himself to be a man of action, he could find his leadership up for auction during the tense weeks of cabinet horse-trading after the votes are counted and the seats filled.

Bertie Embraces DUP
and Sinn Féin

(March 6, 2007)

T he moment Ian Paisley indicated that his Democratic Unionist Party covets the Finance portfolio in a restored Stormont Executive was the signal that today's Stormont Assembly elections are about its sharing the spoils of office with Sinn Féin.

This was a clear signal from the turbulent parson-politician, known as *Dr No* on account of his four decades of iconoclastic opposition to power-sharing with the nationalist community in the North that a deal with Sinn Féin is on.

When the votes are counted, the focus for the first time since the collapse of the Brian Faulkner-Gerry Fitt Sunningdale inter-party government thirty years ago, will not be so much on the ancient tribal division, as on spreading cross-community the financial dividend from the peace process.

Undoubtedly, there will be brinkmanship right up to the March 26 deadline set by Tony Blair and Bertie Ahern for the historic accommodation that will install a ten-member Executive in which Paisley will be First Minister and Martin McGuinness Deputy First Minister.

As the Taoiseach reminded the British-Irish Parliamentary Body on Monday, London and Dublin will take their last offer of power-sharing off the table if the *Demon Doctor* – Faulkner's phrase – still rants about *No Surrender* to the Shinners. The Unionist community's worse nightmare of joint sovereignty of the North by the British and Irish Governments would come into force *sine die*.

Paisley, at 80, has his last chance not only to end his days as the Unionist Moses who led his followers out of forty years in the political desert into the land of shared economic prosperity.

As always, Paisley will exact a hard bargain: this time not on traditional constitutional grounds of protecting the Union – already copper-fastened by the Good Friday and St Andrews Agreements – but on Mammon in the form of Sterling from the British Treasury and Euros from Dublin.

The timing could not be better for Paisley to pull off this financial coup d'etat. With Blair on borrowed time in Downing Street, he desperately needs a settlement in Northern Ireland as his legacy. Chancellor Gordon Brown, equally desperate to move into No 10, will be more than happy to sign the cheque.

With the general election fast-approaching in the Republic, Bertie too wants to go to the hustings with a Northern solution on his *curriculum vitae*, even though this may boost Sinn Féin south of the Border.

But the money, measured in billions of hard cash, will not be handed-over to Ulster's quarrelsome political chieftains without strict conditions being attached to the loot. It will be tied to a definite promise that the North's politicians abandon their mock politics of the Battle of the Boyne and the 1916 Easter Rising, and engage in the delivery politics of the twenty-first century.

Money talks: it is not denominated in either Catholic or Protestant currency. The prudent spending of what will be the North's equivalent of the Marshall Recovery Plan for post-World War Two Europe will be its last chance salon to transform its subsidy sponged-economy into a transformed Ulster Tiger through more inward investment, more North-South trade and more integration in the European Union.

Over the next three weeks, Paisley and his prospective Finance Minister, Peter Robinson, will be revered as statesmen at Westminster and be welcomed in the offices of Blair and Brown as they tie up the biggest economic deal ever negotiated by a Northern administration-in-waiting.

In such a scenario, Gerry Adams and Martin McGuinness will not have the luxury to stand idly-by in Belfast and Mid-Ulster, allowing Paisley's team run off with the credit for securing the cash deal. Watch out, for Adams and McGuinness abandoning their abstentionist policies at Westminster.

Once the marriage of economic and political convenience is consummated by Paisley and McGuinnes at the Stormont nuptials, the most intriguing question for Irish democracy will switch to what future role will be mapped out for Adams, when Sinn Féin turns its attention to achieving its big electoral breakthrough in the Republic.

It is a question which was only partially – and unconvincingly – answered by the Sinn Féin President at his party's Árd Fheis in Dublin last week-end.

Adams left himself wriggle room to run for a Dáil seat in the general election when he said he would love to be a T.D. but did not think this was possible at present. The argument put forward by Adams for not committing himself to Oireachtas politics was that he is the only party leader driving a process from conflict to peace, and this responsibility involves looking after his constituents in West Belfast.

This argument was valid until now but the point is fast approaching when voters, north and south, deserve to know exactly when Adams plans to make himself accountable to the democratic political system.

If Adams is not inside the next Dáil, his influence as a non-elected political leader in the Republic and the North will limit Sinn Féin's capacity to exploit its parliamentary options. He will be an outsider in the Republic with no mandate to meddle in Dáil affairs, and in the North, unlike McGuinness, he will not be Paisley's colleague.

Even with his remarkable communication skills, Adams cannot continue to operate indefinitely as a freelance organiser of a party spanning the jurisdictions of Westminster, Stormont and Leinster House – while not serving as a public representative in any of the three.

By the end of March, Adams, the supreme strategist and public figurehead of the only All Ireland political party, expects to see McGuinness installed in a restored power-sharing Stormont Executive as Deputy First Minister under the leadership of the DUP's Ian Paisley. The Derryman exuded optimism that Paisley will do the deal with Sinn Féin, a move which he described as "one of the biggest political stories in the last 100 years".

By July, south of the border, the Sinn Féin President also has expectations that his party could hold the balance of power in the next Dáil and be implementing a prospective programme of government, possibly as the junior partner with Fianna Fáil in Bertie Ahern's third administration.

While the Shinners stand to benefit from a bounce in the polls in the Republic arising from going into power with Paisley, a doubling of their Dáil seats to 10 may not be enough for them to form, or support indirectly the next Government.

However, even on the most pessimistic scenario, a bigger Sinn Féin parliamentary party will be in a position to exercise considerable influence from the Opposition benches in Leinster House.

Logic should lead Adams to the conclusion that the time is nigh for him to present himself to voters in the Republic by standing for election in one of the Dáil's 43 constituencies. By contesting a Dáil seat, Adams would invest his strong personal standing in demonstrating to voters that Sinn Féin is more than "a slightly constitutional party".

Adams' famed negotiation skills would soften its association with criminality, its anti-establishment appeal and its lack of realistic economic policies, all of which cast it increasingly as a party of protest rather than a catch-all party.

Most pressingly, the party's wobbling around the seven to eight pc share of the vote in opinion polls indicates that its existing Dáil members led by the veteran Caoimhghin Ó Caoláin are not so well-known and who not seen by voters as ministerial material. Nor are its new candidates such as Mary Lou McDonald lighting the heather on fire.

These question marks over Sinn Féin's progress provide compelling reasons for Adams to throw his cap into the Oireachtas ring and create a new momentum. Yet his caution still makes him shy away from doing so. But his radio remarks smacked of an invitation to his supporters to twist his arm and urge him to run for the Dáil along with its five sitting T.D.s, its prospective Dáil candidates and its 54 councillors.

The stark political reality is that none of the Sinn Féin election class of 2007 has the experience and ability of Adams to give credible national leadership in the general election campaign. An enlarged Sinn Féin led by Gerry Adams T.D. after the election would be a more formidable force to be reckoned with.

If Adams is not inside the next Dáil, his influence as a non-elected political leader will limit Sinn Féin's capacity to exploit its parliamentary options. He will be seen as an outsider in the Republic with no mandate to meddle in Dáil affairs.

Meanwhile, Bertie Ahern's Structured Dialogue with religious leaders is a novel attempt to open government doors for the growing numbers of faith communities existing in Ireland's increasingly multi-cultural society. But in his address to its inaugural session in Dublin Castle, Bertie avoided completely the urgent challenge facing his Coalition Government of drawing up a new Constitution appropriate to today's social reality of multi-cultural diversity. The presence of Muslim leaders and Baha'is side by side with Roman Catholic and Anglican leaders, as well as members of the Reformed and Orthodox Churches, highlighted the fast-changing complexion of contemporary religion.

In what struck me as a far too deferential address to religious leaders, Bertie's attack on "illiberal, secularist voices" in Irish democracy diverted attention away from the need for Government today to govern without fear or favour of unelected religious leaders. This is especially incumbent on any Irish Government claiming to uphold the democratic principles of a Republic. The secular autonomy of government does not exclude religious leaders and members having a right to express their views and beliefs – but as interest groups; not as special groups who are now invited to hold regular private meetings with politicians and policy-makers. The gathering exposed the outdated nature of the persistent claims of politicians that Ireland remains an essentially Catholic or even Christian country.

Yet, Bertie ignored addressing the necessity of formulating a new fundamental law to replace Eamon de Valera's seventy year old Constitution, one which was constructed largely in the image of Rome and the Christian Churches active in the Ireland of 1937.

The Taoiseach needs only to read the Preamble to the Constitution to realise that it has passed its sell-by date. This Preamble submits the will of the people of Ireland to "the Most Holy Trinity, from Whom is all authority and to Whom, as our final end, all actions both of men and States must be referred."

Also urgently in need of rewriting in the light of liberal principles arising from the French and American Revolutions are the sections of the Constitution which reflect Catholic social teaching in regard to the family, education and health.

Perhaps it is not so surprising that Bertie, with his All Hallows' connection and his show of Lenten piety, does not want to update the Constitution. But the fervour with which Tanaiste Michael McDowell blessed the Structured Dialogue was further evidence of how the Progressive Democrats have moved away from their early claims of *Standing by the Republic*.

As we approach the general election, we can be sure that the Opposition leaders including Gerry Adams will be as reluctant as Bertie and Michael to touch the Constitution with their barge poles whatever the lip-service they are all giving to a fabled mature modern Ireland.

Entering the Green Age

(March 13, 2007)

The standard light bulb in your home or office is about to become an antiquarian utility of the past as we enter the *Green Age* in earnest. A proposal to impose a tax on or even to ban completely the use of light bulbs is to be brought forward by Environment Minister Dick Roche as part of the Government's new plan to combat climate change. According to the ever-optimistic Roche a levy on the high energy usage of the traditional or incandescent bulb will have the same aim as the recently introduced levy on plastic bags – to persuade consumers to switch to more environmentally-friendly.

This Monday also saw Noel Dempsey published the Government's energy plan that aims to ensure that one third of our electricity supplies come from renewable sources by 2020, an objective dismissed by the Green Party as unrealisable given that Ireland has not met its Kyoto limits and has spent hundreds of thousands of Euro on carbon credits to bridge this deficit.

Almost overnight we have become conscious of the *Green Age* as news bulletin after news story reminds us that Ireland imports 90pc of its energy needs. Fossil fuels like oil and coal have contributed to greenhouse gas emissions being twice as high as should be here, and Ireland's demand for energy is predicted to increase by 30pc by 2020.

The Government's three main goals of achieving security of supplies, a competitive price and consume approach in an environmentally-friendly manner are admirable and long overdue, but political debate will intensify on how these are to be implemented given the poor track record of all Western economies in these areas.

This lurch to Green politics in Ireland – and in Britain which is also introducing its first significant climate change legislation - follows last Friday's landmark decision by the EU Summit in Brussels to commit the 27 member States to binding cuts in greenhouse gas emissions of 20pc, along with meeting tough but popular targets on renewable energy use.

As a crystal-gazing editorial in *The Guardian* pithily predicted, by 2020, the filament bulb in homes will have become a museum piece, just as the coal fire had met its end in the 1970s. But, like many readers, I ask myself the niggling question as to whether Governments will have the political will to effect changes that may already be too late to prevent drastic climate change in our time, let alone for future generations.

A gripping read was provided by a feature in the *Sunday Times* magazine, headlined "Tomorrow's World" in which it predicted a future in which famous cities including Dublin become submerged by the sea, and one third of the world becomes desert, while the rest of the globe struggles for food and fresh water.

Only a few years ago such an article would have been classified in the genre of science fiction, a twenty-first version of Jules Verne or H.G. Wells fantasies. Yet, it must be taken seriously. In particular, I was struck by the conclusion of Mark Lynas, who has spent a year reading every document on global warming at the Radcliffe Science Library in Oxford, that the world is heading for Dante's *Sixth Circle of Hell*.

Almost a week after its Assembly elections, the question still hovers over Northern Ireland, a part of the world that has generated more verbal hot air than its size merits, as to whether the Democratic Unionist Party will agree to going into Government with Sinn Féin by March 26, after both parties consolidated themselves as the North's big two.

The moment Paisley indicated that he covets the Finance portfolio in a restored Stormont Executive was the signal for me that the Stormont Assembly elections were about its sharing the spoils of office with Sinn Féin. For some weeks now I have been convinced that a deal with Sinn Féin is on. I still do, despite the bitter remarks from the DUP about Sinn Féin's need to convince them of their commitment to policing and law and order.

The North can no longer sustain its ancient tribal divisions. The focus will now be on spreading cross-community the financial dividend from the peace process. There will be brinkmanship right up to the March 26 deadline set by Tony Blair and Bertie Ahern for the historic accommodation that will install a 10-member Executive in which Paisley will be First Minister and Martin McGuinness Deputy First Minister.

As Bertie reminded the British-Irish Parliamentary Body last Monday, London and Dublin will take their last offer of power-sharing off the table if the Demon Doctor – Brian Faulkner's phrase – still rants *No Surrender* to the Shinners. The Unionist community's worse nightmare of joint sovereignty of the North by the British and Irish Governments would come into force *sine die*.

Paisley, at 80, has his last chance not only to end his days as the Unionist Moses who led his followers out of forty years in the political desert into the land of shared economic prosperity. As always, Paisley will exact a hard bargain: this time not on traditional constitutional grounds of protecting the Union – already copper-fastened by the Good Friday and St Andrews Agreements – but on Mammon in the form of Sterling from the British Treasury and Euros from Dublin.

The timing could not be better for Paisley to pull off this financial coup d'etat. With Blair on borrowed time in Downing Street, he desperately needs a settlement in Northern Ireland as his legacy. Chancellor Gordon Brown, equally desperate to move into No 10, will be more than happy to sign the cheque.

With the general election fast-approaching in the Republic, Bertie too wants to go to the polls with a Northern solution on his *curriculum vitae*, even though this may boost Sinn Féin south of the Border.

But the money, measured in billions of hard cash, will not be handed-over to Ulster's quarrelsome political chieftains without strict conditions being attached to the loot. It will be tied to a definite promise that the North's politicians abandon their mock politics of the Battle of the Boyne and the 1916 Easter Rising, and engage in the delivery politics of the twenty-first century.

Money talks: it is not denominated in either Catholic or Protestant currency. The prudent spending of what will be the North's equivalent of the Marshall Recovery Plan for post-World War Two Europe will be its last chance salon to transform its subsidy-sponged economy into a transformed *Ulster Tiger* through more inward investment, more North-South trade and more integration in the European Union.

Over the next three weeks, Paisley and his prospective Finance Minister, Peter Robinson, will be revered as statesmen at Westminster and be welcomed in the offices of Blair and Brown as they tie up the North's biggest economic deal ever negotiated by a Northern administration-in-waiting.

In such a scenario, Gerry Adams and Martin McGuinness will not have the luxury to stand idly-by in Belfast and Mid-Ulster, allowing Paisley's team run off with the credit for securing the cash deal. Watch out, for Adams and McGuinness abandoning their abstentionist policies at Westminster, even it is on occasional visits.

Once the marriage of economic and political convenience is consummated by Paisley and McGuinness, Stormont, like Leinster House, will have to come to grips with the new *Green Age*.

New Contract and Covenant

(April 3, 2007)

Enda Kenny's *Contract for a Better Ireland* and the Rev Ian Paisley's *New Covenant* for Ulster with Sinn Féin promise to transform the island, South and North. The Mayoman has taken out a contract, too, to remove Bertie Ahern from the office of Taoiseach, while the most unlikely couple, *Big Ian* and the former IRA commander Martin McGuinness, are evicting the Northern Ireland Secretary Peter Hain from his office in Stormont Castle.

With the general election expected on May 24 or 31, and the Paisley-McGuinness installation in Stormont as First Minister and Deputy First Minister due on May 8, the political landscape is fast altering shape in line with climate change.

The iconic pictures of Protestant Ulster's octogenarian Moses seated in Stormont Castle on Monday alongside his avowed enemy, Gerry Adams, have completely confounded Paisley watchers who predicted that he would go down in history as "Dr No".

Now that he has become not just the undisputed leader of Ulster Unionism, but also the official designated political head of Northern Ireland, any attempt to understand Ian Paisley's mind must focus not just on his role as the founder of the Democratic Unionist Party but give weight to his position as a fundamentalist Protestant evangelist.

The son of a struggling Baptist preacher in County Armagh, the young Paisley's mind was moulded by the folklore memory accorded by the descendants of the Scottish Planters in Ulster to the persecution of their brethren in Scotland by the Stuart Kings.

In his book, *The Crown Rights of Jesus Christ*, Paisley argued that the Covenanters represented both authentic democracy and the correct Scriptural balance in the relationship to be struck between the governed and the governing authority. It was the duty of Christians to defy the will of leaders who were in error.

Ian Paisley can contend that he has saved Ulster Unionism from its past follies as well as leading the IRA to the portals of Stormont. Unlike Moses who crossed the Red Sea only to die in the desert before reaching Palestine, Ian Paisley has proved he can walk on water. This is Ulster's New Covenant.

Indeed, "God Talk" promises to be the spiritual bond which will help promote political dialogue in a divided community and eventually achieve individual trust in the DUP-Sinn Féin-led Executive.

Religion, the centuries-long cancer of sectarian hatred between the feuding Catholic and Protestant tribes, is the new currency of diplomacy in the North. British Prime Minister Tony Blair, an Anglican who attends Mass with his Catholic wife Cherie, has revealed that he "wooed" Doc Paisley, by praying and reading the Bible at their private Downing Street meetings.

Taoiseach Bertie Ahern, he of the black-crossed forehead on Ash Wednesday, sat with his head bowed as *Big Ian* said grace before meals when they met for the first time a few years ago at the Irish Embassy in London for hard boiled eggs.

The most powerful man in the world, US President George Bush has spoken the language of Christian evangelism in his encounters with preacher Paisley, while President Mary McAleese, deeply versed in spirituality, raised the possibility of her meeting Paisley at the Áras, an encounter, no doubt, where they would find time to pray.

In line with this contemporary pattern of theological discourse among political leaders, at their first official face to face encounter at Stormont both the Rev Ian Paisley (predictably) and the Gerry Adams (unexpectedly) invoked the deity when they fixed May 8 in tablets of biblical stone for the formation of the power sharing government.

Paisley, the fundamentalist Bible-thumper who built his long and divisive career on denouncing the Church of Rome as *the Anti-Christ*, had communed for weeks with his God and wrestled with his conscience before agreeing to this historic rapprochement with Catholic nationalism.

In solemnly professing his commitment to lead his Protestant people from "the dark period" in which the IRA waged relentless war on the majority Unionist population, Paisley has pledged to look after all the people of Northern Ireland.

In similar language of Christian reconciliation, Adams, the high priest of republicanism, declared an end to the era of the Orange and Green, and intoned that "now there is a new start with the help of God."

Nor will the historical irony be lost on Paisley watchers that it was Pope Benedict XVI, *the Man of Sin*, who told President McAleese that he felt very strongly that partnership government in the North would be "a powerful Christian witness to the world."

The paradox may be that government meetings at Stormont will begin with a prayer before pursuing a materialistic agenda relating to water charges, road infrastructure, better schools and hospitals. If constitutional difficulties arise, as they will, the maxim of the new Executive will be 'the family that prays together stays together'. They may not yet be family, but the Paisleyites, the Shinners, the SDLP and the Official Unionists are building a broad church as the North moves into the modern world of secular European politics based on dialogue, not demonisation. For once, Ulster may be right.

Enda Kenny's offer at the Fine Gael Árd Fheis to the electorate of a *Contract for a Better Ireland* will either make him Taoiseach or vanquish him as yet another Fine Gael leader who lost the supreme battle to Bertie Ahern. With his own popularity trailing that of Bertie, and with Fine Gael not climbing the opinion polls with the agility of a goat after its mountain fall in the 2002 general election, Enda had to put his personality to the fore of the forthcoming pre-election race.

This was his bid to cast off once and for all the public's lingering lightweight image of him, and to project himself himself as a man of steel, who will deliver a standard of public services required by the Celtic Tiger economy – and if he fails to do so after five years as Taoiseach, he will not lead Fine Gael into the 2012 general election as head of Government.

In making this solemn and unprecedented promise from such a senior politician in the 85 year existence of the Irish State, Kenny has seized the advantage from Ahern whom he contemptuously dismissed as "another man (who last week) stood in this hall and made 53 promises". This challenge could not have come at a better time for the FG faithful, miserably bereft of power and the limelight for a decade, because it coincided with reports of a deep split within Fianna Fáil over Bertie's bag of promises that he announced prematurely – and much to the anger of Finance Minister Brian Cowen.

In contrast, to the spectacle of a jittery Ahern, during his half-hour speech Kenny, boyish-looking in his Bill Clinton styled haircut, sparkled with humour and commitment. The cadence of the sparse prose at time resonated with Clintonesque echoes and even carried with it the promise of a John F Kennedy.

If Enda becomes Taoiseach, you might see him on a walkabout in Castlebar soon with his Northern counterpart, Ian Paisley. As Bob Dylan noted, *The Times They Are A-Changin'*.

Bertie and Ian
Smooch in Farmleigh

(April 10, 2007)

This year's Easter celebrations have witnessed the secular miracle of the Rev Ian Paisley hugging Taoiseach Bertie Ahern like a long lost nephew in the palatial setting of Farmleigh House in Dublin's Phoenix Park.

Journalists were gob-smacked as they watched *Big Ian* jump out of his car last Wednesday and bellow for all to hear and savour: "I must shake hands with this man - give him a good grip."

Like the rest of us, the Lord of Farmleigh could hardly believe his luck as he welcomed *Uncle Ian*, the Benign Neighbour. Mind you, Bertie badly needed a boost after several weeks of doleful news on the home front. This encounter cheered Bertie up, although Paisley reminded his host that he had come from a foreign land.

"Some say hedges make the best neighbours," Paisley intoned, before abandoning his past venom against the South's rescinded irredentist claim of sovereignty over Northern Ireland in favour of his new found political ecumenism. "I do not believe we should plant a hedge between our two countries."

Although Paisley and Ahern had shook hands last autumn at St Andrews in Scotland, they had done so in private, and the Farmleigh grip was a public manifestation of the North's First Minister-designate to make devolution work.

The self-proclaimed proud Ulsterman promised to work to improve relations between the nationalist and unionist traditions, symbolised in his announcement that he would visit the site of the Battle with the Boyne with the Taoiseach, though he refrained from predicting whether he would celebrate the July 12 commemoration of King William of Orange's defeat of King James in 1690 with Bertie Ahern or Enda Kenny!

With the future never brighter for both parts of a divided Ireland, the two political leaders discussed the concrete economic benefits which would emerge from the kitties of Chancellor Gordon Brown and Finance Minister Brian Cowen.

Meanwhile, in Belfast Sinn Féin was announcing the posts which will be taken up by their ministers on the formation of the power-sharing Executive on May 8.

Among them is Ballina's Catriona Ruane, now an Assembly member for North Down who will take charge of the Education portfolio, along with Conor Murphy in Regional Development, Michelle Gildernew in Agriculture. (With Mary Coughlan holding this post in the Republic, this will be the first time two women have ruled over the farmers!)

Significantly, Gerry Kelly, the former IRA prisoner who escaped from the Maze Prison in 1983, will become a junior minister in the Office of Paisley as First Minister and Martin McGuinness as First Deputy Minister. A diplomatic stroke here!

However, a shadow of past sorrows hovered over the historic day with the publication by Patrick McEntee S.C. of the Commission of Investigation into the Dublin and Monaghan bombs in May 1974 which killed 33 persons and injured 300 others.

To the utter disappointment of the relatives of the long-grieving victims, the report failed to establish the suspicion that Loyalists were responsible for the atrocity primarily because the Gardaí had made a mess of their inquiries. The lack of available records prevented McEntee from finding proof of collaboration with RUC or British Intelligence in winding-down their inquiries within weeks of the biggest attack on civilians living in the Republic during *The Troubles*.

Further gloom for Bertie came with the announcement of Senator Margaret Cox that she was resigning from the Fianna Fáil parliamentary party in protest against the Government's failures to deliver its promised investments in the Galway region. Following the resignation of Senator Liam FitzGerald in protest against the selection of election candidates in Dublin North East constituency, all is not well in Fianna-land.

Bertie must be keeping his fingers crossed that the Farmleigh love-in with *Big Ian* will give him a bounce in the polls to counter-act the shambles with which the current Dáil session has wound-down for the two week Easter holidays in advance of election kick-off.

If Bertie announces the election date on May 17, there could be only two days left in the life of the Dáil. If he chooses May 24 that would only provide an extra week for the 29th Dáil and Seanad to pass unfinished legislation including Justice Minister Michael McDowell's messy Criminal Justice Bill.

While Bertie was enjoying his sunshine stroll at Farmleigh, McDowell was causing bedlam in the Dáil, where he took Opposition Leaders' Questions. Like a student debater, he mocked Pat Rabbitte as having been "a half minister at the high chair" of the FG-Labour-Democratic Left Government in the mid-nineties, and he scoffed that Enda Kenny was having "a bad hair day".

As the Labour leader retorted that McDowell would get the high jump from the voters, the Fine Gael leader reminded the Tanaiste that he was on borrowed time in Government as a result of his bailing out the Taoiseach in last September's *Bertiegate* affair over his financial dig-outs from friends in Drumcondra and Manchester.

McDowell's reply that his ethics legislation disallowing senior politicians to receive personal payments such as the €50,000 which Bertie received as Finance Minister from well-wishers on a rainy day will be brought forward as "soon as may be". That strikes me as saying that it would not be passed before the Dáil and Seanad closure.

This issue will resurface in the run-up to the election, however, according to the Irish *Daily Mail* which has reported that the Standards in Public Office Commission is looking into the payments made to him in the 1990s. Its resurfacing could damage McDowell and the PDs more than Bertie and FF. But the *Mail* has editorialised that the "dig-outs return to haunt Bertie".

Hopefully, too, Bertie will not be in need of a nurse in the coming weeks.

Luntz Treats Politics as Showbiz

(April 17, 2007)

D r Frank Luntz, the Harvard pioneer of focus group sampling, is being hailed as the new guru or pope of Ireland's 2007 general election. He has become influential in shaping public opinion, but I'm not sure if he is an infallible guide.

Certainly, in the long run to the election kick-off, Luntz has provided acres of newsprint with his vignettes of the characters and traits of the competing leaders of the main political parties. He is the flavour of the month.

His reverential standing among Irish political commentators is backed up by their awed admiration for his track-record as an adviser to former New York mayor Rudi Guiliani and his assistance to Newt Gingrich when he drew up the Republican Party's contract with America in 1994 to keep its promises or not seek re-election.

Luntz has lauded George W Bush for communicating with American voters but now argues that Bush has lost that skill. His reputation as a political seer soared as a result of his persuading Silvio Berlusconi to enter a similar contract with Italy. His work for the BBC *Newsnight* programme on which his focus group identified David Cameron as the potential leader of the Conservative Party boosted him.

While accepting that Luntz has a talent for spotting political body language and dissecting the mood of voters, I wonder how substantial his advice is. Bush is on the way out, while Giuliani and Gingrich have become yesterday men. The Republicans took a hammering in the recent congressional elections. David Cameron remains his bright hope.

Having missed the first two of his focus group sessions for the RTE *Week in Politics* programme, I watched Sunday's broadcast from Boyle, Co Roscommon, with a mixture of fascination and scepticism at the way in which Luntz elicited reactions from the 32 members of his studio audience.

Luntz predicts Bertie Ahern is strolling to his third successive general election victory, Enda Kenny opposes but does not propose, Pat Rabbitte's straight talking is striking a nerve with voters, Trevor Sargent shouts too loud, and Gerry Adams is Sinn Féin's best asset.

Like the rest of us, Luntz detects that nobody likes the PD leader Michael McDowell, who is blamed for destroying the social pub scene on account of the clamp-down on drink-driving. He is marked out as the politician who caused people to drink less than they would like! For a second time, Luntz has indicated a public preference for the emergence of a Fianna Fáil-Labour government led by Ahern and Rabbitte.

Such is the interest generated by his focus group technique, there is a danger that the Gospel according to Luntz might become the national orthodoxy when voters go to the polls in the 43 constituencies. A self-fulfilling prophecy, perhaps.

What also struck me was that the gathering of the chosen 32 at King House in Boyle was invested with a touch of showbiz glamour by the presence not just of Luntz but also by the television camera, backed up by Seán O'Rourke analysing the comments off-stage with a panel of experts, Terry Prone, Noel Whelan and former Fine Gael TD turned bookie, Ivan Yates.

Would a discussion in a pub with 32 random drinkers, some of whom would not offer opinions to a visiting stranger, a discussion which was being overheard by the four intruders tucked away in the nearby snug, be given any credibility? I doubt it. It would be seen as selective and unrepresentative opinion sampling.

Yet, on the basis of the musings of the Roscommon 32, backed up by his own reading of Enda Kenny's recent Árd Fheis speech in which the Mayoman offer his contract for a better Ireland, Luntz concluded that it did not sell to the RTE audience, and it won't sell nationally.

This was not the response of the Árd Fheis, nor of most commentators who followed it, including myself. There is a fundamental gap here between the armchair judgment of the Roscommon 32 and standard political commentary deriving from actual observation of politicians. If Luntz is correct, Enda is wasting his time.

This brings me to the further point that the election has not even started. The battles in the 43 constituencies have not yet been waged. Events and mistakes in the heat of the hustings will help shape the outcome. Yet, Luntz has pre-determined the outcome with his high profile pontificating. Why not vote the RTE-Luntz way, and scrap the actual election?

This kind of entertainment runs the danger of providing viewers with a *Lazy Voter's Guide*. It offers a voyeuristic technique which carries with it the risk of undermining the actual process of democracy. Subliminally, through the power of television, it is attempting to pre-condition public perception. We are invited to become amateur psychologists of the behaviour of politicians. It may be good for

RTE ratings, but this technique does not necessarily lend itself to the serious debate of complex political and economic issues. It is politics as showbiz.

Meanwhile, the publication of Michael McDowell's Ethics in Public Office Bill is a further betrayal of the founding principles of the Progressive Democrats which will haunt the man known as *the Mad Mullah* on the election campaign trail. This Bill, requiring the Taoiseach, his ministers and senior office holders to seek advance approval for receiving substantial gifts, was the political price McDowell promised to pay for bailing out the Fianna Fáil leader in last September's *Bertiegate* affair over his €50,000 dig-outs from friends in Drumcondra and Manchester during the 1990s.

The declared justification for McDowell's support for Bertie was the fig-leaf assurance that new ethics legislation would be brought in "urgently" to prevent a future *Bertiegate*.

More than seven months after his commitment the publication of the amending Bill has shown how hollow this has proved to be. It has increased the amount of money which politicians can receive without disclosure from €650 to €2,000. Technically, of course, it is a Department of Finance Bill which is defending this first increase of limits on gifts and donations since 1995, and its provision exempting politicians from declaring annual nixers under €5,000.

But in the public eye, this is McDowell's Bill, one which was expected to bear his hallmark in closing-down perks to politicians. It was his opportunity to redeem his self-interested rescue of Bertie last October. Yet, the Bill does not even take the modest reforming step of giving the Standards in Public Office Commission the power to initiate inquiries.

McDowell has many talents, but bluffing is not one of his strengths. Michael's fretting over the disclosure by politicians of free gallons of wine and gourmet dinners in plush suites is far removed from the heady days when the PDs stood for principle.

The *Bertigate* issue took a new twist this week-end with reports claiming that Bertie and his former partner Celia Larkin took a briefcase stuffed with money outside the country. Enda Kenny and Jim Higgins are under pressure to explain the origins of this claim. Otherwise, they face the charge from Fianna Fáil of playing dirty trick against Bertie.

Perhaps we might have to call on Frank Luntz to solve this mystery!

Enda Closes in on Bertie

(April 24, 2007)

The week-end opinion polls have highlighted just how close the general election is going to be as the tide continues to run towards change. *The Sunday Business Post Red C* poll put Fianna Fáil at a lowly 35pc which would mean its worse electoral performance since its foundation eighty years ago.

The same poll showed Fine Gael up four points to 27pc, a position which puts Enda Kenny in striking distance of challenging the ten year supremacy of the FF-PD Government for the next government. Since the start of the year FF has been falling and FG going up. The FG-Labour-Greens vote share is on 47pc, compared with 38pc for the FF-PDS, a gap of nine points.

The *Sunday Independent–Millward-Brown-IMS* poll was not as bad for Fianna Fáil, which is put at 37pc and the PDs on 4pc, compared with Fine Gael at 23pc, Labour 12pc and the Greens on 6pc. Neck and neck. With 20pc don't knows, there is manifest volatility in the electorate. The campaign will be important. The battle on the ground will be as important as the swing of the national pendulum.

As the Dáil resumes this week after its leisurely Easter vacation, the general consensus is that it is in its dying days. Indeed, some commentators have been predicting that Bertie will seek its dissolution this week, or next. Perhaps by the time you read this column, the ground war in the 43 constituencies for the 166 Dáil seats may be officially on.

However, if I were advising Bertie, I would propose to him that the best dates for his going to the country increasingly look like Wednesday May 9 or Thursday May 10. The Taoiseach's choice of this later than expected date for dissolving the current Dáil would mean that the general election would take place on Thursday May 31.

With the week-end opinion polls pointing to a definite momentum in favour of the alternative Fine Gael-Labour-Green administration, a decision by Bertie to keep the Dáil in session for a further three weeks would be deeply frustrating for the Opposition parties.

A leading Opposition strategist told me that the talk among Government sources of the Taoiseach calling the election on the Dáil's return this week, or early next week, is a deliberate diversionary tactic to wrong-foot them.

As all the political parties last week-end conducted intensive door-to-door canvassing, as well as spending heavily on election leaflets and posters, a Government minister confirmed that Bertie's plan is to make the Opposition parties peak too early.

According to Government sources, Bertie's keeping the Dáil in session for two further working weeks in May would enable the Fianna Fáil-Progressive Democrat Government to give a badly needed boost to the flagging property market by introducing and pushing through legislation to reform the highly unpopular stamp duty.

In cabinet, I would imagine, Finance Minister, Brian Cowen, is coming under increasing pressure from both the Taoiseach and the PD leader Michael McDowell to prepare emergency legislation on stamp duty for presentation to the Dáil before its dissolution.

By taking decisive action on stamp duty the Government parties would not only deprive the alternative Fine Gael-Labour government of one of their key election platforms, the popularity of such a pre-election move would help to arrest the downward trend of both Fianna Fáil and the PDs in the opinion polls.

Government and grass-roots feeling within Fianna Fáil is that even if the party announced stamp duty reform as part of its election manifesto, the housing market would remain stagnant for the duration of the campaign.

Immediate Government reform of stamp duty would help calm the taut nerves of Fianna Fáil backbenchers who fear the loss of their seats on account of public anger at the uncertainty in the property market.

This timetable would also give the beleaguered Coalition more time to resolve the nurses strike and the contentious dispute with State hospital consultants.

A further advantage for Bertie in delaying the Dáil's dissolution well into next month is that the general election in the Republic would begin within hours of the installation of the power sharing Executive in the North on Tuesday May 8. The impact on public opinion of the DUP leader, the Rev Ian Paisley, and Sinn Féin's Martin McGuinness taking their seals of office at Stormont would highlight the Taoiseach's major achievement of consolidating the peace in the North. It would also focus attention on Tanaiste Michael McDowell's role in the peace process as Minister for Justice.

An extra bonus for the Taoiseach would be that the general election would kick off just a few days after the bank holiday on Monday May 7.

The choice of May 31 as election day rather than the more mooted May 17 or May 24 would also mean that the FF-PD Government would not face the frustration of campaigning during the early May holiday week-end. Fixing May 31 as polling day would also mean that the election would be over just before a second public holiday on Monday June 4.

Canvassers of all political parties have found that door-to-door campaigning on holiday week-ends is a futile exercise, as so many people head out of Dublin for the country, or if they do remain at home, they spend the valued week-end off in socialising.

Ireland's election may be our preoccupation. But elsewhere in Europe election fever is taking grip, especially in France where Sunday's first round ballot for the Presidency saw a staggering 85pc turn-out. The scene is now set for a *Battle Royal* in the run-off in two weeks time between the Napoleonic conservative Nicolas Sarkosy and the Socialist Ségolene Royal. Either candidate will introduce the France of Chirac and Mitterrand with badly needed reform of its highly cushioned bureaucracy and high taxation.

In Scotland an opinion poll indicated that the Scottish National Party's Alex Salmond is on 35pc of the vote, eight points ahead of Labour. This should make Salmond First Minister in Edinburgh come May 3. This will be a valedictory kick in the teeth to Tony Blair and a pair of handcuffs for Gordon Brown's attempt to keep the 300 year old Union of England and Scotland together.

So the wind of change is swirling around Bertie Ahern. The *Bertiegate* affair has not gone away with half of voters still wanting more information about the payments he received in the 1990s from his cronies in Drumcondra and Manchester.

Bertie's one consolation must be that Enda Kenny again showed a lack of killer punch when the issue resurfaced in the newspapers through Jim Higgins MEP.

Bertie Faces Moment of Truth

(May 1, 2007)

Bertie Ahern's dawn raid on the Phoenix Park on Sunday morning to have President Mary McAleese dissolve the 29th Dáil before her departure for the United States was the weirdest spectacle in the turbulent history of Irish general elections.

Equally bizarre was the Taoiseach's refusal to take questions at the Fianna Fáil press conference in Dublin's Treasury Buildings and his failure to campaign on Sunday morning, while all the election candidates plastered the nation's lamp posts with their promissory posters, beaming faces and lavish advertising slogans. As broadcaster Ryan Turbidy pithily observed, it was like political *mardi gras*.

This unprecedented decision of a Taoiseach to opt for his right of silence on the first day of general election campaign was clearly motivated by his determination to avoid embarrassing questions which would have been fired at him about the Mahon Tribunal. Specifically, he would have found himself bombarded by questions from journalists about whether he felt that the Tribunal should suspend its proceedings or allow builder Tom Gilmartin to begin making his sensational allegations against him in public session at Dublin Castle tomorrow.

With acres of detail already dominating the Sunday newspapers about his leaked statement earlier this month to the Tribunal about payments made to him, and housing benefit in kind in the 1990s, Ahern and his minders decided to take premeditated shelter behind the damage limitation exercise of Omerta.

Ominously for Fianna Fáil, Bertie's reported admissions to the Tribunal differ substantially from the embroidered account of his Drumcondra and Manchester dig-outs which he gave to RTE last September that won him public sympathy and a Dáil bail-out by PD leader Michael McDowell.

Bertie's revised version is of his receiving a briefcase stuffed with €30,000 in cash from businessman Michael Wall in 1994, which he matched with a further €50,000 of his own savings. These were put into two bank accounts opened by his then girlfriend Celia Larkin, enabling him to move into, and later own, a house bought by Wall.

This means that he misled the Dáil and the nation last September. Not only was Bertie economical with the truth nine months ago, he now wants us to shed crocodile tears by giving him the benefit of the doubt that this disguised money trail was necessary to supply him with a permanent address on becoming Taoiseach. It was to spare us the shame of having a nomadic nocturnal Taoiseach conducting the business of the nation!

On the flimsy pretext that journalists had another 23 days in which to quiz him, Bertie bought time yesterday in the desperate hope that the Tribunal will not become the first inquiry in the history of the State to investigate a Taoiseach during the political high tide of a general election campaign. In an otherwise superb display, he had exploited his advantage of determining the timing the election for May 24 with his early morning visit to President Mary McAleese ahead of her departure for the United States. He had followed this up with a heart-on-the-sleeves speech defining the election as attacking issues and policies, not as personal attacks.

The tone and thrust of his scripted address was an anguished plea for voters to re-elect his FF-PD coalition after an Irish decade of achieving peace in the North and providing economic prosperity in the Republic. The alternative would be the squandering of this legacy by giving power to the untried motley crew of Fine Gael, Labour and the Greens who would undo his legacy for years to come.

However, Bertie's *After me the deluge* rhetoric was somewhat undermined by his admission that he did not know if he would win the election.

His uncharacteristic reticence about a Q&A session contrasted, however, with the gung-ho confidence of both Enda Kenny and Pat Rabbitte that they will win, even if Bertie uses the installation of the Northern Executive, his stroll on the Boyne with Ian Paisley and his address to the two houses of the British Parliament for crude electioneering purposes.

Over the next three weeks Bertie will pin his faith that voters will recognise his political achievements and overlook his personal failings. Otherwise, the Irish decade which he referred to will enter the history books as *the Ahern Decade*.

Manchester, Bertie's Waterloo?

(May 8, 2007)

Team captain Bertie Ahern and his disunited Fianna Fáil squad are playing as poorly in the early stages of Election 2007 as his beloved Manchester United did for the whole match against Milan in the European Championship.

Not only has FF's star player, had a disastrous start to the toughest match of his illustrious career, his team-mates are not rescuing him from his woeful performance, they too are playing off-form like headless novices.

In spite of having held the advantage of picking match time and kicking the ball off, the *Teflon Taoiseach* dithered and left the pitch mysteriously in the opening minutes, and on his return he fumbled indecisively with the ball in his own penalty area.

Under pressure from the united Fine Gael-Labour opposition, at one point he left the ball hanging dangerously in the air for a seemingly eternal eight second right in front of his own empty goal before finally blocking it with a bad-tempered sliced kick.

Eventually, Bertie moved the ball out of the penalty area, but only as far as his own corner line where Ronaldo-like he locked himself into the flag pole.

Coming onto the pitch last Thursday to play the role of Milan's weather-beaten hardman Gattuso was the veteran maestro of crusading journalism *Vinnie Brawn*. In doggedly challenging Bertie on his personal finances, Browne completely sidetracked Ahern from his strategic task of presenting FF's game plan contained in its election manifesto and getting his team onto the attack.

Bertie's spirited plea that he had been fouled by the ferocious Browne, aka Gattuso, won applause from gob-smacked FF ministers, deputies, councillors and officials who acted as their man's cheer-leaders. But with FF having changed its tactics on stamp duty and mortgages, the burly and barbecued Brian Cowen has been upping his game, though Mícheál Martin has been proving to be as lame-footed as his fellow Munsterman John O'Shea.

The one consolation for the besieged Bertie is that neither Enda Kenny nor Pat Rabbitte has tackled him on his personal finances with the lethal directness of Milan striker Kaka. Nonetheless, the daily hemming in of the floundering Ahern has enabled Enda and Pat to take a series of free kicks from outside the FF box that are adding to the disarray of the FF defence, while leaving the Mayo duo space to roam around the park without coming under pressure or breaking sweat.

Commentators have been so taken aback by Bertie's slump in form and by FF's jaded turn-out. For so long, Bertie has been Fianna Fáil: it's all round player. So when he has been having a bad patch, and making U-turns on the pattern of play, the others, need to show Cowen-like versatility to keep the team's momentum driving forward.

How the dynamic of the remainder of the big match evolves is yet unknown. It may be that voters will regard Vincent Browne's intervention – unlike his brave and lonely confrontation with Charles J Haughey twenty years ago – as vindictive vanity journalism.

In Browne's showmanship, voters may see the collective media hell-bent on destroying an undoubtedly successful leader and architect of the power-sharing Executive for what seem to them as his arcane domestic finances at a messy time in his personal life. By dint of his aggressive grand-standing, Browne may have alienated a sizable section of voters who will resent journalism acting as referee by usurping the people's constitutional right of deciding the outcome through the ballot-box. Browne may have gifted Bertie an electoral bounce which had eluded him so far. Just as Willie O'Dea and Seamus Brennan were moving up field as the start of a counter offensive, Michael McDowell and the Progressive Democrats staged a weird week-end panto in which they indulged in a bout of conscience beating.

The spectacle of McDowell leaving Government on Saturday and staying in on Sunday exposed disarray in the PDs that is not concealed by their demand for Bertie to make a comprehensive statement of his financial affairs before polling day. The PD monkey is off Bertie's shoulder. Tom Parlon is openly contradicting McDowell and trying to restore a working partnership with FF.

The outstanding issue facing the Bertie camp is when to oblige the PDs with a public *mea culpa* and shift from his position of addressing the issue only at the Mahon Tribunal.

With his triumphant visit to the inauguration of the Executive in Belfast this Tuesday, followed soon afterwards by his Boyne stroll with Ian Paisley and historic address to the Houses of Westminster looming, Bertie will first play the states-man card – and taunt the media to publish and be damned. After his lap of honour in Belfast, Bertie will use his final card of appealing directly to the nation - the last thing Enda and Pat really want. McDowell's response will now be irrelevant to *the Soldiers of Destiny*.

Over this Bank Holiday week-end, Bertie and his minders took stock of a calamitous opening phase to the election, and are pinning their hopes on his having absorbed the worst of the damage, and on his toughness to turn the game around. His future depends on his determination to test the one remaining core value in Fianna Fail - that its leader rules as *Uno duce, una voce*. One leader, one voice.

Brian Cowen's counter-attack on Sunday that Fine Gael leader Enda Kenny was master-minding the attacks on Bertie from the corner of his mouth was a clear indication of solidarity being forthcoming. Bertie knows he must stay on the pitch as team captain until the evening of May 24 when the last ballot box in the 43 constituencies is closed. Only when the votes are counted, and the will of the electorate known, will it be decided whether he secures a mandate for a third term as Taoiseach or not. Until that moment of truth, he has no choice but to battle on in the most dramatic election campaign ever.

Besides, thanks to Eamon de Valera, the godfather of Fianna Fáil and architect of the 1937 Constitution, there is no provision for a Taoiseach to resign during an election campaign and hand over to a successor. Under the Constitution, it is the Dáil that elects a Taoiseach, and as the 29th Dáil which elected Ahern Taoiseach in 2002 has been dissolved, he remains Taoiseach until the 30th Dáil assembles to elect a new Taoiseach.

In other words, Bertie in mid-match – even if he felt personally demoralised to do so – cannot hand his captain's arm-band over to Cowen. Nor are any of the pretenders to the FF throne, such as Cowen, Mícheál Martin, Dermot Ahern or Mary Hanafin, foolish enough to make a leadership move. Party tradition of loyalty to their leader and pragmatic necessity enunciated by Alexander Dumas' *Three Muskateers*, dictate FF's ministers, Dáil candidates and grass-roots supporters to rally to their beleaguered leader to the tune of "One for all, and all for one."

As the Drumcondra druids regrouped, the *Sunday Business/Red C* opinion poll showed FF up two points in popularity, itself a harbinger of a possible Bertie recovery, just as happened last autumn. On the other hand, Browne may have lethally exposed Bertie's vulnerability, and like Manchester United, Fianna Fáil may be heading for defeat.

If so, the epitaph on Bertie's political tombstone may yet read: "Manchester made me. Manchester undid me."

Blair Puts Years on Bertie

(May 15, 2007)

Week three of the general election has begun with the main focus still dominated by the personal finances of Taoiseach Bertie Ahern, as opinion polls show a definite lead opening up for the alternative Fine Gael-Labour Government led by Enda Kenny and Pat Rabbitte.

Yet, the outcome of election 2007 on Thursday May 24 remains difficult to call, not least because it will be the voters who will decide whether Bertie's latest version of his finances, issued on Sunday, satisfies them about the Taoiseach's probity, or casts further doubts on his suitability to serve a third term in the highest political office in the land. His Sunday statement has been accepted by Tanaiste and PD leader, Michael McDowell, who says that there is no longer any obstacle to his doing business with the Fianna Fáil leader after the election.

The one point on which there is all-round agreement is that McDowell has miscued repeatedly on the issue of Ahern's finances since *Bertiegate* surfaced last September. So it is a safe bet to predict that the erratic McDowell is indulging in wishful thinking that the PDs will have enough seats to continue its cohabitation with FF.

Even if McDowell professes to be satisfied by Bertie's lengthy statement, the reality is that it has added further mystification around the Taoiseach's affairs by his disclosure that in October he made an undisclosed provisional payment to the Revenue Commissioners relating to the Drumcondra and Manchester payments and gifts he received in the 1990s when he was Minister for Finance, while suffering the personal trauma of the break-up of his marriage with his wife Miriam.

The introduction by Bertie himself of this admission of potential tax liability in regard to these payments has opened up a fresh cauldron of worms, which will mean that the controversy will continue to haunt him right up to polling day and beyond.

Just as worms wriggle, it will be extremely difficult for Bertie, metaphorically speaking, to wriggle out of further questions which are so preoccupying not only journalists, the Mahon Tribunal of Inquiry but now also the Revenue Commissioners.

Readers who have regaled themselves in the details of purchases made from fashion shops such as Brown Thomas by his former girlfriend Celia Larkin for the house in the north Dublin Beresford estate may take the view that this was not on the scale of Chavret shirts spending by Charles Haughey.

No doubt, in his private dark hours of soul-searching Bertie might have pondered the vicarious pleasure that he could have bestowed the nation if he opted to gift his head in bust form alongside his beloved hanging baskets of pansies in his modest red-brick home that approximates neither to a ranch in the West of Ireland nor to an Abbeville pile!

Sympathy is again cleverly being sought by Bertie. Dolefully, he demurs that the media and other meddlers are prying into the details of his separation from Miriam, and, in turn, causing unnecessary distress to the wider Ahern family. This plea is being spun in spite of the fact that the media and the Opposition politicians have not sought to intrude into these delicate areas.

The real question at issue in September, and even more so today, is that Bertie accepted payments from friends and relative strangers in 1993-4 when he held one of the most important State offices as Minister for Finance. In my view, as I wrote at the time, whatever his reason for accepting such monies, this was irrelevant to the constitutional necessity for Bertie Ahern to have resigned as Taoiseach on their coming into the public domain over a decade later. This he did not do.

Instead, he manipulated the national broadcasting station, RTE, by giving an exclusive and emotional television interview which won him a wave of public sympathy that rendered it virtually impossible for the Opposition to make him accountable in the Dáil, especially when Michael McDowell decided to sacrifice the PDs' core principle of maintaining high standards in Government for their staying in Government.

Nor should it be forgotten that Bertie told Bryan Dobson; "I don't want anyone saying I didn't give the full picture." Today, we have a fuller picture thanks to the leaks from the Tribunal which have surfaced during the election campaign. Nor do we yet have the full picture.

In the light of the most recent revelations, I, like Pat Rabbitte, find it hard to accept Bertie's disclaimer that his Sunday statement contradicts his Dáil September statement that no tax issues were outstanding from either loans made to him by friends in Dublin or financial gifts he received from well-wishers in Manchester.

All this points to the suspicion that Bertie misled the Dáil and the Irish public last September. Not only does he appear to have been economical with the truth nine months ago, he now wants us to shed crocodile tears by giving him the benefit of the doubt that this uncovered money trail was necessary to supply him with a permanent address on becoming Taoiseach, as he thought he would have become in 1994 when Dick Spring instead opted for John Bruton.

This is a sorry mess which Fianna Fáil finds itself on account of Bertie's acceptance of monies. Yet, Bertie's ministers, even the impressive Brian Cowen, continue to claim that the personal integrity of a Taoiseach – any Taoiseach – is irrelevant as an issue in a general election. Bertie Ahern's fitness for office, as distinct for his competence in handling the economy, industrial relations, the North and Europe, will figure large in Wednesday night's television debate between McDowell and Rabbitte.

Ahern's fitness for office will also have to be addressed by Enda Kenny on Thursday evening's debate. Otherwise, Enda will leave himself open to Bertie's counter-charge that Enda has sparse ministerial experience and no experience at all in industrial relations in spite of his pledge to sort out the nurses' strike on becoming Taoiseach.

While Bertie is the architect of his own misfortune in this election, I still would not write him off. He is a wily politician, indeed the most cunning of them all. And he has been playing his record on the North to full political advantage, through the happy circumstances of last Tuesday week's inauguration of the Northern Executive led by Ian Paisley and Martin McGuinness, his visit last Friday to the Boyne with Ian Paisley and his address to the joint Houses of the Westminster Parliament this Tuesday.

Yet, like the disappearance of one half of Laurel and Hardy, or Morecombe and Wise or Podge and Rodge, Tony Blair's announcement that he will bow-out on June 27 raises musings that Ahern, too, is reaching his sell-by date. Blair, unwittingly, did Bertie no favours when in his resignation speech as Prime Minister he wryly admitted that ten years in office was long enough for him and the British public.

By dint of the intimacy of their decade-long working relationship in Northern Ireland and Europe, the Bertie and Tony double act built up a durable image as inseparable twins.

As Bertie accorded the 54 year old Blair an honourable place in Irish history, the Taoiseach would have been forgiven if, inwardly, he winced at his buddy's other eminently exportable remark across the Irish Sea that "sometimes, in a way, you conquer the pull of power by setting it down".

Although Bertie, who will be 56 in September, retains a voracious hunger to win a third term as Taoiseach, and vows to retire in 2011, the endless replays of *the Blair Decade* reminded us that it was in June 1997 that he formed his first Government with the Progressive Democrats just a month after Tony's New Labour landslide victory.

Both leaders exuded youth and promised change: in Blair's case, to revive social solidarity in Britain after the naked greed of the Thatcher Years; in Ahern's lexicon, he pledged to distance a New Fianna Fáil from the corruption of the Haughey Years.

Today, both men wear heavily the physical toll of middle age in vastly changed countries whose citizens appreciate less their achievements and ungratefully begrudge their shortcomings as they await fresher faces to resolve intractable problems.

Unlike Blair, Ahern has no Iraq war to soil his legacy in international affairs, but his cultivation of George W Bush and his blind eye at American fly-overs through Shannon left Ireland aligned to the United States' war against terrorism.

Under Bertie and Blair, Ireland and Britain have enjoyed economic prosperity. Yet, the political agenda in the two neighbouring countries remains stuck over social inequality, the health services, crime, education and grid-lock transport that aggravates the quality of life of young working couples.

Just as Blair's style of leadership increasingly resembled that of the single-minded Thatcher, so too Ahern remained shackled to the Haughey era. Blair is leaving before being disgraced while in office by the 'cash for honours' scandal. Ahern's immediate future is overshadowed by the Mahon Tribunal.

Blair steps down with his record giving him the distinction of winning three successive general elections. The next few weeks will confirm if Bertie can match that record.

While Bertie prides himself on presiding over two coalitions each running five years, perhaps Blair was the more cunning in calling two elections at the end of four years.

Ironically, if Bertie falls to the public's ten year itch and fails to become Taoiseach on June 14, he might be handing in his seal of office to President McAleese 13 days before Tony says his official adieu to the Queen!

Meanwhile, I had the good fortune of getting out of Dublin this week-end to go on the campaign trail in Mayo, though this meant being on the road at 6 a.m. The West was already awake when I arrived in Ballinrobe just before 10 o'clock. There, over 30 able bodied men and women trooped into the Valkenburg hotel for a hearty breakfast and a pep talk from a tall and self-assured woman dressed in jeans and a pullover.

A casual observer would have taken the blonde lady to be a guide bringing pious pilgrims to Knock shrine. But this was deputy Beverley Flynn, in full flight in closed session with her devoted and loyal team of canvassers prior to embarking on a week-end electioneering blitzkrieg of the sprawling Mayo constituency.

As waitresses ferried bacon, egg and rashers to the famished volunteers, Beverly took time off to talk to me.

"Yes", she was confident of holding her seat. "I am getting a great reception on the doorsteps," she said, identifying the local issues as health, poor infrastructure, large class sizes, water charges, rural policing, (not surprising, given that Pádraic Nally lives near Ballinrobe), low incomes of women and farmer discontent at mounting forms-filling.

"No", the issues of her €2m legal bill to RTE and her libel spat with RTE's Charlie Bird were not being raised by voters. Anyway, her payment of the bill was her own personal affair.

"Not so much but occasionally, the question of Bertie Ahern's personal finances is coming up, but I am working flat out on policy matters," she said.

Asked if in a hung Dáil in which Fine Gael-Labour was one vote short of forming a government, would she vote for her fellow Mayoman, Enda Kenny, as Taoiseach, she side-stepped this, saying her sole concern was to get herself elected.

"If I found myself in that situation, I would do what is in the best interest," she added, reminding me of her Fianna Fáil background.

At this point, a wave of excitement swelled the room when her father, the former EU Commissioner, Pádriag Flynn, breezed in, and took his seat at a table, while exchanging chit chat and giving advice to Bev's volunteers.

Beverley returned to the room to address *the Flynnstone Army* and distribute election literature.

"Remember you ask people for their first vote for me. If they say no, ask them to give me a preference. If you come across any problems, take a note and let me known later so I can contact them."

Before Bev and her campaign workers headed for the streets, I saw Pádraig in huddled conversation with her and party activists.

Clearly, though Pádraig is in retirement, he is acting as Bev's chef de cabinet, giving her the advice of his long ministerial experience as *the Messiah of Mayo*. But, contrary to their gift for publicity and showmanship, both Pádraig and Beverley refused to be photographed together. An explanation for this was later given to me by a Fianna Fáil man who said that Beverley is emerging from the shadow of her famous father and is developing her own cult following and personal identity.

Bev is canvassing with the polished aura of a Hollywood diva. Her Castlebar stronghold remains strong, she is sweeping the Erris peninsula, making inroads in the Claremorris-Ballinrobe area, and she will receive transfers in Ballina and throughout rural Mayo.

With opinion polls indicating she will come third in the five-seater, there is a momentum behind her campaign. Indeed, my Fianna Fáil man predicted she will be within range of poll toppers, Fine Gael's Michael Ring, and prospective Taoiseach Kenny.

"There is a lot of sympathy for Beverley over her difficulties with RTE," my FF mole added. "There is also a feeling that she has been hard done by Fianna Fáil. Her top class media performances have reinforced the notion that she has talent and that Fianna Fáil will bring her back into the fold".

This remark reminded me of the TV moment when during his burlesque *Late Late Show* interview Pádraig described her as "a class act." When the votes are counted Mayo people will endorse Bev as *a class act*.

Bertie's Nail-bite

(May 22, 2007)

Harold Wilson's much quoted musing that a week is a long time in politics has retained a remarkable vitality. The late British Prime Minister's phrase came instantly to mind with the publication of the latest opinion polls showing a revitalisation in support of Bertie Ahern and Fianna Fáil.

After three weeks in which Fianna Fáil was on the ropes, its long awaited comeback came with a bang in Monday's *Irish Times tnsmrbi* poll which many readers will have been astonished by. Under the dramatic page one headline "Major surge for Fianna Fáil as alternative loses support", the findings put Fianna Fáil at 41pc, up five points in 10 days, Fine Gael at 27pc, down one, Labour 10pc, down three, the Greens at 6pc, one up, with the PDs are still on 2pc Sinn Féin down one at a strategically positioned 9pc.

These findings reveal a revival in Fianna Fáil fortunes greater than less emphatic trends towards the country's biggest political party registered in polls published in the *Sunday Business Post*, *The Sunday Independent* and Monday's *Irish Independent*.

Taken after last Thursday's Leaders' Debate on RTE *Prime Time* between the Taoiseach and the Fine Gael leader Enda Kenny, *The Irish Times* poll highlights a massive preference for Bertie rather than Enda to run the country for the next five years.

Even if you are disposed to give Bertie victory in the television debate – though I judged it a dreary and scrappy draw which might register as a boost to the Mayo contenders – the polls point to a tight result on Thursday. The FF-PD coalition is neck and neck with FG-Labour-Greens at 43pc.

In this situation the psychological advantage now lies with Bertie, who appears to have survived the shadow surrounding him by the Mahon Tribunal's investigation into his personal finances, and has benefited from the TV debate and other more feisty interviews as well as the huge acclaim given to him in the Westminster Parliament for his role in the peace process in the North.

Bertie is reinvigorated by this poll of confidence in his leadership scoring on the economy, taxation and foreign affairs, but I was astonished by his denial of a crisis in the health services which is being highlighted by the Opposition.

Furthermore, I felt that the Taoiseach's questioning of the expenditure involved in Kenny's *Contract for a Better Ireland* was an instance of masterly confusion-making. The reality is that FG-Labour is setting out its own priorities which are manageable under present budgetary availability, and that they display a determination to improve the shortage of beds in hospitals and provide free GP care for under five year olds that appear lacking in what is being offered by a complacent-sounding Government.

The combination of the four polls, I suspect, will influence undecided voters to stick with the status quo, though it should be remembered that polls give only an indication of first preference intentions and fail to chart the complex web of transfers in the 43 constituencies which will deliver surprises when the boxes are counted on Friday.

If the polls were particularly good for Fianna Fáil, there was something positive for everybody in its findings: PD leader Michael McDowell detected a public swing back to the current administration that has run the economy successfully in the past decade. You must raise your hat to Michael's optimism: even though he remains the most unpopular leader, he sees himself back as Tanaiste with up to ten PDs!

On Monday Enda Kenny and Labour leader Pat Rabbitte maintained that they were not down-hearted with the poll findings which they claim do not reflect the positive response their alliance is getting on the doorsteps.

My own impression is that the mood for a change is stronger than the polls indicate.

For instance, on Saturday morning I accompanied Labour's Finance spokes-person, Joan Burton, during her canvass in the busy Roselawn shopping centre in the Dublin West constituency. Voters approached her as often as she did shoppers. A highlight of the walkabout was when an irate Fianna Fáil supporter came over to tell her that for the first time he would be voting Labour in disgust at "how Bertie Ahern is no longer the representative of the working man."

In the previous few days Burton's helpers had detected an anti-Government swing expressing itself as a late surge to Labour rather than to Fine Gael. "It will be very tight," she said. "But the feed-back I'm getting for my campaign for more schools and better public transport is very good. I have also been getting warm support for women who appreciate my work on their behalf in the Dáil".

To give a second example. My local church, St Joseph's in Dublin's leafy suburb of Terenure momentarily looked as if it was about to become nationally famous for witnessing a remarkable political reconciliation between Michael

McDowell and Enda Kenny. Both men and their supporters turned up outside the church gates to canvass surprised Sunday worshippers as they were leaving the 10 o'clock Mass.

McDowell, dressed in his Sunday suit, appeared to be genuinely taken aback that the casually attired Kenny had chosen the same ecclesiastical spot for a bit of missionary work with the voters of Terenure.

"Hallo, Minister for Justice," the ever affable Enda greeted *the Mad Mullah*. Both men stood together apprehensive that the assembled cameras would depict them engaging in political ecumenism. Or at least that they would try to convert each other to the one true political faith.

Enda immediately ruled out any dialogue when he was asked by the *Irish Independent* if this was to be the occasion of a political rapprochement. "We are here to meet the people, not each other," the Mayoman said, preferring instead to be pictured with Fine Gael's highly presentable new babe, Lucinda Creighton.

McDowell, who had arrived first, was adamant that this was not a Michael-Enda Summit, but that it was by accident that they had chosen the same location at the same time. Non-plussed by the media focus on his rival rather than himself, Michael delivered his messianic message with the passion of an Old Testament prophet. He warned that within months of coming to power of a Left-dominated Fine Gael-Labour administration, the country would find itself in an economic doomsday state, comparable to being consigned to hell after ten years of the Celtic Tiger miracle under FF-PD stewardship.

Enda, after shrugging off the week-end's opinion polls favouring Bertie and predicting that FG-Labour would win, again became the centre of media attention when he showed his paternal instincts for a good photo opportunity with young girls dressed in their first Holy Communion dresses. Ousted from the limelight, McDowell regrouped outside the church yard wishing, no doubt, that John Gormley had turned up to break the Sabbath peace before Judgement Day.

Such vignettes add to the flavour of the most exciting general election in living memory. As decision time approaches on Thursday, we will witness the spectacle of cliff-hangers in numerous constituencies and surprises galore. This could be the prelude to several weeks of intense negotiations among the parties to form a stable administration. The post-election negotiations should be even more exciting than Election campaign 2007.

Bertie's Crying Game

(May 22, 2007)

As one of the 100,000 British-born residents living in Ireland, I felt a deep swell of emotion as I listened to Tony Blair and Bertie Ahern officially lay to rest in Westminster the national antagonisms that have so warped relations between our two island nations. I had tuned into the build-up to the broadcast on my car radio as I was travelling from Mayo to Dublin, methodically deep in W. B Yeats territory having earlier passed through Ballisodare in County Sligo.

The warmth of Blair's introduction of Bertie primed my sense that we were about to hear a major historical speech. But I was unprepared for an oration that would shatter my habitual Glasgow hard-man persona and reduce me to a sobbing jelly-baby!

The benchmark against which to measure the first ever address by a Taoiseach to the joint session of the Westminster Parliament was Eamon de Valera's famous reply in May 1945 to Winston Churchill's ferocious attack on Ireland's neutrality during World War II. "Could not he find in his heart the generosity to acknowledge that there is a small nation which stood alone, not for one year or two, but for several hundred years, against aggression?," Dev intoned, restoring the spirit of patriotism in Irish hearts listening to his Radio Éireann broadcast in their homesteads.

Exactly 62 years after the Churchill-de Valera stand-off, Prime Minister Blair said: "We know full well the history of the Troubles, and the path to reconciliation. Less well known and certainly less well understood has been the part played in it all by the transformation of relations between Britain and Ireland."

With such a generous and heart-felt introduction, I sensed that Bertie Ahern would rise to the occasion by delivering a speech to stand on par with great addresses such as Harold MacMillan's *The Wind of Change* in Africa, John F Kennedy's inspiring Inaugural as President of the United States of America, *Ask what you can do for your country*, and Martin Luther King's *I have a dream*.

Involuntarily, as I crossed the Shannon, my eyes began to moisten. Bertie Ahern's words were pressing emotional buttons in me.

Not since arriving in Dublin 35 years ago to work as a journalist did I ever envisage the elected Taoiseach of the Republic of Ireland stand up in the Mother of Parliaments to represent in an inclusive way not only the people in the 26 counties, but also the nationalists and unionists of Northern Ireland as well as the worldwide Irish diaspora.

The Taoiseach's reference to the story of division and conflict rekindled the perception of Ireland that I gleaned from stories told to me by my grandfather, *Big John*, 'an asylum seeker' fleeing random beatings from Orangemen in Coalisland, County Tyrone, and a refugee from an unviable small farm just before the Great War of 1914. He had come to Protestant Scotland to find work, settling in the pits around the village of Blantyre on the banks of the River Clyde.

Later, lonely after the death of my grandmother Sarah Skelton, from Milltown, County Armagh, whose father had been a boatman on Lough Neagh, *Big John* would invite me to keep him company as we listened to his scratched '78 records, now in my possession, which ranged from the *Bould Fenian Men* to *Kevin Barry*, and from Thomas Moore's sentimental ballads to John McCormack's romantic lyricism. His favourite song was *The Girl from the Co Down*.

Little did I know then that *Big John* smuggled dynamite from the pits to pass onto his brother-in-law Andy Fagan, from County Meath, who was a disciple of the Marxist campaigner and Lenin's representative in Glasgow, John MacLean, for which he was duly rewarded by Irish-born clergy in the archdiocese of Glasgow with excommunication; and that he was the Quartermaster of the Scottish Brigade of Irish Republican Brotherhood, its Director of Purchases.

It was to be as late as 1984 before I discovered the extent of support given by the Irish in Scotland to the cause of Ireland's freedom when I met Michael O'Carroll in Dromore, County Sligo. He confided that he was in 'the movement' in Scotland, and had stayed many a night in Andy's home. In 1919 Andy was host to Countess Markievicz – cited by Bertie as the first woman to be elected to the House of Commons, though she did not take her seat - when she visited the Gaelic Hall in Blantyre. Of how Andy would make furtive visits to Dublin to meet Michael Collins and later to Belfast to rendezvous with Seán Lemass. It was the clandestine activities of the likes of Andy and *Big John* that de Valera had in mind when he said that the chief factor in Sinn Féin's success was the money and materials (ie explosives and guns) from the Irish in Scotland. All of this was confirmed to me by Andy's eldest daughter, Cathie.

By now passing Longford, the tears spilled out from my eyes as if they were rain showers lashing the car wind-screen. Into my mind returned pictures of *Big John* on the day he arrived penniless by boat at Glasgow's Bromielaw, of his finding work in Blantyre after a period in Port Glasgow, of Sarah Skelton and her sister Maggie with her husband Andy joining him in a tenement without basic amenities such as an internal toilet.

Of how my mother, Mary Clark, would often tell me of her sadness that on her side of the family, her uncle Eoin Cassidy, the dux at school in Quarter, had not been able to find work and had gone off to find a better life in Australia, only to die there in an unmarked grave for the indigent Irish, his letter home still full of hope.

At this point I really needed a kleenex to wipe back the tears. This was the first time a Taoiseach was acknowledging the contribution to Irish society of 'immigrants' like myself.

I remembered the many times, too numerous, that I was called 'a Brit, bastard' who should go back to 'the Gorbals' (a notorious slum inhabited by the Glasgow Irish) where I belonged," and worse still that I was 'a planter'. Our hour has come!

I vividly recalled at how, aged 25, arriving in Dublin, a city where I was a complete stranger among 'long-forgotten cousins'. I felt like an Algerian coming to Paris. The Catholic ethos of the Republic was familiar to me, but there was a strand of intolerant triumphalism in Mother Church.

Of how, I felt more comfortable at times in Belfast, despite the strident sectarian violence, on account of having absorbed the best spirit of toleration in the Scottish Presbyterian tradition of *we are all Jock Thomson's bairns* (children).

With 'the Irish Problem' resolved, the future task is not only to make the power-sharing Executive work in Stormont, nationalist and unionist leaders will be called on to develop North-South bodies, as well as making meaningful the East-West dimension of the agreement with the Scots and the Welsh. Neither Bertie and Blair alluded to the fact that as they spoke the devolved Parliament in Edinburgh was poised to elect my good friend, the Scottish National Party leader, Alex Salmond, as that party's first First Minister, ending over fifty years of Labour rule there. I believe, that just as the 1921 Treaty signed by Michael Collins was "a stepping stone" towards Ireland achieving national sovereignty, so Ireland's next Taoiseach will cooperate with Salmond in his pursuit of making Scotland an independent country, at the heart of Europe, like Ireland, but in federal friendship with England, Wales and Northern Ireland as part of a peacefully restructured British Isles.

While appreciating the stoic work for peace done by Ahern and Blair, I was somewhat disappointed that Bertie's speech became too much a mutual congratulation pat on the back for himself and Tony. If only, Bertie had taken the extra time he needed to mention the many other heroes of the peace process, especially John Hume, his speech, splendid as it was, would have ranked as a truly great memorial to the Pantheon of Irish and British Peacemakers.

Bertie Victorious

(May 29, 2007)

Bertie Ahern triumphant. Enda Kenny defiant. Pat Rabbitte despondent. Trevor Sargent expectant. Michael McDowell vanquished. Gerry Adams humbled. Independents with shopping bags – these are the abiding iconic images of Election 2007. The returning officers record the share-out of seats for the 30th Dail as Fianna Fáil 78, Fine Gael 51, Labour 20, Greens, 6, Sinn Féin 4, Independents 5.

We still have to wait until June 14 for the election of Taoiseach and the formation of a Government. Although Enda is bidding for the nomination, the public will be amazed if Bertie is gazumped by the Fine Gael leader.

The post-mortems of the campaign by commentators are providing historians with the first draft of it's dynamics: the media attack on Bertie's personal finances leaked from the Mahon Tribunal, Brian Cowen's gutsy rallying of the Fianna Fáil grassroots and his warnings to the electorate not to risk political stability and economic prosperity for an untried Rainbow formation, Bertie's mastery of the nitty gritty of governance and the economy on his TV debate with Enda, Bertie's glorious days addressing the Westminster Parliament and on the Banks of the Boyne with the North's First Minister, Ian Paisley, and the "squeezing" of the smaller parties and Independents by the campaign's polarisation into a battle between the two main political parties conducted on a presidential style.

Within this framework, it was not surprising that the PDs collapsed, but it was a pleasant surprise for many that Sinn Féin's predicted ascent to power in the Republic faltered. The biggest shock was the defeat of Michael McDowell.

McDowell signed his own political death warrant last September when he saved Bertie Ahern at the height of the controversy over his personal finances. In the light of the Taoseach's success, the nation should be expressing its gratitude to the PD leader, rather than sentencing him to damnation. Instead, it gave his P45 to the PD leader, one of the intellectual giants ever to dominate the Dáil chamber and the national airwaves.

That McDowell's career in Government as Tanaiste is over is largely of his own making as he courted controversy to such a fevered extent that he became the most unpopular political leader in the country. The Minister for Justice alienated not only the Gardaí, but disappointed all sections of society by his failure to implement the biggest police and judicial reform in the history of the State, that he boasted would be his memorial.

A compulsive attention seeker, he had too much to say on every subject. He became a national turn-off whenever he orated in public. Journalists will miss his departure. He was a reporter's dream. He was not short of a quote. He was good company. He was even likeable! He was a Peter Pan of Irish politics who never grew in political maturity as he produced utopia upon utopia as if he was barman pouring pints on a Bank Holiday week-end.

Known as *the Mad Mullah*, he was always in fights. He was a doughty pugilist, with a right hand punch to match Pat Rabbitte's left fist. He could take the blows. This was shown when he lost his Dublin South-East in 1997, but he returned to become Tánaiste and PD leader. It was his desertion from the core PD principle of being the Fianna Fáil watchdog that ensured his demise with PD true believers. On McDowell's tomb-stone may read the words: "Haughey made me. Ahern undid me."

Now that the voters have dealt the nation's politicians with a jumbled deck of cards in the most exciting general election in living memory, an even more riveting game of poker for the title of Taoiseach has begun.

A jubilant Bertie has the upper hand, but an unhinged Enda Kenny has challenged him to play serious poker for the highest stakes in the land. At first glance, most voters will consider that Kenny is bluffing, and that Ahern will face him down, as he did in the presidential-style campaign in the 43 constituencies.

Bertie is in pole position. With the support of the two PDs, Mary Harney and Noel Grealish, he needs a minimum of three extra Dáil votes to secure a majority in the 166 seat chamber which would enable him to be elected Taoiseach for the third time on June 14. (The Ceann Comhairle votes only in the event of a tied vote, and convention is that his casting vote goes to the Government.) As the Taoiseach told *Sky News*, he has the options of entering Government with the PDs plus support from like-minded Independents. He has the Green option. 'Less likely' is coalition with Labour.

When Bertie meets his deputy leader, Brian Cowen, this week, they will work out "a process" to secure power. They could grant Mary Harney her wish of returning to Health. They could cut deals with most, if not all five Independents, Beverley Flynn, Jackie Healy-Rae, Finian McGrath, Michael Lowry, and Tony Gregory. Easy-looking on paper. A manageable majority. But messy. It would question Ahern's objective of forming a stable administration lasting five years. It would essentially be a Fianna Fáil minority government.

Turning either to the Greens or Labour could be even more problematical, given the stated reservation of Trevor Sargent to government with Fianna Fáil, and Pat Rabbitte's reaffirmed ruling out of any deal with FF.

With over two weeks to go before the assembling of the Dáil, FF could lure either party to its side in the national interest. Sargent might be persuaded, but Labour would have to topple Rabbitte, and replace him with either Brendan Howlin or Ruairi Quinn.

A FF-Green administration, with 84 seats, plus two PDs, would be an untried quantity. A FF-Labour formation, on close to a 100, including the PDs, would guarantee durability, but it could force Bertie to concede at least four cabinet posts to Labour and Seanad nominations to the PDs.

However, Kenny, who has refused to concede defeat, yesterday advanced a plausible set of counter-arguments to thwart Ahern. He noted that the electorate has gifted Bertie with a not invincible set of cards, and that his own hand could yet be a winning one.

Kenny pointed out that in comparison to the 89 seats won by the Coalition five years ago, Fianna Fáil has dropped three seats from 81 to 78, and the PDs have slumped from eight to two. This overall drop of nine seats by the outgoing governing partners is hardly the thundering victory hailed in the initial euphoric coverage of Fianna Fáil's recovery from predicted losses.

Tellingly, Kenny also pointed out that the combined strength of Fine Gael, with 51 seats, Labour 20 and the Greens six amounts to 77 seats, only one behind Fianna Fáil and just three below the aggregated FF-PD figure of 80. Another statistic deployed by Kenny, with an eye on Sargent, was that 60 pc of the electorate voted against the FF-PD coalition. Arguing the formation of the next Government was far from clear cut, the Fine Gael leader will talk to Rabbitte, Sargent, and, significantly, Mary Harney.

This is a tantalising move to involve Harney. If she and Grealish joined an alternative government, their numbers would total 79, a lead of one over Fianna Fáil, and a mere four short of the magic 83 figure. Would Kenny be able to win over at least four of the five Independents?

This is unlikely, but not impossible. But it would signal the formation of a potentially unstable FG-Labour-Greens administration dependent on Independents. Such a precarious voting position would bring Sinn Féin's four deputies back into the game. They would offer their four votes to Fianna Fáil from outside government but at a price. Unless Bertie acts quickly and decisively, the electorate might be stuck with 'a hung Dáil' it did not want.

Perhaps the Mayoman's real game is to head a strong Opposition led by Fine Gael, with Labour and the Greens, leaving an insecure Bertie coalescing with PDs and Independents, bolstered in the wings by Sinn Féin.

'Planet Bertie'

(June 5, 2007)

John Gormley, the abrasive chairman of the Green Party, made a colourful and robust speech earlier this year in which he described life on *Planet Bertie*. It was a planet, he said, in which you can sign blank cheques, spend the average industrial wage on make-up, get loans you do not have to pay back and save £50,000 without having a bank account.

Gormley delivered his mock attack on Taoiseach Bertie Ahern at the Greens' pre-election conference last March in Galway. His anti-Fianna Fáil rhetoric was matched by party leader Trevor Sargent, who solemnly condemned FF-ism as a type of religion without values or vision whose annual highpoint was inveigling wealthy pilgrims from the world of big business into tents at the Galway races.

Under the banner that "the Greens are ready for Government", Sargent and Gormley had their platoon of Green delegates excitedly on their feet ready for electoral battle to rid the country of the accursed Fianna Fáil-Progressive Democrat coalition.

That was then. Over this June Bank Holiday week-end Gormley looked like a conspirator who is itching to get into power. He trooped into Government Buildings as head of a Green delegation eager to do a deal with Bertie's Fianna Fáil. They have calculated that the numbers do not stack up for their first preference of a Rainbow Coalition with Fine Gael and Labour.

Sunday's exploratory talks involved Gormley, Dan Boyle, who lost his seat in Cork South Central, and party general secretary Donall Geoghegan for the Greens, while Brian Cowen led for Fianna Fáil accompanied by Seamus Brennan and Noel Dempsey. After what were described as cordial talks, Brennan admitted differences had emerged which would be worked through in coming days. These talks raise the expectation that Bertie aims to form a Government based on a contractual alliance with the six Greens and the two PDs that would give him a relatively secure 86 seat administration in the 166 member Dáil. There is also speculation that he aims to keep sweet three Independents, Jackie Healy-Rea, Beverley Flynn and Michael Lowry. For some time now Bertie has placed increased emphasis on environmental issues aimed at attracting Green Party support. He has rejected nuclear power as a solution to global warming, and promised a 'green energy revolution' to ensure Ireland fully meets its oblibations on climate change. He will pilot energy efficiencies in the State sector, including mandatory use of bio-fuel in transport fuels. All street lighting and traffic systems will become energy efficient. At the spring European Council in March the Governrment supported the EU aim of pressing for an international agreement among developed nations providing for a 30pc cut in greeehouse gas emissions. In the absence of an international agreement, there should be a unilateral cut in EU emission by 20pc.

Before the election Sargent was scathing of Fianna Fáil's promises on green issues, particularly climate change, claiming it had done little in this area in ten years. The Green Party leader accused the Taoiseach of refusing to state how the Government will cut Ireland's CO2 emissions to meet the 20pc unilateral reduction agreed by EU Environment ministers in Brussels.

In the negotiations Fianna Fáil will refuse to reverse its policy of private-public co-location of hospitals. It will stick to its Shannon policy, as Finian McGrath discovered. It will seek Green acceptance of the national roads plan.

Sticking points could be planning law reform, the Greens' attitude to agriculture, and its demands for ending corporate funding of political parties. There is also the question of Sargent's leadership. He has said that he will not lead the Greens into Government with Fianna Fáil, though he would serve as a minister in a Fianna Fáil-Green administration. On one occasion, he ruled out ever sitting around the same cabinet table with Dick Roche, Martin Cullen and Frank Fahey.

If a draft Programme for Government is agreed, the scene will be set for a stormy session of the 700-strong Greens' membership at Dublin's Mansion House next Sunday. It will be a test of Ciaran Cuffe's blog warning: "a deal with Fianna Fáil would be a deal with the devil. We would be spat out after five years, and decimated as a party."

Last September the Labour leader Pat Rabbitte predicted at the height of *Bertiegate* that the Taoiseach would do a deal with Tanaiste Michael McDowell in which "Bertie will do a Lady Di performance." Rabbitte's forecast was inspired by his recall of the famous television interview given by Princess Diana in which she admitted her own foibles that lead to the break-up of her marriage with Prince Charles. Rabbitte proved to be uncannily accurate. As if on cue, a tearful Bertie duly did his Diana act with Bryan Dobson on RTE which waved its spell on the nation, and left Fine Gael, Labour and the Greens impotent to challenge him in Leinster House.

McDowell gave the chastened Bertie absolution for what the nation deemed to be a venial transgression of having taken financial dig-outs from friends and well-wishers in Drumcondra and Manchester when he was Minister for Finance in the early 1990s.

When some seven months later leaks from the Mahon Tribunal appeared in the media at the start of the general election campaign, the new information called into question the comprehensive nature of Bertie's September breast-beating.

So agitated was McDowell with the new revelation that over the first weekend of the campaign, he was on the verge of excommunicating Ahern and taking his distraught PDs into schism. Michael stopped short of this and gave conditional pardon to the Taoiseach provided he issued a further statement. Bertie again duly complied. Michael again granted him pardon.

In this second round, Bertie did not need to invoke the Diana image. The Fianna Fáil grass-roots rallied the sympathy of ordinary voters who had gone through similar difficult traumas in their life which they would not want to be made public. In Bertie's electoral resurrection that left the media at logger-heads with middle Ireland, however, Bertie unexpectedly showed his wounds when he poured his heart out about the "intrusive" media.

Despite his subsequent denial of harbouring brooding intent, his remarks were interpreted as a thinly veiled display of menace towards the Fourth Estate.

The resumption of the Mahon Tribunal last Monday has catapulted him for the third time into defending himself against its statement about "discrepancies" in his financial statement given last April to its lawyers. Specifically, the Tribunal is questioning how a sum purporting to be $45,000 appeared in his AIB bank account in Dublin's O'Connell Street in 1994.

Knowing that the public are turned-off by his personal finances, the Taoiseach's legal representative accused the Tribunal of engaging in a coordinated and malevolent campaign against him. This is Bertie's high-stakes confrontation at a time when Enda Kenny's intermediaries have gone on the offensive to warn Mary Harney, Trevor Sargent and the Independents of the possible risk to stable government of giving their support to the Fianna Fáil leader.

Implicit in this strategy is the hint that, if they side with Bertie, they could suffer a McDowell-style political suicide. Gormley, the scourge of McDowell, needs to contemplate the perils of life on *Planet Bertie*.

Hat-trick for Bertie
the Cunning

(June 12, 2007)

B ertie Ahern will be the proud groom for a third time and Enda Kenny will be the unwilling bridesmaid when the 30th Dáil convenes on Thursday. But as Lanigan's Ball continues its dizzy reels, at the time of writing mid-day Monday it was not yet clear if the Greens would be invited to join the Fianna Fáil fusiliers in the spoils of office.

We still do not know if the Tanaiste will be Fianna Fáil's deputy leader, Brian Cowen, or the Green leader, Trevor Sargent. On Monday morning Bertie made a courtesy phone call to Sargent. Fianna Fáil was responding in writing to a document sent by the Greens on Sunday evening setting out the state of play between the two parties.

The latest indication was that talks might be resumed with a Convention of Green members being summoned for Wednesday evening in the event of a deal being ironed out before deputies meet on Thursday afternoon.

Following the breakdown on Friday of negotiations with the Greens, expecta-tions of a 'hung Dáil' were dispelled when the Taoiseach's spin-doctors revealed over the week-end that backroom diplomacy had ensured that the Drumcondra man was already in a position to lead a Fianna Fáil Government with the support of the Progressive Democrats and four Independents.

It was confirmed that *Bertie the Cunning* has already copper-fastened his first option of a deal with Mary Harney, Jackie Healy-Rae, Beverley Flynn, Michael Lowry and Finian McGrath. Apparently, Bertie and his programme manager, Gerry Hickey, were discreetly stitching up off-stage agreements with the PDs and Independents last week in parallel with the more public acrobatics of the Fianna Fáil-Green talks.

Although the Greens' chief negotiator, John Gormley, was frantically trying to reopen the talks by sending Ahern a document setting out the state of play, the speed of time's 'winged chariot' was militating against their cobbling a last minute programme for Government which has been described by Bertie as "not incompatible."

In turn, Gormley apologised for his recent rhetoric about life on *Planet Bertie*, a climbdown which reflects a more professional attitude towards the Taoiseach, whose personal finances have overshadowed both the election and the negotiations.

On Friday a common navigation route could not be found by the two courting parties in the thicket of climate change, transportation, a carbon tax, education funding, transformation of local government, planning reform, and reform of the health care system. The Greens also objected to Mary Harney.

Fianna Fáil's negotiators, Brian Cowen, Seamus Brennan and Noel Dempsey were too experienced to barter away core policies which would have made Ireland's biggest political party - that identifies itself with the nation - look like an annexed adjunct to Green-land.

Confirmation by Fianna Fáil sources of ongoing talks with Harney, the PD care-taker leader, and Independents indicate that the Drumcondra ward-boss is on course to secure 84 votes in the 166 member Dáil. Even if final details of these financial arrangements are still to be signed on the dotted line, no one doubts that they will not be ready for delivery by Thursday. In that case, the Independents will have forfeited their rights to be called independent. They will have become Bertie's camp followers.

Mary Harney, we are led to believe, will get her wish of returning to Angola as Minister for Health, and her sole PD colleague, Noel Grealish, will march willingly with the triumphant Fianna Fáil divisions.

The icing on the cake for the third term Taoiseach would be the acceptance by a leading Labour deputy of the position of Ceann Comhairle. Already there are signs that Ruairi Quinn, Brendan Howlin and Brian O'Shea are only too eager to be the anointed one. The precedent is being cited of how Seamus Pattison of Labour accepted the office of Speaker in 1997.

Such a defection by a Labour worthy from the Opposition ranks would have a double bonus effect on the Fianna Fáil numbers. It would be a mortal blow to Enda Kenny's outside chance of heading a Fine Gael-led administration. This could be the end of Enda's affair with Labour's Pat Rabbitte, who will come under pressure to adopt a more unilateral policy positioning stance in the incoming Dáil.

At the back of Bertie's memory will be how Charles Haughey's attempt to offer the Ceann Comhairle twenty years ago to Fine Gael's Tom Fitzpatrick failed when he consulted Garret FitzGerald and his parliamentary party – who quickly closed off that bolt-hole.

Bertie will also recall that Haughey had to fall back on offering the Caenn Comhairle's job to Independent Seán Treacy, and only succeeded in becoming Taoiseach thanks to Treacy's casting vote when Tony Gregory abstained.

Little wonder, therefore, that Bertie is on the record in recalling that life in Haughey's minority Government from 1987-89, in which he was Minister for Labour, had difficult times. According to Fianna Fáil handlers, Bertie's favoured formation with the PDs and the Independents will be tight but manageable. They are confident that the previous frontline experience gained 10 years ago with Independents will stand them in good stead.

On June 26, 1997, Bertie was nominated by the 28th Dáil for appointment as Taoiseach for the first time by then President Mary Robinson of a minority Fianna Fáil-Progressive Democrat Government. On top of Fianna Fáil's 77 votes and the four PDs, Ahern secured a majority with the support of three Independents, Harry Blaney, Mildred Fox and Healy-Rae, as well as Sinn Féin's Caoimhghin Ó Caoláin.

In that vote two other Independents, Michael Lowry and Tom Gildea abstained. But Gildea moved quickly to support the Government on the basis of deals made through the then Chief Whip, Séamus Brennan, and Ahern's right hand man, the trusted Hickey.

This time, Michael Lowry wants to join the golden circle of parish-pump camp followers whose constituencies will benefit from Ahern's financial largesse.

Hickey, a former student for the priesthood and a well-read philosopher with a decade's experience of reading Bertie Ahern's enigmatic mind, will still be there to keep the four camp followers inside the Government tent.

Sources in Mayo say that Beverley Flynn will have a cheque for €2.84m in the post to settle her libel dues to RTE, thus avoiding being declared bankrupt before her case is due to be heard in the High Court next Monday. She hopes to return to the Fianna Fáil fold in due course, and be in contention for ministerial office.

However, with Bertie admitting in his statement last Wednesday of a downturn in the economy, managing the camp followers will not be as easy as in 1997 when the Celtic Tiger economy was taking off.

In our tunnel vision about the shape of the next Government, it was uplifting of horizons to hear Ireland's two most famous rock stars, Bono and Bob Geldof lambasting the G8 Summiteers in Germany for their failure to live up to their commitments to end poverty in Africa which they made two years ago in Gleneagles, Scotland. The Heiligendamm communiqué announcing $60bn aid towards treating HIV/Aids, TB and malaria was aptly dismissed by Bono as "bureaubabble" for being a rehash of old promises and pious aspirations.

Hopefully, when we see the line-up of Bertie's third Government, with or without the Greens, it will not be based on a too familiarly parochial Irish version of *bureaubabble*.

Greens 'Rocket Solid' with Bertie

(June 19, 2007)

We knew that Bertie Ahern had done deals with PD caretaker leader Mary Harney and four Independents to form a Government on Thursday, but it was a race against time for him to finalise agreement with the Greens.

By mid-day Wednesday the details of the Fianna Fáil-Green programme for Government rolled out from the respective parties, and on Wednesday evening there was jubilation among the Greens when their special members' convention ratified the accord. But scenes resembling an alleluia gathering of religious evangelicals were overshadowed by the announcement of Trevor Sargent that he would not be going into cabinet and was stepping down as leader.

Sargent stunned the media which was incredulous that he was keeping his pre-election promise. This was an admirable instance of principle in politics. Yet, I cannot help questioning Sargent's logic: he approved the U-turn deal with Fianna Fáil and is to take up the post of Minister of State with responsibility for food. These two actions substantially modify, if not actually negate his self-enunciated principle of non-engagement with Fianna Fáil.

Even before the Dáil assembled it was widely known that the two Green cabinet ministers were John Gormley (Environment) and Eoin Ryan (Communications). Reaction was mixed, with some sections of public opinion elated that climate change and other environmental issues are now centre stage of government policy; others sounded angry that in voting for Fianna Fáil, they had not wanted the Greens.

As the 30th Dáil opened, my mind drifted to the opening day of a newly assembled House of Commons when the leader of the Opposition, Andrew Bonar Law, told Prime Minister Herbert Asquith, "I will have to be vicious with you this session, Sir."

In Dublin, Dáil business is done more graciously than at Westminster. Enda Kenny and Pat Rabbitte were genuinely sincere in their tributes to Bertie Ahern after his election as Taoiseach for a third time.

However, their prospects of bringing-down Bertie within five years looked extremely remote as Kenny and Rabbitte stared across the Dáil chamber at an outwardly invincible Government created by the Taoiseach.

Indeed, the construction of the new administration was best described by former Labour party stalwart Pat Magner as *rocket solid* that would have been a credit to a NASA space worker. With pragmatic skill, Bertie has assembled a partnership Government embracing Fianna Fáil, the Greens, the PDs, contractually supported by Jackie Healy-Rae, Beverley Flynn, Michael Lowry and Finian McGrath. *Fortress Ahern!*

But by early evening after Ahern announced his conservative cabinet line-up with Brian Lenihan the only new FF face in Justice, Kenny plunged his metaphorical dagger into a cynical marriage of convenience in which Mary Harney had turned the once principled PDs into the party of power-driven policy at the front of Bertie's bicycle. The Greens are its back mud guard "lock stock and three pork barrels."

Before the gloves came off, Enda, the new Father of the House, observed wryly that the one area in which he got the better of Bertie's "persistency and permanence" was in length of Dáil service, while Pat acknowledged his truly remarkable achievement to his single-minded focus on politics and public service.

Obviously disappointed that they did not succeed in providing an alternative Fine Gael-Labour Government, Kenny, 56, and Pat, 58, will be called on to display single-mindedness if they are to achieve permanence.

That the Fine Gael and Labour leaders plan to make a fight of it was signalled from the opening moments of the new Dáil when they challenged Fianna Fáil's proposal of John O'Donoghue for the post of Ceann Comhairle by putting forward Labour's Ruairi Quinn. O'Donoghue's resounding margin of victory was a harbinger of the ease of Ahern's election, and an indicator of comfortable majorities for the Government in the foreseeable future.

For Kenny, there was the consolation that he is the indisputable leader of the Opposition with an enlarged party of 51 members who include a youthful crop of newcomers as well as a return of experienced casualties from the 2002 election.

In his post-election interview on Sunday, Kenny described winning an extra 20 seats as a truly outstanding achievement, greater than Jack Lynch's 15 extra seats in his 1977 landslide victory, and Dick Spring's 19 in 1992.

Yet Enda lost, because the Fianna Fáil vote, far from collapsing, had rallied to Bertie whose crowning achievement of a third consecutive election as Taoiseach would not be surpassed in politics in out time. The grit displayed by Kenny in the course of the campaign remained undimmed as he pledged to make Fine Gael the biggest party after the next election. He is now looking for new young candidates for the European and local elections which are only 100 weeks away.

For Rabbitte, disappointed by Labour's return of only 20 deputies, the road ahead will be tougher. Already there is criticism that he did not contest last month's election on Labour's own free-lance identity for change, as did the Greens. With Rabbitte due to present himself for re-election as leader late next year, he needs to reinvigorate his party and quickly recruit a new generation of prospective Labour deputies. He has the opportunity of establishing Labour as the leading voice of the Left, while building on the alliance with Fine Gael.

However, spirited interventions by Sinn Féin's Caoimhghin Ó Caoláin, in which he dubbed Fine Gael as a right wing party which Labour should never have propped up, indicate that the Monaghan man will aim to revive his party's fortunes as a populist third force. Sinn Féin's difficulty is that it will lack speaking time enjoyed by the last Dáil's technical group, because it has only four deputies, three short of the required seven.

But it was Bertie's week. In a round of interviews he anointed Brian Cowen as his successor by the end of the Dáil term and disclosed that he will appoint two or three extra junior ministers this week. Beverley Flynn will be appointed to the junior ranks in mid-term once she sorts out her financial problems with RTE and the courts.

A smiling Bertie was in particularly sparkling form on Saturday evening with Miriam O'Callaghan. He was quite right in ruling himself out for the Presidency in four years time: it would not be his life-style. What struck me most was his enthusiasm for introducing Green policies and for addressing the slow delivery of public services.

Managing and meeting change is the big challenge facing Bertie. A sign of the changing political landscape came this Monday with the arrival in Stormont of the Scotland's First Minister, Alex Salmond, for talks with the North's First Minister Ian Paisley and his deputy Martin McGuinness. As well developing East-West relations promised in his historic address to Westminster, Bertie is hoping to get North-South talks moving soon.

Yet, the ghost of the past came back to haunt us with news over the week-end that Bertie will be called before the Mahon Tribunal early next month to explain his finances in the early 1990s. I bet that I will not be the only one to feel that the electorate has delivered its verdict to Judge Alan Mahon. As Bertie told Miriam O'Callaghan, politics is not about looking back but is about going forward.

With the economy entering difficult conditions and the Mahon Tribunal continuing its probes, Kenny and Rabbitte might console themselves with the famous advice of the unexpected in politics given by another British Prime Minister, Harold Macmillan.

"Events, my dear boy. Events".

Bertie Brings Bev Back

(July 3, 2007)

The willingness of newly elected deputy Dara Calleary to work harmoniously with Beverley Flynn augurs well for Fianna Fáil's healing of its deep divisions in the Mayo constituency.

Whether Flynn's reinstatement in Fianna Fáil ends the rivalry between her Castlebar base and Calleary's Ballina stronghold remains a more dubious prospect, one which may only be addressed by Taoiseach Bertie Ahern's assigning Mayo two junior ministers in his mid-term review of Government places.

Bertie's wooing of Beverley has had the immediate positive effect of focusing the new Government's attention on Mayo's grievances of economic neglect by Dublin during the Celtic Tiger period.

In her talks with the Taoiseach and his right hand man, Gerry Hickey, she indicated that her requirements cover improvements in Mayo's General Hospital, its health services, as well as road rail and airports. Establishing a list of priorities and agreement on the timing of delivery are issues to be resolved and implemented.

Beverley was not in the High Court this Monday when it was confirmed that she has until August 17 to pay the €1.25 million settlement of her failed libel action with RTE. She also dropped her constitutional challenge to the law preventing bankrupts becoming Dáil deputies.

With 10 of the 12 Fianna Fáil councillors in Mayo reportedly supporting her readmission to the party, this could be endorsed by the national executive and the parliamentary party in the near future.

If Beverley received a euro for every inch of press coverage given to her settlement since its disclosure a fortnight ago, not only would she have already cleared her debt, she would have a tidy sum the size of Mount Nephin to spare!

However, much of the coverage has been negative and personalised against *the Flynnasty*. RTE's decision to write off almost €1 million caused a volcanic national eruption spilling over in angry comments to the Joe Duffy Show and in letters to newspapers. These ranged from Kevin Myers who judged both Bertie and Bev acting above the law to Justine McCarthy claiming that the whole episode "serves to cheapen the call to public service".

Lisa Hand's description of Bev as "just an arrogant woman blind to her faults" was an instance of the less acrimonious jibes, while the peeping-Tom sections of the media titillated their readers with pictures of *the Duchess's* Castlebar home with builder Tony Gaughan and their holiday home in Doohoma at "Number One Amnesia Drive"!.

Meanwhile, the theatre surrounding the Flynn deal was further played out in the Dáil when Fine Gael's Michael Ring was expelled by an incandescent Ceann Comhairle John O'Donoghue, and Enda Kenny sought to link Bertie's remarks that Bev would get a junior minister to the Castlebar woman's attempts to resolve her legal and financial difficulties.

I always felt that in pursuing the case against RTE right up to the Supreme Court, while unwisely marginalising herself politically. Once the hullabaloo settles down, whatever the rights and wrongs, it will be good for Dáil and Mayo politics for her to fulfil her father Pádraig's judgement that she is a class act. Her working relationship with Dara Calleary should pay dividends for both Castlebar and Ballina.

A harbinger of summer will come this Thursday when the Dáil adjourns for its long vacation. Beverley Flynn's rehabilitation and the future of the Tribunals of Inquiry will seem very localised compared to the security threat in our neighbouring island.

Following Britain's new Prime Minister Gordon Brown's confirmation that the attack on Glasgow Airport terminal was the concerted action of radical Islamists associated with al-Qaida. Seven terrorist suspects were under arrest, including, significantly, two doctors from overseas, further highlighting that the risk to the UK remains 'critical'.

In the light of the global threat from Islamic terrorism, the old dictum that *all politics is local* seems somewhat dated.

Bertie and People Power

(July 10, 2007)

When Gerry Adams and Martin McGuinness paid their first visit to 10 Downing Street the Derryman said loudly to Tony Blair: "So this is the room where all the damage was done."

According to Alastair Campbell, who was in the cabinet room, it was a classic moment where the different histories of Britain and Ireland played out. This was on Thursday December 11, 1997.

"Everyone on our side thought he was referring to the mortar attack on (John) Major, and we were shocked," Blair's former press secretary discloses in his newly published diaries. "Yet it became obvious from their surprise at our shock that he was referring to policymaking down the years, and Britain's involvement in Ireland."

Correcting their wrong impression McGuinness said: "No, no. I meant 1921," referring to Michael Collins' negotiations with Prime Minister Lloyd George that produced the Treaty giving independence to the 26 counties in Ireland.

Campbell, *the Sultan of Spin* in the Blair years, found McGuinness more impressive than Adams, who "did the big statesmanlike bit, and talked in grand historical sweeps."

In contrast to Adams' Eamon de Valera-like grandeur, McGuinness "just made a point and battered it, and forced you to take it on board," Campbell observed, while eyeing the reaction of the two Irishmen to Blair's remark that he wanted to be able to look the Sinn Féin President in the eye, hear him say he was committed to peaceful means, and he wanted to believe him.

"Both Adams and McG regularly let a smile cross their lips," Campbell writes. Mo Mowlam "got pissed off, volubly, when they said she wasn't doing enough. TB was maybe not as firm as we had planned, but he did ask – which I decided not to brief (journalists) and knew they wouldn't – whether they would be able to sign up to a settlement that did not explicitly commit to a united Ireland."

According to Campbell, Adams was OK on this but McGuinness was not. "Adams said the prize of a lasting peace justifies the risks. Lloyd George, Balfour, Gladstone, Cromwell, they all thought they had answers of sorts. We want our answers to be the endgame. A cobbled-together agreement will not stand the test of time."

Adams "pushed hard on prisoners being released, and the aim of total demilitarisation, and TB just listened. TB said he would not be a persuader for a united Ireland. The principle of consent was central to the process."

As we know, it took another 10 years of intense, on-off negotiations before we arrived earlier this year at the installation of McGuinness as Stormont's Deputy First Minister to the Rev Ian Paisley, while Adams had a disastrous personal outing in the recent Dail elections where he proved himself to be out of touch with thinking south of the Border.

This passage from Campbell's heavily edited diaries to spare the blushes of both Blair and his successor Gordon Brown gives a revealing insight into the dynamic behind closed doors in the relationships of leading politicians. Campbell, who will make a fortune out of his diaries, is under fire for their publication so soon after Blair's departure from office.

The only comparable books to Campbell's which have been written in Ireland are by former Government press secretary to Albert Reynolds, Sean Duignan's *One Spin on the Merry-Go-Round* and Frank Dunlop's *Yes Taoiseach* about his years with Jack Lynch and Charles Haughey.

Gordon Brown has said he will not be reading the book, but I would imagine that it will be packed in the suitcases of quite a few Irish politicians for dipping into during their three month vacation from the 30th Dáil.

Yes, it's that time of year, folks, when the politicians take flight from Leinster House, and Government ministers get on with their briefs without interruption from the Dáil opposition.

Invariably, at this time of the year too, we hear about plans for Dáil reform. On cue, Government Chief Whip Tom Kitt disclosed at the week-end that he will work with the Opposition parties to do so when the Dáil resumes on September 26. He will reconstitute the Dáil Reform Committee which he hopes will meet before Christmas. Whew!

After an exhausting election, which produced Bertie Ahern's macabre Fianna Fáil-PDs-Greens Government supported by Independents that intends to treat the demoralised Fine Gael, Labour and Sinn Féin Opposition like dummies, we may all need a rest from politics.

The interlude, however, provides an opportunity to consider radical parliamentary reform instead of mere tinkering with the archaic Dáil procedures. In this context, it is well worth looking at the package of reforms proposed by Britain's new Prime Minister, Gordon Brown, "to ensure government is a better servant of the people".

Brown's proposals aim to strengthen the powers of members of parliament that have been ceded over the years to centralising governments, notably Blair's. Here in Ireland, too, we have seen the relegation of the Houses of the Oireachtas to the will of government.

The Westminster Parliament is to be given the right to approve major public appointments. Such a move strikes an immediate chord here as ministers prepare to make more than 300 appointments, many of them in the form of party patronage, to State boards and other public bodies before the end of the year. Fine Gael's Jim O'Keeffe wants nominees to the more important jobs to appear before an Oireachtas committee.

Another Brown proposal – of holding general elections on Sundays – is one that would be welcomed here, especially by students who found themselves unable to return to their homes to vote on a Thursday.

While unlike Ireland, Britain does not have a written constitution, Brown has launched a cross-party debate on a new Bill of Rights that could for the first time enshrine the rights and responsibilities of citizens.

What I would urge Taoiseach Bertie Ahern to do in his third administration is to launch a similar cross-party debate to devise a new Constitution to replace the current one which is 70 years old this year, and which, like an old suit, is worse the wear from being a product of a past era and grossly mismatched for a modern multi-cultural society.

An editorial in *The Guardian* highlighted two basic insights in Brown's measures which also equally apply to Ahern's post-election Ireland. First, that constitutional arrangements genuinely matter in defining the kind of society we are. Second, that we can do them very much better than we have been managing to do.

Brown's key point is that people need to have confidence in the way elected politicians go about the task of governance. Unless parliamentary democracy is perceived to be relevant to peoples' lives, it will be unable to deal with the challenges of security from international terrorism, economic change and tense communities.

Ahern, who is renowned for his caution in his ten years as Taoiseach, could take a leaf from Brown's book, and embark on a consultation process that would provide us with a constitution and a system of governance geared to the realities of the opening decades of the twenty-first century.

Above all, Bertie could follow Brown's lead in offering to give more power back to the people rather than making the cabinet room continue to bamboozle people as a secretive and mystifying location where ministers do damage in their name.

Bertie Lauds John Wilson

(July 17, 2007)

I n the archives of the Humbert Summer School is an official Government press release welcoming the School's inception in north Mayo in August 1987 as "an imaginative and courageous new venture".

It was issued by the then Minister for Tourism and Transport, John Wilson, who has died at the age of 84. He hailed the initiative as deserving "the commendation and support of everyone interested in fostering tourism and historical research and discussion".

This Government endorsement gave the fledgling Humbert School the best of starts, especially as its launch in Dublin twenty-one years ago was presided over by Taoiseach Charles Haughey. Between them, Haughey and Wilson put the Humbert School firmly on Ireland's summer school map in a move that a *Western People* editorial greeted as "the genesis of a really significant commitment which can endow the North-West region enormously."

When preparing for the Humbert launch, I contacted John Wilson to brief him on the School's potential as "an intellectual tourism" product. He invited me to join him for breakfast next morning in the Dáil restaurant. It was a most stimulating working breakfast.

Immediately, he gave his personal backing for the project, and began drafting the Government press release. He also put in his diary his commitment to attend the inaugural School with the late Ambassador of France, Bernard Guitton, where they duly unveiled a plaque to Humbert and his French soldiers at Kilcummin.

The following year, 1988, John returned to Kilcummin to open a heritage centre, where standing on the doorsteps he declared, "In its timing, the Humbert School was right on cue, for its arrival has coincided with an upsurge of French interest in Ireland."

The enigma of John Wilson, who went on to become Tanaiste, is that during his long tenure at the centre of Irish political life, his probity ensured that he avoided any hint of notoriety associated with the graft of the Haughey era. Yet, paradoxically, while he was widely admired as a staunch Establishment figure, he never attained the national acclaim in life which accompanied his death.

Lavish tributes paid by Taoiseach Bertie Ahern and his successor in the Cavan-Monaghan constituency, Minister of State, Brendan Smith, portrayed him as a towering giant of the GAA, the academic world, the FF corridors of power and the Cabinet room. That he was a Cavan medallist, a Classical and Gaelic scholar, and that he held seven ministries and the second highest political office in Leinster House over two decades, from 1973-1992, are all indubitably true. These testimonies stand to his distinction as an important personality in recent Irish politics.

Yet, had he been able to hear the cascade of eulogies heaped over his coffin, Mr Wilson, with his Cavan cuteness, would have been the first to question whether he was, indeed, the Icon, the Wise Man and Elder Statesmen of Fianna Fáil that he has been portrayed by colleagues and foes alike.

This picture of a man of unswerving loyalty to the Leader of Fianna Fáil smacks of more than a tincture of political propaganda being mobilised for the present day purpose of healing past divisions within a party now led by the commanding presence of Ahern. It also evades the central but enigmatic question of how a man of Wilson's stature managed to survive unscathed by the scandals of the Haughey days which so preoccupy today's Tribunals of Inquiry.

As a political correspondent who admired Wilson, both as a formidable political operator and a man of culture and humour, I have long reflected on his real place within the Fianna Fáil firmament, and have marvelled at his remarkable instinct for survival at the top. After all, it tells a lot about Wilson's tactical dexterity that he was appointed to high office by three vastly different premiers, Jack Lynch, Haughey and Albert Reynolds.

The key to the Wilson Enigma lies in his republican background as the descendant of a Fenian and the son of a staunch supporter of the Founding Father of Fianna Fáil, Eamon de Valera, as well as his own admiration for the pragmatism of Seán Lemass, and his entry into political life as a supporter of his friend, Jack Lynch.

On his election to the Dáil in the 1973 general election, which was lost by Lynch after 16 unbroken years of FF hegemony, Wilson, a teacher, was the one bright new face which he assigned to his frontbench as spokesman on Education and the Arts.

Tall and distinguished with a crop of curly white hair, Wilson's penchant for peppering his learned but verbose speeches with Latin and Greek quotations marked him out as a rising star in Fianna Fáil, a prognosis which appeared to be borne out with his appointment as Minister for Education after Lynch's tidal election triumph of 1977.

The decisive juncture in Wilson's promising career, however, came in late 1979 with Lynch's retirement, and his support for George Colley in his unsuccessful contest for the leadership against Haughey. This was the fatal fault-line that almost rent Fianna Fáil asunder. It led to the formation in December 1985 of the Progressive Democrats by Desmond O'Malley, Mary Harney and Bobby Molloy.

However, the conundrum surrounding Wilson is that he was retained in office by Haughey in his successive administrations or the Opposition frontbench throughout the turbulent 1980s. The key to Wilson's survival was that he represented the Old Fianna Fáil that pre-dated Haughey's auotocratic and self-serving dominance of the nation's largest political party. In Wilson, Haughey saw a traditionalist who was not powerful enough, nor seething like Colley and O'Malley with ambition for ultimate power. Haughey saw Wilson as a party loyalist who would not threaten his position. A man whom he could control.

Accordingly, Haughey calculated that he did not need to take Wilson out, as he ruthlessly inflicted on the detested Jim Gibbons. For Haughey, Wilson conferred a sense of continuity in a desperately divided party. More than that, Wilson gave an aura of respectability to Haughey's leadership.

Wilson was to live up to Haughey's perception, remaining an obedient servant of the Lord of Kinsealy until his fall in 1992 when Seán Doherty toppled him. Only then did the real Wilson emerge to become the first heavyweight in Fianna Fáil to support the candidature of Albert Reynolds for Taoiseach.

Unless John Wilson left a yet unpublished memoir, or confided his real thoughts to family and friends, we may never know how much he knew of Haughey's corrupt ways. Certainly, he knew how to keep his mouth shut on the hallowed Irish principle of "see no evil, speak no evil".

Perhaps like so many insiders in the Haughey years, Wilson immersed himself in his departmental and party duties, and did not realise the sheer scale of Haughey's venality. After all, it took a man of a younger political generation, Bertie Ahern, some time to come to terms with the Haughey depicted in last year's Moriarty Report.

In lauding Wilson, Bertie is exorcising Haughey's ghost. But he was also honouring a scholarly patriot who swopped the chalk and talk of the classroom for the hurly burly of political life.

In my mind, I retain the picture of John Wilson, on a windswept summer day on Kilcummin Strand, taking a salute to General Humbert – and giving his blessing to the development of cultural tourism in north Mayo.

Bertie Silent on Shannon Pull-out

(August 14, 2007)

A mid the unseasonable August clamour over Aer Lingus's decision to scrap its Shannon routes to London's Heathrow Airport, the comment which I found most pertinent came from the Clare priest-sociologist, Fr Harry Bohan, a long-time champion of the development of the Mid-West.

Describing the Aer Lingus withdrawal as "a wake-up call" for the Shannon region, Fr Bohan remarked that for too long Shannon had been reacting to decisions made elsewhere, and it was time that ownership of the airport was placed in local hands, with the Government wiping off its debts.

Like Fr Bohan, the politician-sociologist, Michael D. Higgins, agreed that the pull-out for strictly economic and commercial reasons was a serious blow, and that the volcanic protests of local business people and public representatives was not an over-reaction. Existing jobs and future investment were now at risk.

The consequences will be felt, not just in the immediate Mid West region, but all along the western seaboard if it is allowed to go ahead, Michael D. thundered. Senior Government ministers cannot continue to bury their heads in the sand and hope that this issue goes away. That is not going to happen.

Arguing that this latest decision made a mockery of proposals for the development of the West, and for the principles of regional development and planning, the outspoken Labour deputy pointed out that when Aer Lingus was being privatised, it was recognised that the Heathrow slots were an important national asset.

Indeed, before the recent general election, the then Minister for Transport, Martin Cullen, gave an assurance that the articles of association of the privatised company would ensure that the slots would be protected. It remains to be seen whether the FF-PD-Greens Government, which has a 25pc stake in Aer Lingus, come out of their summer hideaways and deliver on those assurances.

Certainly, the extraordinary silence of Taoiseach Bertie Ahern and the belated stonewalling of the new Transport minister Noel Dempsey fuelled the ire of the protestors. Fianna Fáil backbenchers and councillors have been to the fore in characterising the decision as being against the national interest, and they feel badly let down by Bertie and his ministers. Had voters known in advance about Aer Lingus's intentions, I am quite sure that Fianna Fáil would have suffered as badly west of the Shannon as their PD colleagues did nationally. A virtual wipe-out. As it is, Bertie has the buffer zone of a further five year mandate and comfortable Dáil majority in which to produce a compromise that will help to restore Shannon's viability, while enabling Aer Lingus to benefit from its expansion into Belfast, with its market of almost two million passengers, compared with the Mid-West's catchment area of some 350,000. Like so many others, I am curious to see what Houdini-style response is made by Bertie, who has used his summer break in Kerry to engage in what Michael D. Higgins described as "soft journalism" with the Sunday Independent. Deputy Peter Power has appealed to Dempsey, as a shareholder, to call for an emergency board meeting of Aer Lingus to suspend the decision, and find a way to resolve the problem. Independent deputy and Government supporter, Jackie Healy-Rea, alarmed about the impact of the decision for his native Kerry has proposed an immediatre recall of the Dáil "to discuss this massive blow to the Shannon region." I strongly suspect that a return of the Dáil would merely add more hot air to the controversy, though it would have advantage of making Bertie and Noel give a fuller account of why they appear to have been caught napping by Aer Lingus – and to begin addressing the resultant problem.

But perhaps Fr Bohan is correct in presecribing more local control of its own affairs by the Mid-West. This, too, I am sure would be the line being advocated by John Healy were he still alive.

However, underlying the Aer Lingus move to Belfast – and the company's warm embrace by the Stormont Executive led by Ian Paisley is a distinct and potentially beneficial shift towards a federal Ireland. The West must act now to ensure that this does not become ust a Dublin-Belfast-Border Regions axis, but widens out to embrace more autonomy for the West and the Midlands.

Emperor Bertie in Divided Nation

(August 21, 2007)

In his famous commentary, *De Bello Gallico*, Julius Caesar, the Roman soldier and statesman immortalised by William Shakespeare, wrote that Gaul was divided in three parts.

If Caesar were surveying Ireland today, his sharp military eye would map out this island in three parts: the economically thriving and populous Dublin-Belfast-Border areas; the sprawling Midlands and the largely underdeveloped Western seaboard.

A commentator of note, Caesar would have been puzzled at the prolonged absence on holiday of our contemporary Emperor and his Roman Senate amid the din of strident protest emanating west of the river Shannon.

What, too, I wonder, would Caesar have made of that noisy little man from Limerick, Willie O'Dea, screaming Armageddon to the masses, while continuing to retain his membership of the exclusive gubernatorial class!

Caesar would have sensed stirrings of rebellion in the misty Celtic air from a restless populace in the snipe grass. For the past two weeks Taoiseach Bertie Ahern and his Government ministers in constituencies across the entire western sea-board have come under intense pressure from the local bellicose tribes to reverse Aer Lingus's decision to pull out of Shannon.

In spite of week-end headlines proclaiming incipient revolt within the cabinet ranks from the triumvirate of O'Dea, Eamon Ó Cuív and the Greens' John Gormley, *the Emperor Bertie*, in Maggie Thatcher's defiant phrase, is not for turning. The Aer Lingus decision to move to Belfast will not be reversed unless Ryanair's *Vercingetorix*, aka Michael O'Leary, pulls off a coup at an emergency board meeting.

In the past week the West has awoke with two fine public interventions. Liam Scollan, managing director of Ireland West Airport Knock, has called for more direct flights to the UK and Europe, more services to key European hubs and more transatlantic routes.

Seán Hannick, chairman of the Council for the West, an organisation supported by the Western Catholic bishops, has called on the Community, Rural

Affairs and Gaeltacht Minister to spearhead fresh moves to bring balanced regional development to the West, specifically requesting Ó Cuív to seize the initiative with his two west of Ireland cabinet colleagues, Minister of Defence Willie *two voices* O'Dea, and Agriculture Minister Mary Coughlan in Donegal. His campaign is also targeting junior western ministers Michael Kitt, Pat *The Cope* Gallagher, and Tony Killeen.

Mayo deputy Dara Calleary, will add his voice this week to the growing movement for a Government rethink on its economic strategy west of the Shannon. Calleary, one of the brightest of the newly elected Fianna Fáil backbenchers, will launch his appeal on Thursday when he addresses the annual Humbert Summer School in Ballina. He will share a platform along with the Clare priest-sociologist, Fr Harry Bohan, and Liam Scollan.

"We need to be positive and pro-active," Calleary says. "We need to play up the cultural and lifestyle qualities as well as the commercial benefits for companies investing in the region."

Noting that while Shannon has received special Government support for decades, Knock airport, built by the late Monsignor James Horan, had to fight on its own to develop routes and attract passengers. "In the past Shannon and the mid-west did little to spread commercial benefits to the west and north west," Calleary adds. "Now that Shannon has taken a hit, we need to look forward to an alliance where we can all work together to build up strong commercial centres across the western seabord."

Hannick, who will also speak at the four-day Humbert School, has appealed to all organisations as well as public representatives, county and town council chairpersons, along the western seaboard from Kerry to Donegal to come together to insist on the implementation of a proper regional development policy.

Following discussions with other western groups, the Council has proposed to the Taoiseach that two leased Heathrow slots and two slots from Belfast should be used to restore the four crucial slots to Shannon. The situation could be reviewed two years hence.

Hannick, a businessman in Killala, argues that the unilateral Aer Lingus decision has highlighted the need for proper, effective balanced regional development. "This is an objective of all Western Development groups," he maintains. "Such an alliance would have as its first priority the front loading of *Transport 21* initiatives for the region, including the Atlantic Road corridor and the Western Rail corridor."

Seán is also demanding that the Government returns the €3.65bn spend designated for BMW region infrastructure that was to have been invested before the end of 2006 and which now has been spent elsewhere. The Council is curious to know where the junior parties in Government, the Greens, the PDs, and the Independents Beverley Flynn and Jackie Healy-Rea stand "in relation to all of this lop-sided preferential treatment which continues to disadvantage the western seaboard".

In the past week I was asked by a journalist Áine Ryan what was the relevance to Mayo of the Humbert Summer School. My reply was that the relevance will be shown on the opening night of this week's School when we have the inspirational Fr Harry Bohan sharing a platform with Liam Scollan and Dara Calleary.

Like Gaulle and contemporary Ireland, Humbert's programme is divided in three parts!

Bertie's Seven Scalps

(August 28, 2007)

Labour Councillor Eamon Tuffy and Fine Gael Councillor Therese Ridge complained that Brian Cowen was not distilling "political wisdom" but was being triumphalist when he delivered a gung-ho analysis in Murphy's Ballina during the John Healy media debate of Taoiseach Bertie Ahern's and Fianna Fáil's third successive general election victory, while pouring scorn on the performance of Fine Gael and its leader Enda Kenny.

"I'm sorry for not apologising for winning the election," the non-plussed Brian replied to laughter from the audience.

Meanwhile, Pat Rabbitte's resignation as Labour leader put the race for his successor higher up the news bulletins than the ongoing Shannon Aer Lingus crisis. The Mayoman's departure prompted public relations consultant Tim Ryan to note that Bertie Ahern has seen off seven leaders of political parties: Rabbitte, Ruairi Quinn and Dick Spring in Labour, John Bruton and Michael Noonan of Fine Gael, Michael McDowell of the Progressive Democrats and Trevor Sargent of the Greens.

Shortly, Mayo's Enda Kenny will come under the spotlight as his leadership of Fine Gael will come under the glare of the media spotlight.

Will Enda become Bertie's eighth scalp?

Can Gilmore Revive Labour?

(September 4, 2007)

The race to succeed Pat Rabbitte as leader of the Labour Party has proved to be a runaway victory for Galway-born Eamon Gilmore, who was anointed by the party grandees and most of his parliamentary colleagues well ahead of Thursday's noon closing date for nominations.

The contest fizzled out when in quick succession former leader Ruairi Quinn, and the inimitable Michael D. Higgins, as well as party chairman Willie Penrose, expressed their support for Gilmore.

As Tommy Broughan dithered, the rally to Gilmore became unstoppable when twice-loser Brendan Howlin announced he would not stand, while Finance spokesperson Joan Burton acknowledged that she had insufficient support to mount a successful challenge.

This non-struggle for the leadership position may reflect a pip-squeak pulse of a jaded party that has never recovered from the public's disillusion with Dick Spring and his adviser Fergus Finlay for coalescing with Fianna Fáil in their 1992 heyday when Les Rouges held 33 seats. It may also be because no one knows what colours Labour sport today.

Much ink has been spilt about Gilmore's earnest youth as a student activist at University College Galway and his early career as a trade unionist mirroring that of his old buddy Rabbitte. Gilmore the younger also followed Rabbitte in their successive jumps from the Workers Party to Democratic Left, and to their taking control of the Labour Party after their merger.

I was surprised that Rabbitte's flight to his burrow did not unearth a more robust scramble for the leadership. Rabbitte's centralising grip of his private office had created resentment among Labour traditionalists. I heard mutterings among them about the Democratic Left experiment having failed.

No such back-lash emerged. Rabbitte may have tipped Gilmore off about his resignation before it became public, thus allowing the Galwayman a head start in mobilising support for his leadership bid. If so, it has been a successful stratagem by the former DL brigade. This may reflect the demoralisation within Labour after Rabbitte's alliance with Fine Gael unexpectedly failed to bring them to power in the May general election.

Gilmore's relative lack of Government experience – he was a junior minister for the Marine in the John Bruton-Dick Spring-Proinsias de Rossa triumvirate of 1995-97 – will be logged against him, as it was against Enda Kenny when he took over a demoralised Fine Gael.

When Gilmore formally takes over from Rabbitte on October 5, commentators will be eager to find out what approach he will take towards Kenny, whether he maintains Rabbitte's FG-Labour cooperation, or steers Labour towards a more independent line designed to check any resurgence from Sinn Féin to his Left.

Like Kenny, Gilmore will spend much of his early days in office, travelling the country in a laborious pursuit of building up his party in the constituencies. Like Kenny, too, he will be expected to make his mark in the Dáil at Question Time.

Much has also been written, too, portraying Gilmore as a dead-pan version of Rabbitte, a slightly pedantic school-master without the cascading witty one-liners that made Pat the darling of the Dáil sketch-writers. Certainly, Gilmore comes across as a more serious thinker than the rumbustious Rabbitte.

But what kind of ideas and policies will Gilmore come up with that can challenge Fianna Fáil's hegemony of Irish politics? What kind of identity does he want to imprint on Labour? What kind of image will be conveyed of Gilmore in the media, which like greyhounds seek to out-run the more slow-moving politicians in setting the national agenda?

It strikes me that in the recent election ideology did not rate highly with Irish voters. To the amazement of journalists, the electorate's late rally to the media-assailed Bertie Ahern rather than to the new contract offered by Kenny and Rabbitte was because they perceived the Fianna Fáil leader as an experienced manager of the economy. Material self-interest of voters, rather than a vision of society, prevailed in the ballot boxes. Now, that we have endured a summer of discontent in the mid-west over the Aer Lingus decision to move from Shannon to Belfast, and an economic down-turn tolls a hair-shirt Budget from Brian Cowen in December, the public mood may be adjusting to a more serious mode.

In her bid for deputy leader, Joan Burton has suggested that Labour should target its appeal not just to the one in ten voters who cast their preference for them, but should reach out to disenchanted voters who found Sinn Féin's anti-establishment rhetoric more attractive. Specifically, Burton, who held her seat in Dublin West by beating the Independent Socialist Joe Higgins, proposes to run on a social justice programme, harnessing an alliance of those idealists who want to tackle growing poverty in Ireland, along with eradicating world poverty. At the same time, she wants to model Labour on European social democratic lines.

Senator Regan Baits Bertie

(September 18, 2007)

RTE'S switchboard was deluged during its *Saturday View* programme with messages for and against Bertie Ahern after his two-day appearance at the Mahon Tribunal in Dublin Castle.

What was striking was that many of the comments about the Taoiseach were libellous, and therefore unreadable, an indication that the country is much more divided about his integrity than the general consensus that most people are indifferent to whether or not he received sums of money for his own personal use in the mid-1990s when he was Minister for Finance and aspirant Taoiseach.

Noting that Bertie has said he would not have taken the monies if he could live that time again when his marriage with Miriam had broken up and he needed a place of his own to live, the Minister for Justice, Brian Lenihan, felt that a substantial body of public opinion is still of the view that what he did was not right, but is not worth removing him from office.

Joan Burton, Labour's Finance spokesperson and candidate for the deputy leadership, however, was convinced that the ground was moving against Bertie, because the political and economic climate has changed since last September when public opinion strongly supported the Taoiseach after his weepy RTE interview with Bryan Dobson, and again in May when he won his third successive general election.

A third participant on the programme, Senator Eugene Regan of Fine Gael, tellingly pointed out that Bertie's two days in the witness box in Dublin Castle had thrown up his evidence in a different light from the versions which he had presented to television viewers, in Dáil debates and in his statements to the media during the election campaign.

According to Senator Regan, the public was for the first time being given a more accurate account of Ahern's personal finances which were quite devastating for the Taoiseach's reputation, details which Fianna Fáil ministers and Bertie himself do not like entering the public domain.

To best situate the prolonged verbal sparring over legal procedure which took place at the Mahon Tribunal between an aggrieved and defensive-minded Taoiseach and its didactic but unapologetic senior counsel Des O'Neill, it is worth looking at what Bertie said a decade ago.

Exactly ten years ago when the Dáil was debating the McCracken Tribunal Report into payments to Charles Haughey and Michael Lowry, the then newly elected Taoiseach Bertie Ahern endorsed its investigative procedures. Speaking in the Dáil on September 10, 1997, he stated that his first Fianna Fáil -Progressive Democrat Government believed following the money trail was the most effective way to progress an enquiry. In this important pronouncement of his Government's position, Bertie set-down for the public record his approval of the method under which Tribunals should operate, as well as the compliant conduct expected of those called to give evidence before these inquiries. The application of this approach to Bertie's sworn evidence in the witness box should have seen the Tribunal procede from the outset on four specific cash lodgements in the mid-1990s involving foreign exchange transactions, worth in today's money some €300,000.

The scene had been set for the Taoiseach's explanation by vivid accounts last Tuesday and Wednesday of how his former landlord Mick Wall handed over a suitcase stuffed with nearly £30,000 in bundles of sterling banknotes at his Drumcondra constituency office on December 3, 1994; and of how two days later Bertie drove his ex-girlfriend Celia Larkin to pick up IR£50,000 in the AIB branch in Dublin's O'Connell Street.

But before the Tribunal could resume tracking this money trail, Bertie took it by surprise when he made the unusual request of issuing a statement, whose purpose was to appeal to the wider public which returned him as Taoiseach. It was a move worthy of the man dubbed by his mentor Haughey as *the most skilful, the most devious and the most cunning* of all politicians.

Ahern galloped through a 15 minute tirade against leaks to the media which he claimed subjected him to an unprecedented attack on his integrity and honesty calculated to do him immense personal and political damage. Insisting that in over thirty years in public office he had never taken a bribe in return for political favours, he bemoaned the "unfairness" of the Tribunal. He demanded to know why it had given such undue attention to twenty untrue allegations made by developer Tom Gilmartin including that he received IR£80,000 from Cork developer Owen O'Callaghan.

This concentration on falsehoods and "forgeries" spread by his detractors was a masterly distraction from the money trail, and was also planned as a bare-knuckled challenge from the Dublin northsider to the Tribunal's credibility.

Bertie's populist appeal to a general public angered by the huge fees paid to lawyers, and his tactical questioning of the Tribunal's methodology, was met head on by O'Neill, who reminded the Taoiseach about its Dáil-mandated procedures which include powers of discovery of personal finances.

It was on this score that O'Neill punctured Ahern's repeated claim of having cooperated fully with the Tribunal, while not accusing him of obstruction. The lawyer made the significant disclosure that when the Tribunal three years ago asked for his banking documentation, the Taoiseach's legal team suggested that these records be confined to January 1, 1989, to December 31, 1992, and be concerned only with payments in excess of IR£30,000.

Such a narrow time-scale would have prevented the Tribunal from discovering the four payments from 1994-5 which it wants Bertie to explain its sources. O'Neill also revealed that the Tribunal was on the point of calling him to a public hearing last year after his failure to meet two deadlines for disclosing information requested by it. The senior counsel also told the head of government that it was his role to put questions, not to answer the politician's questions. This was a caution to Ahern to give what Fine Gael leader Enda Kenny has called answers which leave no ambiguity about who gave him monies, and why he accepted the cash.

By mid-Thursday afternoon, Bertie conceded that he had not previously supplied full information about all the sources of payments to him because new allegations were being put to him all the time.

On Friday, as Bertie still fought his corner – and defended his reputation – it became excruciatingly clear to many of his supporters that he was being worn down slowly by the money trail which he applauded ten years ago. He changed his story about the IR£25,000 dig-outs he received from friends in Drumcondra and Manchester.

Ahead of Bertie's return to Dublin Castle this Thursday, Defence Minister Willie O'Dea, has sabre-rattled against the Tribunal, to the deafened discomfort of the Green members of the Government.

If Bertie has changed his story on his first lodgements, will he do so on the other three? Perhaps crucially will his independent financial consultant prove that he did not make a lodgement in dollars?

Last September, I took the view that Bertie should have resigned as Taoiseach. Nor was I sympathetic to his explanations during the election campaign. His victory made me question the relevance of the Tribunal continuing its inquiry. Now, I am convinced that Bertie has not only failed to clear up the mess of the Haughey era, he is part of that mess.

The Irish political system is on trial.

Poor Misunderstood Bertie!

(September 25, 2007)

Media interviewers are often limited in their scope by the pre-meditated intention of the interviewee to sell an emotional message to the public. An instance of this was 'Badly-Done Bertie's' interview on Saturday from Paris with an over-protective Marian Finucane.

Ahead of his fourth appearance on Monday afternoon at the Mahon Tribunal, the Taoiseach lamented at length that had he not been going through a High Court separation from his wife Miriam, he would still have had a joint bank account with her, and would not have been dependent instead on friends giving him money and renting a house for him. Marian appeared only too willing to hand-out free hankies for a distraught nation!

Advising the public to read his whole testimony, a penance for even the most literate of people, Bertie, who recently turned 56, bemoaned that he would still be dealing with queries from the Mahon Tribunal lawyers when he is an old man! Indeed, his prevarications and changes in his story in the witness box about his financial lodgements in the mid-1990s is putting years on all of us.

TV3's *The Political Party* on Sunday provided Fine Gael leader Enda Kenny his opportunity ahead of this Wednesday's return of the Dáil from its prolonged summer vacation to sharpen his criticism of Ahern, whose loss of memory about the exact nature of five bank transactions worth €300,000 in today's money had "diminished the office of Taoiseach."

As a week-end opinion poll in the *Sunday Business Post* showed only one in three voters believe Bertie Ahern's accounts of his personal finances, the newly appointed Fine Gael Leader in the Seanad, Senator Frances FitzGerald said in her first interview that "the Taoiseach's political capital is in decline."

Even if Bertie's stock is falling, he remains popular and retains the unquestioning support of the Fianna Fáil faithful. With the Tribunal not expected to deliver its verdict for at least two years, his 'decline' promises to be a long one. One which may ultimately prove to be inconclusive.

With Enda Kenny and Labour's Eamon Gilmore about to parade their new front-benches before the resumed Dáil, the Greens, the PDs and Independents appear ready to join Fianna Fáil in their defence of Bertie.

The battle of words over Ahern's finance will run and run in the Tribunal's Dublin Castle as well as the Dáil chamber.

Unless Bertie completely trips himself up in the money trail, we all may age gracefully without becoming any the wiser about who gave him what. Truth is in the ear of the listener, and it is speaking in strange tongues unintelligible to even Michael Ring, Fine Gael's new spokesman for Community, Rural and Gaeltacht affairs although he is not a native Irish speaker. But Michael knows how to run rings round interviewers.

'Leave Bertie Alone'

(October 2, 2007)

E nda Kenny gave his most incisive interview on Sunday radio as leader of Fine Gael when he accused Taoiseach Bertie Ahern of failing to tell the truth during his evidence to the Mahon Tribunal on his personal finances.

"We have a Taoiseach, a head of Government, who cannot explain why very substantial monies went through his accounts, backed up with blind allegiance from Minister after Minister, from his own party, the Greens and PD's," the Islandeady man thundered.

Kenny refused to be diverted throughout the interview from making his central political charge that Ahern has lost his moral authority, and that Ministers are lacking integrity in their "blanket defence" of him.

Detecting a malaise in the Irish political system, Kenny claimed that the message all of this passivity sent out downs every politician, every person in public life and downs the country in the eyes of others who would not tolerate the survival in office of a head of government who had admitted taking money for personal use.

Overnight, Kenny and Labour's new leader, Eamon Gilmore, are no longer impotent Opposition voices doomed to five years of Dáil drift, but have been transformed into moral crusaders agitating against a political system which is still mired in the Haughey era.

With a recent opinion poll in the *Sunday Business Post* showing that two out of three people do not believe Ahern's evidence to the Tribunal, Gilmore's stark warning that the Greens have changed the political culture by their "extraordinary abdication of responsibility" on standards in public office has lodged itself into the Achilles heel of this floundering Government.

This barrage has forced Green Party leader John Gormley, speaking on Sunday on TV3's *The Political Party*, to accept the principle that it was wrong that it was wrong for any politician to accept donations, but he steadfastly refused to criticise the Taoiseach personally.

On cue, in the *Sunday Independent*, his in-house propaganda organ, Ahern defended his acceptance of €300,000 in today's money on the grounds that his unorthodox affairs in the mid-1990s was the result of an unorthodox lifestyle on account of his separation from his wife, Miriam. There was no smoking gun, only a private story of someone who was in public life.

Once again, Ahern is retreating behind an emotional sob-story that aims to distract readers from the main question of who gave him cash, and how did he use it. This evasion is conduct unbecoming of a Taoiseach.

Clearly, Ahern is determined to continue in office for at least another two or three years as if it were business as usual. But it strikes me that he is under-estimating the extent to which the question for the public polity is now one of governance. Can Ministers conduct their responsibilities effectively while the Ahern monies keep haunting them? Can Bertie restore his own authority as head of government? He will try, but as long as the Tribunal continues to probe his affairs, the more we may learn about this dark period of his life.

What before the summer holidays appeared to be Ahern's ingenious assembly of a rocket solid Government majority of FF, the PDs and the Greens, supported by self-interested Independents, now looks more like a wounded whale speared by the Taoiseach's spluttering and untenable evidence to the Mahon Tribunal.

On Sunday evening Gilmore renewed the attack describing Ahern as a lame-duck Taoiseach who was losing his influence inside Fianna Fáil. Increasing attention will now focus on his future, as Fianna Fáil deputies anticipate his departure. Labour's Ruairi Quinn has predicted that this may come far sooner than expected. I would not be surprised if this is so.

Shortly after the Government won the confidence vote in Bertie by a shockingly slim five votes, a senior Fianna Fáil politician approached me in the Dáil and let off stink about the media. As any journalist covering politics knows by rote, there is nothing unusual in Fianna Fáil figures haranguing the media with the mantra of "Leave Bertie alone".

Initially, this was the predictable message on Wednesday evening from this politician who privately admitted that he had voted with the Government, but personally believes the Taoiseach is now irretrievably "damaged political goods".

However, to my surprise, the abrupt "Leave Bertie alone" counsel took a tantalising twist when the FF man added: "If you in the media would only leave Bertie alone, we in Fianna Fáil will take him out".

When I pressed him how widespread his thinking was inside Fianna Fáil, this politician would go no further, though he indicated he was far from being alone in wanting a Brian Cowen succession in the near, if not immediate future.

Before moving on, this former minister demanded that he should not be quoted by name. After he left, his words became louder and louder in my head, as events within the political system, not manufactured by the media, conspired to give Bertie Ahern's supposedly rocket-solid third administration the worse of starts in the first days of a new Dáil term.

The calculated absence of former junior agriculture minister Ned O'Keeffe from Wednesday's crucial vote may be a drip from a tap, but it could also be the first leak within the Fianna Fáil reservoir that could quickly turn into a flood the size of the River Shannon against the sinking Ahern.

Coming close to accusing the Taoiseach of perjury, Kenny has reaffirmed his belief that Ahern has shown himself to be unfit for office, and that his credibility is in shreds. This is not just political rhetoric. Not since the fall of Parnell has there been such a grave question mark over the standing of a leader of the Irish political nation.

With Bertie's credibility at the lowest ebb of any serving Taoiseach, what is vitally at stake now is not just his own personal and political authority, but also that of the whole cabinet.

The moral authority of the Government, based on the fundamental principle of collective cabinet responsibility, is being undermined by the mindless pavlovian defence of their leader by the Fianna Fáil ministers, Mary Harney's amnesia of Progressive Democrat principles of accountability and the ostrich-like head in the sands posture of the Greens, John Gormley and Eamon Ryan.

Kenny's image of the Taoiseach being an egg timer whose sand is running out applies not only to Ahern, but to all members of the cabinet of whatever political persuasion for as long as they stand idly by him. It is not only Gormley and Ryan, but also Harney and the Fianna Fáil ministers who need to recall the electoral demise of Michael McDowell for giving his allegiance to Ahern in the previous Government.

The stink in the cabinet is not coming from the media but from a political elite who put more store in the perks of office than on upholding standards of probity in public life.

I, for one, am increasingly of the opinion that on account of his being economical with the truth a year ago in his television interview with Bryan Dobson, his statements in the Dáil and during the election campaign, Bertie Ahern won the general election on false pretences. He has treated the public with assiduous contempt.

Hallowe'en Horror Show
for Bertie

(October 30, 2007)

Bank Holiday week-ends have been used shamelessly by Governments to make unpopular decisions which they hope will escape the full wrath of the public distracted by the pursuit of leisure during the annual October vacation.

In this expectation Taoiseach Bertie Ahern and Transport Minister Noel Dempsey, have seriously miscalculated the outrage in the public mood which is fired up to give them the Guy Fawkes treatment this Halloween.

Their acceptance of hefty pay rises and the introduction at midnight on Monday of new regulations making motorists caught driving alone on a second provisional licence liable for prosecution has made them look like broomstick bogeymen.

Bertie, the man of the people, became a laughing stock-figure, when he made light of his €310,000 salary that is higher than US President George Bush, French President Nicolas Sarkozy and British Prime Minister Gordon Brown are paid for running bigger countries.

In a reply provocative of a political skit by the late Dermot Morgan, Bertie, smirking, shrugged that he was not living in Chequers, 10 Downing Street, the Elysee Palace or the White House. He was droll enough to suggest that the public would realise that these grandiose perks put his paltry remuneration into proper context.

Drawing attention to his fully-furnished Beresford Avenue home in Glasnevin, which he bought from a builder buddy at a bargain price, was not clever verbal boxing by Bertie, who also forgot to remind us of his State car and chauffeur, his free use of his St Luck's office in Drumcondra, his pension and his regular taxpayer-paid use of stately mansions such as Farmleigh House for wining and dining visiting dignitaries.

The Opposition parties challenged Bertie for so graciously accepting his €38,000 award from the Review Body on Higher Remuneration, at a time when ministers are lecturing us on the need for belt-tightening. His weekly increase of €734 is four times the basic social welfare payment.

These ministerial rises underline a point I have made often in this column that compared with the early days of the State when politicians were badly paid, they have now so feathered their own nests that tax payers are funding a well-heeled "political class."

The molly-codling really took-off when Charlie McCreevy was Minister for Finance in those now seemingly distant days of the dawn of the Celtic Tiger economy. The slogan of our era could be "Enrich yourselves. Join the political class!"

A further instance of the rise of this political class came with Bertie's seigneurial dispersal of patronage to those Dáil deputies who were doled out chairs, vice-chairs and convenorships of Oireachtas Committees, coming so soon after enlarging the overcrowded but under-worked junior minister ranks.

All of this might just be tolerable if ministers managed the country wisely. But the litany of problems in the health services, rising gangland crime, road congestion and shortage of school places in new estates, especially for the children of immigrants, still await solution.

A prime example of ineptitude is Noel Dempsey, who has subjected himself to public ridicule now that it has become known that his Secretary General in the Department of Transport withheld from him for six weeks the news that Aer Lingus would be pulling out of Shannon Airport.

Following his Shannon Airways Debacle, Dempsey has incited road rage with the peremptory announcement that the new safety strategy would be immediately enforced against unsupervised provisional drivers. The apoplectic reaction to this prompted Dempsey to engage in "a political hand-brake U-turn." The law night be forced, or it might not be by Gardaí. Immediately, this was dubbed as another Irish solution for an Irish problem.

To Dempsey's further embarrassment, it became known that the new regulation was news to the Gardaí. He had neither consulted nor even informed them of its introduction. He merely landed them with a huge logistical problem.

In principle, the Government measure requiring learners being accompanied by either professional driving instructors or experienced drivers is sound. This was the practice in Scotland before I crossed the Irish Sea exactly thirty-five years ago this week. The Irish system was too lax and allowed too many untried drivers learn bad and dangerous habits from the word go.

However, the suddenness of its introduction is bound to be disruptive to L-drivers who have become dependent on their vehicles for work, sport or taking children to and from school. A phased-in introduction of the new rule would have been more sensible in view of the inordinate delays facing 431,900 provisional drivers in being given a date for driving test.

Pressure will come on *Dopey Dempsey* to put the regulation's implementation on hold, while praying the testing system speeds up. He himself will be hard put to make up lost ground on his own self-inflicted crash-land that has left his reputation in the ditch.

On another front, this week's funeral of the notorious criminal John Daly has brought the spotlight back on what Dublin Archbishop, Diarmuid Martin, has diagnosed as Ireland's "revolting new culture of violence." This has confronted both the Government and the Catholic Church with acute moral dilemmas. Politicians and churchmen have been united in issuing strong declarations against the drugs-inspired spate of gangland killings and rough vendettas in Dublin and elsewhere such as Monaghan.

Both the Taoiseach and the Archbishop Martin are open to considering the case for re-establishing the non-jury Special Criminal Court to deal with a situation which Justice Minister Brian Lenihan has described as close to a national emergency.

However, Bertie and Dr Martin believe that the point has not been reached of resorting to such a draconian measure, as the court system is still capable of functioning against even para-criminals.

A consensus is emerging that what is most imperatively needed are the allocation of more financial resources for improved Garda intelligence of the criminals, a more effective and beefed-up witness protection programme, new ways of taking evidence from suspects, more gun control and greater Garda presence in housing estates and other shady abodes where the criminals ply their evil trade in human life.

Such a concerted strategy would aim to divide and fragment the villains by instilling a sense of insecurity among them that would severely dent their brazen bravado that they are invincible and untouchable.

The cock-sure hoods must be made nervous and fearful of informers among them their murky ranks. While in the short-term this would most probably lead to an internecine escalation in contract murders of fellow criminals, in the medium term their induced state of paranoia would result in a steady erosion of their operations and power-bases. Middle-rank dealers need to be specially targeted with a view to their squealing on their comrades in arms.

Regretfully, Archbishop Martin's specific proposal for the Taoiseach to convene an emergency summit of community leaders to address the roots of the spiralling social problem of random violence has been rejected by Government on the grounds that this is already being done by Joint Policing Committees involving Gardaí and community representatives.

Bertie should rethink his response to the Archbishop's ideas treating it as one avenue of civic counter-attack against gangland rule. As the political class shows itself out of touch with daily reality of its underclass people, an alliance of the pulpit and the public is urgently needed to help the Gardaí in overcoming the present threat to the stability of society.

Christ Church Bells Toll for Bertie

(November 6, 2007)

O n Sunday I found myself in the same place, at the same time of day and doing the same thing which I did exactly thirty-five years ago. Thirty-five years ago, Bertie had not yet registered as a name in national politics. This time, I wondered if the bells of Christ Church Cathedral were tolling for the beginning of the end of the decade-long Ahern Era.

Bertie, the Celeb Taoiseach

(November 20, 2007)

B ertie Ahern has turned the office of Taoiseach into a branch of celebrity showbiz rather than just attending to the daily grind of governance of an ingrate populace and management of a spluttering economy.

Just look at recent photographs.

Bertie, in bow-tie and dress suit, with his estranged wife Miriam at her CARI charity ball in Dublin's Shelbourne Hotel where a pint of lager now costs €5.80.

Bertie with Boyzone. Bertie with Bono and Bill Clinton at the former US President's fund-raising bash for his wife Hillary.

Bertie with his best selling novelist daughter Cecilia and other literati. Bertie with his grandsons. The Ahern dynasty.

Revealingly, the man who once had a franchise on the anorak cultivating his image of northside Dub, admitted to the Mahon Tribunal that he likes to mix socially with "high net worth" earners of the €50m class.

Astonishingly, he huffed when the public reacted with hostility to his €38,000 a year pay rise, and he was brazen enough to complain self-pityingly about his impoverished status on the international stage compared with other political leaders.

These days it is only the *Hello* magazine style of photo opportunity at a glitzy social function camera that you see Bertie beaming. You see a snarling Ahern when he is confronted for a soundbite from baying journalists. In the Dáil, he is usually grim-faced. In cabinet, he is remote from ministerial colleagues.

As columnist John Drennan has wittily noted, "no one suspected that the cunning one would spend his opening months since the election stumbling around in a fugue of malovelent self-pity."

This new harshness in Bertie's tone and his apparent lack of concern at unfavourable public criticism has been attributed by broadcaster Olivia O'Leary to his now being in touch with his inner feelings as a gurrier. Other commentators have connected his personality change to his dismissive treatment by the Mahon Tribunal lawyers of his changing explanations of how he received substantial sums of money for his own personal use in the 1990s that has persuaded most people that his story does not stand up.

Ahern's own deadline of resigning as Taoiseach when he reaches 60 years is increasingly becoming over-ambitious. He faces further damage to his reputation when he next appears before the Tribunal. He is being talked about as a candidate for one of the senior EU posts in Brussels that are due to become vacant. Psychologically, he is cast as "an already gone" Taoiseach, but one who is determined not to be pushed out.

Nor will Ahern's volatile mood be massaged by a new book edited by Trinity College political scientists Michael Gallagher and Michael Marsh on *How Ireland voted 2007: The Full Story of Ireland's General Election*. It concludes that of Fianna Fáil's six leaders since its foundation Bertie is second bottom in vote-catch power. Gallagher's analysis shows that in his three general elections of 1997, 2002 and 2007 Ahern achieved 40.8pc of the national vote and 47.4pc of seats. Only Albert Reynolds fared worse in his sole general election as leader in 1992 with 39.1pc of the franchise but 41.2pc of seats.

The party founder and icon, Eamon de Valera, who fought 12 general elections, secured an average 43.6pc of the national vote which translated into an average 47pc of Dail seats. In two elections as leader Seán Lemass averaged 45.8pc of the vote with 49.7pc of seats. In three elections Jack Lynch's average register of 45.2pc of the vote gave FF 52.1pc of seats.

Even Charlie Haughey, who failed to win an absolute majority, led Fianna Fáil into five elections with an average 45.2pc vote and an average 47.4pc of seats.

This cold arithmetic prompts Gallagher to take some of the gloss of Bertie's achievement of winning three elections in a row. "While any previous leader who notched up an average support level of 41pc would have had Fianna Fáil TDs searching for a copy of the party's constitution, for the section on how to bring about internal party regime change, Ahern finds himself feted as a leader like no other", Gallagher notes.

Gallagher's colleague, Michael Marsh, also questions a general view that Bertie won the election by outshining Fine Gael leader Enda Kenny in the leader's televised debate. He concludes that some 41pc of voters who made up their minds in the last week of the campaign gave Fianna Fáil their first preference compared with 35pc of those who did not watch Ahern's debate with Kenny.

"Certainly, the voters did not feel it (the debate) was important: only three pc of them offered it as an explanation for their vote," Marsh writes.

Interesting light on the prognosis for future of the Progressive Democrats with two Dáil seats and Sinn Féin with four is also shed in this book.

Gallagher muses that "if the PDs do decide to disband, we can confidently predict that never before has a party that averaged just 5.6pc of the vote in six elections that it contested made such impact on government policy."

Gallagher adds that for Sinn Féin "most of what seemed to be low-hanging fruit have retreated out of easy reach, and it remains to be seen whether 2007 is just a temporary setback to the party's inexorable progress or whether 2002 will come to be seen as Sinn Féin's high water mark."

As the backroom boys of the political parties digest these statistics for future performance, a main focus in the Dáil will be the Government's move to reactivate former Justice Minister Michael McDowell's Bill to put checks, rather than cheques, in the way of future tribunals of inquiry and commissions of investigation.

This Bill, which will be given a second stage reading next week, though its passage into law is not expected until the middle of the next year at the earliest, has been described by Enda Kenny as "sinister". However, it will command popular support, according to a poll showing 88pc agree with the Government's proposed legislation to curb their duration and costs.

Eight out of ten of us are fed up with tribunals which are perceived to have yielded minimal tangible results, but are likely to cost taxpayers a final bill of €1 billion.

Newly released figures of the costs to-date of a decade of tribunals make for interesting reading. The cost so far has totalled €310.9 million. The biggest guzzler is Mahon at €68.5 million, followed by Lindsay, €47m, the Commission to Inquire into Child Abuse €41m, Morris €37.5m, Moriarty €30.5m, the Beef Processing Industry €27m, Barr €19.7m, Dunne €11.5m, McCracken €6.5m, and Finlay €4.7m.

What are grouped as 'others - Barron, Dublin Monaghan Bombings, Madden, Ferns, Neary, Breen and Buchanan, Dean Lyons and Dublin Archdiocese - have cost a further €17m.

With Bertie whinging about his miserable remuneration, most readers will share my anger that these tribunal costs could have been used to combat poverty and other social injustices in Irish society if the politicians had done their jobs properly in the first instance.

Wounded Bertie

(December 4, 2007)

Just as revelations of Ivor Callelly's free painting and decoration of his Dublin home overtook Brian Cowen's pre-election give-aways last year, this week he will be overshadowed by Bertie Ahern's latest troubles at the Mahon Tribunal and news stories linking him to Manchester businessman Norman Turner's plans with the National Lottery for a casino.

The noose is tightening around Bertie's neck, but he is still desperately trying to dig his way out of a deepening hole that is assuming the proportions of a slag-heap. The Opposition believe that the contradictions between Ahern's original account to RTE's Bryan Dobson of the monies he received in 1994 as a "dig-out" from his friends, and his testimony to the Mahon Tribunal are mounting up to further undermine his credibility and political authority.

According to Labour leader Eamon Gilmore Ahern's account has been holed below the waterline by the testimony to the Tribunal by stockbroker Padraic O'Connor.

So it was quite laughable to hear Minister for Defence Willie O'Dea claim, on RTE radio's *Saturday View*, that the Taoiseach's credibility is not in question, that Government ministers are not worried about his declining authority and that many Fianna Fáil backbenchers and supporters do not share the anxieties of Ned O'Keeffe who has resigned the party whip over its failure to address the problems in the health system.

Fine Gael's Charlie Flanagan was persuasive when he asserted that the storm around the Taoiseach is fundamentally corrosive in terms of governance and in ensuring confidence around the cabinet table. The Dobson interview is in tatters. O'Keeffe reflects more the grassroots opinion than admitted by O'Dea, now known as the *Minister for Defending a Drowning Taoiseach*.

Bertie was showing every sign of still being in denial when he was harangued by a battalion of journalists in Dublin on Monday. His reappearance at the Tribunal on December 20 and 21 will be crucial for determining his remaining political life-span as Taoiseach.

Senator Eoin Harris rushed to his defence yesterday when he warned that it was the English-owned Associated Newspapers group which publishes the *Irish*

Mail was trying to topple Ireland's greatest ever Taoiseach. Politics, he claimed, was being corrupted by half-truths and innuendos from the media and politicians such as Fine Gael leader Enda Kenny's reference in a Cork speech to "money-laundering".

An interesting take on all this appeared in *The Mail on Sunday* in an article by historian T. Ryle Dwyer, who pointed out how quickly Taoiseach Jack Lynch left office in late 1979. "Bertie is wounded. Who will be the one to do him the kindness of putting him out of his misery?" he asked.

With the Dáil rising on December 19 for a six week Christmas holiday, the Taoiseach will be looking forward to his planned safari on January 14 to Malawi, Tanzania and South Africa. At least, there are no tigers in Africa!

But past experience has shown that when a Taoiseach is abroad, stirrings take place in his domestic political snake-grass!

Cowen Keeps Eye on Prize

(December 11, 2007)

Brian Cowen is still on course to succeed Bertie Ahern as Taoiseach after delivering his fourth Budget last Wednesday, a cautious but inspiring one which won applause from Government benches, derision from the Opposition and passive resignation from the public.

An ebullient Cowen told the Dáil that his budget provided "significant resources" to allow the Government to address the needs of the most disadvantaged in society, in spite of the more difficult economic situation which the country finds itself confronting since last summer's general election.

The Budget's €900 million social welfare package, on balance, was running slightly above inflation. The improvements in social welfare benefits and child care payments will amount to an extra €957m in 2008 and €980m in a full year. As such, it was presented as demonstrating the Government's commitment to the less well off and the vulnerable by the Minister for Social and Family Affairs, Martin Cullen.

At a news conference at Government Buildings, which I attended with my head reeling from the slick way in which the Government's public relations presentation of the figures puts the best gloss on their supposed largesse, Cullen revealed that Cowen's measures mean that the total expenditure for the Department of Social and Family Affairs for next year will amount to €17bn.

Nearly half of the extra public expenditure allocated by Cowen will be spent on social welfare, and will benefit more than 1.5m people. From the first week in January 42,000 pensioners will receive a €14 weekly rise in their State pensions, while non-contributory pensions will increase by €12 to €212 a week.

Cullen reaffirmed the Government's target of bringing pensions up to at least €300 a week by 2012, and next month too he will raise the carers' allowance, carer's benefit and widow(er) benefit by €14 a week. This will bring the rate for carers aged 66 or over to €232 a week, and for those under 66 to €214 weekly.

Cullen also announced an increase of €200 in the rate of the respite care grant to €1,700 for over 48,000 carers from next June, as part of the plan to raise this to €3,000 a year over the life-span of the Government.

Pledging to increase the pensioner qualified adult allowance to the level of the State pension, Cullen said that an increase of €27 in this budget would bring it to

€200 a week – 90 per cent of the target. This measure should be of special benefit to women not now entitled to a contributory pension.

The back to school clothing and footwear allowance will increase by €209 per child from €180 to €200 for children aged between two and eleven, and from €285 to €305 for children aged between 12 and 22. About 175,000 children will benefit from the expansion of the schools meal programme.

Such figures, on paper, indicate a genuine effort on Cowen's part to tilt scare resources in favour of the less well-off, and as Cullen suggested, it stems from a long tradition in Fianna Fáil of looking after the socially deprived in a way that undermines the Labour Party's capacity to establish itself as a people's party.

Predictably, however, there was a mixed reaction to the budget from care and social groups, many of whose spokespersons were lining up across from Buswells Hotel to give their instant reactions to the bevy of television and radio journalists, while back in their offices their staff inundated news rooms with their views.

The Childrens' Rights Alliance regretted there was no increase in medical cards, bemoaned the reality that the cost of healthcare continues to rise, and that the two euro rise in child allowance "will barely pay for a block of cheese."

Another telling criticism came from Dick Spring's former adviser, Fergus Finlay, now a vocal chief executive with Barnardos, the childrens' charity. While welcoming the modest increases in child benefit, the bearded Fergus argued that Cowen needed to go further in social distribution of wealth to make a real difference to the lives of 100,000 children living in constant poverty.

Even more persuasively Barnardos' director of advocacy, Norah Gibbons, lamented that the Government has an unprecedented opportunity to make a real difference to childrens' lives, but the modest increase in the childcare supplement - the equivalent of €2 a week – is a very poor substitute for the high quality child-care needed.

Meanwhile, back in the Dáil chamber, in spite of the upbeat claims of Cowen and Cullen, Labour's Finance spokesperson Joan Burton expressed the disappointed views of the Opposition, highlighting the small scale of the welfare increases in contrast to the huge rises in the salaries of Government ministers.

Ms Burton pointed out Bertie Ahern's salary increase of €38,000 a year was higher than the industrial wage for one million workers, while most ministers are due a €26,000 hike under the recent awards. Politically, Burton was poking at the Achilles heel of Cowen's budget.

Indeed, at Cullen's news conference I asked him if he had pressed Cowen to increase welfare benefits at a rate proportionate to the ministerial rises. The

Waterford man, a slick talker, gave me the standard line that the ministerial awards came through an independent system after a seven year delay. Bla, bla!

However, I then put it to him that any deserved kudos for the Government's raising welfare above cost of living increases would be wiped out by the public perception that ministers were telling everyone else to tighten their belts while their own bank accounts were bulging. He appeared to concede that the timing of the awards was unfortunate for the Government's public image.

The one budget surprise was Cowen's U-turn on stamp duty, which is largely attributed to Ahern's leaning on him to give a resuscitation jag to the building sector. It remains to be seen if this will have the desired effect, but many economists regard the move as too little too late, and one which amounts to an intervention that will not allow the property market to find its natural level.

In the immediate post-budget situation, signs have emerged of a willingness within the cabinet to postpone their pay rises. Bertie knows only too well that a delay could help in creating a less confrontation climate with the unions when negotiations open next month among the social partners on a new national wage agreement.

That Bertie believes he will still be Taoiseach by next St Patrick's Day was signalled by news of his invitation to address the Houses of Congress in Washington. Another sign of life from battling Bertie came also at the Cáirde Fáil dinner on Friday night when he announced that Fianna Fáil had officially established itself in the North as a recognised political party, a move which received a sneeringly cool response from Gerry Adams at Sinn Féin's week-end of reflection on how to recover from its poor general election performance.

The image of the week must go to Ian Paisley and Martin McGuinness jointly holding the gavel at the podium during a visit to the New York Stock exchange. However, a closer inspection of the photograph showed the North's First and Deputy Ministers being accompanied by Ian Paisley Jnr – his dad's shadow, just as Cowen is still prepared to stand in the shade for Bertie.

Will Lisbon Produce Political Gridlock?

(December 18, 2007)

Many of the tens of thousands of drivers caught up like myself in the recent traffic gridlock in Dublin will not be harbouring kind seasonal thoughts about the politicians who have taken the credit for our recent economic advances in infrastructure development, largely from EU grants and private investment, but immediately run for cover when they are called to explain their abysmal failure to manage prosperity.

Following the Government's climb-down on receiving their pay awards, the Opposition will roar about the lack of traffic plans - not just for Dublin but for all towns and cities around the country in the light of the traffic chaos caused by a truck overturning at the Point Depot – in the last remaining days of the current Dáil session ahead of Christmas.

Despite the commercialisation of the Christmas season, the core of the festivity, based on the birth of Jesus Christ, is still centred for most families in seeing the joy on the faces of children or grandchildren when they open their presents from Santa Claus.

Literally speaking, therefore, it is a huge damper on the seasonal mirth for the Government to find itself engulfed this week in a messy row over school water charges.

Over the week-end representatives of the primary schools asked Environment Minister John Gormley to respond to their fears that bills for water charges up to €10,000 in some cases would cause them serious financial problems, perhaps even bankruptcy. Their plea follows hardline positions adopted last week by both the Taoiseach and the Minister for Education that there is no provision in law for the schools to avoid paying their water charges to local authorities.

Both Bertie Ahern and Mary Hanafin insisted that they had no room to make concessions because the levies were compulsory under a European Union Water Framework Directive.

But this bluff of blaming Brussels was called into question by European Minister Dick Roche when he told Marian Finucane on RTE radio that the EU had no role to play in forcing the water charges on Irish schools. "It is the Irish Government that is responsible for the decision," he said. "It is nothing to do with Brussels. It is our decision as to how we fund our schools".

Fair play to Dick Roche for pointing out that a directive is a general policy decision taken by the Council of Ministers representing the member State governments, who have the power to frame its application in national law.

Both Ahern and Hanafin have been caught out in their misleading attempts to blame Brussels Eurocrats for difficulties which they have brought upon school managers. Worse still, they have claimed that the responsibility in this area belongs to Environment Minister John Gormley – in other words, it ain't Fianna Fáil's mess, let the Greens clean it up!

Such shoddy evasion politics could have a negative effect in the forthcoming referendum on the EU Reform Treaty that was signed in Lisbon last week by the heads of government including Taoiseach Bertie Ahern.

This Treaty is a scale-down version of the Constitution which was negotiated in 2004 under Ahern's Irish Presidency, but was rejected by voters in France and the Netherlands. As the others have opted to have it endorsed in their respective parliaments, Ireland will be only EU State putting the new Treaty to the will of the people in a referendum.

The Treaty provides for a new EU President and foreign minister, as well as an EU diplomatic service, with the aim of enhancing Europe's presence in international affairs, especially as a counter-weight to the dominance of the United State's as the world's sole superpower.

On institutional matters, Ireland will no longer automatically have the right to nominate its own member to the European Commission. It allows for more democratic control over decision-making by the national parliaments and the European Parliament.

Even before the water charges controversy, I detected a distinct nervousness in the Dáil that the referendum could provide an opportunity for voters to register their protest against the political establishment. For instance, Shannon opponents to the Aer Lingus pull-out could seek revenge on the Government for its collusion with this decision.

A senior Labour Party adviser also suggested to me that Bertie Ahern's declining authority on account of his difficulties at the Mahon Tribunal could make him ineffective in leading the Government's campaign for a 'Yes' vote.

The prospect is looming of Ireland causing gridlock in Europe, as well as at home.

Bertie's Last Christmas as Taoiseach

(December 24, 2007)

"I hope you will be leaving Bertie alone this Christmas week", a friend who is not exactly unfriendly towards Fianna Fáil said. From long experience, I know that this kind of unsubtle remark is designed to suggest that a bias or imbalance has crept into my reading of the Taoiseach's finances, and that I should take a seasonal break from the politics of arithmetic.

But there have been too many bad moments at the Mahon Tribunal for Bertie for any objective person still to believe that the man can count correctly!

So incredible has his story become of how he received large payments of cash for his personal use in the mid-1990s – worth €300,000 in today's money - that my prediction is that this will be his last Christmas spent as Taoiseach.

The Taoiseach's two days in the witness box at Dublin Castle last Thursday and Friday were the occasion for ill-tempered slights of the investigating lawyers that show the strain of being unable to get away with bluster is exercising its toll on the Drumcondra ward boss.

Furthermore, the coordinated attacks on the integrity of the Mahon Tribunal by at least six Government ministers via their press spokesman is a sure sign of the growing alarm inside Fianna Fáil that Taoiseach Bertie Ahern is floundering.

A deeper cultural battle is underway involving the right of a judicial body nominated by the Oireachtas to do its work into the affairs of the political leader of the nation without fear from the intimidatory pressure being directed at it by elected ministers who are steeped in an authoritarian mould that is ultimately inimical to the democratic interest.

The tone of the inquiry was lowered by Bertie himself when he claimed that the Tribunal lawyers were trying to stitch him up. This is the language of corner-boy politics. It is an appeal for his side to come to his assistance with their claymores, hammers and sickles.

Foolishly, the ministers have responded with primordial militancy. However, it is crucial to the health of Irish democracy that the Tribunal be allowed to reach its conclusions on the basis of testing forensically the evidence given to it by Bertie and others.

If Fianna Fáil as a political party is committed to honesty in politics, its ministers should be listening carefully to the evidence, and not be merely giving pavlovian loyalty to their leader's assertions. It will be a great day for Irish democracy when the Mahon judges establish the principle that no political personality, however, high the office he or she holds, is untouchable.

Naturally, the Opposition parties have presented the interventions of Ahern's ministers on his behalf as a sinister attempt to hijack the workings of the Tribunal.

Fine Gael's Justice spokesman, Charlie Flanagan, has contended that the challenge from the Fianna Fáil ministers undermines any pretence that they are serious about tackling corruption in Irish politics.

"We did not see this type of interference when Liam Lawlor and Ray Burke were being investigated by the Tribunal," Flanagan notes. "Not since the determined efforts by Fianna Fáil politicians and supporters to defend Charlie Haughey in every circumstance, regardless of the mounting evidence, have we seen such a blinkered defence of a politician under investigation."

Also particularly pertinent are the press releases from Fine Gael Senator, Eugene Regan, not least because they have been causing huge resentment among the FF ministers. Referring to Dermot Ahern, Regan observed: "The Minister for Foreign Affairs says he is astonished by the line of questioning of the Tribunal. It is actually more astonishing that any Fianna Fáil Minister still believes the Taoiseach's explanations as to the source of these very large sums of money."

What will be most worrying to the Taoiseach and his ministers is that the Tribunal has discovered a previously unknown cheque for £5,000 which Ahern used to open two accounts in the Irish Permanent in January 1994. The plot thickens.

Recently turned 56, he spoke the truth when he bemoaned that he would still be dealing with queries from lawyers when he is an old man! Indeed, his prevarications and changes in his story in the witness box about his financial lodgements in the mid-1990s have put years on us all.

However, over the week-end the word from Ahern's associates is that he is determined to stay in office until the 2009 local and European elections – "and beyond".

This is defiant talk, applicable for as long as he holds the support of his ministers and party. But the reality is that they know that Bertie is no longer an asset to them. Most end of year assessments on Ahern's performance have read like his political obituaries.

It was a roller-coaster year of both resounding triumph and humiliating disaster for him. In spite of winning a third successive general election in May and forming what Pat Magner described as "a rocket solid" Government with the PDs, the Greens and Independents in June, by the end of the year his political authority and public standing were waning from the constant drip of revelations from the Mahon Tribunal about his personal finances.

It was the year in which Ahern entered the history books as the longest serving Taoiseach after Fianna Fáil's founder Eamon de Valera. His crowning achievement of a third consecutive election as Taoiseach will not be surpassed in politics in our time.

His decade of patient diplomacy with Tony Blair in the North finally paid-off in March with the formation of a power-sharing executive at Stormont headed by the DUP's Rev Ian Paisley and Sinn Féin's Martin McGuinness.

Yet, he stands accused by Fine Gael leader Enda Kenny of "diminishing" the office of Taoiseach. Labour's new leader, Eamon Gilmore, is adamant that Ahern should resign. At sometime in the New Year, both Opposition leaders will table another motion of no confidence in him.

The yardstick for judging Bertie will not be that he used his public office to accept money for personal use. It will be that he did not tell the full story. As he told Bryan Dobson in his now notorious *Diana* television moment: "I don't want anyone saying I didn't give the full picture."

It is more than likely that Fianna Fáil will continue to stand by Bertie for at least a few more months. But the fuller picture of his finances will continue to drip from the Tribunal.

Perhaps his address to the US Congress, supposedly planned for St Patrick's Day, could be a suitable venue for his *Last Hurrah*.

For his punch-line, he might use the memorable line from Abraham Lincoln: "You may fool all the people some of the time; you can even fool some of the people all the time, but you can't fool all of the people all the time".

Bertie, 'Artful Dodger' of Drumcondra

(January 8, 2008)

Bertie Ahern's spirited New Year attack on what he claims to be his unfair hearing from the Mahon Tribunal almost made me feel sympathetic for his lament that its probing into his bedroom arrangements went beyond the bounds of decency. Once again, Bertie resorted to his old trick of appealing to public sympathy via the national air-waves, complaining that he had been subjected to eight years of Star Chamber treatment from a tribunal that had reached a low point in Irish public life by leaking details of his private tax affairs with the Revenue Commissioners.

Once again, too, he self-pityingly pleaded that he was innocent of builder Tom Gilmartin's allegation that he had received £8,000 from Cork developer Owen O'Callaghan, a charge not yet dealt with by the Tribunal. Bertie is the artful dodger of Drumcondra.

However, his Sunday radio interview with Gerald Barry is back-firing on him, because in the course of the question and answer session, he was forced to admit that he will be going into a new term without obtaining a tax clearance certificate from Revenue. Technically, Bertie may be able to satisfy the Standards in Public Office by furnishing it with documentation showing that he has requested "a certificate of application". This fig-leaf distinction means that the country has the unprecedented situation of being run by a Taoiseach who is not currently compliant with tax law.

This admission was an opening for one of the Taoiseach's *bete noirs*, Fine Gael spokesman, Senator Eugene Regan S.C., to dismiss Ahern's statement about his personal finances and the Mahon Tribunal as "self-serving" and evasive of the crucial issues he should be addressing.

Pithily, Regan summarised the vulnerable points in the Taoiseach's defence: he has not explained why he misled the Irish people and the Dáil about his tax affairs in his infamous 2006 television interview with Bryan Dobson, and why he refused in the Dáil as recently as 26 September 2007 to correct the record. Nor has Bertie explained how a donation given for the Fianna Fáil party by stockbrokers NCB ended up in his own bank account, and why 15 months after the Revenue initiated contact with him about tax liabilities, he still does not have a tax clearance certificate. Furthermore, he has not addressed the latest disclosure of a lodgement to an Irish Permanent Building Society account in January 1994, given that he assured the Irish people on RTE that the so-called loans from friends and gifts from strangers were his only "unorthodox" income at that time.

Against the background of last month's gang bang of the Tribunal by Fianna Fáil ministers who accused it of bias, unfairness and operating outside of the law in its uncovering large lodgements (worth €300,000 in today's value) into his accounts or accounts operated for his benefit, Senator Regan served notice of tabling a Dáil and Seanad motion "to confirm confidence in the tribunal and allow it to continue its work without being undermined".

So the *Bertiegate* affair will continue to distract the Government from getting on with running the country for the foreseeable future. Much political speculation is also focussing on how long ministers can continue to provide blank cheques in defending a severely damaged Taoiseach.

Bertie's Silence
Speaks Volumes

(January 15, 2008)

The old phrase, 'enjoying the life of Reilly', comes to mind as being applicable to Bertie Ahern. While we poor mortals struggle through this bleak and cold January, he simmers in the sunshine of South Africa and Tanzania. Paid air tickets, staying in top class hotels, attending diplomatic receptions, hob-nobbing with African leaders, and being chauffeur-driven to inspect aid projects under Irish auspices – a dream offer which no tour operator can match!

This hot-footing African safari, which is funded by the Irish taxpayer, is a scintillating start to 2008 for Drumcondra Man. It comes after his reported vacation in Lanzarotte. All this jaunting during a six weeks break from the drudgery of being accountable to the Dáil. So it was all the more galling to hear of the Taoiseach's categorical instruction which was given to journalists accompanying him on the African trip on Sunday night by the Government Press Secretary: Bertie would not be taking any questions on the renewed week-end calls for his resignation from Enda Kenny and Eamon Gilmore.

This is a blatant departure from the long-standing convention among political correspondents during a foreign assignment. The established practice is that as well as dealing with the work being undertaken on that specific tour of duty by the Taoiseach – or whatever Government minister – time is put aside for questions to be asked on domestic issues or on breaking news stories from home.

On many occasions abroad I found myself under instruction from news desks back in Ireland to get a hold of Liam Cosgrave, Jack Lynch, Charlie Haughey, Garret FitzGerald, Albert Reynolds, John Bruton and Bertie Ahern for their comments on domestic events which had become topical in their absence. I vividly recall scurrying around the Acropolis in Athens trying to reach Jack Lynch who was among the dignitaries attending the ceremony when Greece acceded to the European Economic Community, as it was then known. I now forget what the issue was, but it was preoccupying the Irish public interest far more than a report on the Greek celebrations! Even Charlie Haughey at his prickliest would revel, verbally and visibly, in the challenge of being diverted from the particular business in hand to comment – or stonewall – on the latest 'nibbling at his bum' by his political opponents. As for Garret and Albert, you couldn't keep them from talking at length on whatever filibuster had been put to them. Those were the days when mobiles and internet were inventions of the future.

Over the past decade, as I personally encountered on a visit to Washington with the media savvy Bertie, he would make time for chats over drinks with correspondents on or off the record on whatever topic that was shooting the breeze. But on Sunday in remote Cape Town this traditional openness was dumped imperiously by a peevish Bertie with his decision to rule out of bounds any questions on the hottest political story of the decade concerning his suitability for high office in regard to his disputed evidence to the Mahon Tribunal about his personal finances and the current withholding of his tax compliant certificate from the Revenue Commissioners.

Bertie's unilateral breach of convention with travelling journalists in refusing to react to the public attacks of the two leading Opposition leaders on his professional credibility as a politician amounted to political censorship more akin to Putin's Russia than a European Union State which accords the Fourth Estate its rightful place in its democratic system.

The fact that Bertie indulged in this sledge-hammer assault on a basic principle of free journalism is all the more alarming when account is taken of his Government's insistence that the Dáil should maintain its discredited habit of taking prolonged Christmas holidays from plenary sessions. This imperious behaviour on Ahern's part merely served to reinforce the impression that he cannot come up with satisfactory answers to the charges of demeaning politics that have again being tossed at him by Kenny and Gilmore. Perhaps worse of all, his self-imposed silence underlined the sad reality claimed by the Opposition that his conduct of State business is being impaired by the ongoing *Bertiegate* saga.

As a skilled, hardened and experienced politician of the first rank, the Bert should be reminded of the dictum that 'if you cannot take the heat, you should get out of the kitchen'. While it is understandable that he feels deeply frustrated by the greater interest in his tax affairs than on his promotion of Ireland's trade and aid activities in South Africa and Tanzania, his firm refusal to respond to the former made it loom larger on his itinerary at the expense of the national interest. It was revealing of the media management exercised by the Taoiseach's handlers that when RTE's David Davin-Power was being interviewed from Cape Town on Monday's *Morning Ireland*, he remarked that as he was speaking an official was listening into the interview by linking into the phone broadcasting-line service. Big Brother Bertie was listening!

My gut feeling on hearing this report was that any journalist worth his or her salt must insist on putting their questions to the Taoiseach without fear or favour, and that at some point he would have to respond publicly or throw an undignified tantrum.

So I was not surprised to hear on the mid-day bulletin that Bertie on his first public engagement in Cape Town had broken his self-imposed silence by retorting that it was "a bare-faced lie" for Kenny to claim that he had not paid his tax bill.

In turn, the Fine Gael media department in Dublin scorned Ahern's comment as a "desperate and dishonest attempt" to distract from his credibility, and reaffirmed its belief that he was still dodging the questions.

A counter-argument being made by Fianna Fáil is that Kenny and Gilmore cynically have raised the stakes on Bertie to boost their own profiles knowing that he is out of the country. Brian Cowen has refused to take Kenny's bait of accusing him of being an accomplice if he does not act against the Taoiseach, while FF backbenchers have scoffed at Gilmore's prediction that their party will move to shaft Bertie once they feel he has become a liability.

The hymn sheet from Fianna Fáil is that Kenny and Gilmore are personalising their attacks on Bertie in desperation after losing last year's general election, and that their accusations are boring the public. This will not deter the Opposition which is convinced that he had misled the Dail both before and since the election. Kenny and Gilmore will continue to taunt Mary Harney and her rump PDs as well as John Gormley's Greens of being "impotent" in a Government that is dominated by Fianna Fáil. This unseemly polarisation of Irish politics will continue and get even dirtier until Bertie bows to the inevitable and resigns as Taoiseach.

This is far from living the life of Reilly, even in sunny Cape Town.

Tide Turning Against Bertie

(January 22, 2008)

Shakespeare's immortal observation that there is "a tide in the affairs of men, which, taken on the flood leads on to fortune" swam unexpectedly into mind as I sat outside a coffee bar enjoying a cappuccino on Thursday in the heart of classical Rome while admiring an awesome view of the Colosseum. The tidal times in the lives of the two men I was reflecting on were Taoiseach Bertie Ahern and Cardinal Seán Brady, the Archbishop of Armagh and Primate of All Ireland. The former is the elected head of Government in Ireland, the latter was the choice of the late Pope John Paul II to lead the Irish Catholic Church into this Millennium. Both leaders need no introduction as they have been in office for over a decade of equally tidal times for Church and State.

The reason for my visit to Rome was to report on Cardinal Brady's taking possession of the titular church of the Christian martyrs, Saints Cyricus and Julitta, where he enchanted the local Italian community by preaching in their native tongue. On this visit I learned that of all the newly created Cardinals at last November's Conclave, the Irishman received the widest coverage of any of them worldwide. Cardinal Brady's growing stature in Rome and abroad augurs well for a possible visit next year by Pope Benedict to the North to support the peace process and celebrate the thirtieth anniversary of the visit to Ireland of his predecessor, the late John Paul.

On my return to Dublin, it again struck me that while the Cardinal's stock is rising, the tide is getting even strong against the Taoiseach. Enda Kenny's interview on Sunday explaining Fine Gael's formal complaint to the Standards in Public Office about Ahern's lack of tax compliance marks a further stage in the Taoiseach's difficulties.

So, too, does the call from PD founder Paul McKay for the party of rectitude either to pull out of Government or disband. Likewise, the equivocal decision by the Greens to allow their Government ministers to vote for a Yes vote in the forthcoming referendum on the Lisbon EU Treaty - but their party members to campaign for a No vote - is messy.

Gormley's failure to secure the two thirds majority needed for the Green Party to adopted a united approach to Lisbon is bad for Government stability and for the success of the Treaty. The Greens' digging their heads in the sand over Bertie's tax affairs is fast becoming a weak spot in the Government.

A Government that was described as being *rocket solid* is now at sea in a turn of the tide in which Bertie Ahern is increasingly caught floundering in misfortune.

Bertie's Lisbon Referendum

(January 29, 2008)

In autumn 2006, however, when leaks from the Mahon Tribunal pointed to his having received large sums of money for his personal use and benefit in the mid-1990s when he was Finance minister, he did his famous interview with Bryan Dobson on RTE television news where he told all, appealed for understanding for this difficult period in his life after his separation from Miriam, and said he had everything about the loans and dig-outs which he received from friends. In retrospect, he said he should not have taken this financial help.

On a wave of public sympathy, the public forgave him. The Opposition leaders Enda Kenny and Pat Rabbitte stalled. Even though more details of his finances were discovered by the media, Bertie went on to win his third general election last summer, but announced that he would be retiring by 60 and would not lead Fianna Fáil into another general election.

Since then, his third term as Taoiseach has been dominated by yet further revelations of other monies, and by his inability to maintain a coherent explanation of his original story and of the provenance of these. His support base within Fianna Fáil has held, and there is a genuine anger felt by his followers that the Opposition and the media should stop sniping at him and await the final deliberations of the Mahon Tribunal. He himself has claimed that a source within the Tribunal has deliberately leaked information to stitch him up.

However, the line of attack on him has broadened, with Kenny and the new Labour Leader, Eamon Gilmore, accusing him of misleading the Dáil and of trying to undermine the impartiality of the Tribunal. Furthermore, it has now been discovered that contrary to his earlier claim that he had cleared up his affairs with the Revenue Commissioners, this was not the case. He enters a new Dáil session this Wednesday without a tax clearance certificate from Revenue, though he has applied for a certificate that meets the less exacting requirement of the Standards in Public Office body.

This preoccupation with Bertie's personal finances, rather than on how he is running – or being distracted from running the country during a period of mounting menace to the national economy has been compounded by the charges from Kenny and Gilmore that he is no longer fit to hold the office of Taoiseach, which he has brought into disrepute.

During the excessively long Christmas recess, Bertie's inability to conduct State business was seen in the focus put on *Bertiegate* at the expense of his promotion of Irish aid projects when he visited South Africa and Tanzania. Last week when he opened Ireland Aid's new office in Dublin's O'Connell Street, his affairs again became the centre of attention. Bertie reaffirmed his intention of staying in office.

Yet, the irony has not been lost on most people that in a week when international financial markets were in turmoil, Ireland's hot topic remained Bertie's personal finances and tax liabilities. But for how long? My prediction that the tide was turning against him has been confirmed in two successive opinion polls carried in *The Irish Times* and *The Sunday Business Post*.

While both polls brought good news for Fianna Fáil by showing its ratings slightly up, its findings made for painfully bad reading for Bertie. The IT survey showed opinion deeply divided with 46pc saying he should not resign and 44pc saying he should step down as Taoiseach, while the SBP, asking a different main question, revealed that a majority 54pc do not believe the Taoiseach's evidence to the Tribunal. Nor would the resignation from the British cabinet of Peter Hain over non-disclosure of money raised during his recent bid for the Labour party's deputy leadership would have cheered Bertie up. It was a reminder of Britain's more honourable tradition of ministerial resignations.

Both polls confirm that Ahern is fast losing the trust of the nation, and his position was made the more galling for FF supporters by the IT finding that Enda Kenny for the first time since becoming leader of Fine Gael is more popular than Bertie. This is most definitely not a comfortable start for the Taoiseach to the new Dáil term which will open with further attacks on his increasingly weakened position as the main story rather than its parliamentary order of business and the Government's response to a bleakening economic situation.

One of the top priorities is the fixing of a date for a referendum on the EU Treaty agreed in Lisbon last December. The week-end polls indicated that Ahern's Government will have a difficult time in securing its passage. The IT poll showed 68pc dissatisfied with the level of information about what is contained in the Treaty, while the SBP found 31pc undecided, as against 45pc for and 25pc against.

There is no room for complacency here on the part of the Government, especially as the anti-campaigners are already in full swing and other issues irrelevant to the Treaty have a tendency to obtrude into public calculations. This Treaty has Ahern's imprint on it, as it is broadly similar to the Constitution which he piloted in 2004 during Ireland's last EU Presidency, but which was rejected by the Dutch and the French. With Ireland the only country in the 27-member

European Union holding a referendum on the Lisbon Treaty, all eyes will be on us. Bertie already has the embarrassing blemish on his record of having been the only Taoiseach since Ireland joined the EU thirty-five years ago to have lost a European Referendum with first Nice Treaty.

In all his current difficulties, Bertie Ahern cannot afford to lose the Lisbon referendum. It will be the biggest test of his career to-date.

Beleagured Bertie

(February 26, 2008)

In his obdurate clinging to office Taoiseach Bertie Ahern continues to debase the fundamental bed-rock of Irish democracy which must be rooted in the transparent integrity of elected public representatives. The continued defence of the beleagured Taoiseach by the Fianna Fáil party, Government ministers and particularly its deputy leader and Minister for Finance, Brian Cowen, is also bringing them into disrepute by association for their defending the indefensible. This sorry state of the affairs for the nation as a whole came into stark focus last Thursday and Friday when Bertie made his most adversarial but self-damaging appearance before the Mahon Tribunal in Dublin Castle.

The revelation that Bertie's former partner Celia Larkin obtained a £30,000 loan in 1993 from FF party funds in his Dublin Central constituency to purchase a house in Phibsboro for two elderly aunts was a shocking insight into the under-belly of parish-pump politics.

Allied to this is Bertie's belated admission of not paying full taxes in that decade, and his continued failure to explain how he used a political donation for £5,000 for his own personal use, which is now the subject of a parallel investigation by the Revenue Commissioners.

The picture that has emerged is far from the impoverished and homeless Minister for Finance of the mid-1990s in post-marital distress that he conveyed on his now infamous RTE television interview in autumn 2006 when the first disclosures of his "dig-outs" from friends in Manchester and Drumcondra were made public.

It has now emerged that the man was awash with money galore, and that he had as many bank accounts as the Sultan of Oman. Nor can he give an adequate and consistent explanation for this bountiful heap of cash.

It was really a new low in Irish political life on Saturday when Bertie at an Ogra Fianna Fáil meeting claimed that he had not been damaged by the loan to Celia Larkin from a B/T account administered by trustees close to him. Worse still, Brian Cowen offered his absolute support for his Taoiseach and lamely excused the Larkin loan on the flimsy grounds that she had paid it back with interest sometime after Christmas.

Over the week-end Fine Gael leader, Enda Kenny, has renewed his offensive against the "blanket-defence" of the hapless Bertie, who will be abroad this week on Government business, and is targeting Cowen for standing-by his wounded leader.

This unseemly circling the wagons around the elusive Bertie contrasts with the recent resignations from the British and Stormont Governments respectively of Peter Hain and Ian Paisley Jnr for lesser demeanours than Bertie has been accused of.

Bertie Acclaims Unionist Giant

(March 10, 2008)

Ian Paisley's decision to step down as First Minister of the Northern Ireland devolved Government this summer has been marked by eulogies from political leaders that he was the ultimate peace-maker to angry tirades by commentators that he was the man who fuelled the sectarian violence for over three decades.

"The established peace and continuing prosperity which everyone in Northern Ireland now enjoys owes a significant debt to the leadership of Dr Paisley," said Shaun Woodward, the North's Secretary of State said.

"I think he will be fondly remembered the people of Ireland, north and south, for the very courageous leadership he showed", was the verdict of Martin McGuinness, his *Chuckle Brother* as Sinn Féin's Deputy First Minister.

"Shed no tears for this roaring bigot. Everything he did was for Ian Paisley", wrote the historian Ruth Dudley Edwards. "The truth about Paisley does not make for pleasant reading", opined Tom McGurk. "Good riddance to that ranting bilious Pied Piper of the North", screamed Eilis O'Hanlon. "I come to bury Paisley, not to praise a dangerous old bigot", scoffed Matt Cooper.

As in so many cases involving a major historical figure during his life-time, both judgements of Paisley as an icon of peace and as a demon figure whose demagoguery incited violence and frustrated moderate political progress so often and for so long are correct.

Indeed, on a number of occasions, I have grappled to find a balance between praising Paisley's achievements and condemning his limitations. I have been absorbed by this question since January 16, 1980, when I hosted a lunch in the members' restaurant of the European Parliament in Strasbourg for the late John *Backbencher* Healy with the leader of the Democratic Unionist Party and his taciturn wife Eileen.

It took place just a few weeks after Charles Haughey had succeeded Jack Lynch as Taoiseach and there were high expectations that Charlie would make a dramatic overture on the North with the relatively new British Prime Minister, Margaret Thatcher.

As we waited, I suddenly sensed that despite all his years as an avid *Big Ian* watcher, Healy had never met him personally. So as Ian and Eileen joined us, I immediately introduced them. Ian instantly shook Healy's hands and told him that he had known his uncle, a Mayoman, who had been a member of the Royal Irish Constabulary stationed in County Antrim prior to Partition. It was a revealing insight into how Paisley needed no lessons from Fianna Fáil about grass-roots politics.

When the attentive waiter brought us our opening dish, Healy and I bowed our heads in silent prayer, while the leader of the Free Presbyterian Church intoned the Lord's blessing over the meal. In relaxed form, Paisley exuded a charm and a humour which were totally at odds with his public image as the fundamentalist Bible-thumper who built his long and divisive career on denouncing the Church of Rome as 'the Anti-Christ', and whose fiery rhetoric had ruined the careers of Unionist leaders, Terence O'Neill, Chichester Clark and Brian Faulkner, and inspired generations of young Loyalists to join para-military organisations.

As Healy, a close confidant of Haughey, talked directly to Paisley about his "Last Hero", the purpose of the meeting gradually dawned on me. Healy stopped being the political pundit and assumed the role of an advocate-emissary bringing a message from Haughey. Healy professed his belief that there were new possibilities opening up to resolve the violence in the North.

Healy told Paisley that the moment had arrived for the brokering of an historic deal between a Fianna Fáil Taoiseach (Haughey) and a Tory Prime Minister (Thatcher).

Several times, he urged Paisley to trust Haughey and negotiate with him. Healy also told Paisley that John Hume, also recently elected to Strasbourg, was another man to do business with.

Paisley listened with great attention, and asked a series of questions of Healy as to what moves he expected Haughey would make, questions which revealed an openness to possible political discourse that was far removed from his 'No Surrender' public posturing.

So well did the lunch go that when Ian and Eileen were leaving, Healy ordered two large glasses of the finest cognac. "The devil's buttermilk will be the ruin of you," Paisley chuckled, as he returned to the chamber.

"Brother Cooney, put this date down in your diary. We have just lunched with the next Prime Minister of Northern Ireland," Healy expansively predicted, as we both sank large cognac brandies in a toast to the Rev Ian Paisley. History did not take the immediate turn sign-posted by Healy. After a period of 'tea-pot' diplomacy, Haughey and Thatcher fell out – and Paisley demonised them both.

Seven years on, I was reporting in the North when *Big Ian* mobilised Ulster Unionists at monster rallies against the Anglo-Irish Agreement agreed by Haughey's successor, Garret FitzGerald, and Mrs Thatcher. It was around this time I met a retired civil servant who had worked in the private office of Terence O'Neill. He assured me that Paisley would never stop saying 'No.'

It was the insight of this civil servant that convinced me in my November 2004 column that Paisley was not for turning. In 1990, Paisley had sat down at Stormont for talks with ministers of Haughey's FF-PD Government, but these broke down. In turn, Paisley had opposed the Downing Street Declaration negotiated by Albert Reynolds and John Major, and later the Good Friday Agreement reached by Bertie Ahern and Tony Blair that gave David Trimble for a short and unsuccessful period in the prime ministerial post which Healy had assigned for *Big Ian*.

Nonetheless, I still clung to the memory of the statesmanlike Paisley I encountered in Strasbourg. After Trimble's demise and Paisley's victory as the undisputed leader of the largest Unionist party, I was still doubtful of a deal with Sinn Féin.

However, I knew Healy's prophecy would come true when in autumn 2006 Paisley agreed to meet the Catholic Primate of All Ireland, Séan Brady. From my many theological conversations over the years with Paisley, I knew instinctively that it was a bigger hurdle for him to meet the Pope of Rome's representative in Ireland than it would be to head a Government with Sinn Féin.

It was after a brush with death from a serious illness, and through the prompting of his wife Eileen who had sat silent at table in Strasbourg, that Paisley made the move last year to lead a Stormont Government predicted by Healy 27 years earlier.

A year in office saw Paisley's triumphs marred by the resignation of his son, Ian Junior, over a tacky property deal, and by grass-roots rumblings from within his own DUP party about his sell-out to Rome and Republicanism.

In John Healy's memory, I raised my glass to *Big Ian* on his arrival in, as I do again on his departure from, the highest office which from January 16, 1980, he was destined to hold. As Taoiseach Bertie Ahern said, Paisley is a giant Unionist figure alongside Carson and Craig.

Bertie Makes
April Fools of Us

(April 1, 2008)

All Fools Day, Tuesday April 1, marks a landmark date in the history of the absurd, Irish-style. On this fantastical day an elected Taoiseach in Ireland initiates a High Court case to prevent his statements in the Dáil about his personal finances from being used by the Mahon Tribunal of Inquiry established by the Oireachtas to investigate political corruption in the planning process.

Counsel for Bertie Ahern contends that statements which he made to the Dáil in September and October 2006 after revelations first appeared in *The Irish Times* about payments made to him when he was Minister for Finance are covered by privilege under the Constitution. Bertie claims that under article 15.13 of the Constitution the Mahon Tribunal is not entitled to cross-examine him on those statements, and that the fact that these were repeated outside the Dáil chamber does not remove that privilege.

This challenge is designed to prevent the Mahon Tribunal obtaining access to advice received by the Taoiseach from a financial expert, Paddy Stronge, about banking transactions conducted through his account in 1993 and 1994. He claims this advice enjoys constitutional or litigation privilege.

A third strand of Ahern's challenge is that he is entitled to the return of all the material and calculations on which the Tribunal relied when putting hypotheses to him that a lodgement into his AIB O'Connell Street Dublin account of IR£28,772.90 by his former partner, Celia Larkin, was the equivalent of either $45,000 or ST£25,000. Under oath, Bertie told the Tribunal that this was neither a dollar nor a sterling lodgement but consisted of IR£16,500 and a further ST£8,000 given to him by friends after a dinner in Manchester.

The fact that the credibility of his original explanations have been ripped apart in various testimonies to the Tribunal – and in its cross-examinations of him to-date – is not deterring him from presenting himself as a champion of constitutional privilege.

Clearly, with his previous evidence in shreds, especially from the admission of his former secretary Gráinne Carruth that it was "a matter of probability" that she had lodged sterling into his Irish Permanent Building account in Drumcondra, his High Court challenge can only be construed as part of a cynical stalling tactic to limit the Tribunal's power of investigation and delay its final report.

Bertie's desperate hope is that a ruling by the High Court will find that he was unfairly treated by the Tribunal. This would trigger calls from the Ahern loyalists demanding the Mahon judges to consider their positions. Its investigation would be in doubt.

If, however, Bertie loses in the High Court, you can be sure our hero will do a runner to the Supreme Court, again to buy more time. All of this is very dignified conduct indeed by a head of Government.

This High Court front is only one of the arenas in which *Battling Bertie* is erecting the barricades around his diminishing ground for manoeuvre. He has been consulting with Brian Cowen and at least four ministers about how he should handle his beloved Dáil on its return this Wednesday from its excessively long Christmas holidays. At issue here is how Bertie should respond to the tepidly minimalist calls from Green leader John Gormley and the PDs' Mary Harney to clarify his position in the light of Carruth's tearful collapse in the Tribunal; and more menacingly, on how to handle the anticipated barrage of questions from Fine Gael leader Enda Kenny and Labour's Eamon Gilmore about the discrepancies between his evidence that lodgements into his savings account were from his salary cheques and were not sterling transactions, as now conceded under caution of perjury by Carruth.

The advice reportedly given to Bertie by his wise ministerial monkeys is, to paraphrase the poet Seamus Heaney, "whatever you say, say nothing". Leave it to the the High Court and your next appearance before Mahon on May 20. At most, give the dumb Dáil cretins a limited explanation in your usually baffling dissection of the English language.

The prolonging of the stalling game was seen on Sunday evening's RTE *Week in Politics* programme when Agriculture Minister, Mary Coughlan, evaded answering five times whether or not she believed Bertie's account of his finances. This was a matter for Judge Mahon to decide, not for Mary to believe or not, she inveighed. He has my full confidence! Coughlan's noble stalling came as the latest *Business Post-Red C* monthly opinion poll showed a drop of two points in Fianna Fáil's ratings. Statistically insignificant, this poll is psychologically significant, because it is the first time that the Ahern cash controversy has dented Fianna Fáil's electoral standing. On the same programme, a wearied Eamon Gilmore repeated his mantra that Bertie is irreparably damaged and should resign.

"Ahern should go now" was the message delivered on Friday evening by Michael Ring, Fine Gael's Community, Rural and Gaeltacht spokesman. Speaking in Carrick-on-Shannon, Mayo's *Mighty Michael* urged Bertie's immediate resignation in order to end the stalemate at Government level and address the economic and health sector crises.

What has been critically wounding is a report in Saturday's *Irish Times* by its Public Affairs Correspondent, Colm Keena, calculating that the total financial transactions under scrutiny by the Mahon Tribunal exceeds IR£452,800 – the equivalent in today's value to €886,830.

This yet unexplained munificence is far from the poor-mouth "down in my luck" claim made by Ahern in his infamously manipulative Bryan Dobson interview.

The End-Game for Bertie is now in sight. His address to the US Congress on April 30 may prove to be his swan-song. His role in bringing peace to Northern Ireland will be played for all its worth. This Thursday Bertie will wrap himself around the 10-year old Good Friday flag when he delivers an address to the Institute of British-Irish Studies at University College Dublin on its legacy. He will hail the Agreement as "a momentous milestone in the history of Ireland", whose tenth anniversary provides a valuable opportunity to reflect on the enormous progress made since 1998.

Bertie's cash controversy, however, is a painful reminder to us all that we are still enmired in the Haughey years of murky financial politics which he pledged to put in the past with clear blue waters of accountability. The reality is that he is a drowning premier.

If Fianna Fáil, the Greens and the PDs do not want to drown with Bertie, they will need to tell him soon that it is time that he jumped ship from the Taoiseach's office and paddled his own rickety canoe.

Bertie Found Himself Trapped

(April 8, 2008)

When I received an e-mail summons to a news conference on Wednesday morning at Government Buildings, I new instantly that it tolled the bell for time on Bertie Ahern's tenure as Taoiseach.

Although the legal team for the Mahon Tribunal had conceded two of his technical complaints the previous day in the High Court, I had detected that it was becoming increasingly difficult for his ministers to get him through politically unscathed to the end of April when he addresses the US Congress in Washington. That handicapped has been removed by himself.

Without acknowledging his receipt in the 1990s of still unexplained monies which became his nemesis at the Mahon Tribunal, he declared that he had never done anything to dishonour the office of Taoiseach, and that the one mistake he had never made was to enrich himself by misusing the trust of the people. For a man renowned for his linguistic howlers, this was a masterly piece of evasive and selective prose.

Flanked by his subdued ministers, his announcement to step-down on May 6 was delivered in a melodramatic atmosphere of finality which released a potent emotional mixture of goodwill associated with the ancestral Irish respect for a tragic funeral and the instant populist canonisation of the deceased.

Few would quibble with the assessment of his heir apparent, Brian Cowen, that Bertie Ahern was the most consummate politician of his era. Yet, contrast this fulsome appraisal with the succinct headline in the *Daily Telegraph*: "Ahern forced to resign over sleaze allegations".

Commentators, anticipating the verdict of historians, have nuanced Ahern's self-portrayal and Cowen's eulogy by balancing his achievements against his fatal Achilles Heel of not only failing to fulfil his promise of cleansing Irish politics of political corruption, but of finding himself trapped in the corrosive culture personified by his political mentor, Charles Haughey.

As with Haughey, Ahern's downfall over his personal finances, and their stealth in concealing the sources of payments for so long, will cast a deep shadow over their stature and ratings. Both men had public service greatness in their bones, but the monies in their back-pockets have cast them as flawed figures wearing hypocritical masks. Notwithstanding Bertie's defiant *Last Hurrah* protestation of doing no wrong and wronging nobody, this down-side will place him with Haughey in the middle of the league table of Taoisigh rather than among the top three champion contenders.

Personally, I found Bertie's resignation speech a sad but inevitable moment. The deserved tributes from President McAleese, Tony Blair, Bill Clinton and Ian Paisley naturally highlighted his contribution to bringing political stability to the North. On the economy, he was judged to be a lucky Taoiseach, enjoying the 'rising tide' of the Celtic Tiger decade but he was also criticised for failing to distribute this wealth more evenly across a society which still has its poor among it, a dysfunctional health system and widespread traffic congestion.

As Brian Cowen ponders the line-up of the Government which he will pilot through stormy economic waters, his equally daunting challenge will be to restore public confidence in the political system and public services after the sinking of *Battleship Bertie*.

Inheriting a united crew and a fair-wind from a *Sunday Business Post-Red C* opinion poll boost of five pc for Fianna Fáil, *Biffo*, who was elected unopposed as the party's President-designate and sole candidate for the office of Taoiseach, will be called upon to reset the ship of State's compass to avoid the rocks on which skipper Ahern foundered.

The nautical reality is that Bertie was forced by adverse circumstances of his own making to abandon the steering-wheel and swim desperately for shore. He had no choice in jumping ship if he was to prevent his third Government from being washed-up on the iceberg of his own hidden personal finances.

No one knew better than Bertie when he took over the helm on his 11-year epic voyage of unprecedented national prosperity that his strategic task was to distance his barque from the stench shoals of corruption associated with the Haughey years.

Indeed, he defined his intended course of direction when he pledged to put clear blue waters between his administration and the murky past which had tainted standards in Irish public life.

It is a national tragedy, as well as a personal one for Bertie, that he did not do so. In spite of his early efforts to introduce more accountable standards in public office, he remained trapped in the corrosive culture personified by his mentor, Charles Haughey. He failed to transcend this 'fixer mentality' by retaining in positions of influence old guard figures such as Ray Burke and the late Liam Lawlor who were subsequently disgraced. Worse still, Ahern's fundamental miscalculation was not to tell the whole story when the revelations first became public in

September 2006 about his irregular finances in the mid-1990s. Just as Richard Nixon's fatal error was to cover-up the break-in of the Watergate building, so too the *Bertiegate* scandal grew in force on account of his incredible yarns to the Dáil and the Mahon Tribunal.

It has taken Bertie 18 tempestuous months of increasingly erratic steerage amid mounting public disquiet to face up to this deception. He was not hounded out of office by the Opposition or the media. His past caught up with him. He had to go.

In making his personally brave but belated decision to jump over-board, Bertie has discovered that his arrival on dry land has helped to shore-up largely intact his considerable achievements as Taoiseach, especially as a peacemaker in the North, notwithstanding the clouds still hovering over him in Dublin Castle.

With his popularity and overall reputation still high in spite of his calamitous exit from office, Ahern now has time on his side to refashion his image as an elder statesman, as did Nixon. In this, he has the especial good-will of his anointed successor.

Cowen Dons Hillery Mantle

(April 15, 2008)

A changing of the guard, old and new, in Ireland's political pantehon will be symbolised this Wednesday when Taoiseach-designate Brian Cowen delivers the graveside oration for Ireland's sixth President, Dr Patrick Hillery, who died on Saturday, aged 84.

The choice of the Tanaiste, at the request of the Hillery family, represents an important step in Fianna Fáil's rediscovery of its republican roots which the Tullamore man stressed at his first press conference as President-elect of the party when he identified himself with Séan Lemass, the pragmatic patriot.

The Taoiseach-in waiting's tribute to Dr Hillery comes after he held talks in Belfast with the North's First Minister-designate, Peter Robinson, which is further focusing minds on future joint all-Ireland economic initiatives.

But Brian Cowen's agile mind is not just concentrating on future public sector reform in dimmer financial times, he is also connecting his style of leadership with former major figures in Fianna Fáil. In Dr Hillery's life and career, Cowen has an ideal model who has been lauded by President Mary McAleese for his "selfless devotion to public service".

Dr Hillery was the Minister for Education who laid the foundations for Donogh O'Malley's introduction of free schooling. As Minister for External Affairs, he made the North an international concern at the United Nations after the Troubles broke out.

His achievements included leading the negotiations for Ireland's membership of the European Economic Community, which he signed with Taoiseach, Jack Lynch, who in 1973 appointed him to the European Commission, where he took the Social Affairs portfolio.

Writing about this period in *A Vital National Interest, Ireland in Europe, 1973-1998*, edited by Jim Dooge and Ruth Barrington, Hillery recalled that in the pre-Accession days, there were no direct flights from Dublin to Brussels, and he sometimes had to drive there a day and a half before the start of meetings of the Council of Ministers. He found his early training as a house doctor in Dublin's Mater Hospital a good preparation for the late night negotiations on unexciting but exacting details such as trade tariffs and fish quotas. During those long nights of hard bargaining, he had to endure poor sandwiches and disgusting cups of coffee.

My first meeting with Dr Hillery was in October 1976 just shortly after I had arrived in Brussels as the European Correspondent for *The Irish Times*. Along with his Caruso-like chef de cabinet, Ed FitzGibbon, he took me for lunch to one of the best Italian restaurants in the Rue Archimede.

When I asked him what it was like being Ireland's first Commissioner, he gently corrected me and said he was the European Commissioner for Social Affairs who was of Irish nationality. He was right. Commissioners take an oath of loyalty to Europe, but the media insists on describing them as cheer-leaders for their respective countries.

The one time Hillery came into open conflict with the Government of Liam Cosgrave was when he supported the Commission in its refusal to give Ireland a derogation from implementing an EEC directive giving women equal payment with men. Although he did not speak the language of feminism, he was committed to improving the status of women.

Appointed to give "a human face" to the increasingly bureaucratic work of the Commission, he admired the West German Chancellor, Willy Brandt, who inspired the move to establish a genuine social policy to off-set the damaging effect for ordinary people from the free market.

Dr Hillery established a Social Fund, but was disappointed that it was smaller than he had hoped on account of the recession following the 1973 Arab oil embargo. The social fund became an important instrument for Ireland's economic development as part of the bigger Structural Funds.

Another vivid memory of the Hillery Brussels years was the day in late 1976 when at the mid-day news conference in the Berlaymont the spokesman announced that the Irish Government had decided not to reappoint him for a second four year term. By coincidence, that evening Hillery was returning to Dublin, and FitzGibbon summoned me to his office for a drink and an informal chat. I veered straight for Dr Hillery and popped the question: "Are you returning to Dublin to the Phoenix Park?"

In his disarming way, the cute Clareman smiled and said: "John, that is the question I will be asked when I arrive this evening at Dublin Airport. What should I say?"

Instantly, I knew that he would be Ireland's next President and I bolted back to my office to file a front-page story predicting that Hillery would succeed Cearbhall Ó Dálaigh, who had resigned from the Presidency that same morning over the "thundering disgrace" jibe made against him by the Minister for Defence, Paddy Donegan.

News of Dr Hillery's death broke during the Marian Finucane programme, where emphasis was placed on how he rescued the Presidency from becoming a party political tool-box. He did so by asserting the independence of the office in 1982 at the height of a potentially damaging constitutional crisis driven by Charles Haughey.

Following the collapse of Garret FitzGerald's first Government when its Budget was defeated in the Dáil on January 27, 1982, FitzGerald went to Áras an Uachtarain to deliver his seal of office to President Hillery with the aim of setting a date for a general election.

However, the Constitution defines clearly that one of the powers of the President is "the absolute discretion" to refuse a dissolution of the Dáil by requiring deputies to elect a new Taoiseach who would appoint his Government without calling a general election".

Hillery consented to dissolve the Dáil and set a date for fresh elections, even though Haughey, then Leader of the Opposition, had issued a public statement, saying: "It is a matter for the President to consider the situation which has arisen now that the Taoiseach has ceased to retain the support of the majority in Dáil Éireann".

Significantly, Haughey, as he was legitimately entitled to do, indicated that he was "available for consultation with the President should he so wish".

Although rumours abounded that Haughey had phoned the Áras that fateful January evening to put improper pressure on the President, Hillery's positive role did not come to light until 'the Áras phone-call row' erupted in October 1990.

The late Brian Lenihan, the Fianna Fáil candidate to succeed Hillery after his two terms in office, was strenuously denying that he had made any phone call on behalf of Haughey, in a dramatic performance on RTE's *Questions and Answers*.

FitzGerald, who was also on the programme, challenged Lenihan's recollection. After Lenihan claimed FitzGerald was talking "fiction", FitzGerald revealed that he was present when the calls came through to Hillery, and he knew how many there were.

This exchange persuaded a research student, Jim Duffy, to make public a tape in which Lenihan had confirmed that he had spoken to Hillery by phone. Lenihan again denied this. His "mature recollection" was that he made no call.

On the Finucane show, FitzGerald disclosed that there were eight calls, and that Hillery was in a rage over the "badgering" from Haughey's ministerial cronies including the late Sylvester Barrett, a fellow Clareman. Had Hillery bowed to Haughey's demands, he would have been viewed as a ceremonial Fianna Fáil puppet-president.

Lenihan lost to Mary Robinson, who, ironically, was campaigning for a more active presidency, a popular appeal especially to women which cast Hillery's as 14 years spent in leisurely retirement on the golf course. Speaking on Saturday, Mary Robinson disclosed that he had not taken her campaign personally, but was privately in favour of this.

Ironically, in view of his being succeeded by a Mayo woman, one of Dr Hillery's cherished memories of his second term, which he found more enjoyable than his stormier first seven years in the Áras, was his visit to Kilcummin and Killala in August 1989 when he declared the Humbert Summer School to be a truly international school.

Although Hillery declined to give a full account of events even in a recent television documentary on the grounds that a reheated controversy would damage the presidency, he received ample vindication in the week-end tribute from Taoiseach Bertie Ahern. In a formal but coded apology for Haughey's machinations, Ahern noted that "in volatile times", Hillery was "a cool head, who exercised his powers wisely, and assiduously protected the independence of Ireland's highest office".

Decoded, Ahern, Haughey's trusted acolyte, admitted that his former *Boss* put improper pressure on Hillery in the messy behind-the-scene power struggle.

History will record Patrick Hillery as a transitional president of substance who was a bridge between the more honorific roles of his predecessors, Douglas Hyde, Seán T O'Kelly and Eamon de Valera, to the more public faces of Presidents Robinson and McAleese.

Further light on his stature will be shed later this year with the publication of an authorised biography by historian John Walsh in which for the first time Hillery will tell his story.

It will be essential reading for both Brian Cowen and Peter Robinson as they take charge of the island of Ireland.

Clergy Canonise Blessed Bertie

(April 29, 2008)

The Taoiseach was declared *Blessed Bertie* with thunderous acclaim by Christian, Jewish and Muslim leaders at a farewell reception in Government Buildings. This is true. I witnessed it. It was like watching a scene from an old-fashioned miracle play rather than a modern soap-opera titled "Disgraced Man Departs in Glory."

Not only did I observe the warmth of the church leaders' valediction for Bertie Ahern, I too felt a surge of affection towards him when he equally warmly shook my hand and thanked me for coming, even though for the past 18 months I had been regularly predicting and calling for his political demise over his irregular personal finances.

Furthermore, when I invited Bertie to be photographed with colleague Patsy McGarry and myself, and asked him to stand for further crucifixion between "two thieves" of the Fourth Estate, he took the joke in good spirits and happily obliged.

The occasion last Tuesday evening was a gathering of the members of the Government's Structured Dialogue with Churches, Faith Communities and Humanists which Ahern set up last year. Speaking on behalf of the members, Cardinal Seán Brady thanked the outgoing Taoiseach for putting religion back on the national agenda, and the Catholic Primate of All Ireland praised him for being the first head of government in Europe to establish an official forum with the churches and faith communities.

After listening head-down to this canonisation, Bertie delivered a remarkable apologia on his attitude to religion in civic society. He said that over the course of his political career he had he had observed a growing hesitation in public debate to refer to religion and the churches, and he even noted a growing hesitation in public debate to acknowledge the very fact of the impact of religion on Ireland's culture and institutions.

Departing from his prepared text, Bertie revealed that this disregard for religion was the one thing which upset him – and in an oblique reference to his travails before the Mahon Tribunal of Inquiry, he quipped that he was not easily or often upset. It was a rare moment of self-revelation from the man described by Fine Gael leader Enda Kenny as *the sociable loner*.

His assurance that the Structured Dialogue would continue after his departure was applauded by the church leaders who privately feared that this official channel of communication with the Government would lapse under his successor, Brian Cowen. Continuity, Bertie said, would be guaranteed by the commitment to it shown by the General Secretary of the Taoiseach's office, Dermot McCarthy.

From conversations with churchmen, I had detected an uncertainty among them about the outcome of the June referendum on the Lisbon Reform Treaty, a section which makes provision for Church-State dialogue in all 27 member States.

This uncertainty has been highlighted in the week-end's *Sunday Business Post-Red C* poll, which showed a dramatic shift in opinion against the Treaty, with support having fallen from 43pc in February to 35pc, while opposition has risen from 24 pc to 31pc, a slender four per cent lead for the Government.

With the undecided remaining static at 34 pc, the pressure is now on Brian Cowen, when he takes over on May 7, to regain the initiative. The shift in the public mood has been widely seen as arising from the disaffection among farmers about EU Trade Commissioner Peter Mandelson's perceived disregard for the Irish beef and dairy industries at the World Trade Talks.

It was no surprise, therefore, that in his 1916 commemoration address at Arbour Hill on Sunday, Bertie predicted that a No vote would have "disastrous" repercussions for this country, not least the agriculture community, and he challenged farmers to rally to the Lisbon agenda, as he was sure that their grievances would be addressed at the WTO talks in Geneva.

The outgoing Taoiseach's timely warning to farmers was met with a cheap and vulgar gibe from Naoise Nunn, the director of the scare-mongering anti-lobby, Libertas, that a 'No' vote would be a disaster for Bertie as there would be no President of Europe' job for him "to run to, where he would be free from the petty concerns of the electorate."

The Government's delay in setting the date for the referendum has allowed Libertas a free-run in the scare-stakes, and it needs to move to explain the issues more fully before June 12. It is a damning indictment of its dilly-dallying that a report from the Electoral Commission has found that 80pc of voters say they do not know or understand the Treaty.

Although the spot-light is now turning on farmers, the Government has been quietly getting church leaders on side. Recently at a special service in Rome to mark the 400th anniversary of the Flight of the Earls, Cardinal Brady called for "a Europe of values" in which the EU respects Catholic Church teaching on ethical issues. The Cardinal warned, however, that in an increasingly technocratic and economic-driven Union, the sense of vision and values which inspired it could be easily lost. This was why he believed that developing the concept of "a Europe of values" remains a critical but unresolved dimension of the European Union. He was referring, of course, to issues such as marriage, family, the origins of life and of death.

His carefully worded address was welcomed in Government circles as signalling the qualified support from the bishops for a 'Yes' vote. At a little publicised meeting in Dundalk, the Minister for European Affairs, Dick Roche, praised Cardinal Brady's homily in Rome as expressing a deep understanding of the positive role played by the European Union in developing peace throughout the continent and indeed in helping to overcome divisions in Ireland.

Roche assured members of the Inter-Church Committee that the Reform Treaty explicitly protects Ireland's constitutional position on the right to life. "Suggestions to the contrary are mischievous and misleading," he said, noting that the Lisbon Reform Treaty reaffirms a guarantee inserted into earlier EU Treaties in the early 1990s stating that nothing in the Treaties can affect the application in Ireland of Article 40.3.3 of the Irish Constitution, the pro-life clause.

"This could not be clearer," Roche said, obviously directing his assurance at ultra-conservative Catholic claims, such as made in last week's *Western People* by Martin Daly. "It has protected Ireland's position for 15 years and will continue to do so under the Reform Treaty", Roche said pointedly, in contrast to Martin's misleading claim that the Lisbon Treaty will put pressure on Ireland's pro-life and pro-marriage culture.

Contrary to the claim by the doyen of *the Moy School of Theology* that our denominational schools and their ethos will be undermined by "intolerant secularism", Roche said one of the most attractive features of the Treaty is the Charter of Fundamental Rights which is given legal status by the Lisbon Treaty.

Take note, Martin, that the Charter explicitly recognises freedom of religion and respect for the rights of parents to have their children educated in conformity with their own religious convictions. "

Furthermore, the Treaty provides for "open, transparent and regular dialogue with the Churches", which Cardinal Brady, Archbishop Diarmuid Martin, Archbishop John Neill, as well as Muslim and Jewish leaders, told Bertie Ahern is "a very valuable initiative".

Along with peace in the North, the Government's own national structured dialogue with the churches and faith communities and humanists is a testimony to *Blessed Bertie.*

Bertie's Long Farewell

(May 6, 2008)

Reflecting on the difficulties in writing a biography of any important public figure, the writer, Russell Braddon, observed shrewdly that real people in real life ignore the demands of narrative and plot in a way that no novelist would tolerate in any fictitious character.

This observation runs aground in regard to the life of Bartholomew Patrick Ahern, who this Wednesday steps down after eleven years as Taoiseach. Bertie's true life story at times reads like fiction.

Heroes, we are taught to believe, do not lead shapeless lives. Yet, at the core of the Ahern idyll is his claim to have become an unlucky casualty in a row between two builders, Owen O'Callaghan and Tom Gilmartin, whose petty planning squabbles enmeshed him in a relentless trawl by the Mahon Tribunal of Inquiry at Dublin Castle into his personal financial details dating from the mid-1990s when he was Minister for Finance but also at that difficult time leading a shapeless life after his separation from his wife Miriam. All this muck-racking by the media distracted the work of Government – and he resigned prematurely in the national interest.

Unlike most people, who throw away their letters, photographs and original documents that provide the straw for the biographer's bricks, the Ahern story ultimately will rest on his possession of the most extensive archives of any figure in Irish public life. His press cuttings alone would clog up Dublin's Phoenix Park twice over!

Paradoxically, the most secretive of modern Irish politicians, next to his mentor Charles Haughey, leaves office with the most expansive collection of public and personal records, much of it on file in Government Buildings for future storage in the National Archive, but also piles of material which have been assembled, with magpie-like diligence, by the Mahon Tribunal lawyers.

What may yet emerge from the Mahon Tribunal remains to be heard and tested, but however mortal or venial that evidence proves to be, historians have not been slow to insist that Ahern will be admired for his peace work in the North, presiding over unprecedented prosperity in Celtic Tiger Ireland and in becoming Taoiseach three times as head of coalitions over which he presided with consummate conciliation and consensus.

During his lap of honour in recent weeks, Bertie, too, has been sedulously crafting his own version of an epic tale for immediate consumption by an avid reading public whose affection for him remains undimmed by his humbling resignation. Like Stephen Dedalus in James Joyce's *Portrait of the Artist*, Bertie is imprinting his indelible soul on the nation's imagination with his own account of his role in contemporary Irish history, one which he hopes will safeguard and consolidate his legacy as Taoiseach.

The working class boy, who grew up under the shadow of Croke Park in Dublin's Drumcondra, and who first cut his political teeth as *the King of the Poster Boys* for a Fianna Fáil candidate in an 1965 by-election, bowed out with an acclaimed address to the joint Houses of the U.S. Congress, bearing the simple but immortal words, "Ireland is at peace." His finest line. His finest moment. His epitaph and Last Hurrah.

Well, not quite his last farewell.

Over the week-end Bertie has been engaged in a round of radio and television interviews recalling with warmth and humour many of the highlights of his extraordinary career. In his leaving, he has found a new eloquence, even in Latin, in his *Noirdside* voice. A fighter to the end, he quoted a line as being his proclaimed family motto: *Per ardua surgo* – "I rise through difficulties".

Of huge particular interest was his rematch interview with RTE's Bryan Dobson against the backdrop of the White House in Washington. Seventeen months after assuring Dobson that he revealed everything about his dig-outs Bertie assured Bryan that there were no other payments to him to be revealed by the horrid Tribunal, other than the more interesting of the fees paid to lawyers!

Writing in Monday's *Irish Independent*, Bertie confided that the last few weeks had been a very emotional experience for him, and that in his last full day as Taoiseach his overwhelming feelings were one of gratitude for the chances of proudly leading the country for 11 years and his great hope for the future. What struck him most in his twenty years at the top in politics, especially since his becoming Minister for Labour in 1987, was not any one decision or another. "What stands out for me is that when we as a nation thought in new ways about old problems, it was then that we found our way forward".

Today Bertie will return the seal of office to President Mary McAleese. On Tuesday he will speak at a ceremony on the Banks of the Bond appropriately with his new found friend Ian Paisley, who is also preparing to depart from his high office. On Wednesday morning for the last time as Taoiseach he will stand at the graves of executed leaders of 1916 in Arbour Hill, leading the nation in commemoration. He will then go to Leinster House to support the nomination of Brian Cowen as Taoiseach.

LIFE AFTER TAOISEACH

Au Revoir, Bertie

"Bertie's most important trait was his ordinariness". - FERGUS FINLAY

"We live in an aspirational society and Bertie embodies what can be achieved.
If he can do it, so can Breakfast Roll Man".
- DAVID MCWILLIAMS

In his resignation announcement as Taoiseach on Wednesday April 2, 2008, Bertie Ahern professed "to submit to the verdict of history". His statement was cunningly crafted with his eye on his legacy and his ranking with the ten other men who had led Irish Governments since Independence in 1921-2. In bracketing himself with Eamon de Valera and Seán Lemass, he subtly wrote the first draft of his autobiography, one which puts the focus on his achievements as an architect of peace in the North through the Good Friday and the St Andrews Agreements, as the reorganiser of the British-Irish relationship, as the skilful manager of the Celtic Tiger economy, as the wizard of social partnerships with business and trade unions, as the unifier of the Fianna Fáil party and the consensus Taoiseach who made coalition governments work, and not least, as the winner of three successive general elections in 1997, 2002 and 2007. While Bertie's reputation as a fixer is second to none, his success in these areas was built upon the work of his predecessors, Garret FitzGerald on Europe, Charles Haughey on social partnership, and Garret and Albert Reynolds on Northern Ireland policy.

Inevitably, notwithstanding Bertie's defiant *Last Hurrah* protestation of "doing no wrong and wronging nobody", the down-side in his record is circumscribed by his failure to fulfil his promise to put clear water between his new Fianna Fáil and the political corruption of the Haughey era, then being investigated and exposed at the Tribunals of Inquiry in Dublin Castle. Indeed, once Haughey was disgraced and Liam Lawlor was dead, the relentless legal-cum-media spotlight turned on Bertie's personal financial affairs. It was this chipping away by the Castle's legal eagles and Castle journalists which compelled his resignation and flight from office. His stirring Dáil declaration of December 1996 came back to haunt him: "The public are entitled to have an absolute guarantee of the financial probity and integrity of their elected representatives, their officials and above all of ministers. They need to know that they are under financial obligations to nobody".

However, by April 2008 Bertie's Government was becoming increasingly paralysed in its conduct of the affairs of State on account of the normal political debate's fixation on his personal finances. "It is a bizarre by-product of the tribunal process that the original allegation that Ahern was bribed by a developer not only receded into the background, but has lost credibility while the spotlight falls on the petty-cash accounts of his complicated and baffling family finances", noted Maurice Hayes.

Sam Smyth reported that sometime the previous week, Bertie had come to the conclusion that standing down was the least bad option open to him and that it would be worse for him to continue as Taoiseach than to resign his position. "By choosing to announce his resignation Ahern retained control of his own resignation," wrote *Irish Independent* Political editor Fionnán Sheahan. Had he left it any later it may have been taken out of his hands and he would ultimately have been forced to go".

Yet the timing of his going completely wrong-footed the media which was focused on an expected ding-dong in the Dáil later that day between the Taoiseach and the leaders of the Opposition, Enda Kenny and Pat Rabbitte. Within 45 minutes of his resignation speech 12,000 listeners to RTE's *Liveline* programme texted their reaction. 55pc supported his decision, while 45pc felt he should have stayed in office. This margin was, no doubt, a subtle tribute to his masterly media finesse and a show of affection for the man in his public coping with personal and professional adversity.

Tony Blair's former press secretary, Alastair Campbell, was convinced that Bertie's contribution to the signing of the Good Friday Agreement, and its consolidation with the formation of the DUP-Sinn Féin partnership government at Stormont in 2007 as modified by the St Andrews Agreement, would be his enduring legacy. "The one thing you'd have to say, looking at it from a British perspective, is his role in the Northern Ireland peace process. Lots of people take different credit. That is their game, but the truth is like a massive jigsaw puzzle and the big pieces fitted together and he was one of the big pieces".

Four attributes in Bertie's make-up were identified by Campbell for this success: his calm and his determination, his understanding of the issues and in particular the way he worked with Tony Blair. "Tony and Bertie", Campbell observed, "could put the views of the parties to the other parties better than the parties themselves, less provocatively or in a way that was more palatable..... Bertie agreed with Tony that this was a once in a life-time, possibly once in a generation opportunity to make it happen".

The record upholds this insight. Still ingrained in the public mind is the memory of how Bertie left the Stormont negotiations to attend his mother's wake, returned to Belfast next morning for a working breakfast with Tony Blair, headed back to Dublin for the funeral and then again returned north to continue the negotiations. According to David Trimble it was Bertie's decision to override his political advice and scale-down the North/South dimension of the agreement that removed "a toxic element" from the negotiation and enabled the Ulster Unionist leader to sign up to the agreement. It was Bertie who confronted "the sacred cow" of Irish republicanism when he agreed to alter the Republic's territorial claim over the North – a move long considered political suicide in the Republic by even Garret FitzGerald and Albert Reynolds - and he won convincingly the ensuing referendum sanctioning its removal from the de Valera Constitution.

Ian Paisley Junior rated Bertie's contribution to the North as "seismic", an evaluation endorsed by Stephen King, the former political adviser to David Trimble, who argued persuasively that when compared with Bertie's predecessors' records in the North, the true scale of his achievement is revealed. "Genuine serious engagement with Unionism was not a new aspiration", King wrote in *The Examiner*. "Garret FitzGerald called it his 'most cherished hope' – but it was only Bertie Ahern who achieved it, proving it could pay dividends. Seán Lemass and Jack Lynch might have lowered the political temperature between north and south a degree, but neither succeeded in establishing lasting political institutions to reflect the north's dual loyalties. Charles Haughey was forced to try to take the Ulster problem to 'a new plane' above Unionists' heads, because his involvement in the arms' crisis made him a political untouchable. He wrecked his (slim) chances of a breakthrough by equivocating over the hunger strikes and earning Margaret Thatcher's 'undying enmity' – Archbishop Robin Eames' words – for appearing to side with Argentina during the Falklands War. Garret FitzGerald succeeded where Haughey failed, concluding the Hillsborough accord, but at the price of alienating unionism and provoking an upsurge in loyalist violence against the north's Catholic community".

Further testimony to Bertie's role in the North has appeared in memoirs produced by the main participants: Bill Clinton in his *My Life*, George Mitchell in *Making Peace*, Jonathan Powell in *Great Hatred, Little Room, Making Peace in Northern Ireland*, and from close observer Deaglán de Bréadún in *The Far Side of Revenge, Making Peace in Northern Ireland*. These are important contributions to what is called "history of the moment".

However, historians will find it impossible to speak of "Ahernism", because Bertie never expressed any interest in ideology, Diarmuid Ferriter concluded. "In terms of what he said and did in public, he will be remembered for his preoccupation with consensus, caution and canvassing". Bertie's 3 Cs! He was fortunate to come to power as the boom years began and lucky to leave office before the recession which is engulfing his successor, Brian Cowen. Thus, Bertie could claim that "Ireland is more prosperous than at any time in our entire history. All levels of Irish society have seen their well-being dramatically improved in the period I served as Taoiseach". Others such as Fr Seán Healy would argue that much more could have been down to address inequality.

According to David McWilliams, author of *The Pope's Children Ireland's New Elite*, the secret of Bertie's success was not his ordinariness but was his capacity to embody the expectations of what an aspirational society could achieve. If Bertie could do it, so too could *Breakfast Roll Man*, David's archetypal figure of Celtic Tiger Ireland. "A Socialist today. A Green tomorrow", mused former Labour Party leader, Pat Rabbitte. "Very few politicians possess the persuasive charms of Mr Ahern or are as good in a one-to-one situation. For the man behind the tent at the Galway Races to be able to present himself to the Greens as a closet environmentalist takes some beating".

Commentators recalled affectionately of how Bertie's many malapropisms – slips of the tongue – were self-evident in themselves to the edification and amusement of a benign public. His distinctive patois was too much of a temptation for the satirical fortnight magazine, *The Phoenix*, which published in bookform its much read fortnightly *Diary of a Nortsoide Taoiseach*. Instances such as "Let's put the dirty linen – the clean linen – on the table". "The world community must build on the road crash for peace in the Middle East". "We shouldn't upset the apple tart".

Since Bertie walked the plank and left *Battleship Bertie*, his period in office is already being looked upon nostalgically as a vanished golden age. But the loss of the Lisbon EU Treaty and the suddenness of the economic recession call for a reassessment of his public presentation to the electorate of European Union issues and his management of the economy. At the time of writing too the Peter Robinson DUP partnership with Sinn Féin is fraught with mutual suspicions. There has been no justice for the McCartney sisters and many other bereaved families. Sectarianism is still smouldering and extreme republicans are targeting the police.

However, these are Cowen's headaches now.

In a new chapter of his eventful life Bertie has diligently begun to create a new identity as an elder statesman, boardroom adviser and popular sports pundit. He contributed a two page book review in the *Irish Independent* on how when he was six years old he fell in love with Manchester United as a result of the team's tragic air crash in Munich in 1958. He launched a website *www.bertieahernoffice.org* which lauds his work in the Northern Ireland peace process. It carries videos and transcripts of his high-profile speeches, including ones in Westminster and the United States Congress. The website design and title is similar to one created by former British Prime Minister Tony Blair. Like Tony Blair, Bertie has joined the international political lecture tour circuit. He has an expensively refurbished office close to the Dáil, where he still is a deputy. There is speculation that he may run for the European Parliament in 2009 or that he has set his sights on becoming President of Ireland in 2011. His future political life will depend on the Mahon Tribunal's findings. Whatever he does, he will still be Bertie, or more exactly, his many different images for different people.

Bertie's Place in History

"History will be kinder to Ahern than it will be to Paisley,
notwithstanding the latter's almost death-bed conversion
to moderation".
- STEPHEN KING, *The Examiner,* April 3, 2008.

I n line with his consensual, non-ideological and pragmatic approach to politics, the public life of Bertie Ahern can be parcelled into a number of critical partnerships: Bertie and Tony Blair, Bertie and Mary Harney, Bertie and Gerry Adams/Martin McGuinness, Bertie and Ian Paisley. Such political promiscuity! That he also forged working bonds with difficult personalities in Gordon Brown and David Trimble, and was welcomed in the White House of both the charismatic Bill Clinton and the George W.Bush, as well as by the ever-changing heads of the EU capitals and institutions, show the force of his infectiously charming persona and people-skills.

In the instant newspaper supplements and broadcast assessments of 'The Ahern Years', historians vied with journalists and politicians in forecasting Bertie's place in the Irish Pantheon of Political Leaders. "History will be kind to Ahern's legacy", opined historian Diarmaid Ferriter, arguing that "even Bertie's fiercest critics must acknowledge how much he contributed to Ireland's political stability over the past decade".

Historians however, will be more detached than his contemporaries. The shadow of Bertie's "unusual" personal finances may place him with Charles Haughey in the middle of the league table of Taoisigh rather than among the top three champion contenders. Historians debate endlessly as to whether the premier league of is headed by W.T. Cosgrave or Eamon de Valera, the State's founding fathers. Though lacking a formal biography, Cosgrave, is revered as the Cumann na nGaedhael leader who consolidated the post-Civil War State, and ensured it had firm institutional foundations and foreign recognition during the gruff Dubliner's precarious decade in power from 1922 to 1932. De Valera, the divisive catalyst of the Civil War and later the enigmatic founder of Fianna Fáil when he abandoned the gun for the ballot box, is principally honoured for being the longest serving Taoiseach who drafted the 1937 Constitution and stood tall in international affairs at the League of Nations in the age of the dictators, Adolf Hitler, Benito Mussolini and Francisco Franco, while maintaining Ireland's neutrality during the Second World War.

However their record has to be balanced against their deference to the Catholic Church which moulded the early State in its devotional and authoritarian ways. They look almost medievalists to us. As John Whyte demonstrated in his classic book, *Church-State in Ireland*, the political auction to catholicise the independent State was begun by its two founding fathers in decades marked by poverty, emigration and repressive puritanism. Their *Dreary Eden* of cross-road dances belongs to a completely different era from today's pluralist, prosperous and multi-cultural Ireland of the Ahern Years.

If Cosgrave's reputation is dimming, de Valera's is holding – even maturing with age. But the key transitional and transforming figure was Lemass. Brief though his time as head of Government was, he has a stronger claim than the two founding fathers to the title of being the greatest Taoiseach. When he at last succeeded the aging de Valera in June, 1959, a new period in Irish politics opened that brought Ireland into the modern mainstream of European life in the swinging sixties through the dismantling of trade barriers in preparation for Common Market membership, through détente with Ulster Protestants in the North and the fostering of a more open outlook in the South through the liberal-isation of censorship. On the Lemass watch, too, a reversal of the population decline took place with the introduction of economic planning under a talented and far-seeing civil servant, T.K. Whitaker. This change in direction helped save Ireland from becoming a failed socio-economic entity and a permanent cultural backwater.

Lemass's successor, the popular Jack Lynch, consummated his predecessor's efforts to join the European Club. The Corkman talked a lot about a pluralist Ireland, but he was aghast when Senator Mary Robinson introduced a Bill in the Senate to legalise condoms. Lynch baulked at removing the ban on contraception, as did his successor Liam Cosgrave. But Cosgrave, like his father, was strong on law and order in his intolerance of IRA subversion. Lynch found himself in the more difficult situation which he faced over the Arms Crisis and his confrontation with his party's republican wing which was conspiring to replace him with Charlie Haughey.

Although Garret FitzGerald's premierships in the 1980s were weakened by economic recession, he advanced the Lemass legacy, not least by calling for the removal of sectarian features in laws passed by W.T. Cosgrave and enshrined in de Valera's Constitution. Yet, Garret's Crusade came unstuck against a reactionary alliance of the Catholic bishops in cahoots with Haughey's Fianna Fáil. His vision of a more pluralist Ireland at peace with the North and supported by Ireland's membership of the European Union has been implemented to a large degree by his successors, Albert Reynolds and Bertie Ahern. Garret's stock is rising with time.

The struggle for the two bottom places is between two Fine Gael leaders, John Bruton and John A. Costello. Bruton, the only one not to take office after a general election, became Taoiseach by accident in late 1994 when Labour's Dick Spring pushed Reynolds from office amid the confusion over the extradition to the North of the notorious paedophile monk, Fr Brendan Smyth. Spring, an aspirant *rotating Taoiseach*, secured a Dáil majority for the formation of the Rainbow FG-Labour-Democratic Left coalition under Bruton. While Bruton succeeded where FitzGerald had failed in introducing divorce, his Unionist leanings made Sinn Féin distrustful of him and the momentum for peace charted by Reynolds in the Downing Street Declaration faltered. Bruton's fatal mistake was to allow himself to be badly advised by Spring to go to the country too soon in 1997, just as the Celtic Tiger economy was taking off. It could have been the Bruton, not the Ahern decade.

Costello, who headed two Inter-Party Governments, from 1948-51 and 1954-57, declared Ireland a Republic but put few, if any obstacles in the way of the Catholic Church's stranglehold of the nation's bedrooms and libraries. Costello was utterly subservient in the Mother and Child controversy in 1950–51, when the Hierarchy, led by the Archbishop of Dublin, John Charles McQuaid, defeated the proposal by the Minister for Health, Dr Nöel Browne, for a free, non-means tested welfare scheme for mothers and children. Costello's docility came close to Ireland's becoming a theocratic State. Browne became a martyred icon, revered in certain quarters above any Taoiseach.

We must await the report of the Mahon Tribunal before settling on Bertie's likely overall place in history. In September Bertie finally got his opportunity to defend his 35 years in public life and to insist that he did not receive any moneys from builder Owen O'Callaghan. On what was expected to be his last appearance in Dublin Castle Bertie told Judge Mahon of his abiding sense of having been treated unfairly during its proceedings over almost nine years – and he reaffirmed that he had never in his public life taken a bribe or a backhander.

In his summary of this bruising encounter for not only Bertie and the Tribunal but also for government politics and the media, Colm Keena, in the *Irish Times*, observed that three years ago Bertie was the politician the public loved the most. However, the years from 2006 to 2008 brought into focus "the man's capacity for truculence and self-pity, created suspicions about his honesty and capacity for deviousness, and made people worried that the man who was famously uninterested in personal gain, might in fact have been in receipt of improper payments while holding high office".

Bertie may have left Merrion Street, but Dublin Castle has not yet gone away. Like Bertie, we wait for the Mahon Judgement.

John Cooney's Rating of Ireland's Top Twelve

1 Seán Lemass: The Modernist Pilot.

2 Eamon de Valera: The Chief.

3 Garret Fitzgerald: The Pluralist Crusader.

4 Bertie Ahern: The Teflon Taoiseach.

5 Albert Reynolds: The Lost Leader.

6 Charles Haughey: The Spirit of Ireland.

7 Jack Lynch: Honest Jack.

8 W.T. Cosgrave: The Founding Father.

9 Liam Cosgrave: The Silent Defender.

10 John Bruton: Johnny Baby.

11 John A. Costello: The Clericalist 'Republican'.

12 Brian Cowen: Biffo's placing – and duration – still unknown

COLUMN TITLES & DATES

POLITICS IN 'BERTIELAND' 2006

POLITICS IN 'BERTIELAND' 2007

POLITICS IN 'BERTIELAND' 2008